Green Trade and Fair Trade in and with the EU

Process-Based Measures within the EU Legal Order

This book explores how EU law constrains the freedom of the EU, the Member States, and private bodies to adopt measures that seek to protect social and environmental interests abroad by placing conditions on production processes in other states. The permissibility of such process-based measures has been examined primarily within the World Trade Organization (WTO) context, but the challenges that they present are equally relevant for the EU internal market system. Ankersmit identifies three core challenges posed by process-based measures from an EU law perspective: extraterritoriality, unilateralism, and the competitive and democratic problems created by private rule-making. It examines these issues in the context of free movement, competition, public procurement, and EU tax law. This book will appeal to academics, policy makers, and practitioners interested in trade and environment, the social impact of trade law, and European and international market regulation.

Laurens Ankersmit is a lawyer at ClientEarth, Brussels, and also teaches EU external relations law at the University of Kent in Brussels. He specializes in the intersection between trade and the environment, having published, taught, and practiced extensively in this area. He is also founder and editor of the *European Law Blog*, the leading blog on EU law issues.

Cambridge Studies in European Law and Policy

This series aims to produce original works which contain a critical analysis of the state of the law in particular areas of European law and set out different perspectives and suggestions for its future development. It also aims to encourage a range of work on law, legal institutions and legal phenomena in Europe, including 'law in context' approaches. The titles in the series will be of interest to academics; policy makers; policy formers who are interested in European legal, commercial and political affairs; practising lawyers, including the judiciary; and advanced law students and researchers.

Books in the Series

Green Trade and Fair Trade in and with the EU: Process-Based Measures within the EU Legal Order
Laurens Ankersmit

New Labour Laws in Old Member States
Rebecca Zahn

The Governance of EU Fundamental Rights
Mark Dawson

The International Responsibility of the European Union: From Competence to Normative Control
Andrés Delgado Casteleiro

Frontex and Non-Refoulement: The International Responsibility of the EU
Roberta Mungianu

Gendering European Working Time Regimes: The Working Time Directive and the Case of Poland
Ania Zbyszewska

EU Renewable Electricity Law and Policy: From National Targets to a Common Market
Tim Maxian Rusche

European Constitutionalism
Kaarlo Tuori

Brokering Europe: Euro-Lawyers and the Making of a Transnational Polity
Antoine Vauchez

Services Liberalization in the EU and the WTO: Concepts, Standards and Regulatory Approaches
Marcus Klamert

Referendums and the European Union: A Comparative Enquiry
Fernando Mendez, Mario Mendez and Vasiliki Triga

The Allocation of Regulatory Competence in the EU Emissions Trading Scheme
Jospehine Van Zeben

The Eurozone Crisis
Kaarlo Tuori and Klaus Tuori

International Trade Disputes and EU Liability
Anne Thies

The Limits of Legal Reasoning and the European Court of Justice
Gerard Conway

New Governance and the Transformation of European Law: Coordinating EU Social Law and Policy
Mark Dawson

The Lisbon Treaty: A Legal and Political Analysis
Jean-Claude Piris

The European Union's Fight Against Corruption: The Evolving Policy Towards Member States and Candidate Countries
Patrycja Szarek-Mason

The Ethos of Europe: Values, Law and Justice in the EU
Andrew Williams

State and Market in European Union Law: The Public and Private Spheres of the Internal Market before the EU Courts
Wolf Sauter and Harm Schepel

The European Civil Code: The Way Forward
Hugh Collins

Ethical Dimensions of the Foreign Policy of the European Union: A Legal Appraisal
Urfan Khaliq

Implementing EU Pollution Control: Law and Integration
Bettina Lange

European Broadcasting Law and Policy
Jackie Harrison and Lorna Woods

The Transformation of Citizenship in the European Union: Electoral Rights and the Restructuring of Political Space
Jo Shaw

The Constitution for Europe: A Legal Analysis
Jean-Claude Piris

The European Convention on Human Rights: Achievements, Problems and Prospects
Steven Greer

Social Rights and Market Freedom in the European Constitution: A Labour Law Perspective
Stefano Giubboni

EU Enlargement and the Constitutions of Central and Eastern Europe
Anneli Albi

Green Trade and Fair Trade in and with the EU

Process-Based Measures within the EU Legal Order

Laurens Ankersmit
ClientEarth, Brussels

CAMBRIDGE
UNIVERSITY PRESS

CAMBRIDGE
UNIVERSITY PRESS

University Printing House, Cambridge CB2 8BS, United Kingdom

One Liberty Plaza, 20th Floor, New York, NY 10006, USA

477 Williamstown Road, Port Melbourne, VIC 3207, Australia

4843/24, 2nd Floor, Ansari Road, Daryaganj, Delhi – 110002, India

79 Anson Road, #06–04/06, Singapore 079906

Cambridge University Press is part of the University of Cambridge.

It furthers the University's mission by disseminating knowledge in the pursuit of education, learning, and research at the highest international levels of excellence.

www.cambridge.org
Information on this title: www.cambridge.org/9781107191228
DOI: 10.1017/9781108120623

First published 2017

Printed in the United Kingdom by Clays, St Ives plc

A catalogue record for this publication is available from the British Library.

Library of Congress Cataloging-in-Publication data
Names: Ankersmit, Laurens Jan, 1984- author.
Title: Green Trade and Fair Trade in and with the EU : process-based measures within the EU legal order / Laurens Jan Ankersmit.
Description: 1 Edition. | New York : Cambridge University Press, 2017. |
Series: Cambridge studies in european law and policy |
Includes bibliographical references and index.
Identifiers: LCCN 2017006774 | ISBN 9781107191228 (Hardback)
Subjects: LCSH: Free trade–Government policy–European Union countries. |
Free trade–Environmental aspects–European Union countries. |
Competition, Unfair–European Union countries. | Direct taxation–Law and legislation–European Union countries. | BISAC: LAW / International.
Classification: LCC HF2036 .A55 2017 | DDC 382/.71094–dc23
LC record available at https://lccn.loc.gov/2017006774

ISBN 978-1-107-19122-8 Hardback

Contents

Series Editors' Preface

This welcome addition to the series *Cambridge Studies in European Law and Policy* engages with one of the most difficult questions raised by the globalization of trade in goods. What if 'we' (in the European Union, that is) are not satisfied by the conditions under which goods, or parts of goods, are made in other countries? What if the conditions under which goods are produced rely on poor labour standards or have an impact on the environment that would not be legal if the goods were produced in the EU? What steps does EU law permit the EU itself, the Member States, and private bodies to take in relation to social and environmental standards outside the EU in the endeavour to change the balance between the principles of free trade, fair trade, and 'green trade'?

The study focuses on process-based measures, which aim to affect the way that products are produced rather than the physical properties of products. It brings into play not only EU law on the free movement of goods, but also principles of non-discrimination and issues of competition law affecting private actors and their choices about, for example, production chains. The book picks up an issue which has been studied more closely in the context of the WTO, but which has received thus far surprisingly little attention in the EU context.

Laurens Ankersmit is well placed to write this study, having had experience in academia, private practise, and the world of NGOs. He has been able to produce a text that will be useful to different academic and practitioner audiences, as well as speaking to the wider moral and ethical issues that underpin these types of development conundrums.

Jo Shaw
Laurence Gormley

Acknowledgements

This book is a substantially revised and fully updated work based on my doctoral dissertation defended on 20 February 2015 at VU University Amsterdam in the Netherlands. The revisions and updates took place during 2016 in Brussels, Belgium and Viitasaari, Finland.

This book is the result of a long-held fascination and curiosity for the societal consequences of trade liberalization, and in particular, its impact on social and environmental interests. I am very grateful for having been given the opportunity and liberty to do academic research on this topic since 2010. I would like to thank Laurence Gormley for recommending me for the research position at VU University and for his encouragement to pursue an academic career.

Two people in particular deserve the most prominent acknowledgement for this book. Gareth Davies for his trust and support as supervisor and for the numerous discussions on EU law and intellectual stimulation. He has been a formidable supervisor, giving me the freedom and feedback that allowed me to complete the research project we started in 2010. Second, I am indebted to Jessica Lawrence. She has been my intellectual sparring partner and counsel for the past six years and has been a tremendous help in finalizing this manuscript.

I am very grateful to several members of the committee of my doctoral defence: Suzanne Kingston, Alberto Alemanno, and Joanne Scott. Their feedback on the dissertation and the discussions during the defence have helped me further improve the manuscript. I would also like to thank Hans Vedder, Jim Mathis, and Harm Schepel for our academic discussions, and Jochem Wiers and Geert van Calster for their support for the project early on.

During my time at VU University Amsterdam, I spent countless hours with colleagues and friends discussing EU law, how to complete dissertations, and many other trivial and not so trivial issues. I would like to thank, in particular, Benedikt, Barend, Juan, Magda, Clemens, Tijmen, Jochem, Wessel, Dimitry, Nik, Luigi, Ulad, Marek, Wouter, Britta, Elmar, Enrico, Geoff, Vanessa, Orla, Marleen, Lianne, and Ioana.

Two institutions have been pivotal in giving me the necessary resources to complete this manuscript. I am grateful to VU University Amsterdam for the (online) library and research facilities and to the Dutch national research organization NWO for funding my research position.

Lastly, I would like to thank Audrey for her love and encouragement, and my family and my friends for their support.

Table of Cases

European Court of Justice

General Court

GATT/WTO and Other International Tribunals

Table of Legislation

EU Directives

EU Regulations

International Legal Sources

Abbreviations

EC	European Community
ECJ	European Court of Justice[1]
ECR	European Court Reports
EU	European Union
GATT	General Agreement on Tariffs and Trade
GC	General Court
PPM	Process and Production Method
TEU	Treaty on European Union
TFEU	Treaty on the Functioning of the European Union
WTO	World Trade Organization

[1] This book refers to the Court of Justice (CJ) of the Court of Justice of the European Union (CJEU) as either 'the Court' or 'ECJ', an abbreviation that has been used for this court since its existence.

Introduction

Introduction

Globalization has without a doubt a profound impact on governments' ability to comprehensively regulate economic life in their jurisdiction. As global supply chains become wider, the jurisdictions in which products are purchased and used increasingly no longer overlap with the jurisdictions in which they were made. The production of goods has become separated from their consumption. As a result, production rules in countries where goods are consumed have become less effective in addressing social and environmental concerns, which may arise far outside of their borders.

Yet, globalization and the accompanying geographic separation of production and consumption are leading to more and more discomfort in societies across the world. People have become aware that the products they buy might be produced in factories with poor labour conditions, by employers who commit human rights violations, and by methods that lead to environmental pollution, contribute to deforestation or overfishing, and harm animal welfare.

The conventional political and legal solution to such civil discontent is, however, neither available nor effective. As a result of global competition, regulating only domestic production is ineffective at preventing these social and environmental harms. However, direct regulation of production taking place outside of a state's borders is neither legally nor politically possible. At the global level, multilateral solutions are also not always feasible. It goes without saying that currently no world government exists, nor is it likely (or even desirable) that such a government would exist in the future to address these social, environmental, and ethical concerns.

The lack of an effective international regulatory framework has resulted in what has been labelled the gap in global governance:

although trade has economically interconnected different parts of the world and has given rise to powerful transnational economic actors, there is no global government, nor sufficient multilateral collaboration, that can deliver and protect collective goods.[1] Civil society and the (often developed) countries where products are marketed see the protection of social and environmental interests by certain (often developing) countries and multinationals as inadequate. However, their efforts have not resulted in the creation of transnational or international law. In most cases, governments are either unwilling or unable to collectively regulate the conditions of production through international agreements, and seem unable to enforce those internationally agreed or national production standards that do exist.[2]

There are a number of reasons for this. First of all, governments might wish to regulate production processes, but be prevented from doing so because of jurisdictional issues. Second, the governments of the countries in which production takes place may be unwilling or unable to regulate production, or enforce their production rules. This becomes a transnational problem if products are sold in markets in other jurisdictions and the people in those jurisdictions care about the way the products are made.

Process-based measures – the focus of this book – are one response to globalization in which both public and private entities attempt to regain control over processes and practices that have crossed borders as a result of globally expanding production lines.[3] Process-based product rules – or

[1] Jurgen Habermas, *The Postnational Constellation: Political Essays* (Cambridge: MIT Press, 2001); Stephen J Kobrin, 'Globalization, Transnational Corporations and the Future of Global Governance', in Andreas Geog Scherer and Guido Palazzo (eds.), *Handbook of Research on Global Corporate Citizenship* (Cheltenham: Edward Elgar Pulbishing, 2008), 249; Sébastien Mena and Guido Palazzo, 'Input and Output Legitimacy of Multi-Stakeholder Initiatives' (2012) 22 *Business Ethics Quarterly*, 527

[2] John Gerard Ruggie, *Just Business: Multinational Corporations and Human Rights* (New York: Norton & Company, 2013)

[3] There are, generally speaking, three other ways in which the EU and its Member States can address concerns regarding production standards in exporting countries. First of all, they can set up assistance programs or support schemes in other countries to encourage producers there to improve production conditions (see for instance the EU's financing instrument for development cooperation DCI: Regulation 233/2014 of the European Parliament and of the Council of 11 March 2014 establishing a financing instrument for development cooperation for the period 2014–2020 OJ 2014 No. L 77/44 and the programs based on it). Second, states can require trading partners to comply with certain international labour and environmental standards both before entering into trade liberalization agreements and suspend the beneficial trade arrangements in case of non-compliance (see for instance, the EU's GSP+ programme: articles 9–16 of Regulation

'PPM rules' (process and production method) as they are known in the WTO context – are rules about how products should be manufactured, rather than about their physical properties. This makes them a distinct conceptual category within trade law. Generally speaking, regulatory practice and discussions about the balance between trade liberalization and the protection of social and environmental norms have focused on the subject of public concerns that materialize at the *consumption* stage. For example, a country may address public concerns about product safety by promulgating consumer safety standards, or concerns about sustainability via environmental packaging requirements. Process-based measures are different because they seek to address social, environmental, and moral considerations at the *production* stage. Shifting the locus of regulation from the place of consumption to the place of production poses a number of challenges to traditional conceptions of trade regulation and liberalization. Under what conditions may states seek to address public interests that materialize outside their territorial boundaries? May they do so without the collaboration or consent of other states? And, since a multiplicity of process-based measures are enacted by private parties, is the state the only entity that can legitimately regulate the marketplace?

Process-based measures are rich in variety: they take various forms, are enacted by different types of actors, and seek to address different public interests. In the EU context, public process-based measures might come in the form of 'command-and -control'-style marketing or import bans by Member States or the EU itself. Such measures include the initial national[4] and later European ban[5] on the marketing of seal products because of the cruel hunting methods employed; the EU ban on

978/2012 of the European Parliament and of the Council of 25 October 2012 applying a scheme of generalized tariff preferences and repealing Council Regulation (EC) No 732/2008 OJ 2012 No. L303/1). Lastly, states can apply trade sanctions to countries that violate human rights. The EU can through its Common Foreign and Security Policy in part or completely interrupt or reduce economic and financial relations with another country (see Chapter II title V TEU and art 215 TFEU).

[4] Besluit van 4 juli 2007, houdende wijziging van het Besluit aanwijzing dier- en plantensoorten Flora- en faunawet en het Besluit vrijstelling beschermde dier- en plantensoorten in verband met het verbod op de handel in producten van zadelrobben en klapmutsen, *Staatsblad* 2007, 253

[5] Regulation 1007/2009 of the European Parliament and of the Council of 16 September 2009 on trade in seal products providing for restrictions on the placing on the market of the European Union of seal products, OJ 2009 No. L286/36 (subsequently amended by Regulation 2015/1775 of the European Parliament and of the Council of 6 October 2015, OJ 2015 No. L262/1)

imports of fur originating from animals hunted in countries that have no ban on the use of leghold traps[6]; the EU ban on cosmetics tested on animals[7]; and the EU import bans on calves and pigs that have not been raised in accordance with EU minimum animal welfare standards.[8] Public process-based measures can also be more 'market-oriented', aimed at nudging the consumer to purchase products that respect certain production standards, or making it more expensive for the producer to use socially or environmentally unfriendly production methods. Such 'market-oriented' measures include, most commonly, labelling and taxation initiatives such as the EU organic[9] and eco labels,[10] national eco-labels such as the Nordic Swan and German Blue Angel programmes,[11] tax measures intended to stimulate consumption of green electricity,[12] green and social procurement rules,[13] social labels for textile products,[14] and the promotion of sustainable biofuels.[15]

In addition to these public measures, a whole range of private initiatives have also sought to regulate products on the basis of how they are

[6] Council Regulation 3254/91 of 4 November 1991 prohibiting the use of leghold traps in the Community and the introduction into the Community of pelts and manufactured goods of certain wild animal species originating in countries which catch them by means of leghold traps or trapping methods which do not meet international humane trapping standards, OJ 1991 No. L308/1

[7] Regulation 1223/2009 of the European Parliament and of the Council of 30 November 2009 on cosmetic products, OJ 2009 No. L342/59

[8] Council Directive 2008/119/EC of 18 December 2008 laying down minimum standards for the protection of calves OJ 2008 No. L10/7; Council Directive 2008/120/EC of 18 December 2008 laying down minimum standards for the protection of pigs, OJ 2009 No. L47/5

[9] Council Regulation 834/2007 of 28 June 2007 on organic production and labelling of organic products and repealing Regulation 2092/91, OJ 2007 No. L189/1

[10] Regulation 66/2010 of the European Parliament and of the Council of 25 November 2009 on the EU Ecolabel OJ 2010 No. L27/1

[11] Information on the Nordic Eco Label can be found on www.nordic-ecolabel.org/about/. Information on the German Blue Angel label can be found on www.blauer-engel.de/

[12] See Chapter 2 Section 2.2

[13] See Chapter 2 Section 2.3

[14] See for instance the Italian textile labelling initative, dubbed the Reguzzoni-Versace Law: Law No. 55 of 8 April 2010 Provisions governing the marketing of textile, leather and footwear products [2010] and the implementing decree Interministerial decree pursuant to article 2.1 of Law 55 of 8 April 2010 – 'Provisions for the sale of textile products, leather goods and footwear' [2011] available at the TRIS website of the Commission http://ec.europa.eu/growth/tools-databases/tris/en/ accessed 23 June 2016. The notification number of Law no. 55 is 2010/286/I, the notification number of the implementing decree is 2010/681/I

[15] Directive 2009/28/EC of the European Parliament and of the Council of 23 April 2009 on the promotion of the use of energy from renewable sources and amending and subsequently repealing Directives 2001/77/EC and 2003/30/EC, OJ 2009 No. L140/16

made. These private initiatives can vary from long-standing, highly organized labelling initiatives to those of a more *ad hoc* nature such as boycotts and media campaigns. Examples of the former include product certification and labelling systems such as Fairtrade, the Forest Stewardship Council (FSC), and the Marine Stewardship Council (MSC).[16] These private labelling organizations are comprised of large numbers of stakeholders, and have a fairly developed organizational structure for developing these process-based standards. Examples of more *ad hoc* measures include Greenpeace's 'Killer' boycott campaign against Nestlé's KitKat candy bar,[17] the Bangladesh Safety Accord,[18] and the Clean Clothes Campaign.[19]

This regulatory behaviour poses challenges to how we understand trade regulation and liberalization. In contrast to more traditional forms of trade regulation,[20] process-based measures go beyond protecting solely domestic stability within the territory of one state, addressing global rather than local concerns. Moreover, process-based measures also challenge our traditional understanding of the role of the state as the primary regulator of the market place, since many process-based measures are enacted by private parties. While the debate surrounding the permissibility of process-based measures has been conducted primarily within the WTO context,[21] the challenges that they present are no

[16] Fred Gale and Marcus Haward, *Global Commodity Governance: State Responses to Sustainable Forest and Fisheries Certification* (London: Palgrave Macmillan, 2011)

[17] The campaign sought to convince Nestlé to stop using palm oil originating from rainforests. Information can be found about this campaign on www.greenpeace.org/international/en/campaigns/climate-change/kitkat/

[18] Information can be found about this accord on www.bangladeshaccord.org/

[19] Information can be found about this campaign on www.cleanclothes.org/

[20] Andrew T. F. Lang, 'Reconstructing Embedded Liberalism: John Gerard Ruggie and Constructivist Approaches to the Study of the International Trade Regime' (2006) 9 *Journal of International Economic Law*, 81, at 86–89

[21] Steve Charnovitz, 'The Law of Environmental PPMs in the WTO: Debunking the Myth of Illegality' (2002) 27 *The Yale Journal of International Law*, 59; Robert Howse and Donald Regan, 'The Product/Process Distinction: an Illusory Basis for Disciplining Unilateralism in Trade Policy' (2000) 11 *European Journal of International Law*, 249; Sanford E. Gaines, 'Processes and Production Methods: How to Produce Sound Policy for Environmental PPM-Based Trade Measures?' (2002) 27 *Columbia Journal of Environmental Law*, 383; Mitsuo Matsushita, Thomas J. Schonebaum and Ptros C. Mavroidis (eds.), *The World Trade Organization: Law, Practice And Policy* (2nd edn, Oxford: Oxford University Press, 2006) 808–811; Jochem-Jurrian Derk Wiers, *Trade and Environment in the EC and the WTO: A Legal Analysis* (Europa Law Publishing, 2002); Erich Vranes, *Trade and the Environment: Fundamental Issues in International Law, WTO Law, and Legal Theory* (Groningen: Oxford University Press, 2009), 319–350; John Howard Jackson, *The World Trading System: Law and Policy of*

less relevant for the EU internal market system, even if there has been considerably less debate within the EU legal context.[22] The EU internal market is also characterized by rules guaranteeing trade liberalization, while at the same time permitting Member States and the EU itself to protect public interests by regulating the marketplace. At the same time, the EU's global ambitions in environmental and human rights policy have tended to make the EU legal system more accommodating towards protecting transnational public interests through trade measures, and its position as the world's largest trading bloc has given the EU the means to effectuate these ambitions.[23]

The aim of this book is to assess how the EU legal system copes with the challenges that process-based measures present to common understandings of how trade is and ought to be regulated. This book identifies three main challenges relating to territoriality, unilateralism, and the public/private divide.

First, public process-based measures challenge traditional notions of territorial jurisdiction, according to which states should only be permitted to regulate matters with a sufficiently close connection to the territory. Public process-based measures aim to address concerns regarding production that takes place outside the territory of the regulating entity. As such, they raise questions about sovereignty, the extraterritorial effects of regulation, and the idea that states should not interfere with other state's domestic affairs (the principle of non-interference).

Second, public process-based measures challenge the historical disfavouring of unilateralism. Process-based measures are often unilateral attempts by one state or regulatory authority to address transnational issues. This unilateral construction is problematic from

International Economic Relations (2nd edn, the Cambridge Massachusetts: MIT Press, 1997) 237–238; Jagdish Bhagwati, *In Defense of Globalization* (Oxford: Oxford University Press, 2007) in particular at 150–158; Geert Van Calster, *International & EU Trade Law: The Environmental Challenge* (London: Cameron May, 2000)

22 L. J. Ankersmit, J.C. Lawrence, and G.T. Davies, 'Diverging EU and WTO Perspectives on Extraterritorial Process Regulation' (2012) 21 *Minnesota Journal of International Law Online*, 58; Gareth Davies, 'Process and Production Method Based Restrictions on Trade in the EU' in C. Barnard (Ed.), *Cambridge Yearbook of European Legal Studies 2007–2008* (Oxford, Hart Publishing, 2008), 69; Wiers, *Trade and Environment in the EC and the WTO: A Legal Analysis*; Calster, *International & EU Trade Law*; Hanna Sevenster, *Eco-imperialisme binnen de Europese Unie; een juridisch probleem?* (W.E.J. Tjeenk Willink, 1998)

23 See Article 3 (5) and 21 TEU; Ian Manners, 'Normative Power Europe: A Contradiction in Terms?' (2002) 40 *Journal of Common Market Studies*, 235; Zaki Laïdi, La norme sans la force: L'énigme de la puissance européenne (2nd edn, Les Presses de Sciences Po, 2008)

the perspective of international norms that give preference to multilateralism and transnational cooperation.

Third, process-based measures challenge traditional understandings of the role of public and private entities in creating and implementing public interest policies. A great deal of process-based regulation is done not through the traditional channels of public regulation, but rather by private entities, for example via self-regulation by multinational corporations or the promulgation of private standards by civil society. Furthermore, many process-based measures do not address market access directly, but are calibrated to nudge consumers into making responsible purchasing decisions, thereby moving away from traditional command-and-control forms of regulation.

These challenges present themselves in various ways within the EU economic legal system, which consists of a number of limiting rules that constrain the possibilities for public and private process-based regulatory initiatives. The rules on the free movement of goods, for instance, limit the range of permissible pecuniary and non-pecuniary obstacles to trade in goods, and as such determine both the scope and conditions under which Member States can invoke a public interest to justify obstacles to trade.[24] In order to determine whether process-based measures are permissible under the EU's free movement regime, it is necessary to determine to what extent Member States can invoke public interest justifications to protect 'extraterritorial' interests and whether they can do so 'unilaterally'. Similarly, rules on public procurement discipline public authorities in their purchasing choices and thus constrain their consumer behaviour. Procurement rules also to a large extent determine the conditions under which public authorities can rely on private regulators in their procurement policies, for instance, by requiring certain fairtrade labels for the procurement of coffee. In addition, competition rules discipline private actors by restricting competition through standardization agreements. And finally, the EU's legal order itself limits the range of actions the EU is competent to take through constitutional principles.

Before moving on to the outline of this book, this introductory chapter will discuss in further detail the three main challenges process-based measures pose to our understanding of trade regulation and

[24] In relation to the free movement of goods, see for instance Article 36 TFEU and Case 120/78, *Rewe-Zentral AG v. Bundesmonopolverwaltung für Branntwein (Cassis de Dijon)* [1979] ECR 650, para. 8. See further Chapters 3 and 4 of this book.

liberalization: extraterritoriality, unilateralism, and the means of regulation. These challenges will also be coupled to the main areas of contention within the EU internal market: the free movement of goods, competition law, public procurement law, and market regulation by the EU. In this way, this section identifies how different areas of EU internal market law are affected by these three main challenges.

I.1 Three Challenges of Process-Based Measures

I.1.1 Extraterritoriality

Process-based measures appear to undermine fundamental jurisdictional principles of international law: the territorial sovereignty of states and the principle of non-interference in the domestic affairs of other states.[25] This challenge can be subdivided into an argument against process-based measures on formal jurisdictional grounds, an argument based on resisting economic coercion, and finally, a pluralist argument based on respect for diversity and disagreement among sovereign states. These arguments are particularly relevant for process-based measures enacted by the EU and by Member States. For the EU, these arguments may be relevant when EU measures are challenged before the EU courts. For Member States, extraterritorial effects of process-based measures may pose challenges in relation to their justification. A public interest justification on grounds of environmental protection may be contested on the basis of extraterritoriality if the measure protects the environment outside the territorial borders of a Member State.

First, from a formal perspective, the principles of state sovereignty and non-interference are enshrined in international law. While process-based measures do not necessarily run afoul of the letter of the legal doctrine of jurisdiction, many commentators and some WTO Panellists have suggested that they do violate its underlying rationale.[26] The *Lotus*

[25] Vranes, *Trade and the Environment*, 97–170 and 319–350; Malcolm N. Shaw, *International Law* (6th edn, Cambridge University Press, 2008) in particular at 211–215, 487–494, 645–696; Matsushita, Schonebaum and Mavroidis (eds.), *The World Trade Organization*, 808–811

[26] GATT Panel Report. *United States – Restrictions on the Imports of Tuna (Mexico)*. Not adopted, circulated on 3 September 1991 (DS21/R - 39S/155); GATT Panel Report, *United States – Restrictions on the Imports of Tuna (EEC)*. Not adopted, May 20, 1994 (DS29/R); Jackson, *The World Trading System*, 237–238; Lorand Bartels, 'Article XX of GATT and the Problem of Extraterritorial Jurisdiction – The Case of Trade Measures for the Protection of Human Rights' (2002) 36 *Journal of World Trade*, 353

case is arguably still the point of reference when it comes to the jurisdiction of sovereign states under international law. In that case, the Permanent Court of International Justice held that it was prohibited for states to 'exercise its power in any form in the territory of another State'.[27] However, it did not follow from this principle that 'international law prohibits a state from exercising jurisdiction in its own territory, in respect of any case which relates to acts which have taken place abroad, and in which it cannot rely on some permissive rule of international law'.[28] The *Lotus* case is thus permissive when it comes to process-based measures, as such measures are not enforced beyond the borders of the regulating state: process-based measures are enforced within the territory of the importing state, by either withholding or placing conditions upon market access.[29]

The *Lotus* doctrine has been criticized in the literature, however, for its overly permissive stance towards state practice regulating conduct abroad.[30] Ryngaert, for instance, has argued for the introduction of a reasonableness test that would allow states to exercise prescriptive jurisdiction beyond their borders only when they have the 'most genuine connection' and/or 'the greatest interest' in the matter at hand.[31] Also following a more stringent logic, GATT panels in the controversial *Tuna – Dolphin* cases in the early 1990s considered a US ban on the import of tuna products from countries that permitted the use of purse seine fishing (leading to high mortality rates among dolphins in certain parts of the world) to be 'extrajurisdictional'.[32]

[27] *Case of S.S. "Lotus" (France v. Turkey)*, [1928] PCIJ Rep Series A No 9 and 10, at 18–19. See Chapter 1 Section 1.2 and Chapter 3 Section 3.1

[28] Ibid.

[29] See also André Nollkaemper, 'The Legality of Moral Crusades Disguised in Trade Laws: An Analysis of the EC "Ban" on Furs from Animals taken by Leghold Traps' (1996) 8 *Journal of Environmental Law*, 237

[30] Shaw, *International Law*, 656; Gerald Fitzmaurice, 'The General Principles of International Law Considered form a Standpoint of the Rule of Law' (1957) 92 *Recueil des cours*, 1, at 56–57; Hersch Lauterpacht, *International Law: Collected Papers* (Cambridge, 1970) at 488–489; Cedric Ryngaert, *Jurisdiction in International Law* (Oxford University Press, 2008), see also The American Law Institute, *Restatement (third) of Foreign Relations Law* (The American Law Institute, 1987) at 402(1)(c)

[31] Ryngaert, *Jurisdiction in International Law*, at 146 and 161

[32] See GATT Panel Report. *United States – Restrictions on the Imports of Tuna (Mexico)*. Not adopted, circulated on 3 September 1991 (DS21/R - 39S/155), para. 5.32; GATT Panel Report, *United States – Restrictions on the Imports of Tuna (EEC)*. Not adopted, May 20, 1994 (DS29/R)

Nonetheless, the application of these jurisdictional rules as a formal basis for opposition against process-based measures is problematic for a number of reasons. First, denying states the right to prescribe under the conditions under which products may be sold in their territory infringes upon the sovereignty of the regulating state. A state may have good reasons to limit market access to products on the basis of their production methods, for instance, because the state is morally opposed to the way a product was made, or because the production method in question resulted in trans-boundary harm such as the case with CO2 emissions. An 'easy' example is Israel's ban on certain non-kosher food products.[33] Second, even if states were deemed to have no jurisdiction to enact process-based measures, this would not mean that there would be no 'interference' with the domestic affairs of the importing country. On the contrary, importing blood diamonds, unsustainable timber, or textile products manufactured by children has an effect on the domestic affairs of another country, too. Positing a jurisdictional barrier to process-based measures is therefore not a normatively appealing argument. For the 'extraterritoriality' argument to have any force, additional elements are needed, requiring a more substantive analysis of the extraterritorial effects process-based measures may produce.

The second argument that uses extraterritoriality as a basis for opposition to process-based measures asserts that process-based measures have economically coercive effects on developing countries and small states heavily dependent on exports for their economy. Opponents of process-based measures have accused western countries of employing them in order to coerce other states to adopt the same levels of protection that exist in the West under threat of withholding market access, using terms such as 'neo-colonialism' or 'eco-imperialism'.[34] This goes to the less formal and more economic heart of the principle of state sovereignty, which seeks to protect states against interference in their domestic affairs. The UN General Assembly, for instance, has condemned economic coercion, in particular against developing countries by

[33] WTO Secretatiat, 'Trade Policy Review, Report by the Secretariat, Israel' (WT/TPR/S/157, World Trade Organization 2006) section 27, 48: '[S]ince December 1994, Israel has maintained a ban on imports of non-kosher meat and meat products. However, the Government permits limited do-mestic production, sale, and consumption of non-kosher meat.'

[34] Bhagwati, *In Defense of Globalization* (Oxford University Press, 2007) 150–158; Matsushita, Schonebaum and Mavroidis (eds.), *The World Trade Organization* 808–811; more descriptive Sevenster, *Eco-imperialisme binnen de Europese Unie; een juridisch probleem?*

declaring that 'no State may use or encourage the use of economic, political or any other type of measures to coerce another State in order to obtain from it the subordination of the exercise of its sovereign rights'.[35] The 1996 Singapore WTO Ministerial declaration similarly stated that members 'reject the use of labour standards for protectionist purposes, and agree that the comparative advantage of countries, particularly low-wage developing countries, must in no way be put into question'.[36] Equally, within international environmental law, developing countries have a special position in relation to common environmental problems. The principle of 'common but differentiated responsibilities' recognizes that developed countries cannot require developing countries to adopt essentially the same level of protection.[37] According to this logic, market access can be used as a tool – a stick – that powerful states use to coerce the less powerful.[38] Jagdish Bhagwati, for example, has made this point, arguing that if countries really care about how products are made in other countries, they should be 'putting their own resources where they claim their moral preferences are'.[39]

Opponents of process-based measures argue that environmental and ethical issues should be dealt with in other fora that are designed to deal with those problems. Trade policy should be concerned with the proper level of trade liberalization and not used as a pressure tool to 'force' others into adopting different production standards. In the *Tuna – Dolphin* decision mentioned above, the Panellists were swayed by this 'economic coercion' argument, stating that the US could not prohibit the import of dolphin unsafe tuna because such a prohibition may 'force other contracting parties to change their policies within their jurisdiction, including their conservation policies', and as such would

[35] Declaration on the Inadmissibility of Intervention in the Domestic Affairs of States and the Protection of Their Independence and Sovereignty, UNGA Res 2131 (XX) (21 Dec 1965) (adopted by 109 votes to none, 1 abstention para 2, See also Charter of Economic Rights and Duties of States, UNGA Res 3281 (XXIX) (12 Dec 1974), article 32; Declaration on the Principles of International Law concerning Friendly Relations and Co-operation among States in accordance with the Charter of the United Nations, UNGA Res 2625 (XXV) (24 Oct 1970)

[36] WTO Ministerial Conference, 'Singapore Ministerial Declaration' (Adopted on 13 December 1996) www.wto.org/english/thewto_e/minist_e/min96_e/wtodec_e.htm

[37] See further Chapter 3 Section 3.1

[38] Bhagwati see above (n 34) notes at 155 'there is also the fear that such an open-ended PPM exclusion would essentially imply that the moral preferences of the powerful nations would prevail, since those of the smaller nations would not be championed in a system where only nations have the legal standing to bring disputes to the GATT.'

[39] Ibid., at 158

seriously impair 'the balance of rights and obligations among contracting parties, in particular the right of access to markets'.[40]

As Panellists in later WTO cases concerning process-based measures have realized, however, economic 'coercion' is to a certain extent inherent in trade relations.[41] Whenever importing countries provide large important markets for exporting countries, producers in those exporting countries will have an incentive to adhere to the standards of the importing country. For instance, the so-called 'California-effect' causes producers in the US and elsewhere to make products that adhere to high environmental product standards so that their products can be marketed in California, a state with higher environmental standards and larger markets than other states and countries. Additionally, economic 'coercion' is to a large extent in the eye of the beholder. Governments and civil society might perceive trade liberalization as leading to low levels of environmental and social protection (the 'race to the bottom' argument). Again, within the WTO, the Appellate Body has taken a more nuanced stance since the very trade-centric views expressed in the first *Tuna – Dolphin* cases. In *US – Shrimp*, for example, the Appellate Body noted that:

> [C]onditioning access to a Member's domestic market on whether exporting Members comply with, or adopt, a policy or policies unilaterally prescribed by the importing Member may, to some degree, be a common aspect of measures falling within the scope of one or another of the [GATT Article XX's public policy exceptions]. ... It is not necessary to assume that requiring from exporting countries compliance with, or adoption of, certain policies (although covered in principle by one or another of the exceptions) prescribed by the importing country, renders a measure a priori incapable of justification under Article XX. Such an interpretation renders most, if not all, of the specific exceptions of Article XX inutile, a result abhorrent to the principles of interpretation we are bound to apply.[42]

Perhaps a distinction can be made between those measures that target the governmental policies of other states and those that do not.[43]

[40] GATT Panel Report, *United States – Restrictions on the Imports of Tuna (EEC)*. Not adopted, May 20, 1994 (DS29/R), 5.26

[41] WTO Appellate Body Report, *United States: Import Prohibition of Certain Shrimp and Shrimp Products*, 12 October 1998 (WT/DS58/AB/R), para. 121

[42] Ibid.

[43] Howse and Regan, 'The Product/Process Distinction: An Illusory Basis for Disciplining Unilateralism in Trade Policy', 249; Charnovitz, 'The Law of Environmental PPMs in the WTO: Debunking the Myth of Illegality', 59

Howse and Regan have argued that this is what separates legitimate process-based measures from illegitimate ones, distinguishing between 'country-based' measures and 'process-based' measures.[44] Country-based measures target a particular country of origin and its laws and policies indiscriminately excluding all products from that origin. Process-based measures, on the other hand, aim solely at the manner of production, so any producers who adhere to the standard can export to the regulating country. In *US – Shrimp*, the 'country-based' aspect of the American rules on imports of certain shrimp was one of the main reasons why the measure was defeated before the Appellate Body.[45] Similarly, the Appellate Body in the 2012 reprise of the *Tuna – Dolphin* case dismissed Mexico's concerns over economic 'coercion' in relation to a process-based measure not targeted at the governmental policy of another Member.[46]

The third and final argument against process-based measures on the grounds of state territorial sovereignty and non-interference is a pluralist argument based on respect for diversity and disagreement among sovereign states. According to this logic, importing states should respect other countries' domestic policy choices, including the way they regulate the manufacturing of goods within their territory. States should treat one another as equals.[47] For pluralists, there are no objective universal truths in world politics, and therefore, one state should not impose its own values on another. If a state wishes to permit child labour, or its population does not value animal welfare or environmental protection, other states should respect such choices and not use trade as a means of imposing 'universal' truths. Pluralism in international law has found renewed vigour in criticizing and challenging universalist arguments over, most notably, universal human rights protection.[48] Non-western states, in particular, have challenged the universality of human rights regimes and insisted that international legal documents

[44] Ibid., see also Section 3.2

[45] WTO Appellate Body Report, *United States: Import Prohibition of Certain Shrimp and Shrimp Products*, 12 October 1998 (WT/DS58/AB/R), para. 161

[46] WTO Appellate Body Report, *United States– Measures concerning the Importation, Marketing and Sale of Tuna and Tuna Products*, May 16 2012 (WT/DS381/AB/R), paras. 335–339

[47] Michael Dougan, 'Minimum Harmonization and the Internal Market' (2000) 37 *Common Market Law Review*, 853–885

[48] See for example Makau Mutua 'Savages, Victims, and Saviors: The Metaphor of Human Rights' (2001) 42 *Harvard International Law Journal*, 201. For a universalist perspective see for example Rosalyn Higgins, *Problems and Process: International Law and How We Use It* (Clarendon Press, 1994)

emphasize the importance of respecting diversity in how states implement their obligations, and sometimes have challenged their validity and use altogether.[49] This argument also has traction within the EU. Article 4 (2) TEU stipulates that 'the Union shall respect the equality of Member States before the Treaties as well as their national identities, inherent in their fundamental structures, political and constitutional, inclusive of regional and local self-government'.[50]

These three arguments related to extraterritoriality – a formal, an economic, and a pluralist argument – are relevant for assessing the legality of process-based measures of the EU and of Member States in the EU legal order. The EU may enact process-based measures that seek to protect interests elsewhere, or seek to 'persuade' other states in changing their policies, and as such may be challenged before the Court. This book will therefore assess to what extent these arguments have any force when challenging EU acts on the basis of that article. Moreover, Member States may seek to do the same which may be opposed on similar grounds but in an entirely different legal context under the internal market rules. Public interest justifications invoked in that context may, then, face these extraterritoriality-related arguments as well.

I.1.2 Unilateralism

Process-based measures also pose a challenge to traditional regulatory paradigms because they are unilateral and not multilateral solutions to transnational problems.[51] This is true in at least three ways. First, unilateralism comes into conflict with the normative preference for cooperation over unilateral action on the international scene. From this perspective, unilateralism can be perceived as illegitimate because those affected or governed by the measures have not been consulted during their development or consented to their application. Second, accepting or resisting the legitimacy of process-based measures has significant impacts on the development of multilateral solutions to transnational problems. Accepting such measures gives those states enacting them a better position at the negotiating table, as they will have a bargaining

[49] For a list of examples of State practice challenging the universality of human rights see Anne F. Bayefsky, 'Cultural Sovereignty, Relativism, and International Human Rights: New Excuses for Old Strategies' (1996) 9 *Ratio Juris*, 42

[50] Article 4 (2) TEU

[51] For a conceptual exploration of multilateralism see James A. Caporaso, 'International Relations Theory and Multilateralism: The Search for Foundations' (1992) 46 *International Organization*, 599

chip – in the form of market access – when negotiating common solutions. Resisting process-based measures, on the other hand, results in a significantly weaker negotiating position for those seeking transnational protection of a certain public interest.[52] And third, as with extraterritoriality, unilateralism may present a legal problem for measures enacted by the EU and by Member States. The EU Treaties enshrine a preference for multilateral solutions, and Member States are bound by the duty of loyal cooperation when acting within the scope of EU law. Again, the unilateralist argument may be relevant when EU measures or Member State measures are challenged.

Process-based measures undermine the normative preference for cooperation over unilateral action on the international scene. Process-based measures face a legitimacy challenge because they were developed without input from the targeted population, and are applied to them without their consent.[53] Unilateral regulation raises legitimacy issues because, when process-based measures fail to take into account the opinions of the people they seek to regulate, these measures violate basic principles of democratic *process*.[54] Unilateral regulation also affects legitimacy in terms of *outcome*, because the rules are not tailored to the individuals and contexts they regulate, and are thus not guaranteed to be maximally effective.[55]

These 'unilateralism' arguments differ from the 'extraterritoriality' arguments discussed in the previous section because they do not try to pigeonhole problems into watertight 'national' compartments confined to the territory of any one state, but rather focus on the *processes and outcomes* of addressing transnational problems. The concern here is that the preferences of the parties affected by process regulation in other countries are not included in the decision making process, and that the individuals regulated do not have an adequate say in the outcomes.

[52] See Daniel Bodansky, 'What's so Bad About Unilateral Action to Protect the Environment?' (2000) 11 *European Journal of International Law*, 339

[53] Bernhard Jansen, 'The Limits of Unilateralism from a European Perspective' (2000) 11 *European Journal of International Law*, 309; Philip Sands, '"Unilateralism", Values, and International Law' (2000) 11 *European Journal of International Law*, 291

[54] Fritz W. Scharpf, *Governing in Europe: Effective and Democratic?* (Oxford University Press, 1999) 7. See also Mena and Palazzo, 'Input and Output Legitimacy of Multi-Stakeholder Initiatives', 527; J. H. H. Weiler, 'In the Face of Crisis: Input Legitimacy, Output Legitimacy and the Political Messianism of European Integration' (2012) 34 *Journal of European Integration*, 825; Mijke Boedeltje and Juul Cornips, 'Input and Output Legitimacy in Interactive Governance' (No. NIG2-01) http://repub.eur.nl/pub/1750

[55] Ibid.

A solution in the form of an agreement (public or private) where all those affected have a say in how they are regulated would remedy this situation and is therefore more legitimate. In the absence of such an agreement, however, the question remains: is it more legitimate to require an importing state to consume goods made in an ethically or environmentally objectionable way, or to prevent those goods from being marketed without consulting the exporting state?

Underlying this objection against process-based measures is the belief that process-based measures are not always protecting a 'legitimate interest', but instead seek to 'level the playing field' or to impose an additional burden on foreign producers to keep them from gaining a competitive advantage over their domestic counterparts.[56] This, in turn, leads some commentators to argue that this form of protectionism undermines the systemic benefits from trade. Specialization and differences between jurisdictions enable certain states to gain a comparative advantage over others and process-based measures can off-set such advantages.[57] However, these arguments only hold true to the extent that indeed competing domestic industry is protected, which is certainly not always the case. Moreover, this point of criticism is equally true for ordinary product requirements. In that sense, it does not necessarily mean that process-based measures do not contribute to the protection of human rights, the environment or other public interests. For instance, measures addressing 'carbon leakage' might indeed prevent firms from relocating to countries with less stringent climate change rules, or help them compete against cheaper imports, but they may equally result in more effective environmental rules.

Concern over unilateralism was at the forefront of the first *Tuna – Dolphin* case, in *US – Shrimp*, as well as in the most recent *EU – Seal Products* case. The first two reports placed particular emphasis on the need to address the transnational problem at the bilateral or multilateral level. In *Tuna – Dolphin*, the Panel noted that the United States had not 'exhausted all options [...] in particular through the negotiation of international cooperative arrangements' before enacting its dolphin

[56] Ankersmit, 'Extraterritorial concerns and trade' (*n* 22), 30–32; Candice Stevens, 'Syntheses Report: Trade and Environment: PPM Issues', in *Trade and Environment: Process and Production Methods* (Paris: OECD, 1994), 7, at 19

[57] Thomas J. Schoenbaum, 'International Trade and Protection of the Environment: The Continuing Search for Reconciliation' (1997) 91 *American Journal of International Law*, 268

protection measures.[58] In *US – Shrimp*, similarly, the Appellate Body attached considerable importance to the fact that the United States had not engaged 'in serious, across-the-board negotiations with the objective of concluding bilateral or multilateral agreements for the protection and conservation of sea turtles, before enforcing the import prohibition against the shrimp exports of those other Members'.[59] Thus, within the WTO, there seems to be a procedural requirement to seek to address a matter on a bilateral or multilateral basis before engaging in unilateral efforts and imposing the 'heaviest "weapon"' of an import ban in a WTO Member's armoury of trade measures.[60]

But what if no agreement can be reached? Can states still unilaterally impose process-based measures? If process-based measures are illegitimate per se, then importing countries can do nothing to address transnational social and environmental concerns by regulating their markets in the absence of a bilateral or multilateral agreement. On the other hand, if importing states are allowed to adopt process-based measures after unsuccessful negotiations, it would still be possible for them to do something about transnational social and environmental problems. The consequences for market access for the exporting Member State might then trigger the exporting Member State to engage in plurilateral negotiations in order to have a say in the outcome. The trade-centric 'per se illegitimate' view was adopted by the Panel in the first *Tuna – Dolphin* case where the Panel felt that if a permissive stance towards process-based measures would be accepted, the GATT would 'no longer constitute a multilateral framework for trade among all contracting parties but would provide legal security only in respect of trade between a limited number of contracting parties with identical internal regulations'.[61]

In *US – Shrimp*, however, the Appellate Body took a more nuanced view. It did not have principled objections against the process-based measure at issue, but did require the United States to be more outwardly

[58] GATT Panel Report. *United States – Restrictions on the Imports of Tuna (Mexico)*. Not adopted, circulated on 3 September 1991 (DS21/R - 39S/155), para. 5.28

[59] WTO Appellate Body Report, *United States: Import Prohibition of Certain Shrimp and Shrimp Products*, 12 October 1998 (WT/DS58/AB/R), para 166. The Appellate Body went on to note that not only were such collaborative efforts recognized in various international legal instruments, but also that a multilateral solution was, in fact, feasible.

[60] Ibid., para. 171

[61] GATT Panel Report. *United States – Restrictions on the Imports of Tuna (Mexico)*. Not adopted, circulated on 3 September 1991 (DS21/R - 39S/155), para. 5.27

oriented in the design of its measure. The United States was required to take into account the particular circumstances and interests of the country affected by the process-based measure and not to require other Members to adopt essentially the same comprehensive regulatory programme in force in the United States.[62] For the Appellate Body, therefore, the failure to take into account the interests of the other Members affected by the process-based measure was key in ruling that it amounted to unjustifiable discrimination. Not only did the US in *US – Shrimp* not engage in serious non-discriminatory negotiations on the subject of sea turtle protection, it also designed the measure in a way that completely disregarded the interests of the Members affected.[63]

Similarly, in *EU – Seal Products*, the Appellate Body noted that the EU had 'not pursued cooperative arrangements to facilitate the access of Canadian Inuit to the IC [Indigenous Communities] exception' to its ban on seal prodcuts, which resulted in arbitrary or unjustifiable discrimination because the application of the measure '[did] not allow for any inquiry into the appropriateness of the regulatory program for the conditions prevailing in those exporting countries'.[64] The points made by the Appellate Body in both *EU – Seal Products* and *US – Shrimp*, demonstrate how the lack of input legitimacy affects the output side of the legitimacy of process-based measures. By not sufficiently taking into account the interests of those affected by the measure, it cannot achieve the desired results. Ignoring those affected can cause a measure to be badly calibrated, making the measure either ineffective or producing undesired side-effects, such as arbitrary discrimination in the case of *EU – Seal Products*.

Within the EU context, the normative preference for cooperation is deeply embedded in the European law and policy, both externally and internally. Externally, the EU envisions itself as an international actor with a strong preference for multilateral solutions to global and transnational problems. The Treaty of Lisbon even introduced a new passage explicitly codifying the EU's preference for multilateralism.[65] Article 21 (1) Treaty on European Union (TEU) states that the EU 'shall promote multilateral solutions to common problems, in particular in the framework

[62] Ibid., para 164 [63] See also Ibid., para 172

[64] WTO Appellate Body Report, *European Communities – Measures Prohibiting the Importation and Marketing of Seal Products*, 22 May 2014 (WT/DS400/AB/R and WT/DS/401/AB/R), para. 5.337

[65] Mark A. Pollack, 'Unilateral America, Multilateral Europe?' in John Peterson and Mark A. Pollack (eds.) *Europe, America, Bush: Transatlantic Relations in the Twenty-first Century* (Routledge, 2003), 115

of the United Nations'.[66] Despite this rhetoric, however, the EU is one of the most prominent enactors of process-based measures and other forms of market-based unilateralism.[67] Internally, the duty of sincere cooperation is one of the cornerstones of EU–Member State relations.[68] The principle[69] is used in a wide variety of situations and requires not only that Member States use EU institutions and procedures to resolve conflicts involving EU law with EU institutions[70] or other Member States,[71] but also to facilitate trade by taking into account the legislative history of a product imported from one Member State into another.[72]

Accepting or resisting the legitimacy of process-based measures, nevertheless, has significant impacts on how multilateral solutions come about. Accepting process-based measures means that importing states can restrict market access in the absence of a common solution, whereas restricting them means that exporting states can continue exporting regardless of such a common solution, creating very different incentives both ways to seek such solutions.[73] Process-based measures may thus be a way to bring 'unwilling' States to the negotiating table to pave the way for stronger regimes for transnational social and environmental protection. Those with a preference for free trade over social and environmental interests, therefore, view process-based measures as a threat to trade regimes and an 'abuse' of free trade to further other policy objectives.

[66] Article 21 (1) TEU [67] See Chapter 1 Section 1.1

[68] John Temple Lang, 'The Development by the Court of Justice of the Duties of Cooperation of National Authorities and Community Institutions under Article 10 EC' (2007–2008) 31 *Fordham International Law Journal*, 1483

[69] Article 4 (3) TEU states that 'Pursuant to the principle of sincere cooperation, the Union and the Member States shall, in full mutual respect, assist each other in carrying out tasks which flow from the Treaties. The Member States shall take any appropriate measure, general or particular, to ensure fulfilment of the obligations arising out of the Treaties or resulting from the acts of the institutions of the Union. The Member States shall facilitate the achievement of the Union's tasks and refrain from any measure which could jeopardise the attainment of the Union's objectives.'

[70] Case 7/71, *Commission v. France* [1971] ECR 1003, para. 48 see also Lang, 'The Development by the Court of Justice of the Duties of Cooperation of National Authorities and Community Institutions under Article 10 EC', 1483, at 1493

[71] Nico Schrijver, 'Case C-459/03, Commission of the European Communities v. Ireland, Judgment of the Court (Grand Chamber) of 30 May 2006, [2006] ECR I-4635' (2010) 47 *Common Market Law Review*, 863–878

[72] John Temple Lang, 'The Duties of National Authorities under Community Constitutional Law' (1998) 23 *European Law Review*, 109; Kenneth A. Armstrong, 'Mutual Recognition' in Catherine Barnard and Joanne Scott (eds.) *The Law of the Single European Market: Unpacking the Premises* (Hart Publishing, 2002), 225 at 239

[73] See Bodansky, 'What's so Bad About Unilateral Action to Protect the Environment?', 339

Part of this book will thus examine to what extent the 'unilateralism' challenge affects the legal feasibility of process-based measures under EU law. This entails an analysis of the legality under EU law of measures enacted by both the EU and its Member States. Does the Court require the EU to conduct the process of law-making in a way that takes into account the interests of outsiders? Is the EU required to make an effort to seek multilateral solutions when enacting process-based measures? Does it require the EU legislator to take into account the interests of the country or people affected by the process-based measure? Moreover, to what extent are Member States required to take such interests into account, or engage in serious across the board negotiations within the EU legal system or with countries outside the EU? Will the unilateral aspect of process-based measures, when resulting in obstacles to intra-EU trade in goods, make them more difficult to justify before the Court?

I.1.3 Who Regulates Whom?

Third, process-based measures challenge our traditional understanding of trade regulation, because a great deal of this type of regulation is not done through traditional public channels, but rather by private entities, either through self-regulation by multinational corporations or by civil society with or without the cooperation of producers operating in other countries. Furthermore, many process-based measures do not address market access directly, but are calibrated to nudge consumers to make responsible purchasing decisions, thereby moving away from traditional command-and-control forms of regulation. Process-based measures, therefore, bring new challenges to traditional notions of *who* regulates, and to what extent this matters from an internal market perspective. What legal challenges do process-based measures face when they have been enacted by the EU itself, by Member States, or by private parties? And what does this tell us about the internal market?

Process-based measures enacted by private parties may, for instance, create obstacles to trade in goods between Member States, or, more specifically, restrict competition between undertakings. The question for EU law, then, becomes whether such obstacles and restrictions are covered by EU free movement and competition law in the first place, and whether such obstacles and restrictions can be justified because they serve public interests even though the norms themselves are laid down by private parties.

Second, process-based measures also require rethinking *whom* they regulate, and how this matters from the perspective of internal market law. Process-based measures can target governments of other countries, creating market-based incentives to change production regulation. They can also target producers, providing incentives for companies to change the ways in which they produce their goods. Finally, process-based measures can target consumers, enabling or nudging them to make socially and environmentally sound purchasing decisions. The choice of *whom* to regulate will impact the legal feasibility of process-based measures within the free movement of goods context, as some types of measures are more trade-restrictive and potentially disproportionate than others.

The way internal market law deals with the question of *who* regulates *whom* through process-based measures gives further insight not only into how process-based measures can best be designed or enacted, but also how the internal market operates and the structural biases that exist within the EU's trading system.

Who Regulates?

Within the EU, process-based measures can be enacted at three different levels: at the EU level, at the Member State level, and through private standard-setting. The question as to *who* regulates fundamentally changes both the permissibility under EU law of a process-based measure and its nature and effectiveness. A measure enacted by the EU, for instance, will face competence issues, and as a result will be designed to remove obstacles to trade between Member States. Regulation at the EU level raises issues with respect to extraterritoriality and unilateralism as well, as the voices of the EU's trading partners are not represented within the EU's legal system.[74] Member State process-based measures may also raise extraterritoriality and unilateralism concerns if they affect the interests of another Member State, requiring the European Court of Justice (ECJ) to make tough choices not only between trade liberalization and the protection of social and environmental interests, but also between trade liberalization among Member States, and among Member States and third States.[75]

[74] See Chapter 1 Section 1.2 and 1.3

[75] Laurens Ankersmit, 'What if Cassis de Dijon were Cassis de Quebec? The Assimilation of Goods of Third Country Origin in the Internal Market' (2013) 50 *Common Market Law Review*, 1387

Even more challenging from the perspective of EU internal market law are process-based measures enacted by private entities. Traditionally, the rules of the EU internal market have been understood as being divided into norms addressed to public authorities – the four freedoms – and norms addressed to undertakings – competition rules.[76] As part of that understanding, it has long been presumed that private parties can only justify restricting competition in violation of internal market rules[77] by demonstrating objective economic benefits, whereas public authorities can justify trade restrictions by citing a wide range of public policy considerations.[78]

Process-based measures enacted by private entities challenge this assumption in two ways. First of all, Private measures may have the same trade restrictive effects as public regulations, calling into question both the effectiveness and uniform application of the free movement of goods provisions within the EU.[79] Boycotts, media campaigns, and certification schemes by private parties may create obstacles to trade in the same way state measures do. There is, thus, a question as to what extent the Court should recognize these activities as having legal implications from the perspective of free movement law. Second, to the extent that private entities are recognized as falling within the scope of the free movement of goods, there is the question of whether they are entitled to rely on public interest justifications. Can private entities legitimately claim to be acting in the public interest? If so, how should we go about recognizing such a claim? Are there any preconditions attached to public

[76] Stefaan van den Bogaert, 'Horizontality: The Court Attacks?' in Catherine Barnard and Joanne Scott (eds.), *The Law of the Single European Market: Unpacking the Premises* (Hart Publishing, 2002), 123

[77] With the entry into force of the Lisbon Treaty all references to a 'common market' have been replaced by references to the 'internal market'. Accordingly, this book treats the concept of 'internal market' as encompassing not only the four freedoms, but also the competition rules, the common commercial policy, and the common agricultural policy, despite the intuition that an 'internal market' is a narrower concept than a 'common market'. For literature on the ambiguity that resulted out of the introduction of the concept 'internal market' see Pierre Pescatore, 'Some Critical Remarks on the "Single European Act"' (1987) 24 *Common Market Law Review*, 9; VerLoren van Themaat and Kapteyn, *Introduction to the Law of the European Communities* (Deventer: Kluwer, 1989), 78; Laurence W. Gormley, 'Competition and Free Movement: Is the Internal Market the Same as a Common Market?' [2002] *European Business Law Review*, 517

[78] Garth Davies, 'Article 86, the EC's Economic Approach to Competition Law, and the General Interest' [2009] *European Competition Journal*, 549

[79] Case C-171/11, *Fra.bo SpA v Deutsche Vereinigung des Gas- und Wasserfaches eV (DVGW)* EU: C:2012:176, Opinion of AG Trstenjak; see further Chapter 2 Section 2.1.4

interest claims in terms of popular support and consent, or is a mere contribution to a recognized public interest sufficient? These same questions apply equally to restrictions of competition by undertakings wishing to pursue public interests such as environmental or social protection, questioning the traditional divide between the rules on the free movement of goods, on the one hand, and the competition rules, on the other hand.

To be sure, there is growing support in the literature for recognizing the significance of law-making outside the realm of the state, and seeking to establish under which conditions such law-making can be considered legitimate.[80] That literature recognizes and accepts a broad range of norms, rejecting both the imposition of a sovereigntist, territorially-based system, as well as universalist ideals. Instead, it advocates a more pluralist solution, managing conflict between hybrid legal spaces through procedural mechanisms, practices and institutions instead of ignoring (sovereigntist territorialism) or eliminating (universalism) them.[81] Managing those conflicts can result in seeking to reconcile competing norms, deferring to jurisdictional differences, or at the very least, requiring judges to explain why deference to international norms is not possible.

If EU law should recognize private public interest measures, how should it go about doing so? As with unilateral regulation, private regulation raises legitimacy issues.[82] When and under which conditions should private parties have the right to rely on public interests to justify restricting trade or competition under EU law? This is not solely a theoretical exercise. Private process-based measures are a particularly appealing form of regulation because they are not bound by the territorial constraints that public measures face. Initiatives such as the FSC or MSC labels can regulate production processes across the globe without being limited by the constraints territorially bound public authorities face.

[80] Harm Schepel, 'Private Regulators in Law' in Joost Pauwelyn, Ramses Wessel, and Jan Wouters (eds.), *Informal International Lawmaking* (Oxford Scholarship Online, 2013), 356; Steven Bernstein and Benjamin Cashore, 'Can Non-State Global Governance be Legitimate? An Analytical Framework' [2007] *Regulation & Governance*, 347; Paul Schiff Berman, 'Global Legal Pluralism' (2007) 80 *Southern California Law Review*, 1155; Julia Black, 'Constitutionalising Self-Regulation' (1996) 59 *The Modern Law Review*, 24; Mena and Palazzo, 'Input and Output Legitimacy of Multi-Stakeholder Initiatives', 527

[81] Berman, 'Global Legal Pluralism', 1155

[82] Mena and Palazzo, 'Input and Output Legitimacy of Multi-Stakeholder Initiatives', 527

If one uses democratic legitimacy theory as a normative basis for determining whether private parties can regulate in the public interest, such regulation would need to be acceptable to the governed. The legitimacy of the public interest claim made by private regulators, then, would depend on the extent to which those affected consent to the rules. The legitimacy of private process-based measures is enhanced if those affected by the activities of the private regulator perceive the *procedure* of law-making as credible or justified because the rules reflect their authentic preferences (input legitimacy).[83] This can be done, for instance, by allowing participation in decision-making by those governed, creating rules that promote deliberation and increase transparency. The more inclusive, consensus-oriented and open the process is, the more legitimate it is from an input perspective.

The output legitimacy of process-based measures, on the other hand, is enhanced if the private entities crafting process-based measures are capable of solving collective problems.[84] The output legitimacy of a process-based measure will be enhanced, for example, if the rule has comprehensive coverage, and thus applies as universally as possible to the actors that it targets. The more free-riders there are to a production standard targeting a specific industry, the less legitimate it will be. Efficacy is also crucial to output legitimacy. This refers to the contribution the rule makes to actually solving the problem at hand. A rule may be poorly designed, either because the rule is too weak to solve the problem or because it has negative side effects. A weak rule suffers from legitimacy problems because the rule does not live up to its promises. Examples include voluntary standards that are not taken seriously, or 'green-washing', where an espoused commitment to environmental goals is not matched by actual contribution to those goals.[85] Another aspect of output legitimacy that is of particular relevance to private transnational regulators is enforcement of norms. Regulators can increase legitimacy by creating transparent certification schemes that are monitored by independent third parties, but their legitimacy suffers

[83] Scharpf, *Governing in Europe: Effective and Democratic?* 7. See also Mena and Palazzo, 'Input and Output Legitimacy of Multi-Stakeholder Initiatives', 527; Weiler, 'In the Face of Crisis: Input Legitimacy, Output Legitimacy and the Political Messianism of European Integration', 825; Boedeltje and Cornips, 'Input and Output Legitimacy in Interactive Governance' (No. NIG2-01) http://repub.eur.nl/pub/1750

[84] Ibid.

[85] Mena and Palazzo, 'Input and Output Legitimacy of Multi-Stakeholder Initiatives', 527 at 540–542

if they only apply self-monitoring.[86] Thus, process regulations are less legitimate if control over compliance is less independent (which is the case with self-monitoring, first and second party monitoring) as there are incentives to cheat.

Input and output legitimacy are complementary, but can also conflict.[87] Input and output legitimacy are complementary in the sense that through adequate representation and participation in norm-making, the interests that a norm protects can be better identified and more effectively pursued. If the norm-maker does not know the interests of the people that will be governed by the norm, it might be difficult to reach the intended results. On the other hand, a lot of input legitimacy can make it difficult to address a particular problem, because it might be hard to find consensus if every stakeholder's preference were taken into account.[88]

Assessing the regulation of production methods by transnational actors through democratic legitimacy theory is not without difficulties, as they do not operate within a single territorial setting, or in a single issue area. Those affected by the rules are thus harder to identify, and encompass not only the persons directly addressed, but also those who experience the positive and negative effects of certain means of production, such as indigenous peoples living in rainforests affected by deforestation. While nation-states have an advantage in this respect, public rules can also have a significant effect on others, and as such can be questionable from a legitimacy point of view.[89] Therefore, Input legitimacy can in both cases be increased where other organizations and governments endorse a process-based rule.

The question is to what extent such legitimacy issues influence the ECJ's decision making when private parties create obstacles to trade or restrict competition through process-based measures. Market regulation by public bodies that is exclusively aimed at environmental protection, for example, does not fall under EU competition rules, even though such regulation can restrict competition among undertakings. Is this any different if the undertakings themselves regulate the market? Under

[86] Ibid.
[87] Boedeltje and Cornips, 'Input and Output Legitimacy in Interactive Governance' (No. NIG2-01) http://repub.eur.nl/pub/1750
[88] Ibid., 11
[89] The prime example here would be a process-based measure by an importing country severely affecting the export opportunities of an important industry in an exporting country.

what circumstances can such private market regulation escape the application of the cartel prohibition of Article 101 Treaty on the Functioning of the European Union (TFEU)? Does it matter that a restrictive agreement has broad grassroots and public support and contributes to a public interest? Similarly, can private parties rely on public interest justifications if the ECJ finds the free movement of goods rules applicable to their trade restrictive conduct? These questions all relate to the blurring of the public-private divide in transnational market regulation, and the Court's response to this change.

Regulating Whom?

Process-based measures also raise interesting issues in relation to whom these regulations target. In addition to command-and-control measures that impose legal requirements on producers, process-based measures can also target governments and consumers. Many process-based measures, for instance, attempt to nudge consumers into making responsible purchasing decisions. Process-based measures can also target the governments of other countries, creating incentives to change their production regulation. This book identifies three principal targets of process-based measures: governments, producers, and consumers, and will refer to these measures as *country-based measures, producer-based measures*, and *consumer-based measures*. The way internal market law deals with the question of whom process-based regulations target gives further insight not only into how these measures can best be designed or enacted, but also into how the internal market operates and the structural biases that exist within the EU's trading system, for example, the way it potentially favours consumer-based over producer-based measures.

Country-Based Measures

The first actor whom process-based measures can target is the government of a trading partner. These type of process-based measures will be referred to in this book as *country-based measures*. A country-based measure, or a 'government policy standard' as Steve Charnovitz calls it, is a measure that seeks to impede or prohibit the marketing or import of a product on the grounds that the country in which it was produced does not have adequate health, environmental, safety, or other legislation in force.[90] Country-based measures featured in the GATT *Tuna–Dolphin* and

[90] Charnovitz, 'The Law of Environmental PPMs in the WTO: Debunking the Myth of Illegality', 59

the WTO *US – Shrimp* disputes discussed above.[91] The measure at issue in *Tuna – Dolphin* was the US Marine Mammal Protection Act, which prohibited the import of yellow fin tuna harvested with purse-seine nets from the Eastern Tropical Pacific Ocean into the United States unless the harvesting country had a marine mammal protection program.[92] In *US – Shrimp Turtle* the United States prohibited the importation of shrimp from countries that did not require shrimp trawlers flying under their flag to use turtle excluder devices.[93] The EU Leghold Trap Regulation is also a country-based measure.[94] Article 3 of Regulation 3254/91/EEC prohibits the importation of pelts into the EU unless the Commission determines that the country of origin has adopted legislation prohibiting the use of the leghold traps or uses internationally agreed humane trapping standards. Each of these measures aims at changing the behaviour of *governments*, not that of producers or consumers. Market access is only granted if a country (rather than individual producers) abides by the importing state's production rules.[95]

Country-based measures have a number of policy advantages for regulators, but also considerable downsides. The main advantage of a country-based measure is that it can result in the greatest degree of environmental and social protection abroad, *if* it results in the exporting

[91] WTO Appellate Body Report, *United States: Import Prohibition of Certain Shrimp and Shrimp Products*, 12 October 1998 (WT/DS58/AB/R)

[92] GATT Panel Report. *United States – Restrictions on the Imports of Tuna (Mexico)*. Not adopted, circulated on 3 September 1991 (DS21/R - 39S/155)

[93] WTO Appellate Body Report, *United States: Import Prohibition of Certain Shrimp and Shrimp Products*, 12 October 1998 (WT/DS58/AB/R)

[94] Council Regulation 3254/91 of 4 November 1991 prohibiting the use of leghold traps in the Community and the introduction into the Community of pelts and manufactured goods of certain wild animal species originating in countries which catch them by means of leghold traps or trapping methods which do not meet international humane trapping standards, OJ 1991 No. L308/1

[95] Country-based measures are, however, still connected to a particular product, and therefore cannot be equated with economic sanctions, which are aimed at cutting economic ties without a specific link between the product and its production process, in order to induce change in government policy abroad. Where country-based measures sanction the marketing of products because their country of origin does not abide by certain production standards *for those products*, economic sanctions target government behaviour that is unrelated to the product that can no longer be imported. To be sure, while many country-based measures are enacted by public authorities, they can also be enacted by private parties too, for instance boycotts of Israeli products because of Israeli settlement policy by non-governmental organizations. See for a list of these boycotts (which do not all call for a boycott of *all* Israeli products) www.ethicalconsumer.org/boycotts/boycottslist/israel.aspx

country changing its laws. All producers in the country of export, irrespective of whether those producers export to the regulating state, will be subjected to the social or environmental production standard. The success greatly depends, however, on the persuasive force of the country-based measure in changing the targeted government's policies. If a targeted government does not change its laws, the measures can be relatively ineffective, since producers adhering to the more stringent production standard are not placed in a competitive advantage over those that do not.

Moreover, country-based measures can be relatively easy for a regulator to monitor. All that is required is to verify whether the country of production has the necessary legislation in place. Alternatively, an importing state can distinguish between adherence to a standard and enforcement of that standard, making expensive monitoring systems unnecessary. Monitoring is, to a significant extent, 'outsourced' to the government of the targeted country. As soon as the importing state is convinced that the exporting country will enact and apply the required production standards, products from that country can be marketed again. Such a system is, practically speaking, easier than sending inspectors of (private) conformity assessment bodies abroad to verify compliance with a process-based standard. Paradoxically, this depends on trust in the other country's ability to enforce a standard that it did not wish to adopt on its own initiative.

Country-based measures are, however, also problematic for a number of reasons. First, because country-based measures target the activities of governments, they are politically sensitive. Such measures risk being subject to accusations of neo-colonialism, paternalism, and economic coercion.[96] The targeted government might object that such measures interfere with its right to self-determination and sovereignty: each country should be able to determine its own levels of protection and not be economically coerced into copying another country's legislation. Of course, much depends on the *de facto* economic dependency of the exporting country on the importing and regulating country's market. Essentially, the exporting country can still do as it pleases, but it might lose access to a market if it does not abide by the country-based measure of the importing state.

In this respect, country-based measures can also be seen as unfair to countries with smaller economies that are more dependent on exports

[96] See Section I.1 and I.2, and Chapter 3 Section 3.1

than countries with large domestic markets.[97] Similarly, it may be unfair to countries with heavily specialized economies that are strongly dependent on the export of one particular product as compared to countries with a diversified and developed economy. If a country's economy is highly dependent on coffee exports, for example, an importing country with a large market for coffee will be in a powerful position vis-à-vis the exporting country's production legislation. Also, those countries that only have few trading partners will suffer more than those that have many trading partners.

Country-based measures also raise extraterritoriality concerns, as the nexus between national interest and the process-based measure is weaker. A measure that requires all tuna to be labelled 'dolphin safe' when sold in the importing country, for instance, demonstrates a stronger link with the interest of consumer protection than a measure that requires all tuna from a particular country – irrespective of the country of destination – to be harvested according to certain dolphin-protection standards.

In addition, country-based measures can be disproportionate and ineffective if targeted governments are not prepared to change their production laws. For example, if a state enacts a country-based measure to combat child labour abroad by prohibiting the marketing of textile products from Bangladesh, the measure would also ban textile products from Bangladesh that were not made using child labour, punishing producers who respect labour and human rights standards and those who do not alike. Only if non-adhering products suffer more than products that adhere to the given production standards, are country-based measures truly effective. In such a situation, non-adhering products are placed at a competitive disadvantage to adhering products, making the country-based measure effective because non-compliance is punished by market forces. However, such a situation is unlikely to materialize, because it is more likely that non-adherence is cheaper and thus results in a better competitive position in the markets of countries that do not have a process-based measure in place.[98] Another practical issue is that if multiple countries decide to enact conflicting

[97] Charnovitz, 'The Law of Environmental PPMs in the WTO: Debunking the Myth of Illegality', 59, at 69

[98] See for this discussion also Howard Chang, 'An Economic Analysis of Trade Measures to Protect the Global Environment' (1995) 83 *Georgetown Law Journal*, 4; Howse and Regan, 'The Product/Process Distinction: An Illusory Basis for Disciplining Unilateralism in Trade Policy', 249, at 270–272

country-based measures, exporting countries are faced with the impossibility of complying with all of them.

Finally, country-based measures are simply discriminatory. Products complying with the required production standard are refused market access solely on the basis of their origin. This discriminatory aspect, it may be argued, is normatively undesirable and should be limited to situations where there is clearly no other option on the table or where the interests at stake are so high that they mandate priority over trade liberalization *and* the principle of non-discrimination.

While these policy considerations are primarily relevant for regulators in choosing their course of action when they wish to address production conditions abroad, they may equally be relevant for the ECJ in determining their legality, in particular, when assessing whether Member State or EU process-based measures comply with the principle of proportionality. The ECJ may consider, for example, that a country-based measure enacted by a Member State is more trade-restrictive than necessary, because producers complying with the underlying production norm are denied access to the market simply because the government of the country of production does not abide by the norm set by the importing Member State.

Producer-Based Measures

Producer-based measures, by contrast, target the behaviour of producers of goods, not that of consumers or the governments of other countries. These measures are designed to prevent producers that do not comply with certain rules from accessing the market of the importing state. Examples of such rules are the EU ban on trade in seal products, the EU cosmetics Regulation, and the FLEGT (Forest Law Enforcement, Governance and Trade) initiative (in particular, the timber Regulation).[99] The seal products ban, for example, prevents seal products from being marketed on the EU internal market unless those seals have been hunted by indigenous peoples as part of their subsistence and not as part of a

[99] Regulation 1007/2009 of the European Parliament and of the Council of 16 September 2009 on trade in seal products providing for restrictions on the placing on the market of the European Union of seal products, OJ 2009 No. L286/36 (subsequently amended by Regulation 2015/1775 of the European Parliament and of the Council of 6 October 2015, OJ 2015 No. L262/1); Regulation 1223/2009 of the European Parliament and of the Council of 30 November 2009 on cosmetic products, OJ 2009 No. L 342/59; Regulation 995/2010 of the European Parliament and of the Council of 20 October 2010 laying down the obligations of operators who place timber and timber products on the market, OJ 2010 No. L295/23. See further Chapter 1 Section 1.1.2.

commercial operation. In addition, seal products can also be marketed if they originate from hunts that are part of marine conservation measures. The cosmetics Regulation bans cosmetics that have been tested for their safe use on animals. The timber Regulation prohibits the marketing of illegally harvested timber within the EU. As such, producers of timber in third countries are denied access to the European market if they do not comply with the legislation of the countries in which they harvest timber.

Public producer-based measures can best be seen as a collective purchasing decision in which a state decides to no longer provide economic incentives to produce in socially or environmentally degrading ways.[100] Producer-based measures are purchasing decisions because they do not attempt to regulate production directly, but only affect the producer's market access. A producer can still harvest shrimp in ways that kill turtles, for instance, but if it does so it will lose consumers for those shrimp products. Unlike with country-based measures, this purchasing decision is not made on the basis of government policy but on the individual conduct of a producer. The purchasing decisions are *collective* because they do not depend on the preferences of the individual consumer in a country. This is different from consumer-based measures such as labelling requirements and advertising restrictions which merely try to nudge or inform individuals about harmful effects of production of certain goods, while leaving the ultimate purchasing decision to the individual consumer.

Producer-based measures can be enacted by private parties as well. Undertakings may, for example, lay down production standards either for themselves and their competitors, or for their suppliers. An example of a private producer-based measure is the agreement by the garment industry to require their suppliers in Bangladesh to respect certain minimum work safety standards.[101]

Producer-based measures can be subdivided into measures that target the entire means of production of a producer and measures that only target the production of the specific goods marketed in the importing country. Charnovitz labels the former as a 'producer characteristics' standard and the latter as a 'how produced' standard.[102] The difference

[100] Davies, 'Process and Production Method Based Restrictions on Trade in the EU', 69 at 70–71

[101] Information can be found about this accord on www.bangladeshaccord.org/

[102] Charnovitz, 'The Law of Environmental PPMs in the WTO: Debunking the Myth of Illegality', 59, at 67

is that in the former case, a producer will be denied market access because some of his production is harmful, even if the goods marketed in the importing country comply with the production rules, whereas in the latter case these, goods can be marketed and the producer can continue producing harmfully with respect to products marketed somewhere else. The former approach is linked to incentivizing general corporate social responsibility, whereas the latter is more narrowly focussed on preventing harmful means of production.

Producer-based measures might be enacted and their legality assessed on the basis of a number of different reasons. Producer-based measures can be an effective means of addressing concerns over production abroad if access to the importing market is an important incentive for producers to change their production methods. In addition, the incentive provided is normally larger than for consumer-based measures, because they prevent *all* consumers – not only those who decide not to buy – from purchasing the offending goods. This can be an important consideration for regulators when consumer and citizen preferences do not overlap.

Second, producer-based measures can result in economically efficient outcomes. Providing incentives for socially or environmentally sound production is more efficient than a blanket rejection of products from countries whose government policies are ethically or environmentally unsound.[103] Because the importing country does not attribute value to economically sound production processes, societal value gets lost, and producers that adhere to sound production processes are denied a market.

In addition, if states were not permitted to enact producer-based measures, this would result in a loss in total welfare.[104] As Gareth Davies has argued:

> [T]he population of this state also give up income if they deprive themselves of cheap imports by having PPM-rules, and if they do so this is because they presumably place a sufficient value on the matters that the PPM-rules protect – the environment, or their own clean conscience. Depriving them of these rules therefore decreases their welfare. This welfare decrease is an externality that is not internalized by the industry in the exporting state, with resulting over-production and loss of total welfare.[105]

[103] Howse and Regan, 'The Product/Process Distinction: An Illusory Basis for Disciplining Unilateralism in Trade Policy', 249, at 270

[104] This can be equally true for consumer-based measures, as discussed below.

[105] Davies, 'Process and Production Method Based Restrictions on Trade in the EU', 70–71; see also Howse and Regan, 'The Product/Process Distinction: An Illusory Basis for

These considerations also highlight a third advantage of producer-based rules for regulators: the nexus with the territory of the regulating Member State is more apparent than with country-based rules. Whereas country-based rules aim to prevent harmful production in the country of origin generally, producer-based rules only target those undertakings that seek to market their goods in the regulating Member State. Producer-based measures are also less politically sensitive, as they are less judgmental of the *politics* of another country, but rather attribute value to the conduct of producers who may not be located abroad. This consideration might be diplomatically more advantageous for regulators, and can influence the ECJ's decision-making too, to the extent that the Court might give preference to preserving good relations among states, in a similar way as the WTO Panellists and Appellate Body Members have done so in the past.[106]

Lastly, policy-makers may give preference to producer-based measures because certain producer-based measures have a cooperative nature, as opposed to the unilateral aspects of country-based measures. The prime example is the EU Timber Regulation, which permits the EU to assist in the enforcement of third state environmental and social rules relating to the harvest of timber. Producers of timber in those countries are confronted with a strong economic incentive to comply with the rules, because otherwise they will not only be breaking the law of their home state, but will also lose access to the entire European market.

Not all producer-based measures have such effects, of course. More often than not, process-based measures reflect different perceptions of the appropriate level of environmental or social protection in relation to the production of goods. The disadvantages of producer-based measures echo the objections to process-based measures more generally: such measures can be perceived as economically coercive and insufficiently reflective of the needs of a particular country or respectful of different values. This is not easily resolved, however, as a rejection of producer-based measures equally infringes upon the autonomy of the regulating state to collectively decide which products it wishes to purchase.[107]

Disciplining Unilateralism in Trade Policy' (2000) 11 *European Journal of International Law*, 249, at 280–285

[106] See Section I.2 [107] See Chapter 3 Section 3.3

These policy considerations can have an impact on the ECJ's assessment of the legality of process-based measures as well. If a measure is not calibrated to address the precise concern of the regulating entity, the Court might find the measure not justifiable under the free movement of goods provisions, for instance. But the same applies for the assessment under EU competition rules. If undertakings develop a producer-based standard because they have evidence that a consumer-based or country-based measure is less effective for reasons listed above, this may affect the reasoning of the Court in assessing the measure at hand.

Consumer-Based Measures

Consumer-based measures aim not at changing the behaviour of governments or producers directly, but rather at changing the behaviour of consumers by encouraging them to purchase environmentally or socially sound products. Examples of consumer-based measures are taxation, mandatory and voluntary labelling rules, bans on advertising, funding or organizing promotional campaigns to raise consumer awareness of production processes, public and private boycotts, and restrictions on where and when certain products may be sold. In addition, this book treats EU public procurement legislation as consumer-based because it sets forth the conditions under which Member State authorities, as consumers, can make purchasing decisions on the basis of social and environmental interests.

Consumer-based measures are an individually oriented market-driven approach to solving social and environmental issues. In that sense, they can be seen as a form of outsourcing governmental responsibility to protect public interests. Alternatively, they can be seen as a private attempt to regulate the market where the government is unwilling to do so. The advantage of consumer-based measures is that they are generally less trade restrictive than country-based or producer-based measures, as they do not prevent access to a market. Products can still be offered for sale, even if they do not comply with a particular production standard, and it is left to the consumer to decide whether he or she wishes to purchase the product or not. Consumer-based measures, even at their most intrusive, only nudge or attempt to influence consumer behaviour, but the consumer is still at liberty to ignore governmental policy. Of course, in some instances, consumer preferences and perceptions are so strong that market access will be denied for a non-compliant product as a result of a consumer-based measure. For instance, there is barely any market in the United States for tuna that is not dolphin-safe, since American consumers feel strongly about dolphin welfare.[108]

For regulators, consumer-based measures also have the domestic advantage of being less intrusive on the individual choice of the inhabitants of the regulating state and therefore less paternalistic. This can be preferable for authorities in a situation in which only a minor part of the population feels strongly about the production process of a particular product or where opinion is strongly divided. For instance, if a part of the population has a strong preference for animal-friendly meat, whereas another part of the population has an equally strong preference for cheap meat, a compromise solution can be a consumer-based measure, allowing individuals to decide for themselves which product they prefer. Government intervention is then limited to correcting information asymmetries or influencing consumer choice for those that do not have strong views on the issue.

As such, there is also a much stronger territorial nexus between the interest protected and the regulating state, as the aim of consumer-based measures is generally strongly connected with the inhabitants of the regulating state. This is more so because that information might also, and in some cases even predominantly, concern domestic production. Opposing a consumer-based measure because it is 'extraterritorial' simply because it may be related to production processes elsewhere will become more difficult because the rule is aimed at properly informing the consumers of the regulating state and can have effects for domestic production too.

Regulators may also favour consumer-based measures over producer-based measures on economic grounds, although the economic picture is complex. In some instances, producer-based measures might be disadvantageous compared to consumer-based measures, because even consumers who do not value a particular process-based attribute must pay a premium, resulting in a loss of welfare. However, this is not always the case. As Howse and Regan point out:

> [W]hether it is true depends on the nature of people's concerns. If all that anyone in the importing country cares about is that her own purchase of shrimp should not encourage the killing of turtles, and if the extra cost of buying turtle-friendly shrimp is no serious object, then indeed labelling requirements solve the

[108] WTO Panel Report, *United States – Measures Concerning the Importation, Marketing and Sale of Tuna and Tuna Products (US–Tuna)*, 15 September 2011 (WT/DS381/R) paras. 7.84–7.89

> problem. People who care about turtles (in this limited way) can just buy turtle-friendly shrimp. The situation is slightly more complicated if the extra cost of turtle-friendly shrimp matters. It may be that some consumer is willing to pay that additional cost if and only if she knows that the turtles will thereby be saved, which depends not just on what she does, but on what others do as well. Here the consumer needs information about collective behaviour, which is not provided just by labelling.
>
> But the most serious problem is further along. It may be that the people who care about turtles do not eat shrimp at all (and conversely the people who eat shrimp do not care about turtles). Now the consumers of turtle-unfriendly are imposing an externality (the death of turtles) on a completely distinct group. It is to prevent this externality (or, as friends of the turtles may view it, this immorality that the process-based restriction is imposed.[109]

In addition, regulators may not prefer consumer-based measures because they have the disadvantages of transaction costs (the sometimes significant effort that goes in gathering and transmitting information relating to production methods) and problems related to an attitude-behaviour gap (the intent of individuals to buy green or ethical is not reflected in actual consumer behaviour), resulting in purchasing decisions not adequately reflecting the consumer's preferences.[110]

Policy-makers might also oppose consumer-based measures because they do not wish to 'outsource' governmental responsibility for important public interests such as environmental and social protection to the consumer. Consumer-based measures can be a means of empowering the consumer to take environmentally and socially conscious decisions, but they also burden consumers with that responsibility. Policy-makers, therefore, might prefer collectively solving social and environmental problems, instead of requiring consumers individually to be aware of these problems every time they go to the grocery store, enter into new electricity supply contracts, or purchase clothing.

In addition, policy-makers might oppose consumer-based measures because of their market driven rationale, which favours consumers and those with resources over non-consumers and people with a lack of

[109] Howse and Regan, 'The Product/Process Distinction: An Illusory Basis for Disciplining Unilateralism in Trade Policy' (2000) 11 *European Journal of International Law*, 249, at 273

[110] Gaëlle Balineau and Ivan Dufeu, 'Are Fair Trade Goods Credence Goods? A New Proposal, with French Illustrations' (2010) 92 *Journal of Business Ethics* 331; M. Darby and E. Karni, 'Free Competition and the Optimal Amount of Fraud' (1973) 16 *Journal of Law and Economics*, 67; S. Lupton, 'Shared Quality Uncertainty and the Introduction of Indeterminate Goods' (2005) 29 *Cambridge Journal of Economics*, 399

resources. Only those who actually consume and are willing and able to pay for the products produced in the way they desire are able to express their preferences. Policy-makers therefore might also want to factor in those who care and value social and environmental protection but do not consume certain products, and are thus not able to express these preferences in market behaviour (for example, vegetarians cannot 'vote with their pocketbooks' to prefer animal-friendly over cheap meat, as they do not purchase meat at all).

Lastly, regulators might not opt for consumer-based measures because they are generally less effective in terms of social and environmental protection and can even be completely ineffective or even counterproductive. Generally speaking (except in cases such as the US dolphin-safe tuna example), a market for environmentally degrading or socially irresponsible products will likely remain even after the enactment of consumer-based measures.[111] This makes such measures less effective than producer-based measures in meeting social and environmental goals. In addition, consumer behaviour in a particular country does not necessarily equate with the political preferences of its citizens. While a large part of the population might be morally appalled by the killing of seal pups and does not wear products derived from them, a small resource-rich part of the population might be willing to pay a significant amount of money for those products.[112] Labelling rules in such a case, or awareness campaigns in such a case can be completely ineffective in terms of animal welfare protection. A large discrepancy between citizen preferences and consumer behaviour can even result in consumer-based measures being counter-productive, as they might result in additional costs for those producers that do adhere to higher production standards, for example, because they have to make additional costs in labelling and certifying their products.

Again, in assessing the justification put forward by regulators in their regulatory choices, these arguments might influence the Court's decision-making in upholding a measure under Article 263 TFEU, the free movement of goods provisions, and EU competition rules. Their effectiveness in the particular context in which the process-based

[111] See above n 108

[112] In addition, vitamin manufacturers also use seal products in their products, resulting either in demand for seal products, even if consumers do not wish to buy certain seal products. This may be the result of a lack of information or indifference when it comes to purchasing vitamin supplements.

measure is situated might enable the Court to determine whether the measure is the least trade-restrictive alternative, for instance, or whether it is not properly designed to achieve the goals the regulators seeks to achieve.

I.2 Outline

This book is about how EU law constrains the EU, the Member States, and private bodies in creating process-based measures that seek to protect social and environmental interests abroad. It will assess the limits set by EU internal market law to the enactment of the different types of process-based measures through the lens of the challenges (extraterritoriality, unilateralism, and private rule-making) identified above and at three distinct levels: the EU, the Member States, and private actors.

At the EU level, this involves discussing and criticizing the legal doctrine on the competence to enact process-based product rules. At the Member State level, it entails analysing the competence of EU Member States to enact process-based product rules under the free movement of goods, including public procurement law. With respect to private actors, it includes assessing the process-based product rules developed by transnational private actors in light of EU competition rules and, to a lesser extent, the rules of the free movement of goods.

Rather than providing an extensive overview of the different areas of law involved, this book will focus on how EU law views the three core challenges posed by process-based measures and complement this legal analysis by addressing the policy context in which process-based measures are formed. Thus, this book not only attempts to answer the legal question whether, for instance, Member States can extra-territorialise their preferences and norms through market regulation under free movement law, but also how such measures can be calibrated to increase their legitimacy. The book therefore allows for a better understanding of both the problems involved in process-based regulation, as well as the nature of the relationship in the EU between economic freedoms and the protection of public interests.

This book will proceed as follows. Chapter 1 looks at the process-based measures enacted by the EU, such as the sustainability criteria for biofuels and the EU marketing ban on seal products, and whether such measures can be challenged before the EU courts on grounds related to extraterritoriality and unilateralism. The EU has enacted a wide range of process-based measures, and the ECJ takes a deferential stance towards the EU legislator in relation to the key challenges posed by process-based measures.

Chapters 2, 3, and 4 assess process-based measures enacted by the Member States. Chapter 2 focuses on process-based measures as restrictions to the free movement of goods. It will examine at the application of the free movement of goods provisions to country-based, producer-based, and consumer-based measures. The scope of these provisions is wide, with only those few consumer-based measures which can be qualified as non-discriminatory selling arrangements falling outside the scope of the prohibition of Article 34 TFEU, and therefore not requiring justification on the basis of ECJ case law or relying on one of the derogations contained in Article 36 TFEU. Furthermore, the free movement of goods provisions also apply to goods from third countries traded within the EU. This enables traders to challenge a range of process-based measures that seek to accomplish social and environmental protection outside the EU.

Chapters 3 and 4 explore whether these process-based measures by Member States are nonetheless permissible under EU law. The chapters, therefore, look into the question of whether Member States can justify process-based measures that create obstacles to trade in goods. It does so by further delving into the issues of extraterritoriality and unilateralism within the context of the free movement of goods. The chapters set out the main arguments in favour of and against accepting justifications for process-based measures through the lenses of extraterritoriality (Chapter 3) and unilateralism (Chapter 4). In this context, procurement and taxation law will be used as examples of how the ability of Member States to enact process-based measures is regulated and how this reflects upon the broader discussions on extraterritoriality and unilateralism. It argues that 'extraterritoriality' is an illusory basis for objecting to process-based measures in EU free movement law, while harmonization and the principle of mutual recognition constrain Member States' possibilities for justifying intra-EU restrictions of trade in goods.

Chapter 5 looks at private initiatives seeking to improve the production processes of goods from an environmental or social point of view, but from the angle of competition law. Competing undertakings may wish to standardize certain production processes or restrict competition in other ways in line with their corporate social responsibility policies. This chapter demonstrates when this may be the case and under which circumstances this may be justified under EU competition law. The chapter therefore assesses under which circumstances such conduct might fall within the scope of Article 101 (1) TFEU, the EU's cartel prohibition, and identifies two approaches that enable undertakings to justify restrictions of competition if the restrictions serve social or environmental interests. The first approach is based on placing the competition goals within the context of the wider aims and ambitions of the EU, and permits restrictions of competition on the basis of a public interest test similar to that of the fundamental freedoms. The second approach seeks to quantify the social and environmental benefits of restrictive conduct on the basis of Article 101 (3) TFEU (the provision that enables undertakings to justify restrictions of competition). The chapter also discusses the legitimacy of public interest claims by private actors, and the relationship between private standardization restrictive of competition and public regulation.

Finally, the concluding chapter summarizes the findings in the various chapters, and paints an overall picture of the legality of process-based measures within the EU legal system and the main legal challenges facing them. The conclusion reflects on the main findings of the book and provides some guidelines on how and under which circumstances process-based measures may be permitted. There is a strong presumption of lawfulness of process-based measures enacted by the EU, whereas Member State process-based measures and private measures are not as easy to maintain, although if properly designed these measures may be found to be compatible with EU law. The conclusion will also place the main findings of the book in the context of more general thinking about the EU's identity as a global actor and approach to globalization.

1 EU Process-Based Measures

Introduction

In its new trade policy document 'Trade for All', the Commission highlights the use of trade to promote social and environmental goals. It states that the EU's trade policy 'will not only project our interests, but also our values' noting that 'responsible management of global supply chains is essential to align trade policy with European values'.[1] Indeed, the EU is the author of a considerable number of process-based measures that seek to address social, moral, and environmental concerns at the production stage. The EU has sustainability criteria for biofuels, illegal logging regulations, rules on conflict minerals, several bans relating to animal welfare issues, rules on illegal, unregulated, and unreported fishing (IUU), and environmental labelling initiatives that address the entire supply chain such as the ecolabel and organic label regulations.

This may come as no surprise if one looks at the EU's wider constitutional mandate for its external relations. Article 3 (5) TEU states that the EU in its relations with the wider world 'shall uphold and promote its values' by contributing to, inter alia, 'the sustainable development of the Earth', 'fair trade', and 'the protection of human rights'. This projection of European values on the rest of the world has many labels from 'enlightenment' to 'colonialism', from 'civic imperialism' or 'eco-imperialism' to 'civilian' or 'normative power'.[2] The way in which the EU seeks to achieve these global ambitions rests not solely on leading by example

[1] Commission, 'Trade for All towards a More Responsible Trade and Investment Policy' (Communication) COM (2015) 497 final, 24

[2] Kalypso Nicoaïdis and Robert Howse, '"This is my EUtopia . . .": Narrative as Power' (2002) 40 *Journal of Common Market Studies*, 767; L. J. Ankersmit, J.C. Lawrence, and G.T. Davies, 'Diverging EU and WTO Perspectives on Extraterritorial Process Regulation' (2012) 21

and diffusing its norms at the international scene, but also on linking its market and economic power to its normative preferences and process-based measures, which are exemplary in that regard.[3] Process-based measures are, in the end, economic instruments that can (seek to) influence social or environmental aspects of production abroad.

One could label this outward-looking aspect of market regulation a form of what Joanne Scott has termed 'territorial extension'.[4] This label describes an increasing number of EU internal market and trade rules that seek to mitigate and manage negative impacts within the EU of practices occurring in other parts of the world. Some of these measures apply to conduct outside the EU even where the link with EU territory or other jurisdictional hooks are very weak.

It is clear, then, that the EU has developed a range of process-based measures that it uses to spread its values in 'the wider world'. However, its use of these instruments is not without limits. EU law may impose several different types of limitations on process-based measures, in particular in light of their transnational reach. In line with the two challenges identified in the introductory chapter, this chapter will assess the ways in which EU law limits the adoption of process-based measures through the lenses of extraterritoriality and unilateralism.

In relation to extraterritoriality, the EU is bound by international law and the EU institutions must respect international customary law, including the rules on international jurisdiction, in the exercise of their powers.[5] This chapter will assess the extent to which these jurisdictional limits constrain the EU in enacting process-based measures. Does

Minnesota Journal of International Law Online, 58; Hanna Sevenster, *Eco-imperialisme binnen de Europese Unie; een juridisch probleem?* (Deventer: W.E.J. Tjeenk Willink, 1998)

3 François Duchêne, 'The European Community and the Uncertainties of Interdependence' in Max Kohnstamm and Wolfgang Hager (eds.), *A Nation Writ Large? Foreign Policy Problems Before the European Community* (London: Macmillan, 1973), 9; Ian Manners, 'Normative Power Europe: A Contradiction in Terms?' (2002) 40 *Journal of Common Market Studies*, 235. To be sure, trade policy is not exceptional in that regard within the EU as the integration of different policy fields is commonplace in the EU Treaties, law and way of thinking generally. Ankersmit, 'Pathways to Conflict', 18; Ernst B. Haas, *The Uniting of Europe: Political, Social and Economic Forces, 1950–57* (Notre Dame: University of Notre Dame Press, 1958); Stephen Weatherhill, 'Competence and Legitimacy' in Catherine Barnard and Okeoghene Odudu (eds.), *The Outer Limits of European Union Law* (Oxford: Hart Publishing, 2009), 19–20; Eloi Laurent and Jacques Le Cacheux, *The EU as a Global Ecological Power: The Logics of Market Integration*, available at www.ofce.sciences-po.fr/pdf/dtravail/WP2010-08.pdf

4 Joanne Scott, 'The New EU "extraterritoriality"' (2014) 51 *Common Market Law Review*, 1343

5 Case C-286/90 *Poulsen and Diva Navigation* [1992] ECR I-6019; Case C-366/10, *Air Transport Association of America and Others v Secretary of State for Energy and Climate Change* [2011] ECR I-13755

the ECJ view process-based measures as complying with the territoriality principle under international law? Are process-based measures required to introduce certain 'safety valves' to accommodate the potentially conflicting prescriptive jurisdiction of third countries?

In relation to unilateralism, this chapter will look into legal limits imposed by EU law on the process of developing process-based measures. Is the EU required to take into account the views of extraterritorial actors that may be affected by process-based measures? Is the EU required to undertake multilateral or bilateral efforts to address a transnational social or environmental problem first? And is the EU required to design its process-based measures in such a way that it takes into account the specific circumstances of third countries that may be affected by process-based measures?

This chapter proceeds as follows. Section 1.1 will outline the EU's three different types of process-based measures. It will start with a discussion of the EU's country-based rules such as the Leghold Trap Regulation, and continue with a discussion of producer-based rules and finally consumer-based rules. In doing so, it will highlight the particular features of these measures in light of the main challenges identified in the introduction (extraterritoriality and unilateralism). Section 1.2 will assess the legality of the EU's process-based measures under EU law from the perspective of extraterritoriality. It will discuss the expansive case law of the ECJ on international jurisdiction in cases such as the *Air Transport Association of America* case. Section 1.3 will assess the legality of the EU's process-based measures from the perspective of unilateralism. Here, the relevance and effect of WTO law, as well as general principles of law and the competence 'enabling function' of the Treaty integration articles will be discussed.

1.1 A Short Overview of EU Process-Based Measures

1.1.1 Country-Based Rules

At the time of this writing, the EU has in place three country-based process-based product measures: the Leghold Trap Regulation,[6] the IUU

[6] Council Regulation 3254/91 of 4 November 1991 prohibiting the use of leghold traps in the Community and the introduction into the Community of pelts and manufactured goods of certain wild animal species originating in countries which catch them by means of leghold traps or trapping methods which do not meet international humane trapping standards OJ 1991 No. L308/1

Regulation,[7] and the ban on imports of conflict diamonds.[8] The three measures are similar in design, but also exhibit significant differences.

The EU ban on imports of pelts from third countries which permit the use of leghold traps is probably the EU's most well-known process-based product rule and has been the subject of considerable academic attention.[9] Article 3 of the Leghold Trap Regulation prohibits the importation of pelts into the EU unless the Commission determines that the country of origin of the pelts has adequate legislation in force that prohibits the use of the leghold trap or uses internationally agreed humane trapping standards.

The ban has not been a complete success and has seen opposition by third countries affected by the ban. As a result, the list of states allowed to export pelts to the EU includes a significant number of countries nowadays, and the Commission itself has, by questioning the legality of the Regulation under WTO law, attempted to deprive the ban of much of its legal force.[10] It is not surprising therefore that the EU was unsuccessful in reaching a multilateral solution to the issue of leghold trapping before enacting the import ban.[11] The country-based standard in place here is probably related to the impossibility of other means of verification of the use of leghold traps in imported pelts.[12]

The IUU Regulation operates quite differently and is for that reason considerably less controversial. The IUU Regulation seeks to combat IUU fishing by, inter alia, banning fishery imports from countries that do not take sufficient action to prevent, deter, and eliminate IUU fishing. Article 12 (1) of the Regulation bans the importation into the EU of fishery products obtained from IUU fishing. This ban is made effective

[7] Council Regulation 1005/2008 of 29 September 2008 establishing a Community system to prevent, deter and eliminate illegal, unreported and unregulated fishing OJ 2008 No. L286/1, 1

[8] Regulation 2368/2002 of the Council of 20 December 2002 implementing the Kimberley Process certification scheme for the international trade in rough diamonds OJ 2002 L258/28

[9] André Nollkaemper, 'The Legality of Moral Crusades Disguised in Trade Laws: An Analysis of the EC "Ban" on Furs from Animals taken by Leghold Traps' (1996) 8 *Journal of Environmental Law*, 237; Nathalie Harrems, 'The Leghold Trap Regulation and Potential Pitfalls during the Dutch Presidency of the EU' [1998] *European Environmental Law Review*, 7

[10] Nollkemper, 'The Legality of Moral Crusades', 243–244, see also Harrems, 'Leghold Trap Regulation'; Commission Decision 98/597/EC of 14 October 1998 amending Council Decision 97/602/EC concerning the list referred to in the second subparagraph of Article 3(1) of Regulation (EEC) 3254/91 and in Article 1(1)(a) of Commission Regulation (EC) 35/97 [1998] L 286/56

[11] See Nollkemper, 'The Legality of Moral Crusades', 242

[12] Ibid., 254

by allowing the importation of fishery products only if they are accompanied by a catch certificate. That catch certificate, in turn, is issued by the competent authorities of the flag state of the fishing vessel that has caught the fish and certifies that its catches have been made in accordance with applicable conservation and management measures. The IUU Regulation is a country-based measure, because Article 31 requires the Commission to blacklist 'non-cooperating countries' which, as a result, cannot export fisheries products into the EU.[13]

While the IUU Regulation is, in principle, a country-based measure, because fishing vessels from a non-cooperating country cannot demonstrate compliance with IUU standards, it differs from the EU Leghold Trap Regulation and other more direct country-based measures discussed in the introductory chapter. First of all, the IUU Regulation adopts a negative listing approach: third countries may export their fishery products into the EU unless they are listed as non-cooperating. The Leghold Trap Regulation operates in the opposite way: all imports are banned, unless a country can demonstrate compliance with the Regulation. The IUU Regulation places the burden on the Commission to demonstrate non-compliance by the third country, whereas the Leghold Trap Regulation places the burden on the importer. While the negative listing approach might impede effectiveness and is less precautionary, it also allows for a less burdensome approach towards third country products.

Secondly, the IUU Regulation is less controversial because its substantive standards are based on international standards, whereas the Leghold Trap Regulation is based on an EU standard. The IUU Regulation aims at combatting IUU fishing by seeking compliance with the relevant provisions of the United Nations Convention of the Law of the Sea (UNCLOS), the United Nations Fish Stocks Agreement (UNFSA), the Food and Agriculture Organization (FAO) Compliance Agreement, and the FAO International Plan of Action (FAO IPOA-IUU), as well as ensuring that third country vessels do not breach the laws of the country in whose waters they are fishing.[14] Because the IUU Regulation primarily seeks compliance with internationally agreed standards rather than the EU's own standards, it is less 'unilateral' than the Leghold Trap Regulation.

[13] See also Article 38 (1) of Council Regulation 1005/2008 of 29 September 2008 establishing a Community system to prevent, deter and eliminate illegal, unreported and unregulated fishing OJ 2008 No. L286/1

[14] See Article 2 (2–4) and Article 31 (3) of the Regulation

Thirdly, the IUU Regulation contains procedural safeguards that accommodate third country interests. Third countries cannot immediately be placed on the list of non-cooperating countries. Article 32 requires the Commission to notify the third country of the possibility that it may be listed as a non-cooperating country and give the country in question adequate time to respond. This 'yellow card' procedure enables the third country in question to provide the Commission with additional information, make inquiries, and potentially remedy the situation. If the situation is not resolved, the Commission may propose that the Council add the third country to the list of non-cooperating countries. The Regulation therefore goes to great lengths to establish a dialogue with the third country in question in order to not only remedy the situation but also follow due process principles before banning imports of fisheries products caught by vessels of that country.

The third country-based measure currently in force in the EU is Regulation 2368/2002, which implements the Kimberley Process Certification Scheme for rough diamonds.[15] The Kimberley Process Certification Scheme is a voluntary scheme set up by exporting and importing countries of rough diamonds in cooperation with the diamond industry and civil society. It consists of recommendations that can be implemented through legislation by participating countries and self-regulation by the diamond industry. The scheme was set up in response to the increasing publicity of the problem of 'blood diamonds' – the sale of diamonds by rebels to fund armed conflict – which threatened the viability of the diamond industry. As a result of the civil wars in diamond-producing countries such as Sierra Leone, there was a significant risk of consumer boycotts, which could damage the image of diamonds as symbols of love.[16]

The Regulation implementing the Kimberley Process Certification Scheme in the EU bans imports of rough diamonds, unless they have been certified by the authorities of the participating producing country as not having been used by rebels or their allies to finance conflict

[15] Regulation 2368/2002 of the Council of 20 December 2002 implementing the Kimberley Process certification scheme for the international trade in rough diamonds OJ 2002 L258/28

[16] Virginia Haufler, 'The Kimberley Process Certification Scheme: An Innovation in Global Governance and Conflict Prevention' (2010) 89 *Journal of Business Ethics*, 403–416, at 407; Clive Wright, 'Tacking Conflict Diamonds: The Kimberley Process Certification Scheme' (2004) 11 *International Peacekeeping*, 697–708, at 699

against legitimate governments.[17] As such, the Regulation seeks to ban diamonds traded or harvested by rebel groups to fund armed conflict, and thereby ensures that only ethical diamonds make it to the European internal market. The Regulation is similar to the Leghold Trap Regulation in that it is based on a positive listing approach, where only the Participants listed in Annex II of the Regulation can export to the EU. However, it is also similar to the IUU Regulation in that it is not truly unilateral, as the Kimberley process is the result of a consensual effort among industry, civil society, and producing and importing countries alike. While the regime is deferential towards participating exporting countries, its effectiveness has been criticized, because it depends on the actual compliance of the recommendations of the participants to the scheme.[18] Effective supervision and enforcement mechanisms against non-compliant participants are mostly absent.

In summary, while the three country-based measures discussed have in common that they ban products because they originated from certain countries, they operate very differently. The IUU Regulation and the ban on conflict diamonds are based on much more consensual substantive standards and to a certain extent are more calibrated to the interests of the exporting country.

1.1.2 *Producer-Based Rules*

The EU has more producer-based rules in place than country-based rules. With the exception of the EU Timber Regulation[19] and the EU Conflict Minerals Regulation,[20] all of these producer-based rules impose

[17] Article 3 of the Regulation

[18] Haufler, 'The Kimberley Process Certification Scheme', 403–416; Wright, 'Tacking Conflict Diamonds', 697–708

[19] Regulation 995/2010 of the European Parliament and of the Council of 20 October 2010 laying down the obligations of operators who place timber and timber products on the market OJ 2010 No. L295/23 ; Commission Implementing Regulation 607/2012 of 6 July 2012 on the detailed rules concerning the due diligence system and the frequency and nature of the checks on monitoring organizations as provided for in Regulation (EU) 995/2010 of the European Parliament and of the Council laying down the obligations of operators who place timber and timber products on the market OJ 2012 No. L177, 16; Commission Delegated Regulation 363/2012 of 23 February 2012 on the procedural rules for the recognition and withdrawal of recognition of monitoring organizations as provided for in Regulation (EU) 995/2010 of the European Parliament and of the Council laying down the obligations of operators who place timber and timber products on the market OJ 2012 No. L115/12

[20] Commission, 'Proposal for a Regulation of the European Parliament and of the Council Setting up a Union System for Supply Chain Due Diligence Self-Certification of

animal welfare standards. The EU seal products ban,[21] the ban on animal-tested cosmetics,[22] the import rules for calves[23] and pigs,[24] as well as the EU slaughtering standards for imported meat,[25] all address animal welfare concerns in Europe. All producer-based measures, in contrast to country-based measures, allow producers to market their products in the EU as long as they comply with the relevant substantive standards. Marketing is thus not dependent on the country of origin.

The EU ban on seal products is probably the most well-known and controversial producer-based measure, both legally and politically.[26] The ban was imposed as a response to concerns by the European public about the way seals were killed around the world.[27] The ban has been challenged before both EU courts (unsuccessfully) and the WTO dispute

Responsible Importers of Tin, Tantalum and Tungsten, Their Ores, and Gold Originating in Conflict Affected and High-Risk Areas' COM (2013) 111 final; see for a discussion of the recently agreed standards below.

21 Regulation 1007/2009 of the European Parliament and of the Council of 16 September 2009 on trade in seal products providing for restrictions on the placing on the market of the European Union of seal products, OJ 2009 No. L286/36 (subsequently amended by Regulation 2015/1775 of the European Parliament and of the Council of 6 October 2015 OJ 2015 No. L262/1)

22 Regulation 1223/2009 of the European Parliament and of the Council of 30 November 2009 on cosmetic products OJ 2009 L342/59

23 Council Directive 2008/119/EC of 18 December 2008 laying down minimum standards for the protection of calves OJ 2008 No. L10/7

24 Council Directive 2008/120/EC of 18 December 2008 laying down minimum standards for the protection of pigs OJ 2009 No. L47/5

25 Council Regulation 1099/2009 of 24 September 2009 on the protection of animals at the time of killing OJ 2009 No. L303/1, 1

26 Robert Howse and Joanne Langille, 'Permitting Pluralism: The Seal Products Dispute and Why the WTO Should Accept Trade Restrictions Justified by Noninstrumental Moral Values' (2012) 37 *Yale Journal of International Law*, 367; Julinda Beqiraj, 'The Delicate Equilibrium of EU Trade Measures: The Seals Case' (2013) 14 *German Law Journal*, 279–320; Peter F. Fitzgerald, '"Morality" May Not Be Enough to Justify the EU Seal Products Ban: Animal Welfare Meets International Trade Law' (2011) 14 *Journal of International Wildlife Law & Policy*, 85–136

27 Methods employed included the use of the Norwegian hakapik (a club with a metal spike), firearms and trapping. All of those methods, in part due to the severe weather conditions in areas in which the seal hunt is conducted, often lead to significant pain and suffering by seals because they are not killed instantly. See European Food Safety Authority, 'Scientific Opinion of the Panel on Animal Health and Welfare on a Request from the Commission on the Animal Welfare Aspects of the Killing and Skinning of Seals' (2007) 610 *The EFSA Journal*, 1–122; Howse and Langille, 'Permitting Pluralism', (n 26), 391

settlement body (partially successfully).[28] After the WTO Appellate Body decision, the EU amended the Regulation to comply with the decision.[29]

In essence, the basic Regulation bans the marketing of all seal products. This means that all products that are derived from seals cannot be sold on the EU internal market. There is, however, an 'indigenous communities' exception[30] and a 'personal use' exception.[31] The 'indigenous communities' exception was introduced to take into account the disparate impact of the Regulation on the way of living of Inuit people and other indigenous communities worldwide.[32] Article 3 of the Regulation allows seal products to be imported if they derive from indigenous communities hunting for their subsistence, making the exception more about how hunts are performed by the hunters overall, rather than about the killing of the specific seal of which the seal

[28] Within the EU Courts two groups of cases can be identified. The first group challenging the basic Regulation 1007/2009 directly includes the cases Case T-18/10, *Inuit Tapiriit Kanatami and Others v European Parliament and Council* [2011] ECR II-5599 and the subsequent appeal Case C-583/11P, *Inuit Tapiriit Kanatami and Others v European Parliament and Council* [2013] ECR I-625. The second group sought to annul both the former implementing Regulation and the basic Regulation: Case T-526/10, *Inuit Tapiriit Kanatami and Others v Commission* EU:T:2013:215 and the appeal Case C-398/13P, *Inuit Tapiriit Kanatami and Others v Commission* EU:C:2015:535. Within the WTO see WTO Appellate Body Report, *European Communities – Measures Prohibiting the Importation and Marketing of Seal Products*, 22 May 2014 (WT/DS400/AB/R and WT/DS/401/AB/R

[29] The 'marine resources' exception has been removed and the 'indigenous communities' exception now requires that animal welfare is taken into account (which was not the case previously).

[30] Article 3 (1) of Regulation 1007/2009 (n 21); The 'indigenous communities' exception permits the marketing of seal products if those result from hunts traditionally conducted by Inuit and other indigenous communities, contribute to their subsistence and the hunt is conducted in a manner which has due regard to animal welfare.

[31] Article 3 (2) under a of Regulation 1007/2009 (n 21) and Article 2 of the Commission Regulation 2015/1850 of 13 October 2015 laying down detailed rules for the implementation of Regulation 1007/2009 of the European Parliament and of the Council on trade in seal products OJ 2015 No. L271/1; The 'personal use' exception permits natural persons to bring seal products into the EU for their personal use.

[32] The exception is created in order to respect the culture and identity of the Inuit people in accordance with the UN Declaration on the Rights of Indigenous Peoples. The ban should not result in the Inuit and other indigenous peoples to abandon their traditional way of life and should therefore take into account the basic human needs of such communities. To that end, Article 3 in the implementing Commission Regulation sets out the conditions which must be fulfilled in order for indigenous communities to market their seal products on the EU internal market. The communities must have a 'tradition' in seal hunting, they must depend on the seal hunt for their living, and they must use or consume the seal products themselves. Certification bodies competent to assess these requirements may issue the attesting document that the seal products imported into the EU have met the criteria specified in Article 3 of the implementing Regulation.

product is derived.[33] The three conditions that need to be satisfied in order to be able to rely on the exception are: 1) the hunt has traditionally been conducted by the community in question; 2) the hunt was conducted for and contributes to the subsistence of the community (the hunt cannot be conducted primarily for commercial reasons; and 3) there has been due regard to animal welfare.[34] Seal-friendly labelling (either voluntary or obligatory) was initially also considered before the WTO challenge, but ultimately rejected because of the disproportionate impact of such measures on economic operators as well as the unsatisfactory results such measures would lead to in terms of the regulatory goals set by the EU.[35]

A process-based measure similar in terms of regulatory goals is the EU ban on cosmetics products that have been tested on animals (Regulation 1223/2009).[36] The Regulation is mostly concerned with ensuring that cosmetics products are safe for human use, but an important part addresses animal welfare concerns.[37] Article 18 of the Regulation bans the marketing of cosmetics products that can only demonstrate

[33] Steve Charnovitz characterizes such a measure a *producer characteristics standard*. The standard is a bit more rigorous in its effects, because products not marketed in the regulating country but produced by the same producer would need to comply with the process-based measure. Steve Charnovitz, 'The Law of Environmental PPMs in the WTO: Debunking the Myth of Illegality' (2002) 27 *The Yale Journal of International Law*, 59–110

[34] Initially this third criterion was not part of the Regulation and was introduced in response to the WTO Dispute Settlement Body rulings. This requirement was considered to be impossible to effectively monitor, due to the remoteness and weather conditions present in the regions where the seal hunt takes place. Seal hunts occur in dangerous conditions often on moving ice where it is very difficult for hunters to take the time for execution and verification of humane killing methods. Recital 11 of Regulation 1007/2009 (n 21)

[35] See the considerations by the Commission, the European Parliament and in the Regulation itself. Commission, 'Proposal for a Regulation of the European Parliament and of the Council concerning Trade in Seal Products' COM (2008) 469 final, 12; European Parliament, 'Report on the Proposal for a Regulation of the European Parliament and of the Council concerning Trade in Seals Products' of 5 March 2009 2008/0160(COD), proposed amendment 10; Recital 12 of Regulation 1007/2009

[36] Regulation 1223/2009 on cosmetic products (n 22)

[37] The purpose of the Regulation is the protection of animal welfare, not the protection of animal rights. This is why animal testing under certain conditions is still allowed for pharmaceutical products, but consumption of products not necessary for basic human needs is prohibited. See Council Directive 86/609/EEC of 24 November 1986 on the approximation of laws, regulations and administrative provisions of the Member States regarding the protection of animals used for experimental and other scientific purposes [1986] OJ L 358/1

compliance with the Regulation's health safety standards[38] on the basis of animal tests. As the ECJ recently confirmed in *European Federation for Cosmetic Ingredients*, this provision prohibits the marketing of cosmetics that demonstrate compliance with the Regulation's health safety standards on the basis of animal tests outside the EU.[39]

In contrast to how the EU seal products ban operates, the Cosmetics Regulation differentiates among products, meaning that it is possible for cosmetics manufacturers to market non-animal-tested products in the EU, even if they have used animal tests for other non-EU products. The extraterritorial effects of the Regulation on producers outside the Union is in part intended. As the Commission notes in discussing a potential lift of the ban, 'any change to the 2013 marketing ban could seriously diminish determination to swiftly develop alternative test methods', and imposing a ban sends 'a strong signal far beyond the cosmetics sector and far beyond Europe'.[40] In addition, 'the possible risks from the 2013 marketing ban can be turned into an opportunity for the Union to set an example of responsible innovation in cosmetics with positive impact beyond Europe'.[41]

A specific feature of the ban is that the approved non-animal-testing methods have been developed internationally. Alternative methods that are validated by the EU are in due regard of the development of validation within the Organization for Economic Cooperation and Development (OECD). Also, the Commission cooperates with the United States, Canada and Japan within the International Cooperation on Cosmetic Regulation (ICCR) in which the International Cooperation on Alternative Test Methods (ICATM) has been developed.[42] In other words, there is considerable multilateral cooperation and shared concern over animal testing within the cosmetics industry. Moreover, the Commission works actively with the industry involved and funds research in order to seek alternative

[38] Article 3 of Regulation 1223/2009 (n 22)

[39] Case C-592/14, *European Federation for Cosmetic Ingredients v Secretary of State for Business, Innovation and Skills* EU:C:2016:703, paras 39–45

[40] Commission, 'Communication from the Commission to the European Parliament and the Council on the Animal Testing and Marketing Ban and on the State of Play in Relation to Alternative Methods in the Field of Cosmetics' COM (2013) 135 final, 6

[41] Ibid.

[42] Commission, 'Report from the Commission to the European Parliament and the Council: Report on the Development, Validation and Legal Acceptance of Alternative Methods to Animal Tests in the Field of Cosmetics (2009)' COM (2011) 558 final

methods of testing.[43] As such, the EU's Cosmetics Regulation is much less unilateral than its ban on seal products.

Three producer-based measures on the importation of animals and meat products operate in a very similar way. As part of a more comprehensive framework laying down minimum standards for the protection of calves and pigs, Directives 2008/119/EC and 2008/120/EC require imports of calves and pigs into the EU to meet minimum animal welfare standards before importation.[44] These Directives thus effectively extend the level of protection granted to calves and pigs within the EU to calves and pigs imported into the EU prior to their importation.

Directive 2008/119/EC on minimum standards for the protection of calves lays down minimum space and living requirements for calves as well as requirements relating to their socialization.[45] Directive 2008/120/EC lays down such requirements for pigs.[46] Article 8 of Directive 2008/119/EC and Article 9 of Directive 2008/120/EC subsequently state that 'In order to be imported into the [EU], animals coming from a third country must be accompanied by a certificate issued by the competent authority of that country, certifying that they have received treatment at least equivalent to that granted to animals of Community origin as provided for by this Directive'.

Similarly, Regulation 1099/2009 lays down the conditions under which animals intended for the production of food and other products may be slaughtered. The Regulation aims at contributing to animal welfare by establishing minimum levels of protection in relation to the conditions under which those animals may be slaughtered.[47] The Regulation requires that animals shall be spared any avoidable pain, distress, or

[43] Cooperation happens through European Partnership on Alternative Approaches to Animal Testing (EPAA). Financing is done through a number of programmes which among others finances the European Reference Laboratory for Alternative Methods to Animal Testing (EURL ECVAM).

[44] Council Directive 2008/119/EC of 18 December 2008 laying down minimum standards for the protection of calves OJ 2008 No. L10/7; Council Directive 2008/120/EC of 18 December 2008 laying down minimum standards for the protection of pigs OJ 2009 No. L47/5

[45] Articles 3, 4 and Annex I of the Directive 2008/119/EC (*n* 23)

[46] Articles 3, 4 and Annex I of the Directive 2008/120/EC (*n* 24)

[47] Council Regulation 1099/2009 on the protection of animals at the time of killing (*n* 25). The Regulation provides for a number of exceptions in chapter I relating to hunting or recreational fishing activities, cultural or sporting events, scientific experiments and poultry, rabbits and hares intended for domestic consumption slaughtered outside slaughterhouses. In addition, in chapter II, the Regulation also grants an exemption to particular methods of slaughter prescribed by religious rites.

suffering during their killing.[48] In particular, the Regulation lists the methods under which animals may be stunned until the death of the animal.[49]

In relation to imports, Article 12 provides that, in accordance with Regulation 854/2004, products of animal origin may only be imported into the EU if they originate from an establishment that has been approved by EU authorities to meet the requirements of inter alia Chapters II and III of Regulation 1099/2009, which contain the substantive obligations in relation to slaughtering.[50] The Regulation provides an exemption to the requirement that animals shall not be conscious or experience sensibility during slaughter for particular methods of slaughter prescribed by religious rites. This exemption equally applies to imports of third countries, as it is listed in Chapter II of the Regulation.

Notably different in terms of regulatory goals and design are the EU Timber Regulation and the very recent EU Conflict Minerals Regulation. The EU Timber Regulation's operation, standards, and aims are different from the other producer-based measures. Not only is the goal of the Timber Regulation different – it aims at combatting illegal logging rather than animal welfare – its standards are based on the forestry and harvesting rules in third countries.

The EU Timber Regulation[51] is part of the EU 2003 Action Plan on Forest Law Enforcement Governance and Trade (FLEGT), which consists of a number of policies for promoting sustainable timber harvesting around the world.[52] FLEGT encourages public authorities to procure sustainable wood, provides for the negotiation of voluntary partnership agreements[53] with third countries in order to promote responsible

[48] Article 3 of the Regulation [49] Article 4 and Annex I of the Regulation

[50] Article 12 provides 'The requirements laid down in Chapters II and III of this Regulation shall apply for the purposes of Article 12(2)(a) of Regulation (EC) No. 854/2004. The health certificate accompanying meat imported from third countries shall be supplemented by an attestation certifying that requirements at least equivalent to those laid down in Chapters II and III of this Regulation have been met.' Regulation 854/2004 regulates, inter alia, under which conditions animal products may be imported into the EU.

[51] Regulation 995/2010 on timber and timber products, Commission delegated Regulation 363/2012 and Commission implementing Regulation 607/2012, see (*n* 19)

[52] European Forest Institute, 'FLEGT Voluntary Partnership Agreements' www.euflegt.efi.int/portal/

[53] Imports from countries that have entered into a voluntary partnership agreement with the EU are 'fast-tracked'. Economic operators on the EU market do not have the same stringent due diligence obligations in relation to timber originating from these countries.

logging, and encourages the timber industry to operate in a responsible and sustainable way. The EU Timber Regulation also prohibits the marketing of illegal timber by economic operators, prohibiting operators from placing illegally harvested timber and timber products on the EU internal market.[54] These operators also have to meet due diligence requirements to make sure that no illegally harvested timber or timber products are placed on the EU internal market.[55] The Regulation falls within the EU's efforts to combat climate change and was adopted in response to reports than an estimated 20% of the timber marketed in the EU was illegally harvested.[56]

The EU Timber Regulation does not set any substantive environmental production standards that need to be met by the country of origin, the producer, or the products exported to the EU. Instead, the marketability of timber depends entirely on whether it meets the legislative requirements of the country of export itself.[57] Thus in contrast to many other process-based measures which put pressure on existing or non-existing production standards in the country of origin, this process-based measure actually *reinforces* domestic production standards.[58] The Regulation bears some similarities with the IUU Regulation, which also seeks to reinforce existing international standards through process-based measures.

While this aspect might make the Regulation much more acceptable for the EU's trading partners, and even desirable, there are also two aspects of the Timber Regulation that are problematic in terms of effectiveness.[59] First of all – and in contrast to the American system – the Timber Regulation only applies to the operators that initially place timber products on the EU market. Traders who buy and sell timber within the EU are under much less scrutiny, since they are only required to identify the operators from whom they bought the timber and the subsequent traders that they supplied. While the consideration here is to avoid placing excessive administrative burdens on traders in timber,

[54] Article 4 (1) of Regulation 995/2010 [55] Article 6 (1) of Regulation 995/2010

[56] See recital 3 of Regulation 995/2010 on timber and timber products (*n* 19)

[57] Article 2 (h) of Regulation 995/2010 further specifies which matters are covered in relation to that legislation in the country of production which mainly relate to property rules and environmental rules.

[58] Recital 14 of Regulation 995/2010

[59] Yulia Levashova, 'How Effective is the New EU Timber Regulation in the Fight against Illegal Logging?' (2011) 20 *Review of European Community and International Environmental Law*, 294. See more critically Dylan Geraerts and Bregt Natens, 'The WTO Consistency of the European Union Timber Regulation' (2014) 48 *Journal of World Trade*, 433

this might create potential loopholes in the system, making it possible for illegally harvested timber to be marketed in the EU.[60] This is because traders – as opposed to operators – are under no obligation to refrain from marketing illegally harvested timber and are not required to have a due diligence system in place.[61] Secondly, Timber Regulation is limited in scope, excluding a major product area of concern: printed materials such as books and magazines.[62] According to Levashova, 25% of all printed products (a total worth of €3.2 billion annually) are imported from China, one of the main sources of illegally imported timber.[63]

Lastly, the EU's institutions have recently agreed upon a mandatory due diligence system to prevent imports of minerals from conflict zones.[64] While the details of the Regulation are still being developed at the time of writing, the trilogue political agreement on the Regulation indicates that it will feature a mandatory due diligence system which would require importers of minerals (tin, tantalum, and tungsten, their ores, and gold) from conflict zones to demonstrate that their activities do not contribute to conflict and the adverse impacts thereof. The proposed Regulation operates within the context of OECD Guidelines for Multinational Enterprises and the UN Guiding Principles on Business and Human Rights.[65]

The EU's producer-based rules are more numerous than the EU's country-based rules and most of them are inspired by animal welfare

[60] Levashova, 'EU Timber Regulation', 295

[61] The European Economic and Social Committee noted in this respect that 'the expected impact of controlling the risk of placing illegal products on the market is progressively reduced as operators in the supply chain get nearer to the final consumer'. See European Economic and Social Committee, 'Opinion on the Proposal for a Regulation of the European Parliament and the Council Laying Down the Obligations of Operators Who Place Timber and Timber Products on the Market' COM(2008) 644 final – 2008/0198 COD' (Brussels, 1 October 2009)

[62] Levashova, 'EU Timber Regulation', 295

[63] Ibid., at 295, see in particular footnotes 49–51

[64] European Parliament, 'Conflict Minerals: MEPs Secure Mandatory Due Diligence for Importers', European Parliament Press release of 16 June 2016. See the initial Commission proposal: Commission, 'Proposal for a Regulation of the European Parliament and of the Council Setting Up a Union System for Supply Chain Due Diligence Self-Certification of Responsible Importers of Tin, Tantalum and Tungsten, Their Ores, and Gold Originating in Conflict Affected and High-Risk Areas' COM (2013) 111 final

[65] OECD, *OECD Due Diligence Guidance for Responsible Supply Chains of Minerals from Conflict-Affected and High-Risk Areas* (Paris: OECD Publishing, 2nd edition, 2013) available at http://dx.doi.org/10.1787/9789264185050-en; UN Human Rights Office of the High Commissioner, 'Guiding Principles on Business and Human Rights' available at http://business-humanrights.org/en/un-guiding-principles

concerns. Some are truly unilateral and have clear extraterritorial effects, such as the EU's ban on seal products, whereas others take a more consensual approach such as the EU Timber Regulation and the EU Cosmetics Regulation. However, all of the EU's producer-based rules seek to address social, environmental, or moral concerns outside the EU.

1.1.3 Consumer-Based Rules

The final category of process-based product rules that will be discussed in this chapter are the EU's consumer-based rules. These rules target the individual consumer, rather than the country of origin or producer of the product in question. These rules do not prevent the marketing of non-compliant products, but merely incentivize or enable consumers to choose compliant products. Four consumer-based rules will be discussed here: the EU Ecolabel scheme, the EU organic label, EU rules on eggs, and the EU's sustainability criteria for biofuels. These rules have both environmental and animal welfare regulatory goals.

Regulation 66/2010 establishes the EU Ecolabel scheme.[66] This is a voluntary labelling scheme that allows products that have a relatively lower impact on the environment during their entire life cycle than other products in their product group to bear the EU Ecolabel sign. The product's impact during its entire life cycle is taken into account in establishing the EU Ecolabel criteria. This means that not only the impact on the environment of the production process, but also other factors such as the durability and reusability of the product and the environmental impact of the packaging after use are taken into account.[67] In addition to environmental criteria, the EU Ecolabel also takes into account the 'social and ethical aspects' of production through reference to international agreements such as International Labour Organization (ILO) standards. Reduction of animal testing is also considered a relevant criterion.[68]

Noteworthy is the relatively large role stakeholders such as NGOs and consumer organizations can play in setting the ecolabel criteria. The Commission, Member States, competent bodies and stakeholders may propose the development or revision of EU Ecolabel criteria for a specific product group after consulting the EU Ecolabelling Board.[69] In that

[66] Regulation 66/2010 of the European Parliament and of the Council of 25 November 2009 on the EU Ecolabel OJ 2010 No. L27/1

[67] Articles 3 (3) (4) and 6 (3) of Regulation 66/2010

[68] Article 6 of Regulation 66/2010

[69] Commission, 'Criteria Development and Revision' http://ec.europa.eu/environment/ecolabel/criteria-development-and-revision.html. See also Article 7 (1) of Regulation 66/2010. The Regulation favours consortiums consisting of more than one interest group.

respect the EU Ecolabelling Board 'observes a balanced participation of all relevant interested parties in respect of each product group'.[70]

The EU Ecolabel is by no means intended to be the exclusive ecolabel on the EU internal market. It operates alongside national and regional ecolabels such as the Blue Angel and Nordic Swan labels. Also, there is some overlap in terms of aims with privately administered environmental labels such as the Forest Stewardship Council (FSC) and Marine Stewardship Council (MSC) labels. There are no provisions in place that prohibit economic operators from advertising the environmental qualities of their products even if the products do not meet specific ecolabel criteria. Only using labels or logos that lead to confusion with the EU Ecolabel system is prohibited.[71] The EU Ecolabel scheme also only applies to a limited number of product groups, and does not include drinks, medicines, fishery products, and food products.[72] With respect to food products, the EU has its own organic labelling scheme which pursues somewhat similar aims as the EU Ecolabel scheme.

The EU Organic Labelling Regulation[73] originates from a wider organic labelling movement in Europe and is an example of how ambiguous the product/process distinction can turn out to be in practice.[74] Consumers of organic products are just as much concerned with the health, safety, and physical quality of food products as they are with the wider environmental, animal welfare, and social justice benefits that derive from organic farming, and both product and process characteristics are reflected in organic farming standards.[75]

Organic farming itself has grass-roots origins and resulted out of a protest against mainstream farming and its environmental impact.[76]

[70] Article 5 (2) of Regulation 66/2010 [71] Article 10 (1) of Regulation 66/2010

[72] Recital 6 of Regulation 66/2010 and Commission, 'Launching a Debate on a Community Approach towards Eco-Labelling Schemes for Fisheries Products' COM (2005) 275 final, on ecolabelling for fisheries

[73] Council Regulation 834/2007 of 28 June 2007 on organic production and labelling of organic products and repealing Regulation 2092/91 OJ 2007 No. L189/1

[74] See the introductory chapter. See also Robert Howse and Donald Regan, 'The Product/Process Distinction: An Illusory Basis for Disciplining Unilateralism in Trade Policy' (2000) 11 *European Journal of International Law*, 249–289

[75] Alberto Alemanno, 'The European Reform of Organic Farming: Balancing Consumer Preferences and Free Movement Imperatives' [2009] *European Food and Feed Law Review*, 406; Matthias Stolze and Nicolas Lampkin, 'Policy for Organic Farming: Rationale and Concepts' (2009) 34 *Food Policy*, 237

[76] Alemanno, 'The European Reform of Organic Farming', 407; see also W.B. Tate, 'The Development of the Organic Industry and Market: An International Perspective' in N. HT. Lampkin & S. Padel (eds.), *The Economics of Organic Farming: An International*

The philosophy behind organic farming is a more holistic, qualitative and ecological approach to farming by respecting natural cycles and equilibria and by excluding the use of artificial products such as chemicals, pesticides, and genetically modified organisms (GMOs).[77] In addition, animal welfare is an important aspect of the organic farming method. In particular, organic farming does not use landless production, and ensures animal-friendly housing conditions, slaughtering methods, and transport of animals. This means that the organic production method is in part related to the physical qualities of the organic produce, but just as much or even more related to the process attributes of organic produce in particular when organic farming leads to a reduced environmental impact at the farming site itself and to improvement of animal welfare.[78]

The aim of Regulation 834/2007 on organic production and labelling of organic products is to regulate under what conditions agricultural produce can be called 'organic' and use the EU organic label.[79] The Regulation establishes an EU logo for organic products, the use of which is mandatory for all pre-packaged food produced within the EU that wishes to label itself 'organic'.[80] The Regulation bans the use of the term 'organic' or related terms for products that do not meet the requirements of the Regulation, unless it concerns non-agricultural products or products that have no connection with organic production.[81] Other national or private organic logos that go beyond the requirements of the Regulation may also be used.[82] Such logos are permitted as long as the products that bear them meet (or exceed) the requirements of the Regulation, and in the case of pre-packaged food, so long as they also bear the EU logo.

The Regulation also regulates the labelling of organic goods of third country origin. These products can be marketed as organic on the EU internal market if they meet organic production standards that are either compliant with or equivalent to the EU organic production standards.[83]

Perspective (University of Wales, Aberystwyth, UK: CAB International, 1994); T. Gieryn, *Cultural Boundaries of Science: Credibility on the Line*, Chicago: (University of Chicago Press, 1999); R. Conford, *The Origins of the Organic Movement*, (Edinburgh, Glasgow: Floris Books, 2001)

77 Alemanno, 'The European Reform of Organic Farming', 407

78 Recital 1 of Regulation 834/2007 (*n* 73)

79 Recital 3 of Regulation 834/2007

80 Article 23 (1) of Regulation 834/2007

81 Article 23 (2) of Regulation 834/2007

82 Recital 26 of Regulation 834/2007

83 See Alemanno, 'The European Reform of Organic Farming' (n 102), 418, Articles 32 and 33 of Regulation 834/2007 and Commission implementing Regulation 1235/2008 of 8 December 2008 laying down detailed rules for implementation of Council Regulation

The organic production requirements[84] do not make any kind of distinction between 'product-related' and 'non-product-related' process rules. For the achievement of the aims of the Regulation, the existence of any residue in the organic product that results from the production method employed is not specifically highlighted. While some organic methods may lead to a detectable change in the product, for instance, in relation to the ban on the use of GMOs[85] and the restriction on the use of external inputs and chemically synthesized inputs,[86] others may not change the physical attributes of the product at all, in particular in relation to animal welfare requirements and limitations on the environmental impact of farming methods.[87] The aim of organic production is to produce products in a more natural way, not necessarily in a way that leads to healthier products.

In addition to the EU organic label, the EU has also introduced a series of marks indicating to consumers the farming methods used in the production of eggs.[88] In essence, EU rules require eggs destined for consumption to be marked according to the producer codes:

0 – for organically[89] farmed eggs;
1 – for free-range[90] eggs;
2 – for barn[91] eggs;
3 – for eggs from caged hens.[92]

834/2007 as regards the arrangements for imports of organic products from third countries OJ 2008 No. L334/25

84 Title III of Regulation 1235/2008 listed in Titles II (objectives and principles for organic production) and III (production rules) and in implementing Commission Regulations. The principles of organic production, and specifically farming, processing of food and feed are further developed in Title III and in implementing Commission Regulations.

85 Article 4 (a) (iii) and 9 of Regulation 834/2007

86 Article 4 (b) and (c) of Regulation 834/2007

87 For example, Article 12 (f) and (g) and Article 14 and 15 of Regulation 834/2007

88 See Article 116 and Annex XIV of Council Regulation 1234/2007 of 22 October 2007 establishing a common organization of agricultural markets and on specific provisions for certain agricultural products (Single CMO Regulation) OJ 2007 L 299/1, Article 9 of Commission implementing Regulation 589/2008 of 23 June 2008 laying down detailed rules for implementing Council Regulation (EC) No. 1234/2007 as regards marketing standards for eggs OJ 2008 L163, 6, and the Annex of Commission Directive 2002/4/EC of 30 January 2002 on the registration of establishments keeping laying hens, covered by Council Directive 1999/74/EC OJ 2002 L30, 44

89 In accordance with Regulation 834/2007 (*n* 73)

90 See Annex II of Commission implementing Regulation 589/2008 of 23 June 2008 laying down detailed rules for implementing Council Regulation (EC) No. 1234/2007 as regards marketing standards for eggs OJ 2008 L163, 6

91 Ibid. 92 Ibid.

Imports of eggs from third countries can be marked similarly if the Commission has established that legislation in those countries offers sufficient guarantees of equivalence with EU legislation.[93] If no such guarantees have been established, the eggs will be marked with the farming method as 'unspecified'.[94]

The last consumer-based rule discussed here is a process-based measure that has drawn considerable criticism and academic attention: the sustainability criteria for biofuels in the Renewables Directive (Directive 2009/28/EC).[95] The sustainability criteria require biofuels to be produced in a sustainable way if they are to be used for the achievement of certain EU climate change objectives.[96] The reason for including the sustainability criteria is that much of the environmental advantage of biofuels would be offset by unsustainable production, potentially even leading to an increase in greenhouse gas emissions. Moreover, growing

[93] IV of Annex XIV of XIV of Council Regulation (EC) 1234/2007 of 22 October 2007 establishing a common organization of agricultural markets and on specific provisions for certain agricultural products (Single CMO Regulation) OJ 2008 L299, 1

[94] Ibid.

[95] Directive 2009/28/EC of the European Parliament and of the Council of 23 April 2009 on the promotion of the use of energy from renewable sources and amending and subsequently repealing Directives 2001/77/EC and 2003/30/EC, OJ 2009 No. L140/16; Joanne Scott 'The Multi-level Governance of Climate Change' in Paul Craig (ed.), *The Evolution of EU Law* (Oxford: Oxford University Press, 2011), 805–835; Kati Kulovesi, Elisa Morgera and Miquel Muñoz, 'Environmental Integration and Multi-faceted International Dimensions of EU law: Unpacking the EU's 2009 Climate and Energy Package' (2011) 48 *Common Market Law Review*, 829–891; Steve Charnovitz, Jane Early and Robert Howse, 'An Examination in Social Standards in Biofuels Sustainability Criteria' (2008) IPC Discussion Paper www.agritrade.org/documents/SocialStnds_Biofuels_FINAL.pdf; Oxfam, 'Another Inconvenient Truth: How Biofuel Policies are Deepening Poverty and Accelerating Climate Change' (2008) Oxfam Briefing Paper www.oxfam.org/en/grow/policy/another-inconvenient-truth; Annie Dufey, 'International Trade in biofuels: Good for Development? And Good for Environment?' (2007) Environment for the MDGS: An IIED Briefing http://pubs.iied.org/pdfs/11068IIED.pdf; Andreas Lendle and Malorie Schaus, 'Sustainability Criteria in the EU Renewable Energy Directive: Consistent with WTO Rules?' (2010) ICTSD Information Note http://ictsd.org/i/publications/86798/; Henry Lee, William C. Clark and Charan Devereaux, 'Biofuels and Sustainable Development' (2008) *Harvard Kennedy School Faculty Research Working Papers Series* www.hks.harvard.edu/var/ezp_site/storage/fckeditor/file/pdfs/centers-programs/centers/cid/publications/faculty/wp/174.pdf; Seita Romppanen, 'Regulating Better Biofuels for the European Union' [2012] *European Energy and Environmental Law Review* 123; See also Emily Barrett Lydgate, 'The EU, the WTO and Indirect Land-Use Change' (2013) 47 *Journal of World Trade*, 159–186; Evdokia Moïsé and Ronald Steenblik, 'Trade-Related Measures Based on Processes and Production Methods in the Context of Climate-Change Mitigation', (2011) *OECD Trade and Environment Working Papers*, 2011/04 http://dx.doi.org/10.1787/5kg6xssz26jg-en

[96] Article 17 of Directive 2009/28/EC

agricultural crops for ethanol and biodiesel creates issues over food and water shortages due to the use of land for biofuels instead of other purposes as well as deforestation and biodiversity issues.[97]

The EU scheme seeks to address these concerns by incentivizing the use of biofuels that meet the sustainability criteria in the Directive. Biofuels that do not comply with the sustainability criteria may still be marketed, but they do not count towards EU or Member State renewable energy obligations and are not eligible for financial support for the consumption of biofuels and bioliquids.[98] This makes non-complying biofuels less attractive on the EU internal market.

The sustainability criteria for biofuels seek to ensure that environmental advantages are not offset by unsustainable production in two main ways. Firstly, the Renewables Directive requires that greenhouse gas emissions savings from the use of biofuels should be at least 60%.[99] Secondly, the Renewables Directive requires that the raw materials of biofuels may not originate from land 'with high biodiversity value', from land 'with high carbon stock', or from peatland.[100] These requirements aim at ensuring that 'greenhouse gas neutrality' is not significantly compromised if 'carbon sinks' such as (tropical) forests, wetlands, and peatlands are cleared for the production of biofuel crops.[101] They also seek to prevent production of biofuels from having a negative impact on biodiversity. Converting biodiverse lands for biofuel production, for example, by clearing forests to grow corn, can have a negative impact on rare, threatened, or endangered species or ecosystems. However, the Renewables Directive only lays down reporting obligations in relation to negative social impact in third countries and developing countries in particular and in relation to indirect land use changes.[102]

97 Dufey, 'International Trade in Biofuels'

98 Article 17 (1) (2) (3) (4) and (5) of Directive 2009/28/EC and obligations under Article 7a of Directive 2009/30/EC of the European Parliament and of the Council of 23 April 2009 amending Directive 98/70/EC as regards the specification of petrol, diesel and gas-oil and introducing a mechanism to monitor and reduce greenhouse gas emissions and amending Council Directive 1999/32/EC as regards the specification of fuel used by inland waterway vessels and repealing Directive 93/12/EEC OJ 2009 L140/88, see Article 7b of that Directive which essentially duplicates the sustainability criteria

99 Article 17 (2) of Directive 2009/28/EC

100 Article 17 (3–5) of Directive 2009/28/EC

101 Recital 70 of Directive 2009/28/EC

102 The reporting obligations are in Article 17 (7) of Directive 2009/28/EC. The increased demand for biofuels can lead to a rise in food prices, affect land rights of local communities and indigenous peoples and lead to infringements of basic labour rights such as forced labour and other forms of labour exploitation.

It is clear that the sustainability criteria have been carefully designed in order to make them WTO compatible.[103] The criteria apply without distinction between imported biofuels from outside the EU and within the EU, there are exceptions to avoid unnecessary trade restrictions, sustainability criteria are based on international standards and scientific evidence,[104] and emphasis is placed on finding plurilateral and non-governmental solutions within the Directive. In relation to the latter, the Directive provides for the possibility of negotiating international agreements with third countries containing provisions that correspond to the EU sustainability criteria and such an agreement would entail recognition of compliance with the Directive.[105] In addition, the Commission may recognize voluntary (inter)national schemes setting standards for the purpose of complying with the sustainability criteria, both also in respect to the sustainability criteria that are not legally binding in the Renewables Directive.[106] Nonetheless, the sustainability criteria have come under criticism for being too weak by not covering a range of important environmental and social criteria. The Commission proposal to amend the Directive has tried to accommodate concerns over the effects of indirect land use change on climate change, but legally binding social criteria remain absent, most likely because of WTO sensitivity in this area.

1.1.4 Potential Future Process-Based Rules

The current EU legislative framework includes two possibilities for introducing future process-based measures, both related to combatting climate change. The first is introducing a form of border tax adjustment

[103] Scott, 'The Multi-level Governance of Climate Change' (*n* 95), Kulovesi, Morgera and Muñoz, 'Environmental Integration and Multi-faceted International Dimensions of EU Law' (*n* 95)

[104] Recitals 69, 82, 85, 92 of Directive 2009/28/EC

[105] Article 18 (4) of Directive 2009/28/EC, note that 'due consideration shall be given to measures taken for the conservation of areas that provide, in critical situations, basic ecosystem services (such as watershed protection and erosion control), for soil, water and air protection, indirect land-use changes, the restoration of degraded land, the avoidance of excessive water consumption in areas where water is scarce and to the issues referred to in the second subparagraph of Article 17(7)' in negotiating such agreements

[106] Article 18 (4) of Directive 2009/28/EC, the Commission has published a Communication on voluntary standard setting schemes: Commission, 'Communication from the Commission on Voluntary Schemes and Default Values in the EU Biofuels and Bioliquids Sustainability Scheme' OJ C 160/1 and taken a number of decisions on recognition of those schemes.

under the EU Emissions Trading Scheme (ETS) and the second involves a more limited measure that introduces a life-cycle approach to fuel production.

Directive 2009/29/EC amends the EU Emissions Trading Scheme (ETS) established by Directive2003/87/EC.[107] The EU ETS was established in order to combat climate change in accordance with the EU's international commitments under the Kyoto Protocol and the United Nations Framework Convention on Climate Change (UNFCCC) regime.[108] To that end an increasing number of industrial sectors within the EU need to participate in the EU ETS and surrender allowances for the amount of greenhouse gasses they emit during a given period. The decrease of the available and tradable allowances makes the EU ETS a market-based instrument to limit the total greenhouse gas emissions within the EU. However, due to the limited participation of other countries under the Kyoto Protocol the EU system is exposed to the risk of 'carbon leakage'.[109] Carbon leakage refers to the situation in which certain industries which are exposed to international competition either lose market share or relocate their production facilities to countries with less stringent climate change policies in order to maintain market share.[110] The disadvantage is not only that reallocation of production or loss of

[107] Directive 2009/29/EC of the European Parliament and of the Council of 23 April 2009 amending Directive 2003/87/EC so as to improve and extend the greenhouse gas emission allowance trading scheme of the Community OJ 2009 L140/63; Commission Decision 2010/2 of 24 December 2009 determining, pursuant to Directive 2003/87/EC of the European Parliament and of the Council, a list of sectors and subsectors which are deemed to be exposed to a significant risk of carbon leakage (notified under document C (2009) 10251) OJ 2010 L1, 10

[108] Kulovesi, Morgera and Muñoz, 'Environmental Integration and Multi-faceted International Dimensions of EU Law' (*n* 95)

[109] See for a discussion on the policy options for carbon leakage in WTO context Joost Pauwelyn, 'Carbon Leakage Measures and Border Tax Ajdustments under WTO Law' in Denise Prevost and Geert van Calster (eds.), *Research Handbook on Environment Health and the WTO* (Cheltenham: Edward Elgar, 2012), see also Kulovesi, Morgera and Muñoz, 'Environmental Integration and Multi-faceted International Dimensions of EU Law' (*n* 95), 858–861

[110] Recital 24 of Directive 2009/29/EC defines carbon leakage as follows: 'In the event that other developed countries and other major emitters of greenhouse gases do not participate in this international agreement, this could lead to an increase in greenhouse gas emissions in third countries where industry would not be subject to comparable carbon constraints (carbon leakage), and at the same time could put certain energy-intensive sectors and subsectors in the Community which are subject to international competition at an economic disadvantage. This could undermine the environmental integrity and benefit of actions by the Community.'

market share would hurt the EU economy, but more significantly that the goals of the EU ETS system would be defeated because the greenhouse gas emissions would continue or even increase elsewhere. Carbon leakage may particularly be pertinent in energy-intensive sectors such as the pulp and paper sector, the chemicals sector, the aluminium, cement, and glass sectors, and the iron and steel sectors.[111]

The ETS Directive requires the Commission to submit an analytical report[112] assessing the situation with regard to energy-intensive sectors that are exposed to significant risks of carbon leakage and appropriate proposals to address carbon leakage in the event that no international agreement on the issue is reached.[113] One of the options available under the ETS Directive constitutes a process-based measure: the inclusion into the EU ETS of importers of products that are produced by the exposed sectors.[114] The Directive requires that such a system would be in conformity with 'the principles of the UNFCCC, in particular the principle of common but differentiated responsibilities and respective capabilities, taking into account the particular situation of least developed countries (LDCs)' as well as with WTO obligations.[115] The EU has so far not opted for including a process-based measure, partially because the Commission is concerned with maintaining an open trading system and the good relations with potentially affected countries,[116] but instead has decided to hand out free allowances to sectors exposed to carbon leakage.

In addition to the sustainability criteria for biofuels, the Fuel Specification Directive (Directive 2009/30/EC) also requires fuel suppliers to reduce life-cycle greenhouse gas emissions per unit of energy by anywhere from 6% to up to 10% by 31 December 2020.[117] These targets could be achieved by blending traditional fuels with biofuels and the promotion of biofuels themselves. However, as the Commission

[111] Pauwelyn, 'Carbon Leakage Measures and Border Tax Adjustments under WTO Law', 2 (n 109)

[112] Article 10a (14–18) of Directive 2009/29/EC

[113] Negotiations are still ongoing under the Durban Platform for Enhanced Action, see Commission, 'Progress towards a Legally Binding Global Climate Framework' http://ec.europa.eu/clima/policies/international/negotiations/progress/index_en.htm

[114] Article 10b (b) of Directive 2009/29/EC [115] Ibid.

[116] Noting that if an effective carbon equalization system 'obviously it would be desirable for such initiatives to be taken together with such partners', see Commission, 'Analysis of Options to Move Beyond 20% Greenhouse Gas Emission Reductions and Assessing the Risk Of Carbon Leakage' COM (2010) 265 final

[117] Depending on Article 9 (1) i and h of Directive 2009/30/EC (*n* 98), see Article 7a of that Directive

indicates, another option would be to take into account flaring and venting during the refining of traditional fuels beyond EU borders.[118] The Commission has undertaken consultations on this point, but has not yet produced any criteria or methodology for calculating life-cycle greenhouse gas emissions from any fuels other than biofuels.[119] Using a life-cycle approach to calculate and regulate the greenhouse gas emissions of conventional fuels has already been introduced outside the EU in California (the 2009 Low-Carbon Fuel Standard, LCFS) and the Canadian province of British Columbia (the 2008 Greenhouse Gas Reduction Act).[120]

1.2 Extraterritoriality

Process-based measures like those described in Section 1.1 may raise concerns over their perceived extraterritorial effects, as they seek to address social and environmental concerns that manifest outside the territory of the regulating entity. As the ECJ has made clear that the EU legislature 'is bound to observe international law in its entirety, including customary international law'[121] and subjects EU acts to judicial review on that basis,[122] the question is whether the Court's

[118] Commission, 'Directive 2009/30/EC amending Directive 98/70/EC on fuel quality: Consultation paper on the measures necessary for the implementation of Article 7a (5)' http://ec.europa.eu/environment/air/transport/pdf/art7a.pdf, 2 and 10

[119] The Commission has implementing powers to establish such criteria on the basis of Article 7a (3) and (5) of Directive 2009/30/EC

[120] Moïsé and Steenblik, 'Trade-Related Measures Based on Processes and Production Methods in the Context of Climate-Change Mitigation' (*n* 95) also Pauwelyn, 'Carbon Leakage Measures and Border Tax Adjustments under WTO Law', 2 (n 109)

[121] Case C-366/10, *Air Transport Association of America and Others v Secretary of State for Energy and Climate Change* [2011] ECR I-13755, para 101; See also Case C-286/90, *Anklagemyndigheden v Peter Michael Poulsen and Diva Navigation Corp* [1992] ECR I- 6019, para 9 and Article 3 (5) TEU

[122] Case C-162/96, *A. Racke GmbH & Co. v Hauptzollamt Mainz* [1998] ECR I- 3655,para 52; Case C-366/10, *Air Transport Association of America and Others v Secretary of State for Energy and Climate Change* [2011] ECR I-13755, para 110. Significantly, 'since a principle of customary international law does not have the same degree of precision as a provision of an international agreement, judicial review must necessarily be limited to the question whether, in adopting the act in question, the institutions of the European Union made manifest errors of assessment concerning the conditions for applying those principles'. The Court will, therefore, maintain a certain level of deference in relation to judicial review of acts that are in breach of customary law, and that furthermore that the act in question either affects rights derived from EU law or that the act creates obligations for the individual.

interpretation of the rules on international jurisdiction imposes limits on the EU legislature when enacting process-based measures.

While international legal scholars generally take a more restricted view on prescriptive jurisdiction under customary international law,[123] the ECJ's case law on jurisdiction broadly follows the permissive stance on international jurisdiction of the Permanent Court of International Justice in *Lotus*: states are permitted to legislate extraterritorially in the absence of a rule that prohibits a state from doing so, as long as that State *enforces* that rule within its territory.[124] The ECJ considers the EU to have complied with international rules on jurisdiction and the territoriality principle in general, so long as the measure in question is enforced within the territory of the EU. Enforcement within EU territory, therefore, constitutes for the ECJ a 'trigger' for the EU's jurisdiction regardless of the broader prescriptive effects of EU rules.

This approach by the ECJ is exemplified in cases such as *Poulsen, Air Transport Association of America*, and, in relation to the General Court, in *Minin*, demonstrates the permissibility of process-based measures under the Court's case law interpreting customary international law.[125]

In *Poulsen* the Court held that EU law could be applied to confiscate salmon caught in waters outside the jurisdiction of the Member States by a ship that was neither registered nor flagged in a Member State,

[123] Cedric Ryngaert, *Jurisdiction in International Law* (Oxford: Oxford University Press, 2008), 21–41: scholars tend to view the customary international law as requiring justification for legislative activity of States through sufficiently strong link to the situation which is covered by the legislation even if it is enforced within the territory of the regulating State.

[124] *Case of S.S. "Lotus" (France v. Turkey)*, [1928] PCIJ Rep Series A No. 9 and 10, at 18–19. The Lotus decision introduced the distinction between legislative and enforcement jurisdiction as a means to limit conflict by force as much as possible while respecting the legislative State's sovereignty as much as possible. Thus, where a State can legislate on any matter wherever in absence of a prohibitive rule, enforcing those rules is strictly limited to the territory of the State unless rules of international law permit the extension of that enforcement. The Permanent Court of International Justice wrote with respect to enforcement jurisdiction, 'the first and foremost restriction imposed by international law upon a State is that – failing the existence of a permissive rule to the contrary – it may not exercise its power in any form in the territory of another State.' On the other hand, the judgment is more permissive in relation to prescriptive jurisdiction, allowing States to exercise jurisdiction over events occurring abroad as long as this is done within the territory of the State exercising jurisdiction and as long as there is no international rule that prohibits this.

[125] Case C-286/90, *Poulsen and Diva Navigation* [1992] ECR I-6019; Case C-366/10, *Air Transport Association of America and Others v Secretary of State for Energy and Climate Change* [2011] ECR I-13755; Case T-362/04, *Leonid Minin v Commission* [2007] ECR II-2003

but was moored in the port of a Member State.[126] The Court held that while the Regulation could not have been applied to the ship in question on the high seas, in the Exclusive Economic Zone, or even in Member State territorial waters, if the ship exercised its right of innocent passage, the Regulation could be applied to the ship 'when it sails in the inland waters or, more especially, is in a port of a Member State, where it is generally subject to the unlimited jurisdiction of that State'.[127]

Similarly, in *Air Transport Association of America* the ECJ found that the application of the EU ETS to aircraft landing and departing from EU airports was not in violation of international law, even though the scheme calculated the emissions on the basis of the whole length of the flight including parts that occurred over the high seas and in the airspace of third countries, because the scheme only applied to aircraft landing and departing from airports situated in the EU.[128] For the ECJ, the aircraft were subject to the 'unlimited jurisdiction' of the EU because they were present in the territory of one of the Member States. The Court found the scheme was not contrary to the principle of freedom to fly over the high seas 'since an aircraft flying over the high seas is not subject, in so far as it does so, to the allowance trading scheme'.[129] The ECJ also emphasized that operators only become subject to the provisions of the Directive when they *choose* to operate a commercial air route departing from or arriving at an airport situated in the EU.[130] This is a highly relevant statement for the legality of process-based measures, which only impose limitations to the extent that a producer or trader *chooses* to export the regulated product to the EU.

The General Court applied this approach in *Minin*, which concerned the imposition of sanctions by the EU following UN Security Council Resolutions to freeze the financial assets of Charles Taylor, certain members of his family, and certain allies who constituted a threat to the peace process in Liberia. Even though the people concerned were not in the EU and the acts committed took place outside the EU,

[126] Case C-286/90, *Poulsen and Diva Navigation* [1992] ECR I-6019, paras 22–27. The Court came to this conclusion because there was no prohibitive rule to the contrary, as was the case in relation to the high seas, the EEZ or in relation to innocent passage.

[127] Case C-286/90, *Poulsen*, para 28

[128] Case C-366/10, *Air Transport Association of America and Others v Secretary of State for Energy and Climate Change* [2011] ECR I-13755, paras 122–125

[129] Ibid., para 126 [130] Ibid., para 127

the General Court found that the EU had jurisdiction because 'the contested regulations apply only to funds and economic resources located in the territory of the [EU] and do not, therefore, have any extraterritorial effect'.[131]

These three cases show that under EU law, as developed by the Court of Justice of the European Union (CJEU) courts, EU legislation complies with the principle of territoriality as soon as it is enforced within the EU, even if such legislation takes into account events occurring abroad. When applying the principle of territoriality, moreover, the ECJ does not make a distinction between enforcement and legislative jurisdiction, considering that the principle has been complied with as soon as the measure can be enforced, by whatever means, within the territory of the Member States. As a result, process-based measures will not violate the principle of territoriality as interpreted by the ECJ, as process-based measures are always enforced either at the border or within the Member States because their aim is to prevent the commercialization of products that do not comply with certain production standards.

The territorial 'trigger' that justifies the EU's jurisdiction is employed loosely, so there is little doubt that process-based measures enforced within the EU's borders would be found compatible with the rules of customary international law as interpreted by the ECJ. This can be seen in *Ebony Maritime*, where the ECJ found that even where actions were undertaken outside EU territory to ensure that EU rules could be enforced within EU territory, this was not contrary to international customary law.[132] Similarly, the ECJ was quick to find a territorial 'trigger' in *Wood Pulp I*.[133] In that case, the ECJ found that the Commission was justified in applying EU competition rules to undertakings established and headquartered outside the EU which

[131] Case T-362/04, *Leonid Minin v Commission* [2007] ECR II-2003, para 106

[132] Case C-177/95, *Ebony Maritime SA and Loten Navigation Co. Ltd v Prefetto della Provincia di Brindisi and others* [1997] ECR I-1111, paras 17–19 in particular. Italian authorities had confiscated a ship and its cargo after NATO/WEU forces had taken control over the ship on the high seas and towed it to the Italian port of Brindisi. This confiscation was done on the basis of Regulation 990/93 imposing sanctions on Serbia and Montenegro as a response to the war in Bosnia.

[133] Joined Cases 89, 104, 114, 116, 117 and 125 to 129/85, *A Ahlström Osakeyhtiö and others v Commission* [1988] ECR 5193. See for a discussion on jurisdiction in this particular case Dieter G.E Lange and John Byron Sandage, 'The Wood Pulp Decision and Its Implications for the Scope of Ec Competition Law' (1989) 26 *Common Market Law Review*, 137–165, 146–152

'implemented' a cartel within the EU internal market, and that domestic presence in the EU (either with or without subsidiaries) was irrelevant in that regard.[134]

Moreover, the Court is unwilling to limit the EU's jurisdictional powers on the basis of any perceived disproportionate extraterritorial effects of the EU's legislative conduct.[135] To the contrary, it has endorsed such effects, especially when the measure is part of an international effort to address transnational issues.[136]

The ECJ has left the door open to challenge EU legislative action on the basis of its extraterritorial effects only in a very limited set of circumstances that could in theory have some relevance for process-based measures. In arguing that there was no violation of customary international law, the ECJ in *Wood Pulp I* first noted that there were no legal obligations in other countries that contradicted the obligations of EU competition rules.[137] Second, the relevant authorities in the other countries concerned did not raise any objections to the application of EU

[134] Joined Cases 89, 104, 114, 116, 117 and 125 to 129/85, *A Ahlström Osakeyhtiö and others v Commission* [1988] ECR 5193, para 17–18. The judgment is usually seen as a qualified version of the effects doctrine in the United States, because it requires perpetrators to 'put that concertation into effect by selling at prices which are actually coordinated' as opposed to applying competition law to conduct which has merely the effect of restricting competition on the internal market. The difference is that the 'implementation' test requires perpetrators to actually sell products on the EU internal market, whereas the effects test could include perpetrators that contributed to the formation of the cartel, but did not actually sell on the EU internal market. Both the Commission and the Advocate General in this case had advocated the adoption of an effects test, albeit one with qualifications. The Commission proposed an effects test where those economic effects were 'substantial' and 'intended' and were 'the primary and direct result of the agreements and practices'. Advocate General Darmon in his elaborate Opinion similarly argued for the adoption of 'the criterion of qualified effect', a test similar to the test proposed by Advocate General Mayras in the *ICI* case. Adovcate General Mayras argued that the EU has jurisdiction over restrictions of competition which have a 'direct and immediate, reasonably foreseeable and substantial effect'. However, Advocate General Darmon rejected the application of the principle of territoriality as a justification for the exercise of jurisdiction since both the conduct and the presence of the members of the cartel were entirely outside the EU.

[135] Case C-366/10, *Air Transport Association of America and Others v Secretary of State for Energy and Climate Change* [2011] ECR I-13755, paras 128–129; Case T-362/04, *Leonid Minin v Commission* [2007] ECR II-2003, paras 107–108

[136] Case C-366/10, *Air Transport Association of America and Others v Secretary of State for Energy and Climate Change* [2011] ECR I-13755, para 128; Case T-362/04, *Leonid Minin v Commission* [2007] ECR II-2003, para 107

[137] Joined Cases 89, 104, 114, 116, 117 and 125 to 129/85, *A. Ahlström Osakeyhtiö and others*, paras 19–20; Case T-102/96, *Gencor Ltd v Commission* [1999] ECR II-753, paras 103–104

competition law in those cases.[138] Third, in *Gencor*, the General Court rejected the argument that the application of the competition rules would affect the vital economic and commercial interests of South Africa, because the applicants had not demonstrated that this was in fact the case.[139]

This potential limitation could, nevertheless, have some relevance in cases involving the legality of process-based measures if this reasoning was used a contrario. The first argument of the Court in *Wood Pulp I* based on conflict of jurisdiction will be difficult to argue in relation to process-based measures, because producers are formally not required to comply with process-based measures; they are only prevented from marketing their goods within the EU.[140] On the other hand and in relation to the second and third arguments, formal complaints or submissions by third country governments or proof that the process-based measure in question affects 'vital' economic interests could potentially be more persuasive. Governments of other states do have the possibility of intervening in a case to substantiate and signal their objections, for instance.[141] What constitutes a vital economic or commercial interest is of course something that is very much dependent on the specific circumstances of a case, but the notion of 'vital' already indicates that the enactment of a process-based measure must seriously and adversely affect the exporting country in question. This situation cannot be ruled out for process-based measures. A country-based measure targeting a country whose economy is largely dependent on the export of one particular commodity might be able to demonstrate that the measure in question economically coerces it in violation of the principle of non-interference.

On the other hand, in *Zuchtvieh-Export* the ECJ recently went as far as explicitly applying Regulation 1/2005 on the protection of animals during transport outside of EU borders to transport taking place in third states, if that transport began on EU territory. This is a strong testimony

[138] Joined Cases 89, 104, 114, 116, 117 and 125 to 129/85, *A Ahlström Osakeyhtiö and others*, para 21; T-102/96, *Gencor Ltd v Commission* [1999] ECR II-753, paras 103–105

[139] T-102/96, *Gencor Ltd v Commission* [1999] ECR II-753, para 105

[140] Case C-366/10, *Air Transport Association of America and Others v Secretary of State for Energy and Climate Change* [2011] ECR I-13755, para 127

[141] Article 40 of the Protocol (no 3) on the Statute of the Court of Justice of the European Union, Consolidated version of the Treaty on the Functioning of the European Union [2012] OJ C 326/47. See, for instance, Case C-428/08, *Monsanto Technology LLC v Cefetra BV and Others* [2010] ECR I-6765

to the ECJ's endorsement of extraterritorial effects of EU rules, as it was the ECJ's interpretation itself that resulted in such effects.[142]

1.3 Unilateralism

Unilateralism is a conceptually distinct challenge to the EU legislature, because it focuses on the process of law-making rather than the territorial division of competences.[143] Unilateralism comes into play with respect to process-based measures because, in contrast to an international agreement, they address a transnational problem without necessarily and/or sufficiently consulting those affected (lack of inclusion or consultation) or taking into account economic, cultural or geographic differences in other countries (lack of calibration). These points were particularly visible in the WTO *US – Shrimp* decision, where the Appellate Body noted that the United States' process-based measure had been adopted without first pursuing a multilateral agreement (lack of consultation), and was a 'rigid and unbending standard' and did not take into consideration 'different conditions which may occur in the territories of those other Members' (lack of calibration).[144]

Despite the EU's constitutional normative preference for multilateralism,[145] it is not immediately apparent that the unilateral aspects of process-based measures would legally constrain the EU legislature within the EU legal order. Perhaps the most developed legal argument against the unilateral aspects of process-based measures can be found in WTO law, and in particular the rulings discussed in the introductory chapter.[146] As the EU is a member of the WTO and the covered agreements are binding upon the institutions,[147] one may wonder whether findings of the WTO Dispute Settlement Body can have a constraining effect on the EU legislature within the EU legal order. The CJEU's case law, however, has been firm and consistent in its refusal to subject EU

[142] See Case C-424/13, *Zuchtvieh-Export GmbH v Stadt Kempten* EU:C:2015:259; Similarly, in *European Federation for Cosmetic Ingredients*, the ECJ found that the EU Cosmetics Regulation prohibits the marketing of cosmetics that demonstrate compliance with the Regulation's health safety standards on the basis of animal tests outside the EU. See Case C-592/14, *European Federation for Cosmetic Ingredients v Secretary of State for Business, Innovation and Skills* EU:C:2016:703, paras 39–45

[143] See the introductory chapter under 'Unilateralism'.

[144] WTO Appellate Body Report, *United States: Import Prohibition of Certain Shrimp and Shrimp Products*, 12 October 1998 (WT/DS58/AB/R), paras 163–164

[145] Article 21 (1) and (2) (f) TEU

[146] See the introductory chapter and in particular *n* there.

[147] Article 216 (2) TFEU

acts to judicial review on the basis of WTO jurisprudence.[148] Neither individuals nor Member States are able to challenge EU acts on the basis of WTO law.[149] The ECJ justifies its rejection of the direct effect of the WTO law generally on the grounds that the WTO is primarily a negotiating forum.[150] As such, the Court is neither willing to intrude upon the powers of the other institutions to negotiate within the WTO, nor is it willing to affect the reciprocal nature of the WTO Agreements by granting them effects that they are not given by the EU's major trading partners.[151]

This view has equally been transposed by the Court to WTO jurisprudence, noting the considerable room for manoeuvre and negotiations under the Dispute Settlement Understanding.[152] The Court has also refused to apply one of the limited exceptions (the *Nakajima* exception[153]) to the denial of direct effect of WTO law to situations in which the EU legislator sought to comply with a decision of the WTO's Dispute Settlement Body.[154] Thus, even where it is clear that the EU legislator has amended or introduced new process-based measures in order to comply with a WTO Dispute Settlement Body decision, this will not be enough to

148 See for a discussion on the legal effects of WTO law in the EU legal order Piet Eeckhout, *EU External Relations Law*, 2nd edn (Oxford: Oxford University Press, 2011), 323–436; Pieter Jan Kuijper and Marco Bronckers, 'WTO Law in the European Court of Justice' (2005) 42 *Common Market Law Review*, 1313; Marco Bronckers, 'The Relationship of the EC Courts with other International Tribunals: Non-Committal, Respectful or Submissive?' (2007) 44 *Common Market Law Review*, 601

149 See Joined Cases 21–24/72, *International Fruit Company NV and others v Produktschap voor Groenten en Fruit* [1972] ECR 1219, paras 19–27 (individuals); Case C-280/93, *Germany v Council* [1994] ECR I-4973, paras 103–112 (privileged applicants); Case C-149/96, *Portugal v Council* [1999] ECR-8395 para 41 (case law confirmed after the establishment of the WTO).

150 See for a reflection of this discussion, among others, Kuijper and Bronckers, 'WTO Law in the European Court of Justice', 1313; Geert A. Zonnekeyn, 'The Status of WTO Law in the EC Legal Order: the Final Curtain?' (2000) 34 *Journal of World Trade*, 111; Eeckhout, *EU External Relations Law*, 323–436

151 Case C-149/96, *Portugal v Council* [1999] ECR-8395 para 40–6; Case C-377/02, *Léon Van Parys NV v Belgisch Interventie- en Restitutiebureau (BIRB)* [2005] ECR I-1465 paras 50–54; Kuijper and Bronckers, 'WTO Law in the European Court of Justice', 1313, 1321

152 Case C-377/02, *Léon Van Parys NV v Belgisch Interventie- en Restitutiebureau (BIRB)* [2005] ECR I-1465 paras 50–54; Case C-351/04, *Ikea Wholesale v Commissions of Customs and Exercise* [2007] ECR I-7723, Opinion of AG Léger

153 In *Nakajima* the ECJ held that it would review the legality of an EU act where the EU intended to implement a particular obligation assumed under WTO law. Case C-69/89 *Nakajima All Precision v Council* [1991] ECR I-2069. See Eeckhout, *EU External Relations Law*, 357–360

154 Case C-377/02, *Léon Van Parys NV v Belgisch Interventie- en Restitutiebureau (BIRB)* [2005] ECR I-1465, para 41

challenge the measure. The WTO Dispute Settlement Body's opposition to unilateralism is therefore of limited value when challenging EU process-based measures within the EU legal order.

Lastly, the Court has even been reluctant to apply the principle of consistent interpretation[155] to decisions made by panels and the Appellate Body within the WTO Dispute Settlement System.[156] It is clear, therefore, that from an EU law point of view WTO law and jurisprudence impose few limits on the EU institutions when adopting process-based measures.

More specifically in relation to potential the lack of consultation with third states regarding the imposition of process-based measures, while EU law and institutional practice does grant affected parties certain participatory rights, the ECJ has not been willing to strike down measures because affected persons located outside the EU have not been sufficiently consulted. Article 11 TEU and Article 2 of the Protocol on Proportionality require the Commission to carry out consultations with affected parties and maintain an open, transparent and regular dialogue with them.[157] The Commission has a long-established practice of carrying out stakeholder consultations.[158] However, this practice merely contributes to the legitimacy of EU rules and reinforces them; it does not result in a legal right that enables non-consulted parties to challenge EU acts on that ground.[159]

[155] Case C-61/94, *Commission v Germany* [1996] ECR I-3989, para 52

[156] Case C-351/04, *Ikea Wholesale v Commissions of Customs and Exercise* [2007] ECR I-7723, para 27–35, note also the Opinion of AG Léger 77–89 urging not to give any effect to those decisions because this would jeopardize the autonomy of the EU legal system. For the *EC – Bed Linen* decision see WTO Appellate Body Report, *European Communities: Anti-Dumping Duties on Imports of Cotton-type Bed Linen from India*, 1 March 2001 (WT/DS141/AB/R); Bronckers, 'The Relationship of the EC Courts with other International Tribunals: Non-Committal, Respectful or Submissive?', 601

[157] Article 2 of Protocol on the application of the principles of subsidiarity and proportionality [2007] OJ C 306/1

[158] Daniela Obradovic and Jose M. Alonso Vizcaino, 'Good Governance Requirements concerning the Participation of Interest Groups in EU Consultations' (2006) 43 *Common Market Law Review*, 1049–1108; see also most recently the proposed interinstitutional agreement on Better regulation http://data.consilium.europa.eu/doc/document/ST-9121-2015-INIT/en/pdf

[159] See Alberto Alemanno, 'The Better Regulation Initiative at the Judicial Gate: A Trojan Horse within the Commission's Walls or the Way Forward?' (2009) 15 *European Law Journal*, 382–400; See, however, Alemanno's analysis on p. 393–396 and Case 282/81, *Ragusa v Commission* [1983] ECR 1234; Case 263/83, *Turner v Commission* [1985] ECR 893; Case T-9/89, *Hüls v Commission* [1992] ECR II-499; Case C-156/98, *Germany v Commission* ECR I-6857; Case T-13/99, *Pfizer Animal Health v Council* [2002] ECR II-3305, para 119.

In *Inuit Tapiriit Kanatami and Others v Parliament and Council*, for instance, the General Court reiterated this stance in relation to the seal products ban and the EU's alleged lack of consultation of Canadian seal hunters by stating that 'in the context of a procedure for the adoption of a Union act based on an article of the Treaty, the only obligations of consultation incumbent on the Community legislature are those laid down in the article in question. Article [115 TFEU] did not impose on the legislature a particular obligation to consult the applicants.'[160] However, the General Court did mention that 'the Union legislature did take account of the particular situation of Inuit communities as referred to in the United Nations Declaration on the Rights of Indigenous Peoples and it is for that reason that it took the view that an exemption for products which result from hunts traditionally conducted by them for the purposes of subsistence should be authorised'.[161] The General Court thereby noted that this exemption was exactly the result of consultation with Inuit communities.[162]

In relation to the potential lack of calibration of process-based measures, the ECJ's standard of review on the basis of the principle of proportionality is deferential towards the EU legislator.[163] The ECJ employs the so-called manifestly inappropriate standard in order to allow broad discretion for the EU legislature in areas in which its action involves political, economic and social choices and in which it is called upon to undertake complex assessments and evaluations.[164] In Inuit *Tapiriit*

Essentially, the clearer and absolute the self-imposed rules are, the easier it is to rely on them before the EU Courts. Moreover, while it is not likely to rely on these documents in order to invalidate measures in which these minimum standards and guidelines have not been followed, they could aid EU courts in determining whether the EU act meets other requirements necessary for the validity of the measure such as the proportionality principle. See C-310/04, *Spain v Council* [2006] ECR I-7285, paras 122–123

160 Case T-526/10, *Inuit Tapiriit Kanatami and Others v Commission* EU:T:2013:215, para 113

161 Ibid., para 115 162 Ibid., para 114

163 Benedikt Pirker, *Proportionality Analysis and Models of Judicial Review: A Theoretical and Comparative Study* (Groningen: Europa Law Publishing, 2013) 249–250, 253–255; Tor-Inge Harbo, 'The Function of the Proportionality Principle in EU Law' (2010) 16 *European Law Journal*, 158, 185; Takis Tridimas, *The General Principles of EU Law*, 2nd edn (Oxford: Oxford University Press, 2006), 139; Case C-84/94, *United Kingdom v Council (Working Time Directive)* [1996] ECR I-5755, paras 57–58

164 Case C-491/01, *The Queen v Secretary of State for Health, ex parte British American Tobacco (Investments) Ltd and Imperial Tobacco Ltd.* [2002] ECR I-11453; Case C-58/08, *Vodafone and Others* [2010] ECR I-4999, Case T-526/10, *Inuit Tapiriit Kanatami and Others v Commission* EU:T:2013:215, para 88

Kanatami and Others v Parliament and Council, the General Court therefore dismissed the applicant's claim that the seal products ban had disproportionate effects on the Inuit communities simply because it had considerable effects on the survival of those communities.[165]

To be sure, some of the EU's process-based measures explicitly seek to avoid or mitigate the unilateralist aspects of process-based measures, for instance, by seeking compliance with the exporting state's production rules as in the EU Timber Regulation or international standards as in the IUU Regulation.[166] Another example is the effort under the EU seal products ban to calibrate the measure in a way that takes into account the way of life of indigenous communities.[167] The Directive establishing sustainability criteria for biofuels expressly permits compliance with the Directive through the negotiation of international agreements.[168] The EU Organic Labelling Regulation sets out through a process of recognition of equivalence several ways in which organic products from third countries can be labelled as organic, without these products necessarily having to comply with identical EU organic production rules.[169] And the IUU Regulation allows for an elaborate consultation mechanism for third countries before they are 'blacklisted'.[170]

This practice of avoiding or mitigating unilateralist aspects of process-based measures can be compared with the more general EU legislative practice of introducing what Scott calls 'safety valves'.[171] These are provisions that seek to prevent 'jurisdictional over-reach' and 'facilitate cooperation and [. . .] reduce conflict between States'.[172] For Scott, such safety valves should be required as a matter of EU law; however, as was demonstrated above, it is hard to find any strong legal ground in the Court's case law to suggest that this is currently the state of the law.

165 Case T-526/10, *Inuit Tapiriit Kanatami and Others v European Commission* EU:T:2013:215, para 97–98

166 Article 4 (1) of Regulation 995/2010 on timber and timber products (*n* 19); Article 2 (2–4), 12 (1) and Article 31 (3) of Council Regulation 1005/2008 (*n* 13), see Chapter 1, Section 1.1.2 for a more elaborate discussion

167 Article 3 (1) of Regulation 1007/2009 (*n* 21); The 'indigenous communities' exception permits the marketing of seal products if those 'result from hunts traditionally conducted by Inuit and other indigenous communities and contribute to their subsistence'

168 Article 18 (4) of Directive 2009/28/EC (*n* 95) see Chapter 1, Section 1.1.3 for a more elaborate discussion

169 Articles 32 and 33 of Regulation 834/2007 (*n* 73)

170 Article 32 of Council Regulation 1005/2008 (*n* 13)

171 Scott, 'The New EU "extraterritoriality"' (*n* 4)

172 Ibid., 1365

If anything, EU law appears to facilitate the adoption of process-based measures rather than imposing legislative limits upon them in terms of unilateralism or extraterritoriality. The remarkable feature of the EU's constitutional system is that since so many of its key legal bases are linked to the completion of the internal market, the adoption of process-based measures is at its basic level relatively unproblematic and even empowers the EU to adopt measures in fields in which it has no competence as such (such as animal welfare), or where EU powers would only lead to minimum harmonization (such as environmental or social protection legislation). The EU does not have the power to lay down animal welfare protection rules, for instance, but it does have the competence to create a level playing field when it comes to agricultural production or trade in animal products, either by removing obstacles to trade or by removing distortions of competition within the internal market, taking into account a high level of animal welfare protection. Thus, for example, EU competence is triggered if measures contribute to the common agricultural policy by laying down the conditions under which products may be marketed as 'organic' or organically produced, while at the same time realizing animal welfare goals.

This systematic feature of EU constitutional law is reinforced by the so-called enabling function of the various policy integration requirements in the Treaties. These articles require EU institutions to integrate certain EU policies and EU interests, such as environmental protection and animal welfare, when implementing and defining EU policies and enacting legislation.[173] The 'enabling function' of these

[173] These consist of, firstly, the 'integration articles': provisions of general application which require coherence between EU policies and integration of interests such as environmental protection and animal welfare in general (and not only integration of various policies in one policy field). Secondly, there are a number of integration articles that are 'tucked away' further in the back of the TFEU. These relate to public health, cultural integration, industrial policy and cohesion. Thirdly, there are a number of provisions within the Charter of Fundamental Rights which require the EU institutions, bodies, agencies and offices of the EU and Member States when implementing EU law to respect these fundamental rights. While the nature of these provisions is different in relation to the 'integration articles', they do require policymakers to refrain from infringing those rights, thus ensuring that those rights cannot be ignored when making EU process-based measures. Lastly, within the field of external relations including common commercial policy, there are additional coherence requirements in Article 21 TEU. See for a discussion of the most discussed of these articles, Article 11 TFEU, Jan H. Jans, 'Stop the Integration Principle?' (2009–2010) 33 *Fordham International Law Journal*, 1533; Nele Dhondt, *Integration of Environmental Protection Into Other EC Policies: Legal Theory and Practice* (Groningen: Europa Law Publishing, 2003); Martin Wasmeier,

integration requirements allows the EU legislator to use a specific legal basis to take into account and achieve policy goals other than the policy goals additional to what would be proper to that legal basis.[174] The Court has on multiple occasions dismissed lack of competence arguments in relation to actions for annulment of acts because those acts pursued other policy goals in addition to the goals of the legal basis used, by referring to the integration articles as an argument that the EU may pursue a variety of policy goals when legislating on a specific legal basis.[175]

Conclusion

This chapter has discussed the current range of process-based measures enacted by the EU, and has argued that process-based measures cannot easily be challenged before the EU courts. Currently, the EU has a number of process-based measures of different types which mainly seek to contribute to environmental and animal welfare goals. No process-based measures attempting to achieve social goals have been enacted, although the Seal Products Regulation does carve out an exception to the marketing ban in seal products for indigenous peoples. To date, only the ban on seal products has been challenged before the EU courts, so far unsuccessfully.

Two challenges – extraterritoriality and unilateralism – process-based measures, identified in the introductory chapter, are not likely to pose significant legal difficulties before the EU courts for EU-enacted process-based measures. The ECJ interprets the territoriality principle broadly, making the extraterritoriality argument employed against process-based measures extremely unlikely to succeed as a matter of EU law. While the EU is committed to multilateralism and public participation in rule-making and the EU institutions are subject to the proportionality principle, the ECJ is equally reluctant to constrain the EU legislature in its ability to regulate in the public interest. The position of WTO law

'The Integration of Environmental Protection as a General Rule for Interpreting Community Law' (2001) 38 *Common Market Law Review*, 159–177

174 Jans, 'Stop the Integration Principle?' (n 173), 1540–1541

175 Case C-300/89, *Commission v Council (Titaniumdioxide)* [1991] ECR I-2867, para 22; Case C-62/88, *Greece v Council* [1990] ECR I-1527, para 20–24; Case C-405/92, *Mondiet* [1993] ECR I-6133, para 27; Case C-336/00, *Republik Österreich and Martin Huber* [2002] ECR-7699, para 33; Case C-180/96, *UK v Commission* [1996] ECR I-3903, para 120; Case T-526/10, *Inuit Tapiriit Kanatami and Others v Commission* EU:T:2013:215, para 42

within the EU legal order, moreover, is not so strong as to enable a successful challenge of EU process-based measures on the grounds of incompatibility with WTO law and jurisprudence. Moreover, EU law requires the EU to integrate social and environmental concerns in its policy, effectively triggering EU competence in such areas through market regulation.

Process-based measures enacted by the EU, as opposed to process-based measures enacted by Member States and private entities, therefore face relatively less resistance within the EU legal order. This demonstrates that if one wishes to enact process-based measures, the choice of who regulates favours the EU itself if one considers the legality of the measure the determining factor. This may be one of many policy factors (effectiveness, subsidiarity, political willingness) to take into account, of course, but one that can expedite the choice for who should regulate.

2 Member State Process-Based Measures as Restrictions on the Free Movement of Goods

Introduction

Chapter 1 discussed the legality of process-based measures enacted by the EU. Chapter 2 now turns inward to examine the legality of process-based measures established by the EU Member States. Member States have regulatory powers that coexist alongside those of the EU, and may wish to enact process-based measures themselves. Indeed, the EU ban on seal products was developed partially in response to Member State rules restricting trade in seal products.[1]

There are several ways in which Member States may take production processes into account in their regulations. As with EU-level rules, Member State measures can range from attempting to encourage consumers to buy socially responsible products through labelling rules, to regulating market access more directly, either by requiring countries of export to have appropriate legislation in place, or requiring producers to demonstrate that their products have not been made in socially or environmentally unfriendly ways.

However, Member States wishing to enact process-based measures face different and more substantial legal challenges under EU law. One of the core aims of the EU is the establishment of an internal market by removing obstacles to trade in goods between Member States and creating a common commercial policy.[2] As such, EU primary and secondary

[1] Regulation 1007/2009 of the European Parliament and of the Council of 16 September 2009 on trade in seal products providing for restrictions on the placing on the market of the European Union of the seal products OJ 2009 L286/36 (amended by Regulation 2015/1775 of the European Parliament and of the Council of 6 October 2015 amending Regulation 1007/2009 on trade in seal products, OJ 2015 No. L262/1, recitals 5–6

[2] See *n* 77 in the Introductory chapter for the notion 'internal market'

legislation limit Member States' ability to regulate products on the basis of their production methods. This is true in at least three ways.

First, Member States are prevented from enacting measures that would impede the free movement of goods within the internal market by Article 34 TFEU's prohibition on quantitative restrictions or 'measures having equivalent effect'. The ECJ's interpretation of 'measures having equivalent effect' in *Dassonville* casts a very wide net, subjecting Member State rules with even potential or indirect effects on the internal market to judicial review by the EU courts.[3] Process-based measures that have the potential to impede trade among the Member States (except for consumer-based measures that can be characterized as selling arrangements within the meaning of *Keck*), therefore, will have to contend with Article 34.

Second, the Treaties grant the EU exclusive competence over the EU's common commercial policy. As such, only the EU has the right to make rules that specifically relate to international trade.[4] Any Member State process-based measures that specifically relates to trade with third states will, therefore, also come under the scrutiny of EU law.[5]

Third, EU secondary legislation regulates Member States' ability to enact process-based measures in various ways. For example, the EU's intricate rules on public procurement impact the ability of Member States to prefer goods that were made in socially responsible ways in their state purchasing decisions.

These three types of limitations imposed by EU rules do not necessarily prohibit Member State process-based measures. Rather, they subject Member State measures to judicial review by the EU courts. Upon review, restrictions on the free movement of goods may be justified on the basis of a non-exhaustive list of public interest grounds either through so-called mandatory requirements or through the derogations contained in

[3] Case 8/74, *Procureur du Roi v Benoît and Gustave Dassonville* [1974] ECR 837, para. 5; Case C-110/05, *Commission v. Italy (motorcycle trailers)* [2009] ECR I-509 paras. 33–37, See for general literature on the free movement of goods and Article 34 TFEU in particular: Catherine Barnard, *The Substantive Law of the EU: The Four Freedoms* 3rd edition (Oxford: Oxford University Press 2010); Laurence W. Gormley, 'Silver Threads Among the Gold . . . 50 Years of the Free Movement of Goods' (2007) 31 *Fordham International Law Journal*, 1637; in Peter Oliver (ed.), *Oliver on Free Movement of Goods in the European Union* (Oxford: Hart Publishing, 2010)

[4] Case C-414/11, *Daiichi Sankyo Co. Ltd, Sanofi-Aventis Deutschland GmbH v DEMO Anonimos Viomikhaniki kai Emporiki Etairia Farmakon* EU:C:2013:520, para. 50

[5] Case 41/76, *Suzanne Criel, née Donckerwolcke and Henri Schou v Procureur de la République au tribunal de grande instance de Lille and Director General of Customs*, [1976] ECR 1921, para. 32

Article 36 TFEU.[6] Moreover, the ECJ's case-law on taxation and public procurement in particular has shown that Member States may, in principle, distinguish products on the basis of their production methods.

This chapter will demonstrate how and when Member State process-based measures fall within the scope of EU law. Section 1 will begin by discussing the limits that Article 34 TFEU and the EU's common commercial policy impose on these measures. It will examine, in turn, how Article 34 and the common commercial policy discipline country-based, consumer-based, and producer-based product-based measures imposed by Member States. Sections 2 and 3 will then discuss the EU's rules on taxation and public procurement, which impose additional limitations on Member States' ability to adopt process-based measures in compliance with EU law. While public procurement decisions and process-based tax measures are consumer-based measures, they fall within their own separate legal regime under EU law.

This chapter will not discuss the extent to which process-based restrictions on the free movement of goods may be justified through mandatory requirements or the derogations contained in Article 36 TFEU. This aspect of the law on the free movement of goods will be discussed in Chapters 3 and 4 in the context of an assessment of the extent to which extraterritoriality and unilateralism challenge the legality of Member State process-based measures.

2.1 Article 34 TFEU and the Common Commercial Policy

2.1.1 Country-Based Measures

As explained in the introductory chapter, country-based measures target governments of other countries, not producers or consumers. Their primary rationale is to induce governments to change their production rules in a way that meets the environmental or social protection levels sought by the importing country. An example is the EU Leghold Trap

[6] Measures that constitute measures of equivalent effect may be justified on one of the public interest grounds set out in Article 36 TFEU or in order to meet imperative requirements. In either case, the measure in question must be appropriate for securing the attainment of the objective pursued and not go beyond what is necessary in order to attain it. See for a general discussion of the case-law on justifying restrictive measures in the sense of Article 34 TFEU Barnard, *The Substantive Law of the EU*, 149–192 and Stefan Enchelmaier 'Article 36: General' in P Oliver (ed.) *Oliver on Free Movement of Goods in the European Union* (Oxford: Hart Publishing, 2010), 215–312

Regulation, which requires governments to ban the use of leghold traps before pelts can be imported into the EU.

Country-based measures can be applied either upon importation of the product or when the product is placed on the market. For example, a Member State could address concerns about child labour either by imposing a rule that prohibits the import of all goods from countries without appropriate legislation in place, or by allowing imports, but prohibiting the marketing and sale of goods from countries that lack such legislation.

If Member State country-based measures are imposed at the border, they will run into Article 34 TFEU, Article 28 (2) TFEU, and the common commercial policy. As Article 34 TFEU prohibits quantitative restrictions on imports and all measures having equivalent effect, country-based measures that restrict the importation of goods from one Member State to another will in principle be prohibited, unless justified for a recognized reason. In *Geddo*, the ECJ held that 'the prohibition on quantitative restrictions covers measures which amount to a total or partial restraint of, according to the circumstances, imports, exports or goods in transit'.[7] If products cannot be imported from one Member State into another because they originate from a country that does not have the required production rules in place, this is a total restraint on imports contrary to Article 34 TFEU.[8]

Member State country-based measures also pose a problem with respect to Article 28 (2) TFEU and the principle of assimilation. According to the principle of assimilation, Article 34 TFEU has 'the same scope' and applies 'without distinction' to products originating in the EU and to those which were put into free circulation.[9] This means that once a good has been legally imported and put into free circulation in one Member State, it must be treated like any other good of EU origin.[10] Applying

[7] Case 2/73, *Geddo v Entie Nazionale Risi* [1973] ECR 865, 879

[8] In any event, border controls have been abolished within the EU since 1 January 1992. See former Article 14 EC (currently Article 26 TFEU) and Stephen Weatherill, 'Union Legislation Relating to the Free Movement of Goods' in P Oliver (ed.), *Oliver on Free Movement of Goods in the European Union* (Oxford: Hart Publishing, 2010), 427–485, at 428–429

[9] Case 41/76, *Suzanne Criel, née Donckerwolcke and Henri Schou v Procureur de la République au tribunal de grande instance de Lille and Director General of Customs*, [1976] ECR 1921, para. 18; Case 119/78, *SA des grandes distilleries Peureux v Directeur des Services fiscaux de la Haute-Saône et du territoire de Belfort*, [1979] ECR 976, para. 26; Case C-30/01, *Commission v United Kingdom* [2003] ECR I-9481, para. 54

[10] Article 29 TFEU and Council Regulation 2913/92 of 12 October 1992 establishing the Community Customs Code OJ 1992 No. L302/1. 'Legally', here, entails compliance with the EU's external border requirements, such as customs duties and quota rules.

an additional process-based 'check' at any stage after import would therefore run afoul of this rule.

If a Member State applied its country-based measure only at its external border, to goods imported directly from third states, it would avoid Article 34 TFEU, which only applies to goods imported from another Member State. However, such a rule would still be caught by the common commercial policy. According to EU law, border measures that amount to quantitative restrictions fall within the scope of the common commercial policy, which is exclusive EU competence, and are therefore prohibited unless specifically allowed by secondary legislation.[11] The secondary legislation applicable in this case is the EU Import Regulation, which provides that products originating in third countries shall be freely imported into the EU and shall not be subject to any quantitative restrictions.[12] However, the Regulation does grant Member States the competence (subject to notification to the Commission) to apply restrictions on public interest grounds that have a comparable function and scope to the derogations contained in Article 36 TFEU.[13]

In addition to being imposed at the border, Member State country-based measures may also be imposed when products are placed on the market. Country-based measures that prohibit imported products – but not domestic ones – from being placed on the market are still generally prohibited by Article 34 TFEU as measures of equivalent effect to quantitative restrictions. *Dassonville* defines measures of equivalent effect to quantitative restrictions as 'all trading rules enacted by Member States which are capable of hindering, directly or indirectly, actually or potentially, intra-[EU] trade.[14] This formula certainly encapsulates Member State country-based measures applied at the point of marketing,

[11] Article 3 (1) (e) TFEU; Case 41/76, *Donckerwolcke* (n 5), para. 32; Case C-414/11, *Daiichi Sankyo Co. Ltd, Sanofi-Aventis Deutschland GmbH v DEMO Anonimos Viomikhaniki kai Emporiki Etairia Farmakon* EU:C:2013:520, para. 50; Case C-137/12, *Commission v Council (European Convention on conditional access services)* EU:C:2013:675, para. 56; see also the cases cited in those judgments; Opinion 1/75, *Understanding on a local cost standard* [1975] ECR 1355; see Piet Eeckhout, *EU External Relations Law* second edition (Oxford: Oxford University Press, 2011), 11–68

[12] Article 1 of Council Regulation 260/2009 of 26 February 2009 on the common rules for imports OJ 2009 No. L84/1. Safeguard measures may be taken however under the conditions specified in the Regulation

[13] Ibid., Article 24; Case C-296/00, *Prefetto Provincia di Cuneo v Silvano Carbone* [2002] ECR I-4670, para. 34

[14] Case 8/74, *Procureur du Roi v Benoît and Gustave Dassonville* [1974] ECR 837, para. 5

since they are only applied to imported products (so-called distinctly applicable measures). In *Commission v Italy (motorcycle trailers)*, for example, the ECJ reiterated settled case law that Article 34 TFEU, among other things, 'reflects the obligation to respect the principle [. . .] of non-discrimination' and that consequently 'measures adopted by a Member State the object or effect of which is to treat products coming from other Member States less favourably are to be regarded as measures having equivalent effect to quantitative restrictions on imports'.[15] Under this logic, applying one set of marketing rules to domestic products and a different set to imported products is a clear violation.

The situation with respect to country-based measures applied to the marketing of third country goods imported directly into the regulating Member State is less clear, because it is not readily apparent that such rules would fall within the scope of the EU's Import Regulation. The ECJ's case law makes a clear distinction between the importing stage and the marketing stage of a product. Thus, in *Carbone* the Court held that rules that apply at the marketing stage are not covered by the EU Import Regulation.[16] According to the ECJ:

> Placing products on the market is a stage subsequent to importation. Just as a product lawfully manufactured within the [EU] may not be placed on the market on that ground alone, the lawful importation of a product does not imply that it will automatically be allowed onto the market.[17]

The Court noted that in the absence of EU rules, 'the Member State into which [goods] are put into free circulation may prevent their being placed on the market if they do not satisfy the conditions laid down for that purpose under national law'.[18] This reasoning also seems to apply to so-called exotic imports where marketing rules only affect products that are not domestically produced or produced in the EU.[19] The General Court seems to have supported this view in *Inuit Tapiriit Kanatami and Others* by finding that the EU marketing ban on seal products, which

15 Case C-110/05, *Commission v Italy (motorcycle trailers)* [2009] ECR I-509, paras. 34 and 37
16 Case C-296/00, *Prefetto Provincia di Cuneo v Silvano Carbone* [2002] ECR I-4670
17 Ibid., para 31 18 Ibid., para 32
19 However, one may wonder whether a country-based measure by a Member State affecting the marketing of goods of third country origin only specifically relate to trade with third countries and therefore falls within the scope of the Common Commercial Policy. See Case C-414/11, *Daiichi Sankyo Co. Ltd, Sanofi-Aventis Deutschland GmbH v DEMO Anonimos Viomikhaniki kai Emporiki Etairia Farmakon* EU:C:2013:520, para 51

overwhelmingly originate from outside the EU, fell outside the scope of the Common Commercial Policy.[20]

However, the situation is different for country-based measures applied to third country goods in free circulation. The principle of assimilation suggests that Article 34 TFEU would apply to the application of such rules and would therefore require justification under either Article 36 TFEU or by reliance on mandatory requirements.[21]

2.1.2 Producer-Based Measures

Producer-based measures target the behaviour of producers of goods, not that of consumers or governments of third countries. These measures are designed to prevent producers that do not comply with the social or environmental production rules set by the importing Member State from having access to its market. An example is the EU cosmetics Regulation, which conditions access to the market on animal friendly production.[22]

Producer-based measures, whether applicable to imported products only or to all products equally, fall under the *Dassonville* definition of 'measures of equivalent effect to quantitative restrictions' if they prevent the marketing of products imported from other Member States. Applying producer-based measures to goods imported from other Member States is therefore a *prima facie* violation of Article 34 TFEU and requires either justification or reliance on one of the derogations contained in Article 36 TFEU.[23] Preventing goods from being marketed because of non-compliance with production rules has trade restrictive effects, even if such rules apply without distinction to imported and domestic goods alike.

[20] Case T-526/10, *Inuit Tapiriit Kanatami and Others v Commission* EU:T:2013:215, paras. 69–70. The General Court found that Article 114 TFEU was the correct legal basis for the seal products ban 'even if it is common ground that the proportion of such products is very small'.

[21] *EMI* a case predating *Donckerwolcke* and *Pereux* suggests that it does not necessarily. See Case 51/75, *EMI Records Limited v Cbs United Kingdom Limited* [1976] ECR 811, 860, para. 16. Note however, that in this case, it appeared that the party in question tried to rely on Article 28 (2) TFEU in relation direct imports from third countries.

[22] See Chapter 1, Section 1.1.2

[23] The *Dassonville* formula is based on trade restrictive effects, including potential and indirect effects, and there is no *de minimis* in its application. Gormley, 'Silver Threads Among the Gold . . . 50 Years of the Free Movement of Goods'; Case 8/74, *Procureur du Roi v. Benoît and Gustave Dassonville* [1974] ECR 837; Case C-110/05, *Commission v Italy (motorcycle trailers)* [2009] ECR I-509, para. 33, for the rejection of an introduction of a *de minimis* test see Case C-67/97, *Bluhme* [1998] ECR I-8093, paras 19–22; Case C-166/03, *Commission v France* [2004] ECR I-6535, para 15

We can analogize the treatment of process-based measures under EU law with the treatment of product requirements. The ECJ in *Keck* defined product requirements as 'rules that lay down requirements to be met by such goods (such as those relating to designation, form, size, weight, composition, presentation, labelling, packaging)'.[24] The Court never explicitly extended this definition to production requirements unrelated to the physical properties of the product concerned. However, Advocate General Van Gerven did so, arguing that production requirements unrelated to the physical composition of the product nevertheless relate 'to the intrinsic or extrinsic characteristics of the product concerned'.[25] In terms of their trade restrictive effects, product requirements and producer-based measures are conceptually very similar. Like producer-based measures, product rules require producers to change how they manufacture goods in order to comply with technical requirements.[26]

Cassis makes clear that product requirements fall within the scope of Article 34 TFEU.[27] In a number of cases the Court applied *Cassis* to mandatory production requirements that had to be met by imported goods. *Humanplasma* is probably the case that most clearly demonstrates that product requirements also cover process-based measures.[28] That case concerned an Austrian measure that prohibited the importation and marketing of blood products if blood donors had received compensation for their donations. The Court first noted that the measure applied to both imported and domestic blood products equally, and that as a result of the measure, blood and blood components lawfully obtained and marketed in Member States that permitted reimbursement for the costs associated with blood donations could not be imported and

[24] Joined cases C-267/91 and C-268/91, *Criminal proceedings against Bernard Keck and Daniel Mithouard* [1993] ECR I-6097, para 15

[25] Joined Cases C-401/92 and 402/92, *Tankstation 't Heuske and Boermans* [1994] ECR I-2201, Opinion of AG van Gerven

[26] Producer-based measures are therefore not necessarily more trade restrictive than product rules, although depending on factual circumstances there may be differences. A labelling requirement can be less trade restrictive than the requirement to use expensive machinery for animal welfare purposes (such as the use of a turtle excluder device in the WTO *US – Shrimp/Turtle* case). Only a 'producer characteristics' standard is more trade restrictive in principle, as it does not permit an undertaking to develop two different production lines for different markets. See Steve Charnovitz, 'The Law of Environmental PPMs in the WTO: Debunking the Myth of Illegality' (2002) 27 *The Yale Journal of International Law*, 59, 67.

[27] Case 120/78, *Rewe-Zentral AG v. Bundesmonopolverwaltung für Branntwein (Cassis de Dijon)* [1979] ECR 650

[28] Case C-421/09, *Humanplasma GmbH v Republik Österreich* [2010] ECR I-12869

marketed in Austria.[29] The Austrian measure was therefore capable of hindering intra-EU trade, and constituted a measure of equivalent effect to a quantitative restriction prohibited by Article 34 TFEU.[30] The ECJ's language in *Humanplasma*, a process-based measures case, follows very closely the language of its product requirements cases, finding that the measure should be presumed unlawful under Article 34 TFEU because it hindered the marketability of blood products that were 'lawfully obtained and marketed' in another Member State.

Another example is the *Beele* case where the ECJ found that Dutch jurisprudence prohibiting the marketing of products that were slavish imitations of products already on the market fell within the scope of Article 34 TFEU.[31] In addition, three cases involving the promotion of production of domestic green electricity should be mentioned: *PreussenElektra, Ålands Vindkraft AB v Energimyndigheten* and *Essent Belgium*.[32] In *PreussenElektra* the Court considered that a German measure requiring electricity suppliers to buy a certain percentage of their supplies from green electricity producers on German territory was a measure capable of hindering intra-EU trade.[33] In *Ålands Vindkraft AB v Energimyndigheten* and *Essent Belgium* national measures requiring electricity distributors on the Swedish and Belgian markets respectively to surrender green electricity certificates which were only granted to domestic green electricity producers were found to be capable of hindering intra-EU trade, because consumers and suppliers were required to buy certificates tied to national production, essentially resulting in favouring domestic production over foreign production.[34] These measures are slightly atypical and cannot be equated squarely with process-based measures, as their aim was more inward looking reserving a percentage of the market for green electricity domestically produced.[35] Such atypical distinctly applicable producer-based rules are thus also covered by Article 34 TFEU.

[29] Ibid., paras 28–29 [30] Ibid., para 30

[31] Case 6/81, *BV Industrie Diensten Groep v. J. A. Beele Handelmaatschappij BV* [1982] ECR 707

[32] Case C-379/98, *PreussenElektra AG v Schleswag AG* [2001] ECR I-2159; Case C-573/12, *Ålands Vindkraft AB v Energimyndigheten* EU:C:2014:2037; Joined Cases C-204/12, C-205/12, C-206/12, C-207/12, C-208/12, *Essent Belgium* EU:C:2014:2192

[33] Case C-379/98, *PreussenElektra AG v. Schleswag AG* [2001] ECR I-2159, para. 71

[34] Case C-573/12 *Ålands Vindkraft AB v Energimyndigheten* EU:C:2014:2037, paras. 65–75; Joined Cases C-204/12, C-205/12, C-206/12, C-207/12, C-208/12 *Essent Belgium* EU:C:2014:2192, paras. 77–88

[35] The measures in *Ålands Vindkraft AB v Energimyndigheten* and *Essent Belgium*, however, did not require domestic consumption of green electricity. Domestically produced electricity

Producer-based measures are also not unambiguously covered by both the Mutual Recognition Regulation and the Notification Directive, but it is likely, in light of the purpose and context of these two pieces of secondary legislation, that Member States are required to follow the procedural rules laid down therein when they enact and apply producer-based measures. The Mutual Recognition Regulation applies to all decisions based on a 'technical rule' if that rule results in the prohibition of the marketing of a product lawfully marketed in another Member State or results in its modification or requires additional testing of that product.[36] A 'technical rule' is further defined as any law, regulation or administrative provision that sets out product characteristics and is either compulsory or prohibits the marketing of non-compliant products.[37] The Regulation does not expressly cover producer-based measures. However, the wording 'such as' indicates that the list of characteristics of products is non-exhaustive, giving ample room to include production characteristics.

The Notification Directive requires Member States to notify to the Commission of any draft 'technical regulations', which covers three categories of rules:

(1) technical specifications;
(2) other requirements;
(3) rules which prohibit the manufacturing, use, marketing, or importation of the product.[38]

The first category – technical specifications – expressly refers to production methods and processes, but limits its coverage to only rules that 'have an effect on their characteristics'.[39] The Court's case law suggests

could also be exported but the producer would still receive certificates that would have to be bought by domestic operators.

[36] Article 2 (1) of Regulation 764/2008 of the European Parliament and of the Council of 9 July 2008 laying down procedures relating to the application of certain national technical rules to products lawfully marketed in another Member State and repealing Decision No 3052/95/EC OJ 2008 No. L218/21

[37] In addition, a technical rule covers any other requirement imposed on a product which affects the life-cycle of the product *after* it has been placed on the market. In relation to these recycling-type of arrangements – the Regulation lists as examples 'conditions of use, recycling, reuse or disposal, where such conditions can significantly influence the composition, nature or marketing of the product or type of product. See Article 2 (2) (b) (ii) of Regulation 764/2008 (*n* 36)

[38] Articles 1 (9) and 8 (1) of Directive 98/34/EC of the European Parliament and of the Council of 22 June 1998 laying down a procedure for the provision of information in the field of technical standards and regulations OJ 1998 No. L204/37

[39] Emphasis added. Article 1 (2) of Directive 98/34/EC

that this excludes measures relating to the production process that do not have an effect on the *physical* characteristics of the product in question.[40] The second category 'other requirements' relates to recycling-type rules that impose conditions on products *after* they have been marketed.[41] The last category, however, refers to all 'laws, regulations or administrative provisions of Member States [...] prohibiting the manufacture, importation, marketing or use of a product'. The ECJ has interpreted this last category of measures as 'particularly intended to cover national measures which leave no room for any use which can reasonably be made of the product concerned other than a purely marginal one'.[42] Although the Court has yet to rule on the matter, it is highly likely that producer-based measures will fall under this notification requirement, since they prohibit the marketing of a product not complying with the production standard.

We now turn to the important question of whether process-based rules can be challenged under Article 34 TFEU if those goods are of third country origin. Article 34 TFEU only applies in relation to trade restrictions between Member States, and as such, direct imports only fall within the scope of EU law to the extent that these rules concern importation and not the marketing of the product.[43] However, while Article 34 TFEU has, following the principle of assimilation, 'the same scope' and 'applies without distinction' when applied to products of third country origin that have cleared customs in another Member State as it does when applied to products originating within the EU, the case-law of the ECJ suggests that

[40] For example, in *Fortuna* – a case concerning a Polish measure that made it impossible to run low-prize gambling machines in places other than casinos and gaming arcades – the Court held that for a measure to fall within the scope of the concept technical specification 'that measure must necessarily refer to the product or its packaging *as such* and thus lay down one of the characteristics required of a product'. Joined Cases C-213/11, C 214/11 and C 217/11, *Fortuna sp. z o.o. and others v Dyrektor Izby Celnej w Gdyni* EU: C:2012:495, para. 28 This is very much similar language employed as used by the Panels in the controversial first *US – Tuna* reports within the GATT framework, but it goes short of explicitly making a distinction between product and process rules, since the case itself does not concern a process-based measure. GATT Panel Report. *United States – Restrictions on the Imports of Tuna (Mexico)*. Not adopted, circulated on 3 September 1991 (DS21/R - 39S/155), para. 5.8; GATT Panel Report, *United States – Restrictions on the Imports of Tuna (EEC)*. Not adopted, May 20, 1994 (DS29/R), para. 5.10

[41] Article 1 (3) of Directive 98/34/EC. The Court has held here that 'the national measures in question must constitute "conditions" which can significantly influence the composition, the nature or the marketing of the product concerned'. See Joined Cases Cases C-213/11, C 214/11 and C 217/11, *Fortuna sp. z o.o. and others v Dyrektor Izby Celnej w Gdyni* EU: C:2012:495, para. 35

[42] Ibid., para. 32 [43] See Section 2.1.1

the principle of mutual recognition only applies to goods 'lawfully produced and marketed in another Member State'.[44]

Cassis therefore suggests that that principle does not apply to goods of third country origin. However, such an interpretation would be somewhat at odds with the rationale of the principle of mutual recognition. That principle, as a decentralized alternative to harmonisation at EU level, seeks to ensure that goods are subject to a single regulatory burden (and not zero or multiple) at the marketing stage by presuming that imported goods which have met the technical rules of one Member State comply with the technical rules of the others.[45] This presumption of equivalence presupposes that within Europe generally similar technical rules apply in the Member States. That presumption can be rebutted if the importing Member State can demonstrate that there is a 'valid reason' for applying its additional technical rules.[46]

Where goods of third country origin can comply with the technical marketing rules of the exporting Member State, the principle of mutual recognition should apply to prevent those goods from being subject

[44] For the principle of assimilation see Article 28 (2) TFEU and Case 41/76, *Suzanne Criel, née Donckerwolcke and Henri Schou v Procureur de la République au tribunal de grande instance de Lille and Director General of Customs*, [1976] ECR 1921, para. 18; Case 119/78, *SA des grandes distilleries Peureux v Directeur des Services fiscaux de la Haute-Saône et du territoire de Belfort*, [1979] ECR 976, para. 26. For the principle of mutual recognition see Case 120/78, *Rewe-Zentral AG v. Bundesmonopolverwaltung für Branntwein (Cassis de Dijon)* [1979] ECR 650, para.14 and the literature below at *n* 47.

[45] Laurens Ankersmit, 'What if Cassis de Dijon were Cassis de Quebec? The Assimilation of Goods of Third Country Origin in the Internal Market' (2013) 50 *Common Market Law Review*, 1387; JHH Weiler, 'Mutual Recognition, Functional Equivalence and Harmonization in the Evolution of the European Common Market and the WTO' in Fiorella Kostoris and Padoa Schioppa (eds.), *The Principle of Mutual Recognition in the European Integration Process* (London: Palgrave Macmillan, 2005), 25–84; Alfonso Mattera 'Principle of Mutual Recognition and Respect for National, Regional and Local Identities and Traditions' in Fiorella Kostoris and Padoa Schioppa (eds.), *The Principle of Mutual Recognition in the European Integration Process* (London: Palgrave Macmillan, 2005), 1; Alfonso Mattera, 'L' article 30 du traité CEE, la jurisprudence "Cassis de Dijon" et le principle de la reconnaissaince mutuelle' [1992] *Revue du Marché Unique Européen*, 13; Kenneth A. Armstrong, 'Mutual Recognition' in Catherine Barnard and Joanne Scott (eds.), *The Law of the Single European Market: Unpacking the Premises* (Oxford: Hart Publishing, 2002), 225; see more critically Gareth Davies, 'Is Mutual Recognition an Alternative to Harmonisation: Lessons on Trade and Tolerance of Diversity from the EU', in Ortino and Bartels (eds.), *Regional Trade Agreements and the WTO Legal System* (Oxford: Oxford University Press, 2006), 265

[46] The Member State in question can rely on mandatory requirements or on the derogations contained in Article 36 TFEU. See Case 120/78, *Rewe-Zentral AG v. Bundesmonopolverwaltung für Branntwein (Cassis de Dijon)* [1979] ECR 650, para.14

to a second regulatory burden when they are subsequently imported into another Member State. If a product of third country origin is good enough to be sold on the French market, it should be presumed to be good enough to be sold on the German market, unless Germany can demonstrate valid reasons for applying additional standards. Most commentators have therefore suggested that the principle of functional equivalence applies to goods of third country origin as soon as they have been 'lawfully marketed in another Member State' or alternatively that such goods should be 'lawfully marketable in another Member State'.[47] This understanding is reflected in the EU Mutual Recognition Regulation which applies to technical rules that would hinder the free movement of a product 'lawfully marketed in another Member State'.[48]

While this approach seems logical for marketing rules generally, the question is whether it should equally apply to producer-based rules. The marketing of a product in one Member State does not necessarily mean that it can be presumed to comply with the process-based measures enacted by the importing Member State. While a Member State of export might have production rules that are functionally equivalent to that of the importing Member State, it may not have process-based marketing measures that are functionally equivalent to those of the importing Member State. To give a hypothetical example, France may have strict labour rules in its country, but it may not have any 'fair trade' rules in place governing the marketing of third country goods. While products originating from France may therefore be presumed to comply with a process-based rule in Germany, third country products imported into and marketed in France and subsequently imported into Germany may not.

[47] Laurens Ankersmit, 'What if Cassis de Dijon were Cassis de Quebec? The Assimilation of Goods of Third Country Origin in the Internal Market' (2013) 50 *Common Market Law Review*, 1387, 1397–1410; Gormley, 'Silver Threads Among the Gold' (*n* 3); Laurence Gormley, 'Some Reflections on the Internal Market and Free Movement of Goods' (1989) 16 *Legal Issues of Economic Integration*, 9–20, 17–18; Mattera, 'L'article 30 du traité CEE, la jurisprudence "Cassis de Dijon" et le principe de la reconnaissance mutuelle'; Jörg Tegeder, 'Applying the Cassis de Dijon Doctrine to Goods Originating in Third Countries' (1994) 19 *European Law Review*, 86–94; Enchelmaier, 'Article 36: General', 231–232; Edmond L. M. Völker, 'Barriers to External and Internal Community Trade' (PhD thesis, University of Amsterdam, 1993, 92–95

[48] Article 1 (2) of Regulation 764/2008 of the European Parliament and of the Council of 9 July 2008 laying down procedures relating to the application of certain national technical rules to products lawfully marketed in another Member State and repealing Decision No 3052/95/EC OJ 2008 No. L218/21

The presumption of equivalence might thus be inappropriate in relation to process-based measures applied to goods of third country origin.

Nonetheless, a deferential approach towards the possibilities of justifying process-based measures or derogating from Article 34 TFEU on the basis of Article 36 TFEU should enable the correct balance to be struck between the completion of the internal market and regulatory autonomy of the Member States. This is a practical solution that avoids a different standard of application of Article 34 TFEU for goods of third country origin in line with Article 28 (2) TFEU, while maintaining the fundamental rationale of the principle of mutual recognition, as well as the regulatory autonomy of Member States to regulate their markets for public interest reasons.

2.1.3 Consumer-Based Measures

Consumer-based measures are not aimed at changing the behaviour of governments or producers directly, but rather at changing the behaviour of consumers. Examples of consumer-based measures are mandatory and voluntary labelling rules such as initiating labels which promote dolphin-friendly tuna products, a ban on advertising cheap meat for animal welfare purposes, funding or organizing promotional campaigns to raise consumer awareness of process-attributes of certain products (such as conflict-free diamonds), government induced boycotts (naming and shaming certain producers), and restrictions on where and when certain products may be sold.[49]

Unlike country-based and producer-based measures, consumer-based measures do not necessarily fall within the scope of Article 34 TFEU. Despite the broad *Dassonville* formula, the ECJ has found Article 34 TFEU not applicable to 'certain selling arrangements', if they are non-discriminatory and do not prevent market access.[50] Because some

[49] See the introductory chapter for a more detailed discussion on the policy rationales of consumer-based measures.

[50] The ECJ did not define the concept of 'certain selling arrangements' in *Keck*. White, in an article predating Keck, suggested that rules concerning 'market circumstances' (rules concerning the time, place, manner and whom sells goods) should fall outside the scope of Article 34 TFEU. See Eric White, 'In Search of the Limits to Article 30 of the EEC Treaty' (1989) 26 *Common Market Law Review*, 235. The ECJ in *Karner* later summarized the *Keck* exception as follows 'provisions concerning inter alia the place and times of sale of certain products and advertising of those products as well as certain marketing methods [are] provisions governing selling arrangement within the meaning of *Keck and Mithouard.* Case C-71/02, *Herbert Karner Industrie-Auktionen GmbH v. Troostwijk GmbH* [2004] ECR I-3025, para. 38

consumer-based measures may fall within the scope of the 'selling arrangements' exception in *Keck*, they may escape the review of the ECJ altogether. Others, however, may be caught by Article 34's prohibition of measures of equivalent effect to quantitative restrictions. This section will proceed in assessing the compatibility of Article 34 TFEU with the five main types of consumer-based measures: labelling rules, advertising restrictions, promotional campaigns, government induced boycotts, and restrictions on the place and time of sale of products with process-attributes.

Labelling Rules

Labelling can be a way to inform consumers about production processes, and therefore enable them to make purchasing decisions on the basis of social and environmental considerations. At the EU level, for example, the EU organic label and EU eco-label inform consumers about the organic and environmental properties of products. At the Member State level, the Italian Reguzzoni-Versace Law is an interesting example.[51] It sets up a system of compulsory labelling for the textile, leather goods, and footwear sectors and requires that in addition to indicating the origin of products, labels must also convy information regarding compliance with national regulations and international standards governing worker health and safety, minimum age of workers and environmental protection.[52] The Reguzzoni-Versace Law is one of the very few government-led initiatives aimed at informing consumers about labour conditions abroad.

Labelling rules can be subdivided into voluntary and mandatory labelling schemes. Mandatory labelling schemes are labelling rules with which an imported product needs to comply before it can be marketed. Voluntary labelling schemes do not prevent the marketing of products if the product is not labelled according to the scheme in question.[53] There is some degree of overlap between these two types of labelling rules,

[51] Law No. 55 of 8 April 2010 Provisions governing the marketing of textile, leather and footwear products [2010] and the implementing decree Interministerial decree pursuant to article 2.1 of Law 55 of 8 April 2010 – 'Provisions for the sale of textile products, leather goods and footwear' [2011] available at the TRIS website of the Commission http://ec.europa.eu/enterprise/tris/index_en.htm. The notification number of Law no. 55 is 2010/286/I, the notification number of the implementing decree is 2010/681/I

[52] Ibid., article 1 (3) of Law no. 55

[53] See for an example of a voluntary scheme addressed under article 34 TFEU Case C-325/00, *Commission v Germany* [2002] ECR I-9977

since in order to protect the integrity of the voluntary scheme, only compliant products are permitted to use the label or any similar tag that would create consumer confusion.[54]

In any event, within the EU context, what matters is the trade-restrictive effects of the rules in question. As soon as a labelling measure requires a product to be modified (whether by removing a label or attaching one), it will be more difficult to market the product. This means labelling rules are measures of equivalent effect to a quantitative restriction under *Dassonville*.[55] In *Morellato*, the Court held that the *Cassis* jurisprudence applies to rules that require products to be modified as 'the need to alter the packaging or the labelling of imported products prevents such requirements from constituting selling arrangements'.[56] Thus, even voluntary labelling schemes may fall within the scope of Article 34 TFEU, as not all products can be marketed without the risk that some products would require adaptation. If a product is labelled as 'fair trade', for instance, but does not comply with the voluntary labelling scheme regulating the use of 'fair trade' labels, and as a consequence the measure in question prevents the marketing of the products, such a measure is a measure equivalent to a quantitative restriction on imports.

The ECJ has therefore held that both voluntary and mandatory labelling schemes can fall within the scope of Article 34 TFEU, which indicates that labelling schemes regardless of their nature constitute product

[54] This issue has surfaced within the WTO where the Appellate Body considered a labelling scheme exhaustively regulating the reference to dolphin-safe tuna, a mandatory labelling scheme, indicating that where such a scheme permitted competition between different (private labels) on dolphin-safe tuna it would not be considered as mandatory. See WTO Appellate Body Report, United States – Measures concerning the Importation, Marketing and Sale of Tuna and Tuna Products, 16 May 2012 (WT/DS381/AB/R), paras 193–195. See for more discussion on this issue Laurens J. Ankersmit and Jessica C. Lawrence, 'The Future of Environmental Labelling: US – Tuna II and the Scope of the TBT' (2012) 39 *Legal Issues of Economic Integration*, 127, at 131–135; Enrico Partiti, 'The Appellate Body Report in US – Tuna II and Its Impact on Eco-Labelling and Standardization' (2013) 40 *Legal Issues of Economic Integration*, 73, at 82–86

[55] Article 2 (1) (b) of Regulation 764/2008 of the European Parliament and of the Council of 9 July 2008 laying down procedures relating to the application of certain national technical rules to products lawfully marketed in another Member State and repealing Decision No 3052/95/EC OJ 2008 No. L218/21

[56] Case C-416/00, *Tommaso Morellato v Comune di Padova* [2003] ECR 9343, paras. 27–30; see also Joined cases C-267/91 and C-268/91, *Criminal proceedings against Bernard Keck and Daniel Mithouard* [1993] ECR I-6097. In paragraph 15 of that judgment the Court defined product rules as 'rules that lay down requirements to be met by such goods (such as those relating to designation, form, size, weight, composition, presentation, labelling, packaging)'

requirements in the sense of *Cassis*.[57] The essential criterion for the Court is whether a labelling scheme has consequences for the actual content (packaging or labels) of the product, regardless of whether the labelling scheme prevents the product from being sold.[58] Even in borderline cases, the Court opts for classifying labelling schemes as product requirements.[59]

Advertising Restrictions

Consumer-based measures can also take the form of advertising restrictions. A Member State may, for instance, ban commercials or other forms of advertising for cheap meat products out of animal welfare considerations. Such measures do not legally prevent products from being sold, but can lead to a *de facto* ban if traders are deprived of effective means of promoting their imported products.[60] While the ECJ has held that advertising restrictions constitute selling arrangements under the *Keck* definition discussed above, it has equally been willing to accept that such measures can have significant effects on market access for imported products.[61]

The key test is whether advertising restrictions restrict market access for imported products more than for domestic products, either because the incumbent already has an established position on a market which the imported product is not able to challenge, or because the advertising restrictions prevent imported goods from being sold.[62] Despite the Court's

[57] Case C-325/00, *Commission v Germany* [2002] ECR I-9977 (voluntary scheme); Case 207/83, *Commission v United Kingdom (origin marking)* [1985] ECR 1207 (mandatory scheme)

[58] Case C-368/95, *Vereinigte Familiapress Zeitungsverlags-und Vertriebs GmbH v. Heinrich Bauer Verlag* [1997] ECR I-3709, para 11

[59] Case C-244/06, *Dynamic Medien Vertriebs GmbH v Avides Media AG* [2008] ECR I-505, paras.33–34. Note however the different view in the Opinion of AG Mengozzi in that case, paras. 48–50. The case concerned labelling rules relating to age classification of DVD's which was compulsory only if the DVD's were sold by mail order for child protection purposes (in shops this protection was carried out by the salespeople). The case is different from most of the *Cassis* type of cases, because not bearing a label was no precondition to marketability: DVD's could be sold in ordinary shops without such authorization, but only to persons above the age of 18.

[60] Case C-412/93, *Leclerc-Siplec v TFI Publicité* [1995] ECR I-179, Opinion of AG Jacobs paras. 38–45

[61] Joined cases C-34/95, C-35/95 and C-36/95, *Konsumentombudsmannen (KO) v De Agostini and others* [1997] ECR I- 3843; Case C-405/98, *Konsumentenombudsmannen (KO) v Gourmet International Products AB (GIP)* [2001] ECR I- 1795; Dimitrios Doukas, 'Untying the Market Access Knot: Advertising Restrictions and the Free Movement of Goods and Services' (2007) 9 *Cambridge Yearbook of European Legal Studies*, 177

[62] It goes without saying advertising restrictions formally distinguishing between imported and domestic products to the detriment of the former are in any event prohibited. See

refusal to apply a *de minimis* test, there is an issue of degree in its case law when it comes to advertising restrictions. If the only effective means of sales promotion is taken away from the trader wishing to sell imported products the Court is more likely to find a violation of Article 34 TFEU than when other effective means of sales promotion remain available.[63]

Nonetheless, it is not entirely clear whether a Member State's ban on advertising for cheap meat products due to animal welfare considerations would be contrary to Article 34 TFEU. On the one hand, a case such as *Douwe Egberts* suggests that such a ban might be problematic. In that case, the ECJ found that a total ban on references to 'slimming' and 'medical recommendations, attestations, declarations or statements of approval' in foodstuffs advertisements was contrary to Article 34 TFEU for two reasons.[64] First, such a measure could 'compel a producer to discontinue an advertising scheme which he considers to be particularly effective'.[65] Second, 'an absolute prohibition *of advertising the characteristics of a product* is liable to impede access to the market by products from other Member States more than it impedes access by domestic products, with which consumers are more familiar'.[66] On the other hand, in *Karner* the Court found that Austrian rules that prohibited retailers from advertising products obtained from an insolvent estate fell outside the scope of Article 34 TFEU in line with *Keck*. The Court distinguished these rules from previous cases[67] because the prohibition in *Karner* did not 'lay down a total prohibition on all forms of advertising in a Member State for a product which is lawfully sold there'. Instead: 'It merely prohibits any reference, when a large number of people are targeted, *to the fact that goods originate from an insolvent estate* if those goods no longer constitute part of the insolvent estate, on grounds of consumer protection.'[68]

Article 2 (3) (m) of Commission Directive 70/50/EEC of 22 December 1969 based on the provisions of Article 33 (7), on the abolition of measures which have an effect equivalent to quantitative restrictions on imports and are not covered by other provisions adopted in pursuance of the EEC Treaty OJ 1970 No. L13/29

63 Compare Case C-71/02, *Herbert Karner Industrie-Auktionen GmbH v. Troostwijk GmbH* [2004] ECR I- 3025 with Joined cases C-34/95, C-35/95 and C-36/95, *Konsumentombudsmannen (KO) v De Agostini and others* [1997] ECR I- 3843

64 Case C-239/02, *Douwe Egberts v Westrom Pharma* [2004] ECR I-7007

65 Ibid., para 52

66 Ibid., para 53

67 Joined cases C-34/95, C-35/95 and C-36/95, *Konsumentombudsmannen (KO) v De Agostini and others* [1997] ECR I- 3843; Case C-405/98, *Konsumentenombudsmannen (KO) v Gourmet International Products AB (GIP)* [2001] ECR I- 1795

68 Case C-71/02, *Herbert Karner Industrie-Auktionen GmbH v. Troostwijk GmbH* [2004], para 42, emphasis added.

Both cases are equally relevant for process-based measures, but it seems that a ban on specific advertising means such as brochures of cheap meat in supermarket for animal welfare reasons could be defended on the basis of *Karner* as long as other means of advertising remain possible. If all references to cheap meat in advertising are prohibited, by contrast, it seems that *Douwe Egberts* suggests that such a rule falls within the scope of Article 34 TFEU and requires justification or derogation under Article 36 TFEU.

A problematic aspect of the ECJ's case law in that sense is that while the Court highlighted the grandfathering nature (protecting the incumbent) of advertising restrictions, it did not elaborate upon the discrimination test it introduced. It assumed these effects or left it up to the national court to verify. Yet, it is central to determining a violation of Article 34 TFEU. This issue is particularly important for process-based advertising restrictions, because in a number of cases there will be no domestic counterpart to which the imported product can be compared. Products such as textile products or tropical timber are barely manufactured in many Member States. In these advertising cases the Court simply refers to 'domestic products', not 'similar domestic products', or 'domestic products which are in competition with the imported product', or 'like products'. If the comparator truly is just any domestic product, the reference to discrimination is superfluous and collapses into a general market access test, as there will always be a domestic product that is not affected by the advertising restrictions even if there is absolutely no economic relationship between the domestic product and the imported product.

Promotional Campaigns

Another way of inducing the consumer to buy products with certain process-attributes is through promotional campaigns. Governments can fund public awareness campaigns for things like animal welfare at farms, corporate social responsibility abroad, or sustainable energy production'. These campaigns can be targeted to create awareness of a particular government-run label or may promote a certain way of doing business with which undertakings can affiliate themselves. They can also be entirely informative, raising an issue, but not connecting it specifically to the purchase of products, for example by sponsoring a documentary on labour practices in Bangladesh that might have subsequent chilling effects on the consumption of imported textile products.

The case law on promotional campaigns mainly concerns discriminatory practices by Member State governments, and it is not entirely clear whether public awareness campaigns – aside from those that attempt to induce consumers to buy domestic goods – fall within the scope of Article 34 TFEU.[69] On the one hand, such measures may have potential and indirectly trade-restrictive effects. On the other hand, the effects may be seen as *too* uncertain and indirect.[70] The latter approach seems the more sensible one, so long as imported products are not specifically targeted.

The two leading cases in this area are *Commission v Ireland (Buy Irish)* and *Apple and Pear Development Council*. In *Commission v Ireland (Buy Irish)* the Court made clear that government-sponsored campaigns aimed at promoting domestic goods over imported ones solely on the basis of the origin of the product was contrary to Article 34 TFEU, as this was a means of substituting 'domestic products for imported products and was liable to affect the volume of trade between Member States'.[71] *Apple and Pear Development Council* concerned, among other things, a government-funded publicity and promotion campaign which promoted (1) apples and pears in general, (2) English and Welsh apples and pears, and (3) certain varieties which are typical of English and Welsh production. The Court considered only the second type of promotion to be contrary to Article 34 TFEU, because it promoted domestic goods 'solely by reason of their national origin'.[72]

However, Article 34 TFEU did not apply to promotion campaigns aimed at (1) promoting certain products in general, or (3) particular qualities of those products, *even if* those qualities where typical of national production. The ECJ held that a promotional campaign therefore may draw attention 'to the specific qualities of fruit grown in the Member State in question or from organizing campaigns to promote the sale of certain varieties, mentioning their particular properties, even if those varieties are typical of national production'.[73] The Court dismissed the argument put forward by the Commission that campaigns promoting certain varieties might result in the exclusion of varieties originating from other Member States. According to the ECJ:

[69] Janja Hojnik, 'Free Movement of Goods in a Labyrinth: Can Buy Irish Survive the Crises?' (2012) 49 *Common Market Law Review*, 291

[70] Thomas Horsley, 'Unearthing Buried Treasure: Art 34 TFEU and the Exclusionary Rules' (2012) 37(6) *European Law Review*, 737

[71] Case 249/81, *Commission v Ireland* [1982] ECR 4006, para 25

[72] Case 222/82, *Apple and Pear Development Council* [1983] ECR 4087, para 18

[73] Ibid., para 19

It is true that such a distortion of the conditions of competition, which would be incompatible with the proper functioning of the common organization of the markets, might occur in a market where the publicity measures related exclusively or essentially to certain varieties to the exclusion of the others, that consideration cannot justify the prohibition of all publicity campaigns whereby an organization such as the Development Council draws attention to the properties of certain varieties and indicates the uses for which those varieties are specifically suitable.[74]

Promotional campaigns aimed at creating awareness or even promoting specific process-attributes of products relating to animal welfare, fair trading, labour standards, and environmental protection would therefore generally seem to fall outside the scope of Article 34 TFEU. This is true even where such schemes draw attention to such process-attributes that are typical of domestic production. Last, the combination of setting up a label for domestic products only with a promotion campaign for that label can constitute a measure of equivalent effect to a quantitative restriction.[75]

Government-Induced Boycotts

A more negative and *ad hoc* way of inciting consumers to make socially and environmentally responsible purchasing decisions is to name and shame undertakings through government-induced boycotts. An example of this is the black-listing by the Dutch trade minister Ploumen of undertakings that were unwilling to sign the Accord on Fire and Building Safety in Bangladesh.[76] Other potential examples of such conduct could be the naming and shaming of multinationals for polluting the global environment (oil spills for example), violating human rights, or being complicit in corruption.

[74] Ibid., para 21

[75] See Case C-325/00, *Commission v Germany* [2002] ECR I-9977. In paragraph 23 the Court held that such a 'scheme has, at least potentially, restrictive effects on the free movement of goods between Member States. Such a scheme, set up in order to promote the distribution of agricultural and food products made in Germany and for which the advertising message underlines the German origin of the relevant products, may encourage consumers to buy the products with the CMA label to the exclusion of imported products'. See further Malcolm A. Jarvis, 'Case C-325/00, Commission v. Germany, Judgment of the Court of Justice of 5 November 2002. Full Court' (2003) 40 *Common Market Law Review*, 71

[76] NRC Handelsblad, 'Bangladesh Kledingconflict loopt op' (26 November 2013); see for the Accord: 'Accord on Fire and Building Safety in Bangladesh', available at www.bangladeshaccord.org/

The analysis under Article 34 TFEU should be relatively similar to that for promotional campaigns, although there is only one case dealing with the issue of public statements 'naming and shaming' a company. In *Lehtinen* the ECJ found that discriminatory or unsubstantiated statements made in relation to a particular type of imported goods with a negative impact in the sale of such goods led to a breach of Article 34 TFEU.[77] *Lehtinen* was a relatively 'easy' case for the Court. The public official in question had made public statements about foreign products on his own initiative, contrary to the assessment made by his boss, and in a public capacity. The official's comments led to considerable publicity, and as a public official he was in the position to influence consumer behaviour. Moreover, the statements violated the procedures set in secondary law to deal with exactly the issue of unsafe machinery despite being certified by a certification organisation. This meant that Finland was also in breach of the duty of loyalty, as it did not follow the procedure agreed to collectively by the EU legislature.

However, it would be problematic to extrapolate from *Lehtinen* to other cases in which these aggravating circumstances are not present. Consider, for example, the situation in which a minister of a government of a Member State has evidence of serious human rights violations occurring the factories of a textile undertaking, presents this evidence in newspapers and on television, and urges the population not to buy the products of this company. Should the ECJ engage in judicial review over such statements? On the one hand, there may very well be trade-restrictive effects, and it would be preferable to have some sort of marginal review in order to check whether the claims are substantiated and not aimed at keeping imported products off the market. On the other hand, such judicial review would limit national politicians holding public office from expressing their concerns in public, hampering the national democratic process of public deliberation, especially if the ECJ maintains its

[77] Case C-470/03, *A.G.M.-COS.MET Srl v Suomen valtio and Tarmo Lehtinen* [2007] ECR I-2749, para. 65. However, the case is not that straightforward because it was closely connected to the proper functioning of the Machinery Directive. The main problem for the Court was that Finland did not comply with the procedures set out in the Directive enabling Member States to prevent unsafe machinery from being marketed in Finland. The Court itself recognized that public officials were very much at liberty to prevent vehicle lifts from being placed on the market if they ascertain that the machinery is liable to endanger the safety of persons and property, but only in accordance with the Directive. The Court noted that 'the competent authorities neither ascertained that there was a risk, nor took measures to withdraw the lifts at issue in the main proceedings from the market, nor a fortiori did they inform the Commission of any such measures'.

restrictive stance on the freedom of expression in this regard.[78] It would be advisable, therefore, if, in line with the case-law on promotional campaigns, to only consider Article 34 TFEU breached if there is evidence that the statements made by public officials are purely discriminatory or unsubstantiated. This would avoid Article 34 TFEU from being invoked in every instance where a public official makes statements that might indirectly and potentially have an effect on the marketability of imported products, and limit judicial review of public statements to those statements that are aimed at keeping imported products off the market on the basis of their origin.

Restrictions on Where and When Goods May Be Sold

The last type of consumer-based measures fall squarely within the *Keck* exception for certain selling arrangements: restrictions on where and when goods may be sold. Provided that such measures do not prevent market access or impede it in comparison with domestic products, Article 34 TFEU is not breached. Measures that fall within this category are, for example, permitting only the sale of animal-friendly products in certain public places, such as public markets, or maintaining more generous opening hours for organic-only shops.

The application of the *Keck* criteria by the Court in relation to these consumer-based measures is, however, far from coherent, and such measures may still require justification. Whereas in *Commission v Greece (infant milk)* the Court held that Greek rules requiring processed milk for infants to be sold in pharmacies constituted a selling arrangement and fell outside the scope of Article 34 TFEU, the Court in *Ker Optica* held that a prohibition of selling contact lenses over the Internet did violate Article 34 TFEU.[79] The explanation probably lies in the fact that *Commission v Greece (infant milk)* was a relatively early case decided soon after the decision in *Keck*, as well as the fact that selling over the Internet is by definition a means to penetrate a new market in another Member State, and therefore is more closely related to the case law on advertising restrictions. The language in *Ker Optika* resonates with that of the advertising cases: the prohibition of sales over the Internet, according to the

[78] In *Lehtinen* the Court rejected reliance on the freedom of expression by a public official: 'Member States, however, cannot rely on their officials' freedom of expression to justify an obstacle and thereby evade their own liability under Community law' (para. 72).

[79] Case C-108/09, *Ker-Optika bt v ÀNTSZ Dél-dunántúli Regionális Intézete* [2010] ECR I-12213; Case C-392/91, *Commission v Greece* [1995] ECR I-1648

Court, 'deprives traders from other Member States of a particularly effective means of selling those products and thus significantly impedes access of those traders to the market of the Member State concerned'.[80]

A lot depends, in that respect, on how the ECJ applies the test laid down in *Keck* in paragraphs 16 and 17. However, this application is far from coherent. In some cases the Court places emphasis on rooting out protectionism with respect to domestic products. In other cases, discrimination against foreign traders is central to finding a violation. In *Ker-Optika*, for instance, the Court held that a prohibition on selling contact lenses over the Internet 'does not affect in the same manner the selling of contact lenses by Hungarian traders and such selling as carried out by traders from other Member States' without looking into the origin of the contact lenses themselves.[81] In some cases, the Court has moved on from the conditions laid down in paragraph 16 of *Keck* to looking at whether a measure satisfies the conditions laid down in paragraph 17.[82] This means that non-discriminatory selling arrangements that prevent market access can also fall under the prohibition of Article 34 TFEU. Often the ECJ applies both paragraphs.[83]

When the ECJ compares the treatment of domestic and imported products, it usually does so in relation to a particular class of products, for instance domestically produced versus imported tobacco.[84] In *Commission v. Greece (infant milk)* the Court explicitly transferred the discrimination test contained in Article 110 TFEU[85] to Article 34 TFEU. It held that certain selling arrangements would be covered by Article 34 TFEU 'if it was apparent that the legislation at issue protected domestic products which were similar to processed milk for infants from other Member States or which were in competition with milk of that type'.[86] That reference has not found its way into the case law of the ECJ again, although the Court does usually stick to comparing similar products. Similarity is nowhere defined by the Court, however, and it is not clear if

[80] Case C-108/09, *Ker-Optika*, para. 54 [81] Ibid., para. 55

[82] Case C- 239/02, *Douwe Egberts NV v Westrom Pharma NV* [2004] ECR I-7007, para. 51; Case C-531/07, *Fachverband der Buch- und Medienwirtschaft v LIBRO Handelsgesellschaft mbH* [2009] ECR I-3717, para. 20;

[83] Case C-405/98, *Konsumentenombudsmannen (KO) v Gourmet International Products AB (GIP)* [2001] ECR I- 1795, paras. 21–25; Case C-141/07, *Commission v Germany* [2008] ECR I-6935

[84] Case C-387/93, *Giorgio Domingo Banchero* [1995] ECR I-4683, para. 40; Case C-405/98, *Konsumentenombudsmannen (KO) v Gourmet International Products AB (GIP)* [2001] ECR I-1795

[85] Article 110 TFEU prohibits discriminatory and protectionist product taxes, see for a discussion below Section 2.2.2

[86] Case C-392/91, *Commission v Greece* [1995] ECR I-1648, paras. 18–19

the Court will only look at physical similarity or similarity from the point of view of the consumer,[87] or also similarity from the point of view of the regulator.

Sometimes, the ECJ does not pin itself down to making comparisons within a particular class of products.[88] The overarching idea expressed in its judgments seems to be to prohibit protectionist selling arrangements by introducing a crude economic assessment of whether a measure modifies the conditions of competition to the detriment of imported products.[89] The Court uses the terminology 'discriminatory' and 'protectionist' indiscriminately, despite the latter being a more economic concept and not confined to rooting out discrimination solely on the grounds of origin. It is clear, however, that it is not necessary for the measure in question to impede market access for *all* imported products. The Court has held that:

> [For] a national measure to be characterised as discriminatory or protective within the meaning of the rules on the free movement of goods, it is not necessary for it to have the effect of favouring national products *as a whole* or of placing *only imported products* at a disadvantage and not national products.[90]

This is in line with the case-law of the Court in relation to Article 110 TFEU, in which it is immaterial if certain domestic products are treated even more disadvantageously than similar imported products when those imported products are treated less advantageously than other similar domestic products.[91]

The ECJ is also yet to determine whether the prohibition of discrimination in selling arrangements also entails a form of most favoured nation obligation. So far, it has only compared foreign traders with domestic traders, or domestic products with imported products, and has not looked

[87] Case C-405/98, *Konsumentenombudsmannen (KO) v Gourmet International Products AB (GIP)* [2001] ECR I-1795, paras. 21–25

[88] Case C-254/98, *Schutzverband gegen unlauteren Wettbewerb v TK- Heimdienst Sass GmbH* [2000] ECR I-151, para. 27

[89] Gareth Davies, 'Understanding Market Access: Exploring the Economic Rationality of Different Conceptions of Free Movement Law' (2010) 11 *German Law Journal*, 671–704, available at www.germanlawjournal.com/index.php?pageID=11&artID=1264

[90] Joined Cases C-1/90 and C-176/90, *Aragonesa de Publicidad Exterior and Publivía* [1991] ECR I-4151, para. 24; Case C-254/98, *Schutzverband gegen unlauteren Wettbewerb v TK- Heimdienst Sass GmbH* [2000] ECR I-151, para. 27; Case C-141/07, *Commission v Germany* [2008] ECR I-6935, para. 39, emphasis added

[91] Case C-213/96, *Outokumpu Oy* [1998] ECR I-1777 paras. 34–36; Case C-152/89, *Commission v Luxembourg* [1991] ECR I-3141, paras. 20–22

at distinctions among similar imported products from different third country origins. *Keck* indicates only a national treatment obligation: that only selling arrangements that prevent or impede market access for foreign products more than domestic ones falls within the scope of Article 34 TFEU.[92]

In relation to the situation in which there is no domestic production of a particular type of good, the ECJ has reached contradicting results. This relates to the so-called exotic import problem: measures can be extremely burdensome on imports, but as long as there is no domestic production that benefits, there is no protectionist effect. However, that does not mean that the measure is not discriminatory, if the reason for the existence of the measures is based on the origin of products. In *Commission v. Greece (infant milk)* the ECJ took the more limited protectionist view. It held that because there was no domestic production of processed infant milk or competing products, Article 34 TFEU did not apply. The application of Article 34 TFEU 'to a national measure for the general regulation of commerce, which concerns all the products concerned without distinction according to their origin, cannot depend on such a purely fortuitous factual circumstance, which may, moreover, change with the passage of time'.[93] If such would be the case, according to the Court, 'this would have the illogical consequence that the same legislation would fall under Article [34] in certain Member States but fall outside the scope of that provision in other Member States'.[94] The Court appears to contradict itself here, because reasoning *a contrario* this would mean that the application of Article 34 TFEU depends on the existence of domestic production, making the same legislation either fall within the scope of Article 34 TFEU or not in different Member States depending on domestic production.[95]

In *Morellato,* the ECJ appears to have reconsidered its position. The Court held in that case that an Italian rule (which it classified as a selling

[92] Joined cases C-267/91 and C-268/91, *Criminal proceedings against Bernard Keck and Daniel Mithouard* [1993] ECR I-6097, para. 17. This might be explained by the fact that the case itself did not concern a situation where the measure at issue treated similar imported products of different origin differently. *Keck* actually concerned two French products: Picon Beer and Saté Rouge Coffee. See Laurence Gormley, 'Reasoning Renounced? The Remarkable Judgment in Keck & Mithouard' (1994) 5 *European Business Law Review*, 63

[93] Case C-392/91, *Commission v Greece* [1995] ECR I-1648, para. 17 [94] Ibid.

[95] The Court admits as much in the following paragraph where it states that '[t]he situation would be different only if it was apparent that the legislation at issue protected domestic products which were similar to processed milk for infants from other Member States or which were in competition with milk of that type'

arrangement) requiring pre-baked bread to be packaged *after* it was baked in order to sell the bread as ready for consumption did fall within the scope of Article 34 TFEU, even if there was no domestic production of pre-baked bread. It held that:

> [W]here there is no manufacture of the product at issue in the Member State of import, such a requirement, although it applies without distinction, disadvantages imported products only, in that it discourages their import or makes them less attractive to the final consumer. If that were the case, which it is also for the national court to determine, that requirement would constitute an obstacle to imports and would therefore be caught by the prohibition in Article [34] of the Treaty, unless it could be justified by a public-interest objective which takes precedence over the requirement for the free movement of goods.[96]

In conclusion, it is therefore difficult to say *in abstracto* whether consumer-based measures are exempted from Article 34 TFEU or whether they require justification. Measures that permit only the sale of animal-friendly products in certain public places, such as public markets, or that maintain more generous opening hours for organic-only shops would need to be assessed in accordance with the ECJ's crude case law on whether they prevent market access or impede market access for imported products in relation to domestic products.

2.1.4 *The Personal Scope of Article 34 TFEU and Its Horizontal Effects*

In recent years a discussion has emerged whether Article 34 TFEU should not only apply to state measures but to private actions as well.[97] Those in

[96] Case C-416/00, *Tommaso Morellato v Comune di Padova* [2003] ECR I-9343, para. 37

[97] See for those generally in favour: Christoph Krenn, 'A Missing Piece in the Horizontal Effect "jigsaw": Horizontal Direct Effect and the Free Movement of Goods' (2012) 49 *Common Market Law Review*, 177; Case C-438/05, *International Transport Workers' Federation and Finnish Seamen's Union v Viking Line ABP and OÜ Viking Line Eesti* [2007] ECR I-10779, Opinion of AG Maduro, Case C-171/11, *Fra.bo SpA v Deutsche Vereinigung des Gas- und Wasserfaches eV (DVGW)* EU:C:2012:176, Opinion of AG Trstenjak; G R Milner-Moore, *The Private Accountability of Private Parties under the Free Movement of Goods Principle* (Harvard Jean Monnet Working Paper 9/95) available at www.jeanmonnetprogram.org/archive/papers/95/9509ind.html. See for those opposing such extension Harm Schepel, 'Constitutionalising the Market, Marketising the Constitution, and to Tell the Difference: On the Horizontal Application of the Free Movement Provisions in EU Law' 18 (2012) *European Law Journal*, 177; Jukka Snell, *Goods and Services in EC Law: A Study of the Relationship Between the Freedoms* (Oxford: Oxford University Press, 2002), 139; Stefaan van den Bogaert, 'Horizontality: The Court Attacks?' in Catherine Barnard and Joanne Scott (eds.), *The Law of the Single European Market: Unpacking the Premises* (Oxford: Hart Publishing, 2002), 123; Kamiel Mortelmans, 'Towards Convergence in the Application of the Rules on Free Movement and on Competition?' (2001) 38 *Common Market Law Review*, 613.

favour of such extension base their reasoning on ensuring the effectiveness and uniform application of Article 34 TFEU. Christoph Krenn, for instance, points out that 'private regulation' and 'private governance' – meaning rules that are drafted by private actors alone or in the form of 'co-regulation' with the State – pose a threat to the effectiveness of Article 34 TFEU. Krenn argues that

> private regulation or 'private governance' – meaning rules that are no longer drafted by the State but by private actors alone or in the form of 'co-regulation' with the State – is not a new phenomenon, but is significantly growing in importance and frequency. Private regulation spans diverse sectors, such as sports regulation, social and employment law, food safety, Internet regulation or environmental governance. On a global scale this weakens national governments, gives further rise to multinational corporations and supply chains and leads to the 'proliferation, diversification and internationalization of new social movements and their strategies'.[98]

Krenn concludes from this that 'the *effet utile* justification of horizontal direct effect appears applicable to Article 34 TFEU'.[99]

Opponents of applying Article 34 to private actions base their reasoning on the text of Article 34 TFEU and its origins,[100] the context in which Article 34 TFEU operates (in particular in relation to securing the effectiveness of the EU competition rules[101]), and preserving the autonomy and fundamental rights of private individuals.[102] Even proponents of

See further Julio Baquero Cruz, *Between Competition and Free Movement: The Economic Constitutional Law of the European Community* (Oxford: Hart Publishing, 2002), 123; Gareth Davies, 'Freedom of Contract and the Horizontal Effect of Free Movement Law' in Dorota Leczykiewicz and Stephen Weatherill (eds.), *The Involvement of EU Law in Private Law Relationships* (Oxford: Hart Publishing, 2013), 53

98 Krenn, 'A Missing Piece in the Horizontal Effect "jigsaw"' (*n* 97), 201–202

99 Ibid., at 203. Advocate General Maduro has expressed similar views on extending the personal scope of the freedom of establishment to private individuals, see Case C-438/05, *International Transport Workers' Federation and Finnish Seamen's Union v Viking Line ABP and OÜ Viking Line Eesti* [2007] ECR I-10779, Opinion of AG Maduro, paras. 37–40

100 See also Snell, *Goods and Services in EC Law*, 129

101 Mortelmans, 'Towards Convergence in the Application of the Rules on Free Movement and on Competition?', 613; Bogaert, 'Horizontality: The Court Attacks?' with doctrinal support in Joined Cases 177 and 178/82, *Criminal proceedings against Jan van de Haar and Kaveka de Meern BV* [1984] ECR 1797, paras. 11–12

102 Christopher Brown, 'Case C-112/00, Eugen Schmidberger, Internationale Transporte und Planzüge v. Austria' (2003) 40 *Common Market Law Review*, 1499; Loïc Azoulai, 'The Court of Justice and the Social Market Economy: The Emergence of An Ideal and the Conditions for its Realization' (2008) 45 *Common Market Law Review*, 1335; Niamh Nic Shuibhne, 'Settling Dust? Reflections on the Judgments in Viking and Laval' (2010) 21 *European Business Law Review*, 681; Anne Davies, 'One Step Forward, Two Steps Back?

horizontal effect recognize these negative effects and have sought to limit horizontal application of Article 34 by proposing various *de minimis* tests.[103]

Applying Article 34 horizontally could place substantial limitations on the ability of private parties to enact process-based measures. Activists, politicians, journalists, undertakings, non-governmental organizations, and citizens can influence patters of trade, and persuade producers to change their production processes directly, or through consumer behaviour. These activities can range from public-private cooperation with minor private involvement, for example, reliance by governments on private certification organisations for public production standards, to entirely private actions, such as private labelling initiatives and campaigns against certain multinationals operating abroad or even entire countries. Sometimes these activities result in lasting and coherent regulation of products. For example, private 'fair trade' and environmental labels such as the Marine Stewardship Council (MSC) label and the Forest Stewardship Council (FSC) certify that a product adheres to environmental and social production standards.[104] Other activities are of a more *ad hoc* nature, responding to a particular event featured in the media. These can include organized campaigns to boycott products from specific undertakings or countries.[105] Examples are the 'killer' boycott organized by Greenpeace against Nestlé for using palm oil leading to rainforest destruction in KitKat candy bars,[106] and the Clean Clothes Campaign.[107] If such activities fell within the scope of Article 34 TFEU, its application would be considerably broadened.

Thus far, it appears that the ECJ has been reluctant to extend Article 34 to private process-based measures. In contrast to the other fundamental freedoms, the Court has found that Article 34 TFEU only applies to

Laval and Viking at the ECJ' (2008) 37 *Industrial Law Journal*, 126; see Case C-271/08, *Commission v Germany* [2010] ECR I-7091, Opinion of AG Trstenjak, paras 75–84

[103] Krenn, 'A missing piece in the horizontal effect "jigsaw"' (*n* 97), 209; Case C-438/05, *International Transport Workers' Federation and Finnish Seamen's Union v Viking Line ABP and OÜ Viking Line Eesti* [2007] ECR I-10779, Opinion of AG Maduro, paras. 37–40

[104] Fred Gale and Marcus Haward, *Global Commodity Governance: State Responses to Sustainable Forest and Fisheries Certification* (London: Palgrave Macmillan, 2011)

[105] Examples of boycotts against countries are the boycott against South Africa during apartheid and more recently against Israel.

[106] Information can be found about this campaign on www.greenpeace.org/international/en/campaigns/climate-change/kitkat/

[107] Information can be found about this campaign on www.cleanclothes.org/

State measures.[108] In *Commission v. Italy* the Court stated that 'the subject of [the free movement of goods] chapter is *State intervention* in intra-[EU] trade by measures in the nature of prohibitions, total or partial, on import, export or transit, according to circumstances'.[109] Similarly, in *Sapod-Audic* the Court held that contractual provisions between private parties relating to an environmental labelling scheme 'cannot be regarded as a barrier to trade for the purposes of Article [34] of the Treaty since it was not imposed by a Member State but agreed between individuals'.[110] Again in *Vlaamse reisbureaus*, the CJEU affirmed that 'Articles [34 and 35] of the Treaty concern only public measures and not the conduct of undertakings'.[111]

However, the Court has carved two major inroads into this principle, and the recent *Fra.bo* judgment seems to stretch the public/private distinction to its limits, as it stated that Article 34 TFEU also applies when 'in the light of inter alia the legislative and regulatory context in which it operates, the activities of a private-law body [...] has the effect of giving rise to restrictions on the free movement of goods *in the same manner as do measures imposed by the State*'.[112]

State Involvement

The first inroad is the broad reading of when a measure can be attributed to the activities of a Member State. First, all acts or measures taken by public bodies that create obstacles to the free movement of goods fall under the prohibition of Article 34 TFEU. This means that measures

[108] Although in Case 58/80, *Dansk Supermarked A/S v A/S Imerco* [1981] ECR 181, a case never recited again by the Court, the Court did state that 'it is impossible in any circumstances for agreements between individuals to derogate from the mandatory provisions of the Treaty on the free movement of goods'. The reasons for this deviation will be explored further below and can be attributed to the peculiar features of the exercise of intellectual property rights on the EU internal market.

[109] Case 7/68, *Commission v Italy* [1968] ECR 424

[110] Case C-159/00, *Sapod Audic v Eco-Emballages SA* [2002] ECR I-5031, para. 74

[111] Case 311/85, *VZW Vereniging van Vlaamse Reisbureaus v VZW Sociale Dienst van de Plaatselijke en Gewestelijke Overheidsdiensten* [1987] ECR 3821, para. 30. See also Joined Cases C-46 and 48/93, *Brasserie du Pêcheur SA v Germany and the Queen v Secratary for State and Transport ex parte: Factortame Ltd and Others* [1996] ECR I-1131, para. 54 where the Court stated that 'article [34 TFEU] imposes a prohibition *on Member States*'. In *GEMA* Advocate General Warner concluded that 'One must first bear in mind that, when Article [34] refers to a "measure", it means a measure taken by a Member State; it does not mean a measure taken by a private person' see Joined Cases 55 and 57/80, *Musik Vertrieb v GEMA* [1980] ECR 167, Opinion of AG Warner at 174

[112] Case C-171/11, *Fra.bo SpA v Deutsche Vereinigung des Gas- und Wasserfaches eV (DVGW)* EU: C:2012:453, para. 26

taken by central, regional and local authorities are covered, as well all measures stemming from public bodies.[113] Moreover, branches of government are bound by Article 34 TFEU, including independent public bodies, the judiciary, and even statements made by a public official if that official appears to represent governmental authority.[114] Thus, process-based measures set up by regional or local governmental bodies, such as an Italian regional label for sustainably produced cow milk, will not escape the application of Article 34 TFEU if those measures materially result in obstacles to trade in goods.[115]

Second, Article 34 TFEU covers measures of bodies in which the Member State has *controlling influence* within the activities of private bodies.[116] What matters is not the formal legal status of a body, but the degree of influence the Member State has over its activities, its composition, and its finances.[117] If such a body is *de facto* under Member State control, its measures may fall under the scope of Article 34 TFEU.

Third, the Court has also considered measures of private bodies to be State measures where those measures can be attributed to the *delegation* of regulatory powers by Member State authorities to such private bodies. The difference with the situation in which the Member State has

[113] Case 45/87, *Commission v Ireland (Dundalk water)* [1988] ECR 4929, para. 12, paras. 12–23; Case 58/80, *Dansk Supermarked A/S v A/S Imerco* [1981] ECR 181; Case C-1/90 *Aragonese de Publcidad v Departamento de Sanidad* [1991] ECR I-4151, para. 8

[114] In *Dundalk Water* the Court held that the Dundalk Urban District Council fell within the personal scope of Article 34 TFEU since it was 'a public body for whose acts the Irish Government is responsible' (para 12); Case C-470/03, *A.G.M.-COS.MET Srl v Suomen valtio and Tarmo Lehtinen* [2007] ECR I-2749, para. 58 (public official conduct); Case 58/80, *Dansk Supermarked A/S v A/S Imerco* [1981] ECR 181, para. 12 (judiciary)

[115] Decree of the Director-General No 138 of 27 September 2012, approved by the Regional Council with Resolution No 1744 of 11 October 2012 establishing the collective trademark named "Agricoltura Ambiente Qualità" (Agriculture Environment Quality - AQUA), aquality trademark granted by The Friuli-Venezia Giulia region [2012]

[116] This is comparable to the 'nexus-test' in the US State action doctrine: if there is sufficient involvement of the state with the private individual's actions there is 'state action'. Mattias Kumm and Victor Ferreres Comella, 'What Is So Special about Constitutional Rights in Private Litigation? A Comparative Analysis of the Function of State Action Requirements and Indirect Horizontal Effect' in András Sajó and Renáta Utiz (eds.), *The Constitution in Private Relations: Expanding Constitutionalism* (The Hague: Eleven International Publishing, 2005), 265–283; Stephen Gardbaum, 'The "Horizontal Effect" of Constitutional Rights' (2003) 102 *Michigan Law Review*, 387

[117] Case C-325/00, *Commission v Germany* [2002] ECR I-9977, paras. 17–19; Case C-302/88, *Hennen Olie BV v Stichting Interim Centraal Orgaan Voorraadvorming Aardolieprodukten and State of the Netherlands* [1990] ECR I-4639, para. 15; Case 249/81, *Commission v Ireland* [1982] ECR 4006, paras. 15–23; Case 222/82, *Apple and Pear Development Council* [1983] ECR 4087, para. 17

controlling influence over a private body is that the private body in the situation of delegation can act independently, but its powers stem from Member State regulation.

The important decision in *Fra.bo* is a good example of Member State delegation of regulatory powers that result in private parties being bound by Article 34 TFEU. That case concerned the refusal of a private law body in Germany (DVGW), not controlled or funded by the state, to certify certain copper fittings made by the Italian company Fra.bo as compliant with German legislation. This national regulatory arrangement is much like the EU's 'new approach' to harmonization, where products certified by private European standardization organizations are presumed to comply with the essential requirements laid down by the EU legislature.[118] For the ECJ the question was whether 'in the light of inter alia the legislative and regulatory context in which it operates, the activities of a private-law body such as the DVGW has the effect of giving rise to restrictions on the free movement of goods in the same manner as do measures imposed by the State'.[119] The ECJ found that this was the case. Because DVGW certification automatically resulted in conformity with German legislation, and it was *de facto* the only body that was in the position to certify, because of consumer preferences for DVGW certificates on the German market, the ECJ concluded that 'in such circumstances, it is clear that a body such as the DVGW, by virtue of its authority to certify the products, in reality holds the power to regulate the entry into the German market of products such as the copper fittings at issue in the main proceedings'.[120]

Fra.bo makes clear that even if a private body is financially and legally independent of the State its measures can still be found to fall under Article 34 TFEU if the State has delegated regulatory responsibility to that body. As Schepel has noted, 'what the Court of Justice is answering is really a question about the compatibility of the German regulatory framework' and not so much about the activities of the private certification body in question.[121]

[118] Harm Schepel, 'Case C-171/11 Fra.bo Spa v Deutsche Vereinigung des Gas- und Wasserfaches' 9 (2013) *European Review of Contract Law*, 186 at 192

[119] Case C-171/11, *Fra.bo SpA v Deutsche Vereinigung des Gas- und Wasserfaches eV (DVGW)* EU:C:2012:453, para 26

[120] Ibid., paras. 27–29

[121] Harm Schepel, 'The New Approach to the New Approach: The Juridification of Harmonized Standards in EU Law' 20 (2013) *Maastricht Journal of European and Comparative Law*, 521, at 527

Indirect Horizontal Effect

The second inroad into the horizontal application of Article 34 is the recognition that Member States may be responsible for the activities of their inhabitants or undertakings within their own borders when these persons create obstacles to trade. The ECJ's case-law on the application of the duty of loyalty has created positive obligations of the part of Member State authorities to ensure the free movement of goods, even when those authorities do not themselves factually create obstacles to trade.[122]

Applying the doctrine of loyalty widely in the context of the horizontal application of Article 34 (which the Court has not done so far) could have enormous ramifications, requiring Member States to actively police individual conduct that may result in an obstacle to trade. For process-based measures, this would mean that Member States might begin to prohibit private environmental labels that create unjustifiable obstacles to trade, actively prevent media reports that could damage the reputation of imported products or their manufacturers, and prohibit any demonstration targeted against certain imported products or undertakings making such products.[123] Such a neoliberal police-state is probably not what the Court intended with its judgments in *Commission v France (angry farmers)* and *Schmidberger*. The better reading of these cases is that the Court imposes a good faith obligation of the part of the Member States which does not require them to go out of their way to facilitate the free movement of goods, but rather to avoid a situation of lawlessness and violence or – admittedly more constraining – to respect basic good governance principles in balancing the interests of all those affected by State (in)action.[124]

Under the ECJ's current case law, a violation of Article 34 TFEU only appears to occur if the Member State in question has manifestly wrongly assessed the balance between individual freedoms and the free

[122] Case C-112/00, *Eugen Schmidberger, Internationale Transporte und Planzüge v Republik Österreich* [2003] ECR I-5659, paras. 57 and 59; Case C-265/95, *Commission v France* [1997] ECR I-6959, paras. 31 and 32, emphasis added

[123] An example would be requiring a prohibition against the recent March Against Monsanto, the world's largest producer of GMOs and products containing GMOs.

[124] Wolf Sauter and Harm Schepel, *State and Market in European Union Law: The Public and Private Spheres of the Internal Market Before the EU Courts* (Cambridge University Press, 2009), 99; Damien Chalmers, Gareth Davies, and Giorgio Monti, *European Union Law; Cases and Materials* (second edition, Cambridge University Press, 2010), 760

movement of goods.[125] Even then, this may only result in obligations for the Member State, not for the individual directly. The Member State becomes a sort of 'mediator' between private parties.[126] The limited effect is clear from the Court's case law: Member States enjoy 'a wide margin of discretion' in determining whether a 'fair balance' was struck between the interests of traders and the interests of the individuals restricting trade where it involves the protection of their fundamental rights such as the freedom of expression.[127] Member States only violate Article 34 TFEU if in light of the serious nature of the breach of Article 34 TFEU, a Member State's assessment is 'manifestly inadequate'.[128]

2.2 Taxation

In addition to the limits imposed by Article 34 and the common commercial policy on Member State process-based measures, EU law may pose additional hurdles in the form of its rules on taxation. Taxation is one of the most common means of influencing consumer behaviour, and product taxation specifically is subject to Treaty Articles 30 and 110 TFEU as well as secondary legislation. Subject to these rules, Member States can use taxes to incentivise consumers to buy green electricity, organic and fair trade products or other environmentally or socially responsible products As such, taxation is a consumer-based measure, but because it is subject to its own set of rules under EU law it is treated separately here.

2.2.1 Articles 30 and 110 TFEU

Article 30 TFEU prohibits customs duties and charges of equivalent effect between Member States.[129] Therefore, Member State process-based

[125] Eva Julia Lohse, 'Fundamental Freedoms and Private Actors – towards an "Indirect Horizontal Effect"' 13 (2007) *European Public Law*, 159; Schepel, 'Constitutionalising the Market, Marketising the Constitution, and to Tell the Difference', 177, at 192

[126] Lohse, 'Fundamental Freedoms and Private Actors – Towards an "Indirect Horizontal Effect"', 159

[127] Case C-112/00, *Eugen Schmidberger, Internationale Transporte und Planzüge v Republik Österreich* [2003] ECR I-5659, paras. 69–82, in particular paras. 81–82

[128] C-265/95, *Commission v France* [1997] ECR I-6959, para. 52

[129] A charge of equivalent effect to customs duty is defined by the Court as any pecuniary charge, however small and whatever its designation and mode of application, which is imposed unilaterally on goods by reason of the fact that they cross a frontier and which is not a customs duty in the strict sense. See Case 24/68, *Commission v Italy* [1969] ECR 193; Joined Cases C-441/98 and C-442/98, *Michaïlidis* [2000] ECR I-7145, para. 15

customs duties are not permissible on imports from other Member States. Moreover, Article 3 (1) (a) TFEU stipulates that the customs union is EU exclusive competence, thus prohibiting Member States from imposing their own customs duties.

However, Member States may still levy internal process-based product taxes, subject to the discrimination prohibition in Article 110 TFEU. Distinguishing charges of equivalent effect to customs duties from internal product taxation is nevertheless not a straightforward exercise, because process-based tax rules may only apply to imported products in the absence of domestic production and therefore could be considered a charge of equivalent effect to a customs duty instead of an internal product tax. The key element is whether the tax burden on a product results completely from the fact that it crossed the frontier.[130] In addition, as soon as the charge relates to a general system of internal dues applied systematically and in accordance with the same criteria to domestic products and imported or exported products alike, is does not constitute a charge of equivalent effect to a customs duty.[131] If a levy on an 'exotic' import is part of a general system of internal taxes, for example, charges on fruit or tropical products, the tax falls within the scope of Article 110 TFEU prohibiting discriminatory internal taxation and not within the scope of Article 30 TFEU. However, it is unclear whether a process-based product tax that is levied on products for which there are no domestic equivalents (for example, a Finnish tax on both domestic and imported unsustainably produced pineapples) might be considered a charge of equivalent effect to a customs duty. It is submitted that this should not be the case if the process-based tax is levied as an excise duty or consumption tax, rather than a tax that is applied upon importation.

The ECJ has decided a number of cases concerning process-based tax measures under Article 110 TFEU and it has not only shown deference to

[130] A frontier is not necessarily equivalent to a border of a Member State. The Court has held that a frontier can also mean a frontier internal to a Member State. In Case C-163/90, *Legros* [1992] ECR I-4625, paras. 16–17, the Court held that 'A charge levied at a regional frontier by reason of the introduction of products into a region of a Member State constitutes an obstacle to the free movement of goods which is at least as serious as a charge levied at the national frontier by reason of the introduction of the products into the whole territory of a Member State. The effect of such a regional levy on the unity of the Community customs territory is not altered by the fact that it is also charged on goods from the other parts of the territory of the Member State in question.'

[131] Case C-389/00, *Commission v Germany* [2003] ECR I-2001; see also Commission, Free Movement of Goods: Guide to the application of Treaty provisions governing free movement of goods (Luxembourg: Publications Office of the European Union, 2010), 32

Member State process-based taxation, but has actually *required* Member States to incentivize social and environmental protection abroad where domestic socially or environmentally friendly production is favoured through product taxes. Article 110 TFEU prohibits, first, higher taxes on imported products that are similar to domestic products and, second, it prohibits product taxation that is protectionist.[132] In line with the considerable fiscal autonomy of Member States,[133] the Court has given Member States broad policy discretion to differentiate tax rates of products for public policy reasons. Crucially, it has allowed Member States to differentiate between products on the basis of their production methods if such a distinction can be explained by public policy reasons.[134]

Three cases highlight how the Court allows Member States to do so: *Chemical Farmaceutici* (alcohol production), *Bobie* (small breweries), and *Outokumpu Oy* (green electricity).[135] In *Chemical Farmaceutici*, the ECJ held that Article 110 TFEU does not prevent Member States from taxing products differently 'on the basis of objective criteria, such as the nature of the raw materials used or the production processes employed'.[136] Such a distinction is permitted under EU law 'if it pursues economic policy objectives which are themselves compatible with the requirements of the Treaty and its secondary law and if the detailed rules are such as to avoid any form of discrimination, direct or indirect, in regard to imports from other Member States or any form of protection of competing domestic products'.[137] In that sense, it was key for the ECJ that the tax was applied to domestic and imported products alike.[138]

Chemical Farmaceutici can be contrasted with both *Bobie* and *Outokumpu Oy*, where national tax rules also applied different rates to products on the basis of their production methods, but did not extend that differentiation to imported products. In both cases imported products that were similar to domestic products were taxed at a higher rate and were therefore in violation of Article 110 TFEU. In *Bobie* the Court had

[132] See for a more general discussion Catherine Barnard, *The Substantive Law of the EU*, 51–69

[133] See Barnard, *The Substantive Law of the EU*, 52–53

[134] See also for a discussion Gareth Davies, '"Process and Production Method"-based Trade Restrictions in the EU' in Catherine Barnard (ed.), *The Cambridge Yearbook of European Legal Studies 2007–2008* (Oxford: Hart Publishing, 2008), 69–97

[135] Case 140/79, *Chemical Farmaceutici SpA v DAF SpA* [1981] ECR 2; Case 127/75, *Bobie Getränkevertrieb GmbH v Haptzollamt Aachen-Nord* [1976] ECR 1080; Case C-213/96, *Outokumpu Oy* [1998] ECR I-1777

[136] Case 140/79, *Chemical Farmaceutici SpA v DAF SpA* [1981] ECR 2, para. 14

[137] Ibid.

[138] Ibid., para 16

absolutely no difficulty with the tax policy that favoured small and medium-sized breweries. However, the Court did find it a problem is such a tax policy would lead to higher taxes imposed on similar imported products or would protect domestic products.[139] In *Outokumpu Oy* the Court came to essentially the same conclusion with respect to different rates of tax on energy products that distinguished products on the basis of their origin. The Court held that Article 110 TFEU 'does not preclude the rate of an internal tax on electricity from varying according to the manner in which the electricity is produced and the raw materials used for its production, *in so far as* that differentiation is based, [...] on environmental considerations'.[140] Nonetheless, the tax violated Article 110 TFEU because it did not solely distinguish between methods of production for environmental policy reasons, but in fact, on the basis of origin of a product, even if this was only so in certain cases.[141]

This means that if a Member State decides to tax a product less because it is made in a certain way for public policy purposes, this is allowed as long as that reduced rate applies indiscriminately to imported similar or competing goods that meet the same production standards. The Court thus effectively promotes social and environmental interests abroad by requiring the extension of the lower rate to goods produced in another Member State.

2.2.2 *Member State Taxation in the Context of Secondary Legislation*

Where EU legislation provides for minimum harmonisation, process-based product taxes for social and environmental policy reasons are more feasible if additional taxes are introduced, rather than exempting products from taxes introduced at EU level. The three relevant directives governing indirect taxation – the VAT Directive, the General Arrangements Directive,

[139] Case 127/75, *Bobie Getränkevertrieb GmbH v Haptzollamt Aachen-Nord* [1976] ECR 1080, paras. 3–10

[140] Case C-213/96, *Outokumpu Oy* [1998] ECR I-1777, para. 31

[141] Ibid., para. 35. Interestingly, the ECJ brushed the Finnish objections that it was practically not possible to verify the method of production of foreign electricity aside as 'practical difficulties cannot justify the application of internal taxation which discriminates against products from other Member States' (para. 38). In *PreussenElektra*, however, a later case on the application of Article 34 TFEU, the Court did allow the German government to apply a directly discriminatory measure in relation to the promotion of green electricity because among other things 'the nature of electricity is such that, once it has been allowed into the transmission or distribution system, it is difficult to determine its origin and in particular the source of energy from which it was produced'. See Case C-379/98, *PreussenElektra AG v Schhleswag AG* [2001] ECR I-2099, para. 79

and the Directive on taxation of energy products and electricity – offer a limited set of possible exemptions and reduced rates. However, there are a number of provisions that enable Member States to introduce new taxes as long as those taxes do not jeopardize the proper functioning of the harmonized rules.

The VAT Directive, which establishes a general consumption tax on products within the EU, offers only limited possibilities for exceptions and reduced rates, none of which are relevant for process-based tax measures. This is in line with the nature of the tax as a general consumption tax and its purpose of achieving neutrality in competition.[142] However, the Directive does allow for additional taxes to be levied as long as such taxes cannot be characterized as 'turnover taxes'.[143] Taxes that apply specifically to a number of products, which is essentially the idea behind process-based taxes, are therefore compatible with the VAT Directive.[144]

The General Arrangements Directive also provides that Member States may levy taxes on products other than excise goods,[145] as well as additional taxes on excise goods (energy products and electricity, tobacco, and alcohol and alcoholic beverages) but in the case of the latter only for specific purposes and not for purely budgetary reasons, making process-based tax measures still possible.[146]

Directive 2003/96/EC on taxation of energy products and electricity imposes an excise tax at EU level for energy products and electricity.[147] The Directive lays down minimum levels of excises that Member States must levy on energy products and electricity as well as a number of obligatory as well as facultative exemptions for those excise duties. While the Directive is not entirely environmentally friendly because

142 Recitals 5 and 7 of Council Directive 2006/112/EC of 28 November 2006 on the common system of value added tax OJ 2006 No. L347/1

143 Article 401 of Directive 2006/112/EC on the common system of value added tax

144 Case C-437/97, *Evangelischer Krankenhausverein Wien v Abgabenberfungskommission Wien* [2000] ECR I-1157, para. 22; Case C-435/03, *Banca popolare di Cremona Soc. coop. arl v Agenzia Entrate Ufficio Cremona* [2006] ECR I-9373, para. 28; Case C-119/08, *UAB Mechel Nemunas* [2009] ECR I-12, para. 37; Case C-49/09, *Commission v Poland* [2010] ECR I-619, para. 46

145 Article 1 (3) of Council Directive 2008/118/EC of 16 December 2008 concerning the general arrangements for excise duty and repealing Directive 92/12/EEC OJ 2008 No. L9/12

146 Article 1 (2) of Council Directive 2008/118/EC, see for 'specific purposes' Case C-437/97, *Evangelischer Krankenhausverein Wien v Abgabenberfungskommission Wien* [2000] ECR I-1157, para. 31

147 Council Directive 2003/96/EC of 27 October 2003 restructuring the Community framework for the taxation of energy products and electricity OJ 2003 No. L283/51

energy-intense businesses receive favourable treatment,[148] Article 15 does enable Member States to exempt products totally or partially from the excise duties for certain energy products and electricity that has environmental benefits. Member States may, for instance, exempt fuels from renewable resources (such as biofuels) and products used for pilot projects developing environmentally friendly projects.[149] In addition, green electricity may be exempted.[150] Environmental process-based tax measures in relation to energy products and electricity are still possible either through introducing exemptions or by applying additional taxes on environmental grounds.

2.3 Public Procurement

Another way that EU law may limit the ability of Member States to enact process-based measures is through the operation of public procurement rules. Through their public procurement decisions, Member State authorities can 'lead by example' and provide economic support for socially or environmentally friendly goods. The EU public procurement regime – part of the EU internal market acquis[151] – is treated here

[148] The Directive stipulates that (1) Member States shall exempt fuels used for planes and vessels navigating EU waters from taxation in Article 14 (1) (b) and (c) (2) Member States are allowed to apply tax reductions in favour of energy-intensive business on the consumption of energy products in Article 17 (3) excludes the use of energy products and electricity for mineralogical processes from the scope of the Directive in Article 2 (4) (b). See for a discussion Jolanda van Eijndthoven, 'Energy Taxation at European Level: What does It Do for the Environment and Sustainability?' (2011) 20 *EC Tax Review*, 283–290

[149] Article 15 (1) (a) [150] Article 15 (1) (b) and (d)

[151] Recital 1 of Directive 2014/24/EU of the European Parliament and of the Council of 26 February 2014 on public procurement and repealing Directive 2004/18/EC OJ 2014 No. L94/65 states that '[t]he award of public contracts by or on behalf of Member States' authorities has to comply with the principles of the Treaty on the Functioning of the European Union (TFEU), and in particular the free movement of goods, freedom of establishment and the freedom to provide services, as well as the principles deriving therefrom, such as equal treatment, non-discrimination, mutual recognition, proportionality and transparency.' See also Berend Jan Drijber and Hélène Stergiou, 'Public Procurement Law and Internal Market Law' (2009) 46 *Common Market Law Review*, 805–846; Sue Arrowsmith, 'The Purpose of the EU Procurement Directives: Ends, Means and the Implications for National Regulatory Space for Commercial and Horizontal Policies' (2011–2012) 13 *The Cambridge Yearbook of European Legal Studies* (Oxford: Hart Publishing, 2012), 1–47; Case 45/87, *Commission v. Ireland (Dundalk Water)* [1988] ECR 4929, paras. 18–19;Case C-507/03, *Commission v Ireland (An Post,* [2007] ECR I-9777, para. 27; Case C-380/98, *University of Cambridge* [2000] ECR I-8035, para. 16; Case C-19/00, *SIAC Construction* [2001] ECR I-7725, para. 32

as consumer-based, because it sets forth the conditions under which Member State authorities, as consumers, can make purchasing decisions on the basis of social and environmental interests.

To begin with, EU law does not generally require Member States to make environmentally or socially conscious purchasing decisions. Member States are required to purchase socially or environmentally friendly goods only in a limited number of instances (such as when procuring energy efficient office equipment), none of which involve social or green production conditions.[152]

However, EU law does permit Member States to voluntarily include environmental and social standards in their public procurement decisions. Distinguishing products on the basis of their production methods is an explicit and prominent feature of EU public procurement law and the legal discourse surrounding it. Production processes, as well as fair trade criteria, are explicitly mentioned in Directive 2014/24/EU as a means enabling contracting authorities to procure socially or environmentally friendly goods.[153]

Moreover, despite the initial opposition of the Commission, the ECJ has on multiple occasions recognized that Member States may distinguish between products on the basis of their social or environmental production characteristics when procuring such goods.[154] The Court has held that contracting authorities may take into account social and environmental considerations in their procurement decisions, for instance, by procuring green electricity (in *EVN Wienstrom*) or organic and fair trade produce (in *Max Havelaar*) irrespective of the fact that the social and environmental considerations were not part of the material substance of the products in question.[155]

In general, therefore, EU public procurement law is permissive and enabling when Member State authorities wish to base their procurement

152 Anja Wiesbrock, 'An Obligation for Sustainable Procurement? Gauging the Potential Impact of Article 11 TFEU on Public Contracting in the EU' (2013) 40 *Legal Issues of Economic Integration*, 105; Peter Kunzlik, 'From Suspect Practice to Market-based Instrument: Policy Alignment and the Evolution of EU Law's Approach to "green" Public Procurement' [2013] *Public Procurement Law Review*, 97–115

153 Articles 42, 67 and 70 of Directive 2014/24/EU of the European Parliament and of the Council of 26 February 2014 on public procurement and repealing Directive 2004/18/EC OJ 2014 No. L94/65; see also recitals 74 and 97 of that Directive

154 Case C-448/01, *EVN AG and Wienstrom GmbH v Republik Österreich* [2003] ECR I-14527; Case C-368/10, *Commission v Netherlands (Max Havelaar)* EU:C:2012:284

155 Case C-368/10, *Commission v. Netherlands (Max Havelaar)*, para. 91, Case C-448/01 *EVN AG and Wienstrom*, paras. 32, 34, 39, and 42 in particular

decisions on ethical, social, or environmental considerations.[156] Contracting authorities can undertake social, environmental, or ethical public procurement in three ways. First, they may include production standards as part of the 'technical specifications' of the product they wish to purchase (for example, by specifying that they wish to purchase organic coffee).[157] Second, they can decide to award purchasing contracts on the basis of environmental or social standards through 'award criteria' (for example by awarding a contract for coffee purchasing to a vendor selling organic coffee).[158] Third, Member State authorities can require the winning bidder to perform the contract in a way that takes social and environmental considerations into account, including criteria that relate to the upstream – or production stage – level of the supply chain through 'conditions for performance of contracts' (for instance by specifying that coffee supplied by a vendor must meet fair trade criteria).[159]

Each of these features of the Directive allows contracting authorities to differentiate goods on the basis of their process methods. However, the Directive and the ECJ's case law suggest that contract performance conditions may not be equivalent in effect technical specifications. This is because literature,[160] and guidance documents by the Commission,[161] suggest that tenders can be rejected *a priori* only for non-compliance with

[156] See generally Sue Arrowsmith and Peter Kunzlik (eds.), *Social and Environmental Policies in EC Procurement Law: New Directives and New Directions* (Cambridge: Cambridge University Press, 2009) and Case C-513/99, *Concordia Bus Finland Oy Ab, formerly Stagecoach Finland Oy Ab v Helsingin kaupunki and HKL-Bussiliikenne* [2002] ECR I-7213, para. 56; Case 31/87, *Gebroeders Beentjes BV v State of the Netherlands* [1988] ECR 4635, para. 37; Case C-225/98 *Commission v France* [2000] ECR I-7445, para. 50

[157] What to buy is defined by the 'technical specifications' in the public supply contract documents regulated by Article 42 (1) of the Directive.

[158] Award criteria are regulated by Article 67 and in particular 67 (2) and (3) of the Directive, see also recital 97 of the Directive.

[159] This can be done through so-called conditions for performance of contracts regulated in Article 70 of the Directive. See in particular recital 97 of the Directive. See further Sue Arrowsmith, 'Application of the EC Treaty and Directives to Horizontal Policies: A Critical Review' in Arrowsmith and Kunzlik (eds.), *Social and Environmental Policies in EC Procurement Law*, 206–212; Marc Martens and Stanislas de Margerie, 'The Link to the Subject-Matter of the Contract in Green and Social Procurement' [2013] 8 *European Procurement & Public Private Partnership Law Review*, 15; Case 31/87 *Gebroeders Beentjes BV v State of the Netherlands* [1988] ECR 4635, paras. 37–38

[160] Arrowsmith, 'Application of the EC Treaty and Directives to Horizontal Policies: A Critical Review', 206–212

[161] Commission, 'Buying Social – A guide to taking account of social considerations in public procurement' (2010), 47

technical specifications.[162] By contrast, anticipated non-compliance with performance conditions cannot result in *a priori* exclusion of tenderers during the procurement procedure.[163] This differentiation, however, would seem to be contrary to the EJC's holding in *Storebaelt* that a contracting authority cannot accept a bid that does not comply with the tender conditions.[164] It would also be contrary to Article 56 of the Directive, which provides that contracts shall be awarded on the basis of award criteria, provided that the contracting authority has verified in accordance with Articles 59 to 61 that 'the tender complies with the requirements, conditions and criteria set out in the contract notice or the invitation to confirm interest and in the procurement documents'.[165]

This distinction between technical specifications, on the one hand, and award criteria and performance conditions, on the other, is problematic from the perspective of process-based measures. This is because the Court and the current Directive appear to make a subject-matter distinction, considering fair trade standards as 'performance conditions', and environmental standards as technical specifications.[166] Article 42 (3) (a) of the Directive specifically refers to 'environmental characteristics' as a part of technical specifications. By contrast, other parts of the Directive are more elaborate, including social standards in procurement considerations, and suggesting that the concept of technical specifications is to be narrowly construed in this respect, by only allowing for the inclusion of environmental standards as characteristics of the products to be supplied.[167] Moreover, the ECJ, in interpreting the previous Directive in *Max*

[162] If undertakings do not accept such conditions, however, their bids must be refused according to the Commission, basing its views on Case C-243/89, *Commission v Denmark (Storebaelt)* [1993] ECR I-3353 see the Buying Social guide at 43, footnote 78

[163] Arrowsmith, 'Application of the EC Treaty and Directives to Horizontal Policies: A Critical Review'

[164] Case C-243/89, *Commission v Denmark (Storebaelt)* [1993] ECR I-3353, para 39–45; see also Kunzlik, 'From Suspect Practice to Market-based Instrument: Policy Alignment and the Evolution of EU law's Approach to "green" Public Procurement' and by analogy Case C-448/01 *EVN AG and Wienstrom* (n 154), paras 47–50

[165] Article 56 of Directive 2014/24/EU (n 151)

[166] This does not imply that all social process-attributes cannot be technical specifications, but that to the very least social trading conditions fall under contract performance conditions. This will be discussed further below.

[167] Article 43 on the use of labels (discussed in section IV) refers to 'environmental, social or other characteristics'. Conditions relating to the performance of the contract and exclusion grounds equally are explicitly connected to environmental and social considerations. The article on award criteria – Article 67 – is even more elaborate. Award criteria may include qualitative, environmental and/or social aspects and may comprise social, environmental, and innovative characteristics and trading and its conditions.

Havelaar, held that fair trade criteria fall outside the scope of technical specifications, refusing to characterise them as either product characteristics or manufacturing conditions. This implies that at least certain social considerations at the production stage of a product cannot be formulated as technical specifications, and must instead be formulated as either award criteria or performance conditions.[168] If the ECJ maintains its approach in *Max Havelaar*, excluding all social standards from 'technical specifications', there is a risk that social policy is disadvantaged in comparison with environmental policy in public procurement decisions. If this were the case, a tender could be rejected *a priori* on the basis of failure to meet environmental criteria, but not certain social ones. It is therefore suggested that a tender should also be rejected on grounds of non-compliance with conditions relating to the performance of the contract.[169]

As can be seen from the foregoing, EU law gives contracting parties considerable room to include social, environmental, or ethical considerations in public procurement decisions. Nonetheless, there are a number of legal constraints imposed on contracting authorities when they do so.

First of all, such considerations must be linked to the 'subject matter of the contract'.[170] This originally judge-created legal test is a specific application of the principle of proportionality.[171] It implies that social and environmental criteria unrelated to the supplies in question cannot be taken into account by procuring entities. In *EVN Wienstrom*, a case on the procurement of green electricity, the ECJ held that '[a]n award criterion that relates solely to the amount of electricity produced from renewable energy sources in excess of the expected annual consumption, as laid down in the invitation to tender, cannot be regarded as linked to

This is an explicit reference to the use of fair trade criteria as an award criterion, something that was already accepted by the Court in *Max Havelaar*.

168 Case C-368/10, *Commission v Netherlands (Max Havelaar)* (n 154), para 74

169 Case C-243/89, *Commission v Denmark (Storebaelt)* [1993] ECR I-3353, para 39–45; see also Kunzlik, 'From Suspect Practice to Market-based Instrument: Policy Alignment and the Evolution of EU Law's Approach to "green" Public Procurement' and by analogy Case C-448/01 *EVN AG and Wienstrom* (n 154), paras 47–50; Article 56 of Directive 2014/24/EU (n 151)

170 The link to the 'subject matter of the contract' can be found throughout the Directive, including in the Articles on technical specifications, award criteria, and contract performance conditions. However, the required link to subject-matter of the contract cannot be found in Article 57 discussed further below. See further Martens and de Margerie, 'The Link to the Subject-Matter of the Contract in Green and Social Procurement'

171 Case C-513/99 *Concordia Bus* (n 156), para. 64

the subject-matter of the contract.'[172] This means, in essence, that procuring entities can only place social and environmental production standards on the specific goods supplied to them and not to goods producers supply to other customers. As a result, this means that the Court permits 'product-characteristics' criteria, but sanctions 'producer-characteristics' criteria.[173] 'Producer-characteristics' are only permitted, to a limited extent, as selection and exclusion criteria which relate to the conduct of undertakings, and not to the selection of supplies.[174]

Moreover, selection criteria (which refer to the ability of tenderers to perform a contract rather than the characteristics of the goods supplied) must also be related to the subject-matter of the contract.[175] In addition, the use of selection criteria is limited and cannot serve as a means to encourage general corporate social responsibility norms through procurement policy. The exhaustive[176] list for selection criteria contained in Article 58 (4) consists of criteria of a more technical rather than policy oriented character.[177] In *Max Havelaar,* the Court made clear that these provisions can by no means be interpreted as allowing contracting authorities to request information on businesses' corporate social responsibility policies.[178] Thus, contracting authorities cannot take a company's environmentally or socially irresponsible conduct into account, unless

[172] Case C-448/01 *EVN AG and Wienstrom* (n 154), paras. 67–68; see also Case C-368/10, *Commission v Netherlands (Max Havelaar)* (n 154), para. 90

[173] Steve Charnovitz, 'The Law of Environment "PPMs" in the WTO: Debunking the Myth of Illegality' (2002) 27 *The Yale Journal of International Law*, 59–110

[174] Articles 56–58 of Directive 2014/24/EU (n 151)

[175] Article 58 (1) of Directive 2014/24/EU (n 151)

[176] Joined Cases C-226/04 and C-228/04, *La Cascina Soc. coop. arl and Zilch Srl v Ministero della Difesa and Others* [2006] ECR I-1347, paras. 21–22, see Sue Arrowsmith, 'A Taxonomy of Horizontal Policies in Public Procurement' in Arrowsmith and Kunzlik (eds.) *Social and Environmental Policies in EC Procurement Law*, 104. By way of exception, Member States may also exclude undertakings to ensure equal treatment in accordance with Joined Cases C-21/03 and 34/03, *Fabricom SA v Belgian State* [2005] ECR I-1559

[177] Two criteria may be relevant for verifying the ability of undertakings to produce the goods supplied in an environmentally friendly or socially responsible way. Part II (c), (d), (g), and (k) (ii) refer to 'a description of the technical facilities and measures used by the economic operator for ensuring quality and the undertaking's study and research facilities'; 'an indication of the supply chain management and tracking systems that the economic operator will be able to apply when performing the contract'; 'an indication of the environmental management measures that the economic operator will be able to apply when performing the contract'; 'certificates drawn up by official quality control institutes or agencies of recognised competence attesting the conformity of products clearly identified by references to technical specifications or standards'.

[178] Case C-368/10, *Commission v Netherlands (Max Havelaar)* (n 154), para 106–107

that conduct is specifically related to the product they are buying. The EU public procurement regime, therefore, does not permit contracting authorities to encourage corporate social responsibility.

The only exception to this is the limited possibility to exclude tenderers on the basis of violations of social and environmental legislation or other grave professional misconduct. One of the key new aspects of Directive 2014/24/EU is to ensure that undertakings are not awarded contracts when they do not comply with social and environmental legislation.[179] More than before, undertakings may and, in some instances, must be excluded from a tender procedure if they have violated national, European, and international social and environmental laws. Article 57 (1) (f) requires contracting authorities to exclude undertakings which have been subject of a conviction by final judgment for reasons of child labour. Moreover, contracting authorities may exclude undertakings for violation of social, labour, and environmental norms referred to in Article 18 (2) (Article 57 (4) (a)) and grave professional misconduct which renders its integrity questionable (Article 57 (4) (c)).[180] The latter option could enable contracting authorities to exclude companies that have been found liable for damages that are connected with harmful production in developing countries. An example would be excluding a multinational oil company from public tenders because it has been held liable for causing environmental damage in a developing country such as Nigeria.[181]

Thus, while EU procurement law strengthens the existing national, European, and international legal framework of social and environmental protection, it does not permit contracting authorities to reward undertakings that go beyond legal requirements. As noted above, the use of procurement policy to encourage corporate social responsibility generally and beyond mere compliance with social and environmental legislation is not permitted. This is at odds with the EU's policy on corporate social responsibility, which is to encourage actions by companies over and above their legal obligations towards society and the

[179] Article 18 (2) of Directive 2014/24/EU (*n* 151)

[180] See for the interpretation of 'grave professional misconduct' Case C-465/11, *Forposta SA and ABC Direct Contact sp. z o.o. v Poczta Polska SA* EU:C:2012:801, para 26–30

[181] Rb. Den Haag, 30 januari 2013, LJN BY9845, BY9850, en BY9854 (olielekkages Oruma, Goi en Ikot Ada Udo); Liesbeth Enneking, 'Zorgplichten van multinationals in Nederland: "Second best" zo slecht nog niet?' [2013] *Nederlands Juristenblad*, 607; Aukje van Hoek, 'Het proces tegen Shell wegens olielekkages in de Ogonidelta (Nigeria)' (2013) 62 *Ars Aequi*, 482

environment.[182] This is remarkable, since the Commission considered in its Communication on a renewed strategy for Corporate Social Responsibility 'the need to promote market reward for responsible business conduct, including through investment policy and public procurement'.[183]

Last, EU public procurement law is moving in the direction of imposing certain requirements relating to good governance when contracting authorities wish to base their purchasing decisions on social and environmental production standards of goods. The new procurement Directive, for instance, allows procurement decisions to be made on the basis of, and reference to, fair trade, green, or other labels, which was not allowed under the previous Directive.[184] This will make it much easier for procuring entities to buy socially or environmentally friendly products and reduce the fragmentation of the procurement market.

However, this change also raises questions about the labels, and the standards on which they are based. The Directive in that respect requires the standards to be developed through a procedure in which all relevant stakeholders may participate. In particular, the last three conditions imposed in Article 43 (2) of the Directive on labels suggests that the standards and processes developed by labelling organisations must be inclusive, transparent, accessible, and procedurally fair. This is an indication that the EU seeks to promote basic levels of good governance in relation to private standard setting organizations, promoting labels that are have a certain level of democratic legitimacy through public procurement legislation.

Conclusion

This chapter has found that most Member State process-based measures (except for a number of consumer-based measures that can be characterized as selling arrangements within the meaning of *Keck*) can be characterized as quantitative restrictions on imports or measures of equivalent effect. As such, those measures will require a justification or will need to rely on the derogations listed under Article 36 TFEU in order to be applied to imported products from another Member State. Moreover, EU tax and procurement rules may discipline Member State process-based measures.

[182] Commission, 'A renewed EU strategy 2011–14 for Corporate Social Responsibility' (Communication) COM (2011) 681 final, 3

[183] Ibid., 5 [184] Article 43 (1) and recital 75 of Directive 2014/24/EU (*n* 151)

The reason Member State process-based measures fall within the scope of Article 34 TFEU is because the broad effects-based doctrine of the ECJ causes such measures to be characterized as obstacles to the free movement of goods. In addition, the ECJ's case law on the personal scope of Article 34 TFEU ensures that Member State involvement in the development of process-based rules by private parties may trigger the application of Article 34 TFEU and as such judicial review by the EU courts.

Article 34 TFEU also disciplines process-based measures applied to goods of third country origin that have been traded within the EU. The principle of assimilation enables traders in such goods to rely on Article 34 TFEU in the same manner as traders in goods of EU origin as soon as they have cleared customs in any Member State. Moreover, goods of third country origin traded within the EU can rely on the principle of mutual recognition established in *Cassis* as long as they comply with the technical rules of at least one Member State even if they have not been 'lawfully produced' in another Member State.

Article 34 TFEU does not, however, apply to third country goods that have not been traded in the EU, since Article 34 only governs trade between Member States, and the exclusive nature of the EU's common commercial policy is likely to only discipline Member State border measures. Moreover, not all consumer-based rules fall within the scope of Article 34 TFEU. While it is clear that labelling rules fall within the scope of *Cassis* because they require a modification of the product or its packaging, it seems that promotional campaigns and government-induced boycotts fall outside the scope of Article 34 TFEU altogether as long as they do not discriminate against imported products or impede market access. Advertising restrictions, on the other hand, fall within Article 34 TFEU if they deprive traders of the only effective means of sales promotion. Yet, just as is the case with restrictions on where and when goods may be sold, the application of the *Keck* criteria and especially the discrimination test therein has not been fully crystalized. However, as the Court tends to apply Article 34 TFEU in border situations, it is safest to assume that when in doubt, a justification or reliance on Article 36 TFEU will be necessary.

In relation to taxation, Member States are still very much competent to introduce additional process-based taxes, but their options to reduce tax burdens imposed by EU legislature is more limited. Nonetheless, there is considerable leeway in introducing new process-based taxes for specific public policy reasons. All harmonized tax rules at EU level permit such additional taxes and Articles 30 and 110 TFEU only prohibit discriminatory taxation in the form of a prohibition on customs duties and discriminatory internal taxation. The Court has given Member States substantial freedom to introduce product-specific taxes for public policy reasons, only prohibiting taxes that negatively affect imported goods solely on the basis of origin. In particular, the Court has explicitly stated that Member States can differentiate among products on the basis of their production methods. Interestingly, the Court requires that similar or competing foreign products that meet a Member State's production standards must also be allowed to profit from any provided lower tax rate. Therefore, domestic incentives to produce in an environmentally or socially friendly way are extended extraterritorially, enabling foreign producers to compete at lower prices if they comply with the environmental norms of the Member State to which their products are destined.

Last, EU public procurement law generally enables contracting authorities to make green and social purchasing decisions. The ECJ's case law and the current Public Procurement Directive enable contracting authorities to explicitly take such considerations into account, irrespective of whether those concerns form part of the material substance of the goods procured. Nonetheless, EU public procurement law does impose certain constrains on contracting authorities. Contracting authorities must generally link process-based considerations to the subject-matter of the contract, limiting their ability to reward undertakings for their general corporate social responsibility policies. Only requiring compliance with applicable social and environmental legislation is still possible as a more general consideration. The EU and its Member States are thus limited in their ability to encourage Corporate Social Responsibility through market incentives, contrary to what EU policy would suggest.

3 Extraterritoriality within the Free Movement of Goods

Introduction

Most Member State process-based measures fall within the scope of EU free movement law. To the extent that such measures qualify as quantitative restrictions on imports or measures having equivalent effect, such measures will require justification either on the basis of case-law based justifications accepted by the ECJ or by reliance on the derogations in Article 36 TFEU. Reliance on public interests to justify other restrictions to the free movement of goods, such as tax and public procurement measures, also occurs within EU tax and public procurement law.

What makes process-based measures a conceptually distinct category of market regulation is that they seek to address social and environmental concerns that manifest themselves outside the Member State's jurisdiction.[1] In relation to 'ordinary' product rules, the nexus between

[1] Gareth Davies, 'Process and Production Method-based Trade Restrictions in the EU' (2007) **10** *The Cambridge Yearbook of European Legal Studies*, 69; Robert Howse and Donald Regan, 'The Product/Process Distinction: An Illusory Basis for Disciplining Unilateralism in Trade Policy' (2000) **11** *European Journal of International Law*, 249; Steve Charnovitz, 'The Law of Environmental PPMs in the WTO: Debunking the Myth of Illegality' (2002) **27** *The Yale Journal of International Law*, 59; André Nollkaemper, 'The Legality of Moral Crusades Disguised in Trade Laws: An Analysis of the EC 'Ban' on Furs from Aimals taken by Leghold Traps' (1996) **8** *Journal of Environmental Law*, 237; Lorand Bartels, 'Article XX of GATT and the Problem of Extraterritorial Jurisdiction: The Case of Trade Measures for the Protection of Human Rights' (2002) **36** *Journal of World Trade*, 353; Nicolas De Sadeleer, *EU Environmental Law and the Internal Market* (Oxford: Oxford University Press, 2014), 358–364; Jochem Wiers, *Trade and Environment in the EC and the WTO* (Groningen: Europa Law Publishing, 2002), 347–366; Hanna Sevenster, *Eco-imperialisme binnen de Europese Unie; een juridisch probleem?* (Deventer: W.E.J. Tjeenk Willink, 1998); Martin Hedemann-Robinson, 'Defending the Consumer's Right to a Clean Environment in the Face of Globalisation. The Case of Extraterritorial Environmental Protection Under European Community Law' (2000) **23** *Journal of Consumer Policy*, 25

the regulating Member State and the social and environmental concern addressed in process-based measures appears to be either weaker generally, or weaker than that of the State of production, since there is no direct physical trace of the concern in the product itself. The object of concern is still located in the country of production, and not necessarily in the country of import. Process-based measures, for instance, seek to mitigate the use of child labour or the use of polluting factories in other countries, by making the marketing of products originating from such factories more difficult, either by preventing the marketing of those products through compulsory labelling schemes or by other means. Ordinary product rules, by contrast, address concerns of which the nexus with the jurisdiction of the regulating Member State is more apparent: for example, when a Member State regulates the contents of products intended for human consumption on public health grounds.

The question then becomes whether the ECJ when interpreting the room for Member States to rely on public interests in justifying restrictions on trade, places any territorial limits on such justifications. On the one hand, one could argue that Member States should 'mind their own business' when regulating their markets. Process-based measures interfere with the producing State's right to set its own level of protection, in line with its own needs and societal preferences. On the other hand, one may wonder why free movement law should restrict the sovereignty and regulatory autonomy in the field of social and environmental policy of an importing Member State. Restricting such freedom equally 'interferes' with a Member State's right to set its own levels of protection, only in this case that of the importing Member State rather than the exporting Member State. A territorial limitation could therefore potentially indicate an inherent bias of market liberalization over social and environmental interests.

The answer to this question in free movement law is by no means straightforward and the ECJ is yet to develop a clear and concise doctrine on the issue. This chapter seeks to outline and contrast the main arguments for and against such a territorial limitation of public interest justifications with reference to case-law of the ECJ supporting these arguments. Section 3.1 outlines six main arguments in favour of such territorial limitation. These range from jurisdictional grounds, perceived economic coercion, objections against paternalistic use of trade measures, to a call for tolerance and diversity among Member States. Section 3.2 subsequently discusses arguments against such territorial limitation. These arguments include unjustified limitation of Member States to address trans-boundary harm, such as the effects of climate change, or may address deeply felt ethical or moral values among the population of a particular Member State. In light of these arguments, Section 3.3 concludes and seeks to problematize the notion of 'extraterritoriality' in trade relations as a clear-cut rule for separating 'good' from 'bad' market regulation.

3.1 Arguments in Favour of a Territorial Limitation of Public Interest Justifications in Free Movement Law

As a preliminary issue, an argument against process-based measures on formal jurisdictional grounds is not likely to succeed before the ECJ. Opposing process-based measures, because it would amount to an 'unreasonable' exercise of prescriptive jurisdiction,[2] would go against the unequivocal case-law of the ECJ on jurisdiction of the EU itself. As we have seen in Chapter 1, the ECJ's permissive case-law has resulted in upholding many measures on grounds that the measures were enforced within the EU despite their obvious extraterritorial effects and intent.[3] Process-based measures enacted by the EU therefore do not violate international rules on jurisdiction as interpreted by the ECJ simply because such measures only apply to goods within EU territory. It is unlikely that the ECJ would interpret these rules of customary international law any differently when it comes to the jurisdiction of Member States, simply because there is no apparent reason why these rules would be any different for Member States. Since only products imported into the territory of the Member State are subject to measures that may create obstacles to trade, one may infer from the ECJ's case-law on jurisdiction that these goods are subject to the 'unlimited jurisdiction' of a Member State.[4]

[2] Cedric Ryngaert, *Jurisdiction in International Law* (Oxford: Oxford University Press, 2008), 214–215

[3] See Chapter 1 Section 1.2; Case C-286/90, *Anklagemyndigheden v Peter Michael Poulsen and Diva Navigation Corp* [1992] ECR I- 6019, paras. 22–28; Case C-177/95, *Ebony Maritime SA and Loten Navigation Co. Ltd v Prefetto della Provincia di Brindisi and others* [1997] ECR I-1111, paras. 17–19; Case C-366/10, *Air Transport Association of America and Others v Secretary of State for Energy and Climate Change* [2011] ECR I-13755, paras. 122–125

[4] In this context, it is important to recall that production abroad is not regulated directly, but merely incentivized through market access. Producers in other countries remain free to produce as they like, ignoring process-based measures. Targeted producers will not have their factories closed down by government officials, nor will they be prosecuted on the basis of those rules, but will only suffer economically through the loss of a market.

3.1.1 *Doctrinal Reasons*

A first argument in favour of a territorial limitation of public interest justifications in free movement law that can be made is doctrinal: the ECJ simply finds such a limitation to exist. While the ECJ's case law is mostly ambiguous and largely absent on this issue, there are a number of cases which provide some support that Member States for such territorial limitation. It should be noted, however, that there is also doctrinal support against such a view which will be discussed in more detail in Sections 3.2 and 3.3.

In *Nertsenvoederfabriek*, the Court was suspicious of the justification invoked by the Netherlands government of an export restriction of poultry offal relating to the protection of public health. For the Court, it did not 'appear' necessary, in relation to exports, for reasons of public health for the Netherlands government to oblige all poultry offal producers to dispose of the poultry offal at licensed undertakings in the Netherlands 'provided that the conditions relating to health laid down by those provisions are satisfied with respect to removal and transport *on national territory*'.[5] The Court seemed to imply that health risks that might occur across the Dutch border were not a legitimate concern for the Dutch government but the issue of extraterritorial health protection was not specifically addressed: not by the Court nor by the Dutch government.

Alpine Investments also provides support for territorially limiting the scope of justifications in free movement law. *Alpine Investments* concerned a Dutch prohibition on cold-calling services made, among others, from the Netherlands to other Member States. The Court in that case held that 'the protection of consumers in the other Member States is not, as such, a matter for the Netherlands authorities'.[6]

The most unequivocal statements on the issue come from Advocate General Trabucchi in his Opinion in *Dassonville*. In this case, the Advocate General viewed measures seeking to protect industrial and commercial

Process-based measures are, thus, only enforced within the territory and the market of the country enacting them, providing a territorial basis for jurisdiction.

5 Case 118/86, *Openbaar Ministerie v Nertsvoederfabriek Nederland BV* [1987] ECR 3883, para. 16, emphasis added.

6 Case C-384/93, *Alpine Investments BV v Minister van Financiën* [1995] ECR I-1141, paras. 43–44. The Court went on to state that, on the other hand, the protection of the good reputation of the Dutch financial sector was a ground for justification. These matters are of course inextricably linked, complicating the issue of extraterritorial justifications and derogations. This issue will be discussed further below.

property, namely, the protection of a designation of origin ('Scotch' whiskey) through a mandatory certificate as unlawful because it protected British commercial property and not Belgian commercial property. The Advocate General held that

> States can derogate in the said manner only for the purpose of the protection of their own interests and not for the protection of the interests of other States. Thus, for example, restrictions on freedom of movement, which a State can introduce on the basis of this rule for the protection of public health, cannot in any case justify restrictions on exports of products considered harmful for the purpose of protecting the public health of the populations of other Member States.
>
> Article 36 allows every State the right to protect exclusively its own national interests. Consequently, for the purpose of protecting industrial and commercial property, each State can restrict the freedom of movement of goods only with reference to the protection of individual rights and economic interests falling under its own sphere of interest.[7]

The Advocate General reiterated his views in *Kramer* concerning Dutch fishing quota to protect a common interest of the Member States (preserving marine resources): the 'essential spirit and purpose of this exempting clause [should have … a] genuinely unilateral character, confined to a particular State, which results from the fact that the interest for which Article 36 provides protection is essentially national and internal to the State.'[8]

Indirect doctrinal support against extraterritorial justifications and derogations also comes from the interpretation of secondary legislation by the ECJ in *Gourmetterie van den Burg* and *Compassion in World Farming*. In *Gourmetterie van den Burg*, the Court interpreted the Directive on the conservation of wild birds as not permitting the Dutch government to prohibit the sale and possession of red grouse, a non-endangered and

[7] Case 8/74, *Procureur du Roi v Benoît and Gustave Dassonville* [1974] ECR 855, Opinion of AG Trabucchi, para. 5

[8] Joined cases 3, 4 and 6–76, *Cornelis Kramer and others* [1976] ECR 1279, Opinion of AG Trabucchi, 1325. The Advocate General realizing the problematic aspects of his stance added that exceptionally, pending Union action, Member States may adopt measures for the pursuit of common interests. He considered that 'Notwithstanding the cogent formal objections set out above, this consideration, which is one of substance, might perhaps make it possible to rely, even if only for a limited period, on the provision in Article 36, the essential purpose of which is to protect the basic assets of each individual State even although this does not involve conflict between the State's own interests and the common interests but the protection of its own interests pending their protection in the wider field of the Community.'

non-migratory species only occurring in the territory of the United Kingdom. According to the Court, the exception contained in the Directive permitting Member States to take more stringent measures was confined to the territory of the Member State in question in relation to non-migratory and non-endangered wild birds. The Court held that Member States are required to adopt the protective measures contained in the Directive, 'but are not authorized to adopt stricter protective measures than those provided for under the directive, except as regards species occurring within their territory.'[9]

Compassion in World Farming also concerned the interpretation of a Directive, but this time the Directive in question provided for textual support for territorial limitations in contrast to the Directive at issue in *Gourmetterie van den Burg*. The case concerned the export of veal calves from the United Kingdom to countries that permitted the 'veal crate system', which was detrimental to the welfare of veal calves. The ECJ found that the Directive did not allow a Member State prohibit exports for animal welfare considerations related to farming outside that Member State's territory.[10] The Directive stipulated that 'Member States may, in compliance with the general rules of the Treaty, maintain or apply *within their territories* stricter provisions for the protection of calves than those laid down in this Directive.'[11] On that basis the Court held that it was 'clear from the wording of Article 11(2) of the Directive, first, that the measures permitted on that basis, which are limited to strictly territorial boundaries, may relate only to cattle-farms falling within the jurisdiction of the Member State in question and, second, that such measures may be adopted only in compliance with the general rules of the Treaty'.[12]

[9] Case C-169/89, *Gourmetterie van den Burg* [1990] ECR I-2151, para. 12; this territorial limitation did not follow from the text or purpose of the Directive, and has been severely criticized in literature. E. H. Pijnacker Hordijk, 'Oordeel over verenigbaarheid van verbod van invoer en verhandeling van uitheemse vogelsoorten met art. 36 EEG-Verdrag en Richtlijn inzake het behoud van de vogelstand' [1991] *Sociaal-Economische Wetgeving*, 261–271; Martin Hedemann-Robinson, 'Defending the Consumer's Right to a Clean Environment in the Face of Globalisation. The Case of Extraterritorial Environmental Protection Under European Community Law' (2000) 23 *Journal of Consumer Policy*, 25, at 36 and references there.

[10] Council Directive 91/629/EEC of 19 November 1991 laying down minimum standards for the protection of calves OJ 1991 No. L340/28

[11] Case C-169/89, *Gourmetterie van den Burg* [1990] ECR I-2151, para. 12, emphasis added

[12] Case C-1/96, *The Queen v Minister of Agriculture, Fisheries and Food, ex parte Compassion in World Farming Ltd.* [1998] ECR I-1251, para. 59

3.1.2 Paternalism

A second argument in favour of a territorial limitation for public interest justifications in free movement law is that extraterritorial measures can be paternalistic. Member States should not take measures to protect the population or interests of other Member States, since Member States should be able to decide for themselves whether they need the level of protection the other Member State 'thinks' it needs. The ability and right of a Member State or a third state to make its own determination on its levels of social or environmental protection are so important that no Member State has the right to interfere with these choices for the sole reason that it knows what is best for the exporting state. Anti-paternalists would argue that an exporting state is always in the best position to assert what is in its interest and that interference with that principle will in the end result in every state being worse off.[13]

Crucially, the argument against paternalism is based on the notion that the regulating Member State is not acting in its own self-interest, but *exclusively* in the interest of the other Member State. A process-based measure that could be considered paternalistic, for instance, is where a Member State prohibits the marketing of a product that has been made in a factory in another Member State, which polluting and health harming effects occur entirely within that Member State, on grounds that the population of the other Member State needs to be protected. Enchelmaier, for instance, has argued that 'altruism has its limits in the eyes of the law: despite the absence of a clear ruling from the Court on the point, it seems plain that Member States may not rely on this provision to impose their standards or morals on others, save where human health and life are at stake'.[14]

Anti-paternalistic thinking can be extrapolated from a number of judgments of the Court and Opinions of Advocates General. In *Alpine*

[13] See for literature on paternalism in the context of the relationship between the state and the invidual: Donald VanDeVeer, *Paternalistic Intervention: The Moral Bounds on Benevolence* (Princeton: Princeton University Press, 1986); Anthony Ogus, 'The Paradoxes of Legal Paternalism and How to Resolve Them' (2010) **30** *Legal Studies*, 61–73; Gerald Dworkin, 'Paternalism' in R.A. Wasserstrom (ed.) *Morality and the Law* (Belmont: Wadsworth, 1971); Joel Feinberg, 'Legal Paternalism' (1971) **1** *Canadian Journal of Philosophy*, 101; See for thinking about paternalism in the context of international law Joshua James Kasner, *Rwanda and the Moral Obligation of Humanitarian Intervention* (Edinburgh: Edinburgh University Press, 2013)

[14] Stefan Enchelmaier 'Article 36: General' in P. Oliver (ed.) *Oliver on Free Movement of Goods in the European Union* (Oxford: Hart Publishing, 2010), 215–312, at 237

Investments, the Court held that 'the protection of consumers in the other Member States is not, as such, a matter for the Netherlands authorities'.[15] In the context of paternalism, one could argue that the consumers protected were consumers of other Member States. As such, it should be up to those consumers themselves or their governments to decide whether they wish to be protected against cold calling. This reasoning can also be applied to the Court's judgment in *Nertsenvoederfabriek* where the Court suggested that reliance on the human health derogation was limited to people living within the territory of the regulating Member State.[16] The protection of human health of people exclusively living in other Member States is a matter for the Member States themselves, as any interference restricts the liberty for those Member States to decide on their own level of protection.

Anti-paternalistic reasoning can also be found in Advocate General Léger's Opinion in *Compassion in World Farming*. According to the Advocate General, 'Article 36 does not allow a Member State to restrict its exports on account of extra-territorial circumstances which, even though they produce effects within its population, *do not affect on its own national territory the interest protected by this provision*.'[17] If Article 36 would be allowed to be construed more broadly and allow Member States to protect animals beyond their own borders through export restrictions, 'would in practice mean giving Member States the right to monitor, and even to influence, the practices or rules applied by the other Member States'.[18] Similarly, the Advocate General used an anti-paternalist argument in *Hedley Lomas*, a case concerning an export prohibition of live sheep by the United Kingdom out of concerns that certain slaughterhouses in Spain did not comply with EU rules, when he held that '[o]nly the Member State within whose territory the protective measure must be adopted is in a position to ensure that the measure is strictly necessary and to check that it is being complied with.'[19]

[15] Case C-384/93, *Alpine Investments BV v Minister van Financiën* [1995] ECR I-1141, para. 43

[16] Case 118/86, *Openbaar Ministerie v Nertsvoederfabriek Nederland BV* [1987] ECR 3883, para. 16

[17] Case C-1/96, *The Queen v Minister of Agriculture, Fisheries and Food, ex parte Compassion in World Farming Ltd.* [1998] ECR I-1251, Opinion of AG Léger, para. 113

[18] Ibid., para. 115

[19] Case C-5/94, *The Queen v MAFF ex parte Hedley Lomas* [1995] ECR I-2557, Opinion of AG Léger, para. 33

3.1.3 Economic Coercion

A third argument against reliance on justifications and derogations for matters occurring outside the territory of the regulating Member State is that this would result in economic coercion. As a result of process-based measures aiming at regulating conduct abroad, the regulating Member State is seeking to force another Member State to incorporate the importing Member State set of values and standards, interfering with the Member State's right to self-determination. This argument is closely related to the argument against paternalism, as it is also based on a principled argument against non-interference and in favour of self-determination, and it might equally lead to accusations of neo-colonialism and economic imperialism. According to this argument, process-based measures interfere with its chosen level of environmental and social protection within its own territory. This might be considered objectionable, because the process-based norm impedes on the liberty of the producer State to determine its own levels of environmental and social protection for persons and objects within its own territory, and consequently, its right to self-determination. Developing countries, for instance, might argue that they should be able to determine their own pace for development and not necessarily incorporate higher or different environmental or labour standards.

The difference with the argument against paternalism is that the argument against economic coercion applies irrespective of whether the Member State is acting exclusively in the interest of the other Member State or in its own self-interest and evolves solely around the use of economic power to obtain political results.

In the international context, the UN General Assembly has condemned economic coercion generally and in particular against developing countries by declaring that 'no State may use or encourage the use of economic, political or any other type of measures to coerce another State in order to obtain from it the subordination of the exercise of its sovereign rights.'[20] The 1996 Singapore WTO Ministerial declaration similarly

[20] *Declaration on the Inadmissibility of Intervention in the Domestic Affairs of States and the Protection of Their Independence and Sovereignty*, G.A. Res. 2131(XX) para. 2, U.N. GAOR, 20th Sess., Supp. No. 14, at 11, U.N. Doc. A/6014 (1965). *See also Charter of Economic Rights and Duties of States*, G.A. Res. 3281 (XXIX) art. 32, U.N. GAOR, 29th Sess., Supp. No. 31, at 50, 55, U.N. Doc. A/9631 (1974); *Declaration on the Principles of International Law concerning Friendly Relations and Co-operation among States in accordance with the Charter of the United Nations*, G.A. Res. 2625 (XXV), U.N. GAOR, 25th Sess., Supp. No. 28, at 121, U.N. Doc. A/8082 (1970)

stated that members 'reject the use of labour standards for protectionist purposes, and agree that the comparative advantage of countries, particularly low-wage developing countries, must in no way be put into question'.[21]

In relation to environmental protection in particular, one may refer to the 'special position' of developing countries under international law. Born out of the general international law principle of equity, the principle 'common but differentiated responsibilities' recognizes that, while developing and developed countries alike have a common responsibility to protect the environment, developing countries should not bear the exact same economic and social burden as developed countries.[22] Accordingly, public interest justifications in the free movement context should be territorially limited in order to prevent the importing Member State from coercing exporting developing countries into following the preferred production rules of the importing Member State.

3.1.4 *Tolerance for Diversity*

Applying the argument of economic coercion more specifically within the EU context and the relationship between Member States, one could argue, fourth, that extraterritorial effects of process-based measures are particularly problematic, since the EU is founded on the basis of tolerance for diversity. Indeed, the preamble of the Treaty on European Union states the desire 'to deepen the solidarity between their peoples while respecting their history, their culture and their traditions'. Moreover, Article 4 (2) TEU stipulates that 'the Union shall respect the equality of Member States before the Treaties as well as their national identities,

[21] WTO Ministerial Conference, 'Singapore Ministerial Declaration'(Adopted on 13 December 1996) www.wto.org/english/thewto_e/minist_e/min96_e/wtodec_e.htm

[22] *Report of the U.N. Conference on the Human Environment, from the U.N. Conference in Stockholm, Sweden [Stockholm Declaration]* (Stockholm, 16 June 1972), U.N. Doc. A/CONF.48/14, 11 I.L.M. 1416 (1972), principle 23; *United Nations Rio Declaration on Environment and Development* (13 June 1992), 31 I.L.M. 874 (1992), principles 6, 7, and 11; Article 3 (1) of United Nations Framework Convention on Climate Change OJ No. L33/13. Concluded on behalf of the EU by the Council in Council Decision 94/69/EC of 15 December 1993 concerning the conclusion of the United Nations Framework Convention on Climate Change OJ 1994 No. L33/11; Michael Hertel, 'Climate-Change-Related Trade Measures and Article XX: Defining Discrimination in Light of the Principle of Common but Differentiated Responsibilities' (2011) **45** *Journal of World Trade*, 653; The Centre for International Sustainable Development Law, 'The Principle of Common But Differentiated Responsibilities: Origins and Scope' (Montreal, 2002)

inherent in their fundamental structures, political and constitutional, inclusive of regional and local self-government'.[23]

As Dougan argues, extraterritorial application of laws would undermine the fundamental idea that the EU is built upon the tolerance for diversity among Member States. He notes that prohibiting extraterritorial measures is sensible because 'the rationale for tolerating regulatory differentiation within the [EU] legal order is to respect legitimate domestic diversity in the social/welfare spheres, even if this comes at the cost of maximum economic freedom; but to recognize the extra-territorial pursuit of one Member State's policy choices would permit one national identity to force itself upon other Member States which have chosen to adopt an alternative stance, on threat of economic sanction through the imposition of barriers to trade where the latter refuse to tow the line. Such a possibility would seem to undermine not only the rationale for regulatory differentiation but also the basic principles of equality and solidarity upon which the integrity and acceptability of the [EU] system depends.'[24]

According to this argument, process-based measures cannot be justified or derogated because Member States do not respect other Member States' different levels of protection and solutions to environmental and social problems. A process-based measure requiring products to be made according to the higher production standards of the importing Member State insufficiently takes into account that the exporting Member State may have other priorities and problems than the specific environmental or social problem of the importing Member State.

3.1.5 *Calibration and Proportionality*

A final argument in favour of a territorial limitation for public interest justifications in free movement law is that measures seeking to regulate matters outside the territory of the importing Member State will often be disproportionate. In particular, the regulating Member State would not be in the position to calibrate the measure in a way that it contributes effectively to the concern addressed. Moreover, the extraterritorial interference of the regulating Member State inadequately takes into account the particular circumstances prevalent in the producer State.

[23] Article 4 (2) TEU
[24] Michael Dougan, 'Minimum Harmonization and the Internal Market' (2000) **37** *Common Market Law Review*, 853–885, 873

As a consequence of this lack of calibration, the process-based standards of the importing country may not adequately address the social and environmental concerns targeted.

This argument is less bipartisan in the sense that it does not result in accusations of paternalism or economic coercion, but focuses more on the actual contribution the measures make to the public interest invoked. It nonetheless does share similar traits with those concerns. It argues that the country of regulation might not always be able to adequately calibrate a measure to address concerns over production elsewhere, simply because practices and facts are largely unknown to it. However, this does not result in a rejection of a reliance on justifications and derogations outright. It depends on the facts of the case.

This view is best reflected in the Opinion of Advocate General van Gerven in *Gourmetterie van den Burg*. The Advocate General did not rule out *a priori* the possibility of relying on Article 36 TFEU for the protection of animal life in other Member States.[25] In applying the principle of proportionality, the Advocate General found that a ban on imports of the protected species in question may 'exert a positive influence on the population of the species in the Member State in which it occurs' but that the import ban was nevertheless disproportionate, because first, the importing Member State in question without cooperating with the exporting Member State could not take into account certain interests (in this case, farming interests) and second, because 'an absolute prohibition of imports in the Netherlands is out of proportion, in my view, to the small contribution which such a prohibition is capable of making in concreto – by discouraging the killing of the bird species in question in the United Kingdom – to the achievement of the objective pursued, namely, the improvement of stocks of bird species which is not endangered and whose protection is not a priority under [Union] law'.[26] One of the reasons the Advocate General therefore found the measure

[25] Case C-169/89, *Gourmetterie van den Burg* [1990] ECR I-2151, Opinion of AG Van Gerven, paras. 8–9

[26] The Advocate General added that this was particularly so because 'the measure was adopted on the basis of a unilateral appraisal of the interests involved, that is to say without taking account of interests which may warrant or justify the hunting of that species. Much of the proportionality test applied by the Advocate General is inherently connected with the issue of unilateralism – the adoption of standards without cooperation of other involved States – and this issue will be further addressed below.

disproportionate because of the inability of the Netherlands to properly address the issue of conservation of red grouse in the United Kingdom.[27]

3.2 Arguments against a Territorial Limitation of Public Interest Justifications in Free Movement Law

While there may be good reasons limiting the territorial scope of justifications and derogations in free movement law, there are equally valid reasons for Member States to regulate matters occurring outside the territory of the regulating Member State. Indeed, the EU's own legislative practice is a testament to this.[28] More often than not, the regulating Member State has valid reasons to adopt measures with extraterritorial effects and the location of concern can equally be worded as having a nexus with the territory of the Member State.[29] And even where such a link is less apparent, there are a number of arguments to permit such derogations and justifications, in particular, where the concern is one shared between Member States. Striking down such rules, then, may equally interfere with the regulatory autonomy of a Member State to protect public interests even where such rules are not necessarily discriminatory, protectionist, or even unnecessary. This section will elaborate upon legal arguments against a territorial limitation of public interest justifications in free movement law.

3.2.1 Textual, Legal-Systematic, and Doctrinal Reasons

One may argue that there is no textual support in the first place in Article 36 TFEU itself that suggests that there is a territorial limitation to the derogations upon which Member States may rely.[30] In contrast to secondary EU legislation, which explicitly provides for territorial

[27] Advocate General Léger in *Compassion in World Farming* also had similar reservations to potentially banning the exports of veal calves to another Member State 'for reasons based on a practice which is largely unknown to it.' Case C-1/96, *The Queen v Minister of Agriculture, Fisheries and Food, ex parte Compassion in World Farming Ltd.* [1998] ECR I-1251, Opinion of AG Léger, para. 77

[28] Joanne Scott, 'The New EU "extraterritoriality"' (2014) **51** *Common Market Law Review*, 1343

[29] Organisation for Economic Co-operation and Development (OECD) 'Processes and Production Methods (PPMs): Conceptual Framework and Considerations' (OECD 1997); Nicolas De Sadeleer, *EU Environmental Law and the Internal Market* (Oxford University Press, 2014), 301–308

[30] This point is also considered by Advocate General van Gerven in Case C-169/89 *Gourmetterie van den Burg* [1990] ECR I-2151, Opinion of AG Van Gerven, para 7

limitations in relation to more stringent measures that go beyond the minimum requirements set by those rules, there is no such territorial limit in primary law itself.[31] The derogations from the other fundamental freedoms do not contain any explicit language on the territorial scope of the derogations. The text only indicates that the provisions on the fundamental freedoms shall not preclude Member States from achieving certain legitimate non-economic policy aims of Member States without specifying whether these policies may only be achieved on the territory of that Member State.

Article 36 TFEU, in particular, does not state that restrictions can only be justified on grounds of public morality, public policy, *within the territory of the Member State* or on grounds of public morality, public policy etc. *proper to that Member State*.[32] On the derogation related to the protection of *national* treasures, possessing artistic, historic, or archaeological value presupposes some kind of territorial limitation.

A territorial limitation to public interest justifications is also problematic from a legal-systematic point of view. Article 36 TFEU states that both Articles 34 and 35 shall not preclude prohibitions or restrictions on imports, exports, or goods in transit justified on the grounds listed. It does not make a distinction between the grounds listed that can be relied upon for import or for export restrictions. In that respect, imposing such a territorial regulatory limitation would undermine and put the *effet utile*

[31] See for instance Article 11 of Council Directive 2008/119/EC of 18 December 2008 laying down minimum standards for the protection of calves OJ 2008 No. L10/7 and article 34 of Regulation 834/2007 on organic production and labelling of organic products OJ 2007 No. L189/1

[32] By contrast, in the WTO context such reference is explicitly made in the SPS Agreement. The SPS Agreement regulates trade restrictions applied by Members of the WTO for the protection of public health. Such trade restrictions are called sanitary and phytosanitary measures. Such measures, according to Annex A1 of the SPS Agreement, are measures applied:

(a) to protect animal or plant life or health *within the territory of the Member* from risks arising from the entry, establishment or spread of pests, diseases, disease-carrying organisms or disease-causing organisms;

(b) to protect human or animal life or health *within the territory of the Member* from risks arising from additives, contaminants, toxins or disease-causing organisms *in* foods, beverages or feedstuffs;

(c) to protect human life or health *within the territory of the Member* from risks arising from diseases carried by animals, plants or products thereof, or from the entry, establishment or spread of pests; or

(d) to prevent or limit other damage *within the territory of the Member* from the entry, establishment or spread of pests.

of the derogations contained in Article 36 TFEU at risk for restrictions of exports.[33] This would lead to a restrictive reading of those derogations and justifications whereby, for example, restrictions of exports of sheep on the basis of slaughtering methods employed abroad would no longer be permitted on grounds of the protection of health and life of animals despite the fact that Article 36 TFEU explicitly states that Article 35 TFEU shall not preclude such prohibitions in the absence of harmonization.[34]

As such, reliance upon Article 36 TFEU seems, in principle, to be possible for all grounds of derogation for export restrictions. The Court, in its case-law on export restrictions, has never explicitly ruled out the possibility of relying on Article 36 TFEU to prohibit exports for the protection of the life and health of humans, animals, and plants for instance. There are a couple of well-known cases that deal with export controls and export licenses for primarily waste recovery and waste disposal in other Member States where the Court grappled with the issue of the location of the interest that a Member State sought to protect. In those cases the Court has given indications that it assesses and values the location of the interest to be protected. However, it has also left space for the protection of interests that are not or only partly located in other Member States. In *Inter-Huiles*, for example, the ECJ's reasoning suggests that if the French authorities could establish that the environment would be protected less effectively in other Member States it would be possible to justify export restrictions on those grounds.[35] In *Dusseldorp*, the ECJ rules that with regard to extraterritorial protection of human health and the environment, 'such a justification would be relevant if the processing of oil filters in other Member States and their shipment over a greater distance as a result of their being exported posed a threat

[33] Rodolphe Munoz, 'Case C-1/96, The Queen v. Minister of Agriculture, Fisheries and food, ex parte Compassion in World Farming Limited. Judgment of 19 March 1998, [1998] ECR I-1251' (1999) 36 *Common Market Law Review*, 831, at 839; see also Geert Van Calster, 'Export Restrictions – A Watershed for Article 30' (2000) **25** *European Law Review*, 335

[34] This is all the more problematic since the Court in *Gysbrechts* applied the *Groenveld* criteria as to include de facto discrimination of exports. See Case C-205/07, *Criminal proceedings against Lodewijk Gysbrechts and Santurel Inter BVBA* [2008] ECR I-9947, paras. 38–44; Case 15/79, *Groenveld* [1979] ECR 3409, para. 7: 'national measures which have as their specific object or effect the restriction of patterns of exports and thereby the establishment of a difference in treatment between the domestic trade of a Member State and its export trade in such a way as to provide a particular advantage for national production or for the domestic market of the State in question, at the expense of the production or of the trade of other Member States.'

[35] Case 172/82, *Syndicat national des fabricants raffineurs d'huile de graissage and others v Groupement d'intérêt économique "Inter-Huiles" and others* [1983] ECR 555, para. 14.

to the health and life of humans.'[36] The Court focused on the issue of transport as well as the processing of the waste abroad. In other words, a Member State would actually be able to justify export restrictions on grounds of extraterritorial protection of human health or the environment if a Member State can establish that the level of protection abroad is lower than its own.

In the context of secondary legislation, the Court has explicitly endorsed extraterritorial protection where such protection was not prohibited nor required in the text of the legislation at issue. *EU-Wood-Trading* concerned the objections by German authorities to a shipment of wood waste from Germany to Italy for recovery. In interpreting Regulation 259/93/EC, the Court came to the conclusion that not only could German authorities object to the export of waste on health and environmental grounds in the Member State of destination, but also that they could do so on the basis of their own levels of protection. The Court held that the objections of authorities of dispatch 'may be based on considerations connected not only to the actual transport of the waste in each competent authority's area of jurisdiction but also on the recovery planned for that shipment.'[37] This implies, according to the Court, 'that those authorities, in assessing the risks which such recovery would entail for human health and the environment, may take account of all relevant criteria in that regard, including those which are in force in the State of dispatch, even if they are stricter than those of the State of destination'.[38] In *Zuchtvieh-Export*, the ECJ found that Regulation 1/2005 on the protection of animals during transport applies outside of EU borders to transport taking place in third states, if that transport began on EU territory.[39] Similarly, in *European Federation for Cosmetic Ingredients*, the ECJ found that the EU Cosmetics Regulation may prohibit the marketing of cosmetics that demonstrate compliance with the Regulation's health safety standards on the basis of animal tests outside the EU.[40]

[36] Case C-203/96, *Chemische Afvalstoffen Dusseldorp BV and Others v Minister van Volkshuisvesting, Ruimtelijke Ordening en Milieubeheer* [1998] ECR I-4075, para. 46; see also Case C-209/98, *Entreprenørforeningens Affalds/Miljøsektion (FFAD) v Københavns Kommune* [2000] ECR I-3743, para. 45

[37] Case C-277/02, *EU-Wood-Trading GmbH v Sonderabfall-Management-Gesellschaft Rheinland-Pfalz mbH* [2004] ECR I-11957, para. 43

[38] Ibid., para 46

[39] Case C-424/13, *Zuchtvieh-Export GmbH v Stadt Kempten* EU:C:2015:259

[40] Case C-592/14, *European Federation for Cosmetic Ingredients v Secretary of State for Business, Innovation and Skills* EU:C:2016:703, paras. 39–45

Moreover, the Court has also endorsed the protection of consumers abroad as a justification for export restrictions contradicting its earlier statements made in *Alpine Investments*. In *Gysbrechts*, the Court held that Belgian export restrictions relating to distance contracts could, in principle, be justified on grounds of consumer protection.[41]

3.2.2 Trans-Boundary Harm

A second strand of argument against a territorial limitation of public interest justifications in free movement law is that such a geographic demarcation is ill equipped to deal with transboundary issues. A Member State might, for example, still have an interest in regulating the production process of a product abroad because it is harmed by that production process. Since regulating production directly is not possible, a Member State could simply decide not provide any market incentives to continue production. For instance, environmental pollution can have trans-boundary effects, resulting in the effects of environmentally degrading production being felt in the Member State of import and not necessarily in the country in which the product is produced, such as climate change or emissions of hazardous substances in a border area. Most obvious examples are the consequences of acid rain resulting from industrial activity abroad and climate change related problems. Member States might want to prevent that their environment gets damaged by providing funds for industrial activity elsewhere.

In such instances, it would be logical that a Member State should be able to protect the environment on its own territory. In *Commission v. Germany*, the ECJ found that German legislation requiring a permit for shipment of dangerous and toxic waste outside Germany compatible with EU secondary legislation because 'the disposal of hazardous waste in another Member State, particularly an adjacent Member State, may have serious environmental consequences in Germany and justify a refusal to allow a shipment to that State'.[42] Other

[41] Compare Case C-384/93, *Alpine Investments BV v Minister van Financiën* [1995] ECR I-1141, paras. 43–44 with Case C-205/07, *Criminal proceedings against Lodewijk Gysbrechts and Santurel Inter BVBA* [2008] ECR I-9947, paras. 47–49. See Wulf-Henning Roth, 'Case C-205/07, Lodewijk Gysbrechts, Santurel Inter BVBA, Judgment of the Court of Justice (Grand Chamber) of 16 December 2008' (2010) **47** *Common Market Law Review*, 509. This change of direction by the Court might have very well been inspired by both practical reasons and the fact that there was EU harmonization in the area; the Belgian measures in principle reinforced and contributed to the EU's policy on consumer protection.

[42] Case C-422/92, *Commission v Federal Republic of Germany* [1995] ECR I-1097, para. 41

examples are the many free movement cases involving green electricity in which Member State authorities sought to mitigate the effects of climate change, a quintessential transboundary issue, by promoting domestically produced green electricity. The ECJ had no difficulty in finding that measures combatting climate change constitutes a legitimate public interest.[43]

3.2.3 Protection of Universal or Common Interests

Third, a territorial limitation of public interest justifications in free movement law is problematic when a common or 'universal' interest is at stake which the importing country seeks to address, for instance, the preservation of endangered species or the protection of biodiversity.[44] This presupposes a shared interest between the producer and importing country, but is similar to the prevention of trans-boundary harm in that there is a self-interest of the regulating Member State as part of a larger community at stake. In *Van der Feesten*, for instance, the Court accepted the necessity of national measures aiming at protecting species of birds that for part of common EU heritage.[45] The protected interest is thus not unilaterally recognized by the importing Member State, even if it concerns a transboundary problem, but is an interest that both the exporting country or Member State and the importing Member State share and recognize. Such common interests can usually be found in international treaties and documents, as well as in EU legal sources itself.

An interesting and somewhat odd example within free movement law in which a common interest was at stake and explicitly mentioned by the Court was *Josemans*. The case concerned a Dutch measure combatting drug tourism in a border town of the Netherlands. The measure at issue, despite being discriminatory because it targeted non-residents, was also

[43] Case C-379/98, *PreussenElektra AG v Schleswag AG* [2001] ECR I-2159, paras. 73–81; Case C-573/12, *Ålands Vindkraft AB v Energimyndigheten* EU:C:2014:2037, paras. 77–82; Joined Cases C-204/12, C-205/12, C-206/12, C-207/12, C-208/12, *Essent Belgium* EU:C:2014:2192, paras. 90–95; in the context of taxation see Case C-213/96, *Outokumpu Oy* [1998] ECR I-1777, paras. 31–33

[44] Case C-510/99, *Procureur de la République v. Xavier Tridon* [2001] ECR I-7777, see also Marcel Brus, 'Case C-510/99, Procureur de la République v. Xavier Tridon' (2003) **40** *Common Market Law Review*, 169–178

[45] Case C-202/94, *Criminal proceedings against Godefridus Van der Feesten* [1996] ECR I-355, para. 3; Hanna Sevenster, *Eco-imperialisme binnen de Europese Unie; een juridisch probleem?* (Deventer: W.E.J. Tjeenk Willink, 1998); Jochem Wiers, *Trade and the Environment: A Legal Analysis* (Groningen: Europa Law Publishing, 2000), 134

defended by bordering Member States.[46] The Court found the measure to be justified as it concerned 'both the maintenance of public order and the protection of the health of citizens, at the level of the Member States and also of the European Union.'[47] The Court emphasized EU secondary legislation and the international commitments both the EU and its Member States entered into against the use and trade in illicit drugs in this regard.[48]

The free movement cases on green electricity discussed above are also good examples. In all of these cases, the ECJ noted that combatting climate change was a goal of both the EU and of its Member States and noted the international commitments entered into in that regard.[49] These arguments were made by the ECJ in addition to the point that promoting renewables protect the health and life of humans, animals and plants, a justification listed in Article 36 TFEU. In *Ålands Vindkraft*, the ECJ also noted that the Treaties state that combatting climate change is one of the energy objectives that must guide EU energy policy, whereas in the other cases, the ECJ referred to the goals of EU environmental policy in the Treaties.[50]

Another example is *Gysbrechts*, where the Court held that Belgium could justify an export restriction in distance selling contracts that made it more difficult to sell to consumers in other Member States on grounds of consumer protection.[51] The Court did not, as was the case in *Alpine Investments*, make a distinction between consumers located in Belgium and consumers located elsewhere. This could be explained by the fact that the measure in question sought to reinforce common EU policy on consumer protection. The Court highlighted the complementary nature of the Belgian measure in question to existing EU legislation which

[46] Case C-137/09, *Marc Michel Josemans v Burgemeester van Maastricht* [2010] ECR I-13019, paras. 61 and 64

[47] Ibid., paras. 65–66 [48] Ibid., paras. 67–68

[49] Case C-379/98, *PreussenElektra AG v Schleswag AG* [2001] ECR I-2159, paras. 73–81; Case C-573/12, *Ålands Vindkraft AB v Energimyndigheten* EU:C:2014:2037, paras. 77–82; Joined Cases C-204/12, C-205/12, C-206/12, C-207/12, C-208/12, *Essent Belgium* EU:C:2014:2192, paras. 90–95

[50] Case C-573/12, *Ålands Vindkraft AB*, para. 81; Joined Cases C-204/12, C-205/12, C-206/12, C-207/12, C-208/12, *Essent Belgium*, paras. 94; Case C-379/98, *PreussenElektra AG v Schleswag AG* [2001] ECR I-2159, para. 76

[51] Case C-384/93, *Alpine Investments BV v Minister van Financiën* [1995] ECR I-1141, para. 56. This omission by both the Advocate General and the Court has been noted by Roth. See Roth, 'Case C-205/07, Lodewijk Gysbrechts, Santurel Inter BVBA, Judgment of the Court of Justice (Grand Chamber) of 16 December 2008', 509

sought to protect consumers, but did not prohibit suppliers from requiring credit card numbers in advance. It held that the Belgian measure aimed at protecting consumers and, 'in particular, the effectiveness of the right of withdrawal guaranteed' to the consumer by the Directive in question.[52] At the time of *Alpine Investments*, consumer protection was not yet a recognized goal of the EU itself and there was no relevant secondary legislation in place regulating consumer protection on financial markets.[53] In contrast, at the time *Lodewijk Gijsbrechts* was lodged, strengthening consumer protection was an explicit goal in the EC Treaty which contained a Title on consumer protection.[54]

It is thus clear that Member States are willing, and are justified to restrict trade for the pursuit of common interests. To the extent permitted by secondary legislation,[55] process-based measures could contribute to those common interests. The Court has even endorsed the only process-based measure that has come before it – a measure that was discriminatory – on grounds that it contributed to a goal that is shared among the Member States of the EU. Of particular interest in this sense is the promotion of fair trade and respect for labour standards in developing countries through measures which may restrict the free movement of goods. While not unlike the EU's environmental goals (this goal appears to be covered by the Treaties[56]), the ECJ has not referred to these provisions in a free movement of goods case.[57] In the public

[52] Case C-205/07, *Criminal proceedings against Lodewijk Gysbrechts and Santurel Inter BVBA* [2008] ECR I-9947, para. 48

[53] Alpine Investments was lodged on April 28th 1993, the treaty of Maastricht that modified the EEC Treaty to include consumer protection as a goal only entered into force on Novermber 1st 1993.

[54] Article 3 para 1 (t) EC and Title XIV and Article 153 EC

[55] See Chapter 4 Sections 4.1 and 4.3.

[56] Internally, the EU's ambition is according to Article 3 (3) TEU 'full employment and social progress', combatting 'social exclusion and discrimination, and shall promote social justice and protection, equality between women and men, solidarity between generations and protection of the rights of the child'. These goals find their complement externally in Article 3 (5) TEU, as the EU aims to promote and uphold these values in its relations with the wider world, by contributing to 'solidarity and mutual respect among peoples, free and fair trade, eradication of poverty and the protection of human rights, in particular the rights of the child'. In addition, the Charter of Fundamental Rights contains a number of provisions which aiming to protect labour rights. Title IV of the Charter lists a number of core labour rights in this respect, which include the right to collective bargaining (Article 28 Charter), fair and just working conditions (Article 31 Charter), and the prohibition on child labour (Article 32 Charter).

[57] Only in *Oebel* did the Court establish that a Member State could justify restrictions on trade in bakery products in order to 'improve working conditions'. However, that case

procurement case *Commission v. Netherlands (Max Havelaar)*, the ECJ did not refer to these goals, but did accept that the Dutch province of North Holland was permitted to award a public supply contract for coffee and tea on the basis of fair trade criteria which 'seek to promote the interests of small-scale producers in developing countries while maintaining trading relations with them which take into account the actual need of those producers, and not only the dictates of the market'.[58]

3.2.4 *Public Morality*

Fourth, a territorial limitation of public interest justifications in free movement law is also problematic because a Member State might be morally opposed to a method of production abroad and does not want products stemming from such production to be marketed inside its territory. The Member State in question is then not so much concerned with the physical harm done to its flora and fauna, or its population, but rather opposed to the method of production because of a socially shared belief among its population. An obvious example of this type of process-based measure with extraterritorial effects is found in a third country: Israel bans imports of non-Kosher food.[59] As we have seen in Chapter 1, the EU itself has adopted numerous process-based measures on animal welfare grounds.[60] Another example would be where the importing country does not want to be complicit in child labour by allowing the sale of textile products on its market made by children. The difference with a defence on the basis of common values is that public morality can be truly unilateral and inherent to a particular population of a Member State.[61]

concerned the protection of domestic workers in the bakery industry against night work and only indirectly protected workers abroad through restrictions on transport times of bakery products. Nonetheless, the Court did refer to international labour standards (ILO Convention no 20) that Germany and other Member States sought to implement with the restrictions at issue. See Case 155/80, *Summary proceedings agains Sergius Oebel* [1981] ECR-1993, paras. 11–13

[58] Case C-368/10, *Commission v Netherlands (Max Havelaar)* EU:C:2012:284, para. 89

[59] WTO Trade Policy Review Body, 'Trade Policy Review, Report by the Secretariat, Israel' (24 March 2006) WT/TPR/S/157/Rev.1, section III, paras 27, 48 (noting: 'since December 1994, Israel has maintained a ban on imports of non-kosher meat and meat products. However, the Government permits limited domestic production, sale, and consumption of non-kosher meat.').

[60] Chapter 1 Section 1.1

[61] In addition, public morality can be seen as something that is perceived by the population of a particular country, and not something that can be verified by science, which may be the case, for example, with the protection of endangered species and the mitigating the effects of climate change.

Public morality is a well-known ground for justification under free movement law.[62] The Court has maintained that in relation to justifications on grounds of public morality within free movement law that 'in principle, it is for each Member State to determine in accordance with its own scale of values and in the form selected by it the requirements of public morality in its territory'.[63] Although such deference is coupled with the procedural proportionality requirements of coherence and consistency, it is clear that there is room within the free movement law to accommodate moral and ethical diversity within the EU.[64] Such a right to diversity is well recognized within the Treaties.[65]

It is obvious that prohibiting morally based process-based measures for reasons of extraterritoriality would, contrary to what Dougan has suggested (see Section 3.1 in this chapter), permit the *other* national identity to force itself upon importing Member States which have chosen to adopt an alternative stance.[66] Despite this, and the Court's usually generous stance when it comes to trade restrictive rules based on cultural and moral values of Member States, the Court has denied reliance on public morality derogations in relation to two high profile morally induced process-based measures: the potential UK veal cow export ban to countries permitting the 'veal crate system' in *Compassion in World Farming* and the Polish ban on GMOs and products containing GMOs based on the catholic and humanist beliefs of the Polish population.[67] In both cases, the existence of secondary legislation aiming at removing

[62] Floris de Witte, 'Sex, Drugs & EU Law: The Recognition of Moral and Ethical Diversity in EU Law' (2013) **50** *Common Market Law Review*, 1545; Case 34/79, *Regina v Maurice Donald Henn and John Frederick Ernest Darby* [1979] ECR 3795, paras. 15–16; Case C-275/92, *Schindler* [1994] ECR I- 1039; Case 121/85, *Conegate Limited v HM Customs & Excise* [1986] ECR 1007; Case C-65/05, *Commission v Greece* [2006] ECR I- 10341; Case C-244/06, *Dynamic Medien Vertriebs GmbH v Avides Media AG* [2008] ECR I-505

[63] Case 34/79, *Regina v Maurice Donald Henn and John Frederick Ernest Darby* [1979] ECR 3795, paras. 15–16

[64] Witte, 'Sex, Drugs & EU Law: The Recognition of Moral and Ethical Diversity in EU Law', 1545

[65] The preamble of the TEU notes that the Union desires 'to deepen the solidarity between their peoples while respecting their history, their culture and their traditions'. Similarly, Article 3 (3) TEU states that the Union shall 'respect its rich cultural and linguistic diversity' and Article 4 (2) TEU states that 'the Union shall respect the equality of Member States before the Treaties as well as their national identities, inherent in their fundamental structures, political and constitutional, inclusive of regional and local self-government'.

[66] Dougan, 'Minimum Harmonization and the Internal Market', 853–885, 874

[67] Case C-1/96, *The Queen v Minister of Agriculture, Fisheries and Food, ex parte Compassion in World Farming Ltd.* [1998] ECR I-1251; Case C-165/08, *Commission v Poland* [2009] ECR I-6843

obstacles to trade made the Court unwilling to permit reliance on public morality as a separate ground for justification.

Thus, in *Compassion in World Farming*, recourse to Article 36 TFEU was no longer possible on grounds of public morality since the Directive at issue aimed at harmonizing rules concerned with the protection of animal health. The Court concluded that 'in reality, public policy and public morality are not being invoked as a separate justification but are an aspect of the justification relating to the protection of animal health, which is the subject of the harmonising directive'.[68] The Advocate General, by contrast, did consider a derogation on grounds of the protection of public morality still possible, emphasizing that the concept of public morals should be interpreted with the necessary judicial restraint.[69]

In *Commission v. Poland*, the Court was not convinced that the Polish ban on GMOs and products containing GMOs was adopted on moral grounds. The Court held that Poland had insufficiently demonstrated that the laws in question were adopted on religious and ethical considerations, setting a high standard of proof.[70] The Court found that mere convictions shared by the majority of parliament were insufficient to prove that the legislative intent of the GMO ban was to protect public morality.[71] These cases are indicative of a high level of scrutiny of the ECJ of public morals justifications with extraterritorial implications in free movement law. The level of scrutiny employed can be explained by the existence of harmonized rules in the area which had as their

[68] Case C-1/96, *The Queen v Minister of Agriculture, Fisheries and Food, ex parte Compassion in World Farming Ltd.* [1998] ECR I-1251, para. 66

[69] Case C-1/96, *The Queen v Minister of Agriculture, Fisheries and Food, ex parte Compassion in World Farming Ltd.* [1998] ECR I-1251, Opinion of AG Léger, paras. 104–106. The Advocate General noted that 'it is no part of the Court's task to judge values characterizing the public morality of a Member State and which are therefore quite specific to it' and stated that 'the fact that a Member State should consider that harm unjustifiably caused to the life or health of domestic animals, even for economic purposes, through the use of a particular rearing method is a matter of public morality in that State does not appear to be manifestly contrary to Article 36.' The Advocate General did add, however, that there must be 'objective scientific evidence that the rearing system in question causes unreasonable harm to the health or life of animals and that the measures adopted must be proportionate to the aim in view, which is for the national court to judge.'

[70] Case C-165/08, *Commission v. Poland* [2009] ECR I-6843, paras 52–60; Niamh Nic Shuibhne and Marsela Maci, 'Proving Public Interest: The Growing Impact of Evidence in Free Movement Case Law' (2013) **50** *Common Market Law Review*, 965, at 981–982

[71] See also Witte, 'Sex, Drugs & EU Law: The Recognition of Moral and Ethical Diversity in EU Law', 1545

explicit aim the elimination of obstacles to trade among Member States, an issue returned to in Chapter 4.

3.2.5 Practical Reasons

Fifth, territorially limiting public interest justifications in free movement law might have impractical implications and should be avoided for the sake of simplicity and effectiveness. In relation to process-based measures, there may be no genuine attempt to induce extraterritorial effects, but these effects are the consequences of domestically oriented process-based regulation. This is particularly visible in relation to consumer -based regulation, such as labelling measures and promotional campaigns. A Member State may, for example, choose a more market related instrument to stimulate rather than require a domestic industry to produce according to higher social and environmental production standards. Thus, instead of requiring domestic farmers to respect high animal welfare standards, a Member State may set up a labelling system or a promotional campaign which enables consumers to decide whether they want to incentivize farmers to farm in a more animal-friendly way.[72] This can be a reflection of government policy to enable a part of population which feels strongly about animal welfare to make purchasing decisions accordingly, while allowing other parts of the population that values a lower price more to purchase cheaper animal products. In order to protect the cohesion and coherence of this policy, imported products are also subjected to such labelling rules, even if they are voluntary. Producers may be prohibited from passing off products as 'animal-friendly' if they do not comply with the labelling requirements, or may be even required to provide information on the welfare of the animals used for the products in question.

[72] The Court has been fairly permissive in relation to such measures intending to inform consumers about certain qualities of products. In *Apple and Pear Development Council*, a case concerning a promotional campaign to promote British fruit, contains a number of interesting statements of the Court as regards the permissibility of promoting certain aspects of products as long as it is not solely related to the origin of the product. While promotional campaigns 'intended to discourage the purchase of products of other Member States or to disparage those products in the eyes of consumers [... or] advise consumers to purchase domestic products solely by reason of their national origin' are not permitted, a promotional campaign may draw attention 'to the specific qualities of fruit grown in the Member State in question or from organizing campaigns to promote the sale of certain varieties, mentioning their particular properties, even if those varieties are typical of national production.' See Case 222/82, *Apple and Pear Development Council* [1983] ECR 4087, paras. 18–19

Such consumer protection may result in the protection of social and environmental interests abroad to the extent that it results in less demand of products made in environmentally or socially degrading ways. While a regulating Member State may not be primarily concerned with inducing these effects, it would be impractical and contrary to the aims of protecting consumers to introduce labelling requirements only for domestic production. The Court appears to understand that sometimes extraterritorial protection of interests as a 'by-product' is simply the most feasible way of designing legislation. Consider the Belgian rules in *Gysbrechts,* for example. The Belgian measure in question protected all consumers in distance selling contracts, irrespective whether they were resident in Belgium or not.[73] In contrast to *Alpine Investments,* however, the Court did not consider the protection of consumers in other Member States to be an issue, and did not make a distinction between consumers located in Belgium and consumers located elsewhere.[74] If it would have decided along those lines, Belgium would have been faced with the complexity of introducing two types of rules: a more stringent regime for consumers located in Belgium and a more relaxed regime for consumers located elsewhere. This would result in a lower level of protection for non-Belgian residents: a discriminatory approach which is contrary to the aims of the Directive to protect consumers irrespective of their location.[75]

Other examples are the ECJ tax rulings on process-based measures discussed in Chapter 2 (Section 2.2.1).[76] In those cases, the ECJ required domestic incentives to produce in an environmentally friendly way to be extended extraterritorially, enabling foreign producers to compete at

[73] Case C-205/07, *Criminal proceedings against Lodewijk Gysbrechts and Santurel Inter BVBA* [2008] ECR I-9947

[74] Case C-384/93, *Alpine Investments BV v Minister van Financiën* [1995] ECR I-1141, para. 56. This omission by both the Advocate General and the Court has been noted by Roth. See Roth, 'Case C-205/07, Lodewijk Gysbrechts, Santurel Inter BVBA, Judgment of the Court of Justice (Grand Chamber) of 16 December 2008', 509. Roth however criticized the Court for its approach, suggesting that each Member State should only be responsible for the protection of its own consumers in line with *Alpine Investments*.

[75] The Directive in question was Directive 97/7/EC of the European Parliament and of the Council of 20 May 1997 on the protection of consumers in respect of distance contracts OJ 1997 No. L144/19.

[76] Case 140/79, *Chemical Farmaceutici SpA v DAF SpA* [1981] ECR 2; Case 127/75, *Bobie Getränkevertrieb GmbH v Haptzollamt Aachen-Nord* [1976] ECR 1080; Case C-213/96, *Outokumpu Oy* [1998] ECR I-1777

lower prices if they comply with the environmental norms of the Member State to which their products are destined.[77]

Another practical reason against territorial limitation of public interest justifications in free movement law is that this might compromise the effectiveness of social and environmental legislation at home. In the context of process-based measures a Member State might introduce such a measure to ensure the effectiveness of a social or environmental measure regulating domestic production. The most notable examples in this regard are measures introduced to prevent 'carbon leakage': the reallocation of production to countries with less stringent environmental standards, making the stringent environmental production standards useless, since the same amount or even more (through transportation among others) of emissions is released elsewhere.[78] A Member State may seek to introduce a process-based measure in order to preserve the effectiveness of the regulatory goal. The EU itself has a practice of territorial extension of its rules in order to combat evasion of those rules by rule-subjects.[79]

3.2.6 *Desirable for Others*

Lastly, one could argue that a territorial limitation of public interest justifications in free movement law is unwarranted because it would frustrate the ability of Member States to assist or contribute to social or environmental objectives of another country, Member State, or even a particular group. A Member State might, for instance, seek to protect social and environmental interests at the production stage of products

[77] In this context, it is interesting to note that practical reasons may also be a reason for Member States to withhold market access or beneficial treatment of imported goods, since it may be more difficult for Member State authorities to verify compliance of those goods with production standards, for instance. The ECJ has made contradictory statements in that regard, but it is submitted that the Member State in question must be open to receiving proof that a product complies with a particular process-based standard. Compare Case C-213/96, *Outokumpu Oy*, paras. 38–39 with Case C-379/98, *PreussenElektra AG v Schhleswag AG* [2001] ECR I-2099, para. 79. See also Case C-213/96, *Outokumpu Oy* [1998] ECR I-1780, Opinion of AG Jacobs, para. 5

[78] Joost Pauwelyn, 'Carbon Leakage Measures and Border Tax Ajdustments under WTO Law' in Denise Prevost and Geert van Calster (eds.) *Research Handbook on Environment, Health and the WTO* (Cheltenham: Edward Elgar, 2012); Kati Kulovesi, Elisa Morgera and Miquel Muñoz, 'Environmental Integration and Multi-faceted International Dimensions of EU law: Unpacking the EU's 2009 Climate and Energy Package' (2011) **48** *Common Market Law Review*, 829, at 858–861

[79] Scott, 'The New EU "extraterritoriality"', 1343, 1359

elsewhere in collaboration with the country of production. Through such measures, the country of import helps out the country of production with maintaining its level of protection by reducing incentives for producers and traders to ignore social and environmental interests in the country of production. The most typical example of this is the EU FLEGT initiative which, in collaboration with developing exporting countries, seeks to prevent the EU market from being used to market illegally harvested timber in the country of production.[80] As such, there is no real issue of 'neo-colonialism', 'eco-imperialism', or economic coercion, as such measures seek to avoid that a few individuals can exploit the anarchical nature of international trade to the detriment of larger societal interests which may be felt in both the importing and exporting countries.

Such measures might still be challenged on the basis of Article 34 TFEU which can be invoked by any individual trader losing access to a market of a Member State for goods originating in the EU but also for third country goods in free circulation.[81] Unlike the WTO, which dispute settlement system is based on resolution of disputes between sovereign states (and the EU), the EU internal market system permits individuals to challenge measures that restrict access to the market of a Member State. Thus, even if trading partners (implicitly) agree on trade barriers between them, such barriers can still be struck down through recourse to Article 34 TFEU. This can lead to paradoxical situations in which multiple Member States seek to defend a trade-restrictive measure, while only one individual seeks its abolishment. In *Dassonville*, the United Kingdom defended the Belgian (process-based) measures protecting the designation of origin and the certificate of authenticity required for the sale of Whiskey ('Scotch' Whiskey).[82] In *Josemans*, France, Belgium, and

[80] See Chapter 1 Section 1.1.4

[81] See Chapter 2 Section 2.1 and Laurens Ankersmit, 'What if Cassis de Dijon were Cassis de Quebec? The Assimilation of Goods of Third Country Origin in the Internal Market' (2013) **50** *Common Market Law Review*, 1387

[82] Case 8/74, *Procureur du Roi v Benoît and Gustave Dassonville* [1974] ECR 837, at 844–845. While the United Kingdom was a Member State of the European Economic Community at the time, trade restrictions were still permitted. The case itself concerned parallel imports from another Member State, France. The Accession Treaty 9 Treaty of Accession of Denmark, Ireland, and the United Kingdom (1972) OJ L 73, 27.3.1972) specified that quantitative restrictions were to be abolished between the United Kingdom and the Member States upon accession, but that measures having equivalent effect to such restrictions should be abolished by 1 January 1975 at the latest. Thus at the time of reference (11 January 1974) and judgment (11 July 1974) of the ECJ measures of

Germany defended the Dutch discriminatory measures aiming to prevent drug tourism.[83] In cases such as *Exportur v LOR* and *Ravil*, Member States defended each other's trade restrictions based on bilateral agreements to protect designations of origin.[84]

Despite, or maybe because of this, the Court is permissive towards justifications that protect extraterritorial interests with the (implicit) consent of other Member States. In *Commission v. Belgium (Dassonville II)*, the Court held that the amendments to Belgian law and the liberalization efforts made between the United Kingdom and Belgium in order to comply with the *Dassonville* judgment were satisfactory.[85] In *Josemans*, the ECJ had no difficulty in finding that the Dutch discriminatory ban on non-residents from coffeeshops could be justified *inter alia* on grounds of protection of public health as argued by the German government.[86]

Similarly, the ECJ has found on a number of occasions that bilateral cooperation between Member States resulting in trade restrictions was justified. In *Bauhuis*, the ECJ stated that veterinary inspections for livestock destined for export that replaced such inspections of the importing Member State were permissible.[87] In *Exportur v LOR*, the Court upheld trade restrictive measures taken as a result of a convention concluded by France and Spain to protect the geographic denominations on each other's territory. According to the Court, Article 36 'does not preclude such protection from being extended to the territory of another Member State' by means of concluding such a convention.[88]

This argument may even be extended to a situation in which an exporting country is largely indifferent towards both restrictions of trade that may result out of the enactment of process-based measures, but those negatively affected by production may strongly support initiatives by importing countries to reduce demand for the products that are

equivalent effect to quantitative import restrictions were still permitted between the United Kingdom and the other Member States but not between the original six Member States themselves.

83 Case C-137/09, *Marc Michel Josemans v Burgemeester van Maastricht* [2010] ECR I-13019, paras. 61 and 64

84 Case C-3/91, *Exportur v LOR* [1992] ECR I-5553; Case C-469/00, *Ravil SARL v Bellon import SARL* [2003] ECR I-5085

85 Case 2/78, *Commission v. Belgium* [1979] ECR 1762, paras. 41–44

86 Case C-137/09, *Marc Michel Josemans v Burgemeester van Maastricht* [2010] ECR I-13019, paras. 61–66

87 Case 46/76, *W.G.J. Bauhuis v the Netherlands State* [1977] ECR 6, paras. 43–47

88 Case C-3/91 *Exportur v LOR* [1992] ECR I-5553, para. 39; See also Case C-469/00, *Ravil SARL v Bellon import SARL* [2003] ECR I-5085

produced in environmentally or socially degrading ways. For example, a developing country may be indifferent towards the imposition of stricter worker protection in their factories by importing countries, but the workforce and labour unions may strongly support such measures. In particular, there might be public-private cooperation between societal stakeholders in both countries in order to protect workers in developing countries.[89] There may therefore be a certain global solidarity among different parts of the global population which is only detrimental to a few individuals operating those factories.

In that sense, the case-law mentioned above whereby the ECJ accepts that trade restrictions are justified even where Member State authorities seek to protect public interests in other Member States or third countries might not be all that surprising if one considers that the Court itself requires Member States to be 'other-regarding' when it applies the principle of mutual recognition and, more generally, the principle of proportionality in free movement law. Often the Court strikes down national rules and practices because they insufficiently take into account the interests of the 'outsider' in free movement.[90] This is most visible in the case-law of the Court on the mutual recognition of conformity assessment procedures or technical regulations. In those cases the Court explicitly requires Member State authorities to take into account the legislative history of a product in the territory of another Member State.[91] More generally, one could argue that the case-law of the Court on the free movement of goods reflects an idea that Member States, as co-regulators of the internal market, need to take into account the interests of the EU as a whole, and should not regulate from a purely national perspective. As Maduro has argued,

> we can no longer allow Member States to take decisions from a purely national perspective. State regulation is now almost always regulation of the common market as well. Within the framework of the European Economic Constitution, Member States should take all interests affected into account when regulating the common market. This includes out-of-State interests. Member States should

[89] An example is the Bangladesh Fire and Safety Accord of the garment industry and labour unions supported by, among others, the Dutch government, the United Nations and the ILO. See www.bangladeshaccord.org/

[90] Miguel Poiares Maduro, *We the Court: the European Court of Justice and the European economic constitution: a critical reading of Article 30 of the EC Treaty* (Oxford: Hart, 1998)

[91] Case 272/80, *Criminal proceedings against Frans-Nederlandse Maatschappij voor Biologische Producten BV* [1981] ECR 3277, paras. 14 and 15

be able to make different policy judgments. What we should not permit is that they ignore out-of-States interests in the making of those judgments.[92]

If this is true, the question then becomes which extraterritorial interests should be taken into account by the regulating Member State. Should this only be the interests of traders, or can this also be the interests of a broader group, including social and environmental interests in addition to economic interests? Maduro, for one, does not suggest that this should be the case:

One of the advantages of the present proposal is that it does not assume a priori that market integration is more legitimate than State regulation. Rather, it operates at the level of the correction of State legitimacy problems. It is not intended to replace national policy-making with market integration rationality, but to correct and improve national policy-making so as to expand its democratic basis. This would require Member States to internalise within their national political processes all the interests affected by their regulation of the common market or, alternatively, to include national interests which can represent out-of-State interests within their national political processes.[93]

De Witte and Azoulai have also further elaborated upon this requirement to take the interests of 'outsiders' into account when regulating markets. De Witte has argued for instance that free movement law is a 'sophisticated elaboration of the idea of "no taxation without representation". It seeks to extend national democratic practices to take account of unrepresented interests in an attempt to equate the objects and subjects of rule. In essence, it tackles the most evident externality of democracy: the fact that its norms might affect citizens, interests or institutions that are not represented in the institutional process-, did not have a chance to voice their concerns, and that the norms expressed by theat institutional process might therefore contain a parochial basis.'[94]

Azoulai's notion, however, comes closer to only representing those who take advantage of free movement, not those who may suffer the consequences of it. He argues that Member States must '*recontextualize* the decision-making process at national level … to take account of interests coming from or situated in other Member States, which are

[92] Maduro, *We the Court: The European Court of Justice and the European Economic Constitution*, 171
[93] Ibid., 171–172
[94] Witte, 'Sex, Drugs & EU Law: The Recognition of Moral and Ethical Diversity in EU Law', 1545, 1553

not only interests of *firms but also of citizens, workers or students.* They also have a "*re-programming*" function to the extent that they should lead the national authorities to adapt their policies to the objectives of integration. The application of free movement provisions is based on an engagement on the part of the Member States to "denationalize" their normative standards. It demands a profound turnaround of national practices.'[95]

The relationship between legitimacy and taking social and environmental interests abroad into account is complex and raises issues of unilateralism or non-cooperation. On the one hand, taking the interests of everyone affected by free movement into account is less biased towards deregulation and against social and environmental protection. It is crucial to realize that giving market access to imported products is not value neutral in itself-depending on the products granted access to the market, such access may incentivize others to harm the environment or provide funds for factory owners that employ children, and importing cheap textile products from a country with unsound labour practices induces more of those practices. Similarly, exporting large quantities of weapons to another country is unlikely to go without consequences.[96]

3.3 Problematizing and Framing Justifications and Derogations in Light of Extraterritorial Effects

As Sections 3.1 and 3.2 have shown, there are reasons to favour and to oppose a territorial limitation of public interest justifications in free movement law. In some instances, the Court appears to be suspicious of justifications that appear altruistic and do not address a clear domestic concern; in others, the Court is oblivious to such issues. However, more often than not, a Member State will have an interest in regulating matters that appear extraterritorial. If it would be otherwise, the measures in question would probably not even be adopted.

This double-sided nature of derogations and justifications, which appear at first sight 'extraterritorial', is evident in the case-law of the

[95] Loïc Azoulai, 'The Court of Justice and the Social Market Economy: The Emergence of an Ideal and the Conditions for its Realization' (2008) 45 *Common Market Law Review*, 1335, 1342–1343

[96] On the other hand, there is the significant question of understanding as a regulating country what is the 'right' thing to do. It is one thing to take into account the interests of others abroad, it is quite another to not give them a say in how this should be done. This will be considered in more detail in Chapter 4.

Court. In *Alpine Investments,* for instance, while the Court conceded that the prohibition on cold-calling to customers outside the Netherlands for reasons of consumer protection of consumers in other Member States 'is not, as such, a matter for the Netherlands authorities', the Court added that 'the nature and extent of that protection does none the less have a direct effect on the good reputation of Netherlands financial services.' As such, 'maintaining the good reputation of the national financial sector may therefore constitute an imperative reason of public interest capable of justifying restrictions on the freedom to provide financial services.'[97]

The Court recognized that there may be two sides to that particular coin, since it is not oblivious to the fact that also persons may be affected in both Member States. Advocate General Jacobs was, in that respect, even more explicit than the Court. He held that 'there can be no doubt that the concern to protect consumers and the concern to safeguard the reputation of the Netherlands securities markets may justify the imposition of restriction on the free movement of services'.[98] In particular, those concerns could not be separated 'since unfair or abusive practices against foreign investors by financial intermediaries established in the Netherlands may well affect adversely the integrity of the Netherlands financial markets'.[99] This interconnection between extraterritorial and territorial aspects of public interests was more explicitly recognized in the public security cases *Richardt*, and *Werner and Leifer. Richardt*, dealt with the seizure by Luxembourgish authorities of goods destined for the Soviet Union. In that case, the Court held that 'the concept of public security within the meaning of Article 36 of the Treaty covers both a Member State's internal security and its external security'.[100] In *Werner*, concerning the export restriction of dual-use goods to Libya, the Court held that

> it is difficult to draw a hard and fast distinction between foreign-policy and security-policy considerations. Moreover, as [Advocate General Jacobs] observes in point 46 [of his Opinion], it is becoming increasingly less possible to look at the security of a State in isolation, since it is closely linked to the security of the international community at large, and of its various components. So, the risk of a

97 Case C-384/93, *Alpine Investments BV v Minister van Financiën* [1995] ECR I-1141, paras. 43–44

98 Case C-384/93, *Alpine Investments BV v Minister van Financiën* [1995] ECR I-1141, Opinion of AG Jacobs, para. 69

99 Ibid., para. 77

100 Case C-367/89, *Richardt v "Les Accessoires Scientifiques"* [1991] ECR I-4621, para. 22

serious disturbance to foreign relations or to peaceful coexistence of nations may affect the security of a Member State.[101]

Similarly, the Court implicitly rejected Advocate General Trabucchi's suggestion in *Dassonville* that the measure in question was aimed at protecting British intellectual property and could not be upheld because Article 36 TFEU could only be relied upon to protect 'national' interests defined as individual rights and economic interests falling under the 'own sphere of interest'.[102] However, trademark rights and geographic indications also function as an indication to the consumer of what they are buying and where the product comes from, and as such, seek to inform consumers located within the territory of the regulating Member State.[103] The Court implicitly rejected the approach taken by the Advocate General in *Commission v. Belgium (Dassonville II)*.[104]

This point was made even more clearly by the Court in *Beele*. Dutch case-law prohibited the marketing of products that were slavish imitations of other products already marketed in the Netherlands. In *Beele*, this resulted in the protection of Swedish (not a Member State at the time) cable ducts against competition from German imitations. Following Advocate General Trabucchi, one could argue that there was absolutely no *Dutch* interest in protecting a Swedish manufacturer from German competition in the Netherlands. The Court ruled otherwise. It held that 'national case-law prohibiting the precise imitation of someone else's product which is likely to cause confusion may indeed protect consumers and promote fair trading'.[105]

Concerns over extraterritoriality, especially in relation to moral considerations, are therefore to a certain extent something which is in the eye of the beholder.[106] Any restriction imposed by a transnational

[101] Case C-70/94, *Fritz Werner Industrie-Ausrüstungen GmbH v Federal Republic of Germany* [1995] ECR I-3189, paras. 26–27

[102] Case 8/74, *Procureur du Roi v Benoît and Gustave Dassonville* [1974] ECR 855, Opinion of AG Trabucchi, para. 5

[103] William Cornish, *Intellectual Property: Omnipresent, Distracting, Irrelevant?* (Oxford: Oxford University Press, 2004), 89

[104] Case 2/78, *Commission v. Belgium* [1979] ECR 1762, paras. 13–17; see however later Case 251/78, *Denkavit Futtermittel v. Minister für Ernährung, Landwirtschaft und Forsten des Landes Nordrehein Westfalen* [1979] ECR 2269; Case C-205/89, *Commission v. Greece* [1991] ECR I-1361

[105] Case 6/81, *BV Industrie Diensten Groep v J.A. Beele Handelmaatschappij BV* [1982] ECR 707, para. 9

[106] L.J. Ankersmit, J.C. Lawrence, and G.T. Davies, 'Diverging EU and WTO Perspectives On Extraterritorial Process Regulation' (2012) 21 *Minnesota Journal of International Law Online*, 58

adjudicator on the importing country's right to determine its own moral preferences and standards or attempt to solve trans-boundary or global problems is an unjustified constraint on the right to regulate its markets within its own territory, which goes well beyond prohibiting discriminatory or protectionist measures. To complicate the picture even further, a Member State may not have any extraterritorial effects in mind with its regulation, but is merely trying to satisfy demands of its own population to properly inform consumers about the production methods employed for certain products. Consumer protection, here, clearly has a link with the territory of the regulating Member State, yet at the same time can produce substantial extraterritorial effects if consumers in one country care about a process-based issue enough to have a significant impact on the patterns of trade between Member States.

An adjudicator deciding on the legal permissibility of process-based measures under free movement law not only needs to walk on this globalized tight-rope of competing claims of self-determination, but also is required to find an adequate balance between social and environmental protection and the free movement of goods. A judgment striking down process-based measures because they are extraterritorial inevitably results in a reduced level of environmental or social protection, while a judgment endorsing such measures results in creating additional barriers to trade, through a multiplicity of production standards prevailing in the EU and third countries. In fact, the choice made by an adjudicator to strike down or not measures on grounds of 'extraterritoriality' highlights a choice over whether the free movement of goods provisions are about uniting national markets in a 'single market having the characteristics of a domestic market' or being intrusive on regulatory autonomy of Member States more generally in favour of free trade within the internal market.[107] Furthermore, a choice to permit labelling on consumer protection grounds because there is a clearer link with the territory instead of an outright ban reflects a political preference for individual choice over collective decision making. This can be less effective, in particular, if the group of consumers of a product is ignorant or indifferent over process-based concerns, while the population at large does care about the issue.

In addition, one may wonder why the Court would strike down a measure that serves a public interest recognized in the EU Treaties,

[107] Case 207/83, *Commission v. United Kingdom (origin marking)* [1985] ECR 1201, para. 17

international agreements, or secondary legislation. The limitation of public interests into rigid territorial compartments without taking into account the broader European interest at stake would appear to be contrary to an international organization which aspires to achieve more than simply trade liberalization. Indeed, as Section 3.2 has shown, the existence of a European interest is often explicitly mentioned by the Court in condoning measures with extraterritorial protective effects. This is not to say that process-based measures which result in extraterritorial social and environmental protection should always be permitted if such measures contribute to a goal of the EU itself. Rather, the proxy 'extraterritoriality' seen in an absolute sense seems to be ill-fitted to address legitimate objections that one may have against such measures. The core problem is not so much that process-based measures might have the effect of protecting social and environmental interests abroad-any measure liberalizing or restricting trade has effects in other countries. 'Extraterritoriality', 'non-interference', or 'sovereignty' are therefore problematic concepts in an increasingly interdependent world, especially if one uses these concepts in a trade context where there is always a relationship between two countries which are not committed to full autarky.

Just as denying market access has consequences in other parts of the world, granting market access may equally have an impact by, for example, incentivizing others that harm the environment or provide funds for those that do not respect core labour standards. Nonetheless, there remains the issue whether a Member State can decide on such problems unilaterally, without the cooperation or consent of the people or governments of countries that may be affected (positively or negatively) by such rules. It is this issue which the next chapter seeks to address.

4 Unilateralism within the Free Movement of Goods

Introduction

As we have seen in Chapter 2, most Member State process-based measures fall within the scope of EU free movement law and to the extent that such measures fall within the scope of Article 34 TFEU, they will require justification either on the basis of case-law based justifications accepted by the ECJ or by reliance on the derogations in Article 36 TFEU. In addition, reliance on public interests to justify other restrictions to the free movement of goods, such as tax and public procurement measures, occurs within EU tax and public procurement law.

Chapter 3 discussed the extent to which free movement law imposes or should impose any territorial limitations to such justifications. The chapter suggested that extraterritoriality as a concept to discipline process-based measures in free movement law is neither unequivocally supported in the case-law of the ECJ, nor is it a desirable or suitable means to constrain Member State regulatory autonomy.

However, process-based measures face a second challenge in free movement law: unilateralism. Process-based measures can be seen as problematic, because they are unilateral and not multilateral solutions to transnational problems. Process-based measures therefore face a legitimacy challenge because they were developed without input by the targeted population, and are applied to them without their consent.[1] Unilateral regulation raises legitimacy issues because, when process-based measures fail to take into account the opinions of the people they seek to regulate, these measures violate basic principles of democratic

[1] Bernhard Jansen, 'The Limits of Unilateralism From a European Perspective' (2000) 11 *European Journal of International Law*, 309; Philip Sands, "Unilateralism', Values, and International Law' (2000) 11 *European Journal of International Law*, 291

process.[2] Unilateral regulation also affects legitimacy in terms of *outcome*, because the rules are not tailored to the individuals and contexts they regulate, and are thus not guaranteed to be maximally effective.

These 'unilateralism' arguments differ from the 'extraterritoriality' arguments discussed previously because they do not try to pigeonhole problems into watertight territorial compartments, but rather focus on the *processes and outcomes* of addressing transnational problems. The concern here is that the preferences of the parties affected by process regulation in other countries are not included in the decision-making process, and that the individuals regulated do not have an adequate say in the outcomes.

This chapter aims at investigating how EU free movement law on derogations and justifications deals with the challenge posed by unilateralism. Is there a legal obligation within free movement law to cooperate, consult, or in other ways take into account interests of or within other Member States and third countries when designing and applying process-based measures to imported goods from other Member States?

On the one hand, one might think that a Union fundamentally based on cooperation between Member States is hostile towards attempts by Member States to regulate production throughout the Union through market access unilaterally and without the consent or cooperation of other Member States. The proper route seems to be to agree on production standards multilaterally, either at EU level or at international level, instead of conditioning access to its market on the basis of standards determined by the importing Member State alone. One of the fundamental principles of EU law is, in that respect, that of sincere cooperation between Member States and the EU institutions which requires them to assist each other in carrying out tasks which flow from the Treaties.[3]

[2] Fritz W. Scharpf, Governing in Europe: effective and democratic? (Oxford University Press, 1999) 7. See also Sébastien Mena and Guido Palazzo, 'Input and Output Legitimacy of Multi-Stakeholder Initiatives' (2012) 22 *Business Ethics Quarterly*, 527; J. H. H. Weiler, 'In the Face of Crisis: Input Legitimacy, Output Legitimacy and the Political Messianism of European Integration' (2012) 34 *Journal of European Integration*, 825; Mijke Boedeltje and Juul Cornips, 'Input and Output Legitimacy in Interactive Governance' (No. NIG2-01) http://repub.eur.nl/pub/1750

[3] Article 4 (3) TEU. The principle of sincere cooperation also requires Member States to 'take any appropriate measure, general or particular, to ensure fulfilment of the obligations arising out of the Treaties or resulting from the acts of the institutions of the Union' and to 'facilitate the achievement of the Union's tasks and refrain from any measure which could jeopardise the attainment of the Union's objectives'.

On the other hand, the function of Article 36 TFEU is explicitly to allow Member States to unilaterally protect the public interests contained therein pending EU rules to protect the matter collectively. Equally, recourse to mandatory requirements by Member States is permitted 'in the absence of common rules' protecting the interest which the Member State seeks to protect.[4] Such interests are therefore not dependent on collective action at EU level, but can be protected *pending* EU action. EU free movement law is thus not based on free trade without unilateral rules protecting interests nor free trade with collective rules protecting *common* public interests, but rather, free trade with collective rules protecting common public interests the existence of obstacles to trade insofar as Member States enact legislation to protect public interests. As the Court stated in *Cassis*, 'obstacles to movement within the [EU] resulting from disparities between the national laws relating to the marketing of the products in question *must be accepted* in so far as those provisions may be recognized as being necessary in order to satisfy mandatory requirements'.[5]

Regulating the internal market is, after all, a *shared* competence, something that Member States are entitled to regulate pending EU action and in conformity with primary law.[6] The EU trade system thus permits frontrunners and regulatory leadership in environmental and social protection and does not condemn them. This is not surprising, since there is no *legal* means which permit Member States to initiate legislation that seeks to protect the environment or workers at EU level. With the right to propose secondary legislation at EU level firmly in the hands of the Commission, Member States have no formal legal means to initiate regulation of production standards consensually. Thus, while one might prefer European cooperation to address the issues process-based measures seek to address, Member States are, legally speaking, not able to initiate such cooperation.

This chapter identifies three main legal obstacles process-based measures face within free movement law that are linked to the challenge of unilateralism. The first legal obstacle is harmonization adopted in the context of the proper functioning of the internal market. Such rules seek to establish a level playing field, and unilateral derogation from them by applying more stringent rules is only possible if those rules do not

[4] Case 120/78, *Rewe-Zentral AG v. Bundesmonopolverwaltung für Branntwein (Cassis de Dijon)* [1979] ECR 650, para. 8
[5] Ibid., emphasis added [6] Article 4 (2) (a) TFEU

protect the interest relied upon, only results in partial harmonization, or by use of the limited possibilities in Article 114 (4–9) TFEU.[7]

The second legal obstacle is the principle of mutual recognition. In applying technical rules, Member States need to take into account whether imported products comply with functionally equivalent rules of other Member States. This implies that Member States cannot require a product to comply with a process-based measure, by requiring a certificate of conformity for instance, if that product has already been produced according to functionally equivalent production rules in the Member State of origin.

The third and final legal obstacle is the principle of sincere cooperation in relation to the *enforcement* of existing EU rules on production within the EU. If the EU already has production rules in place, a Member State cannot condition market access upon compliance with those EU rules. Member States must, in full mutual respect, trust each other in the fulfilment of the tasks that flow from the Treaties. The EU legal system has remedies in place to enforce compliance by a Member State that does not comply with agreed production standards, and therefore economic 'retaliation' is not an option. However, the picture is more complicated when other Member States consent to such process-based measures or where third countries are involved.

This chapter will assess these three legal obstacles in turn (Sections 4.1 to 4.3) and argue that outside these constraints, unilaterally deciding on the level of social and environmental protection (going beyond the level of protection determined at EU level) is in principle permitted under free movement law, especially if such rules contribute to a wider goal that the EU seeks to aspire itself (Section 4.4).

4.1 More Stringent Rules in the Context of Common Rules for the Operation of the Internal Market

The first legal obstacle process-based measures face within free movement law that is linked to the challenge of unilateralism is harmonization adopted in the context of the proper functioning of the internal market or in the context of the common organization of an agricultural market. Such harmonized rules seek to establish a level playing field and

[7] See for a detailed discussion of these exceptions Nicolas De Sadeleer, *EU Environmental Law and the Internal Market* (Oxford: Oxford University Press, 2014), 415–438

unilateral derogation from them by applying more stringent rules is only possible if those rules do not protect the interest relied upon, only results in partial harmonization, or by use of the limited possibilities in Article 114 (4–9) TFEU.

Rules adopted on the basis of these internal market legal bases aim at approximating the laws of the Member States in order to prevent obstacles to trade or distortions of competition arising from them. This means that process-based measures can no longer be enacted if the EU has adopted rules which protect the same interest of the process-based measure in question. If it would be otherwise, the competence to regulate the internal market would be meaningless. The goal of internal market legislation is not only approximating laws to reach a common level of protection, but also by doing so removing obstacles to trade among Member States. This goal would be affected if Member States could still rely on the specific derogations and justifications to enact more stringent rules than in place at EU level.[8]

As a consequence, the Court denies Member States the possibility to rely on the derogations of Article 36 or mandatory requirements for the specific objective of the EU rules in question. For the ECJ, the use of such derogations and justifications is precluded where secondary rules provide for harmonization of the measures necessary to achieve the specific objective which would be furthered by recourse to those derogations or justifications.[9] This means that if the EU has already adopted rules on the protection of the welfare of calves in the context of the common organization of the market – rules which explicitly aim to level the playing field – Member States can no longer enact process-based measures to set higher standards for the welfare of calves and which result in trade restrictions.

This is different for rules adopted on other legal bases. If rules are adopted in the context of another EU policy, for instance, under the heading of environmental protection, process-based measures should be permitted to the extent that they strengthen the level of protection set by the EU rules and comply with EU law and the free movement of

[8] Robert Schütze, 'Supremacy Without Pre-emption? The Very Slowly Emergent Doctrine of Community Pre-emption' (2006) 43 *Common Market Law Review*, 1023, at 1041

[9] Case C-99/01, *Criminal Proceedings against Gottfried Linhart and Hans Biffl* [2002] ECR I-9375, paras. 24–25; Case C-1/96, *Compassion In World Farming* [1998] ECR I-1251, para. 47, and Case C-112/97, *Commission v Italy* [1999] ECR I-1821, para. 54; for mandatory requirements see Case C-102/96, *Commission v Germany* [1998] ECR I-6871, para. 21 and Case C-99/01, *Criminal Proceedings against Gottfried Linhart and Hans Biffl* [2002] ECR I09375, paras. 24–25

goods provisions in particular. The logic of this is that protecting the environment does not depend on creating a level playing field, and therefore more stringent rules do not necessarily undermine the rules adopted at EU level. As such, if a Member State wishes to go beyond the level of protection set at EU level this is not necessarily problematic from an environmental perspective. As long as those rules are not contrary to the rules in place or undermine their proper functioning, there is no legal problem if such rules create trade barriers between Member States. The same reasoning applies for consumer protection, social policy, and public health. This is supported by the Treaty texts which state that only minimum harmonization is possible in those areas.[10]

This bifurcated approach is reflected in the case-law of the ECJ. If rules are adopted with the primary aim of removing obstacles to trade, as is the case with EU rules adopted for the common organization of agricultural markets or for the proper functioning of the internal market, the Court is less willing to accept more stringent measures adopted by Member States that result in obstacles to trade between Member States. If, on the other hand, rules are adopted of which the primary aim is the protection of the environment or consumer protection, the Court is more willing to accept obstacles to trade that may result out of more stringent measures. The Court's case-law even suggests that it is willing to endorse extraterritorial effects of the higher level of protection, since such additional measures further contribute to the goals set by the EU rules and strengthen the EU legal regime in place. As Dougan notes,

> one must conduct a contextual analysis to determine whether the relative emphasis of [EU] policy falls on free movement and regulatory uniformity, or on social protection and differentiation. Where minimum harmonisation occurs within a common organization of a market, the Community legislature must implicitly have conceived of its potential impact in the least economically disruptive terms possible and to have viewed the attainment of the relevant welfare imperatives as a goal entrusted primarily to the [EU] rather than the Member States (CIWF). By contrast measures adopted under the specific Treaty basses on consumer or environmental protection are concerned primarily with social regulation, not economic integration and one might expect that the Court would take a more serious view of the need for high standards of welfare protection and a

[10] A Member State may introduce or maintain more stringent measures on the basis of Articles 153 (4), 168 (4) (a), 169 (3), 193 TFEU. This requirement is not explicitly mentioned in Article 168 (4) (a), but seems to be nonetheless the case see Case C-421/09, *Humanplasma GmbH v Republik Österreich* [2010] ECR I-12869

correspondingly more generous approach to the role of the Member States in attaining it, interpreting their rather trite minimum harmonization clauses accordingly.[11]

The issue is most apparent in the case of minimum harmonization. In the case of minimum harmonization, EU rules allow Member States to adopt more stringent rules. However, the Court's case-law suggests that in the context of internal market rules, more stringent rules can only be applied to domestic industry and not to imported products, making it no longer possible to apply process-based measures to imported products that comply with the rules of that particular type of EU legislation. On the other hand, more stringent rules may be applied to imported products if the objective of secondary legislation is environmental protection, for example. This can be seen by contrasting the judgment in *Compassion in World Farming* with the judgments in *Aher-Waggon* and *EU-Wood-Trading.*[12]

As explained above, *Compassion in World Farming* concerned the question as to whether the United Kingdom could restrict exports of veal calves to other Member States which used the veal crate system which was banned in the United Kingdom but permitted in other Member States. Directive 91/629/EEC laying down minimum standards for the protection for calves, adopted on the basis of the current Article 43 TFEU, provided for a level of animal welfare protection lower than the rules in place in the United Kingdom. Moreover, the Directive allowed for generous time limits which permitted postponement of the implementation of the Directive. However, the Directive did permit Member States to take more stringent measures. Article 11 (2) of the Directive provided that 'Member States may, in compliance with the general rules of the Treaty, maintain or apply *within their territories* stricter provisions for the protection of calves than those laid down in this Directive'.[13] The Directive thus maintained a territorial limitation with respect to more stringent measures for the protection of calves. However, strictly speaking, the export prohibition applied to calves present within the territory of the United Kingdom.

[11] Michael Dougan, 'Minimum Harmonization and the Internal Market' (2000) 37 *Common Market Law Review*, 853–885, 876–877

[12] Case C-1/96, *The Queen v Minister of Agriculture, Fisheries and Food, ex parte Compassion in World Farming Limited* (n 9); Case C-389/96, *Aher-Waggon GmbH v Bundesrepublik Deutschland* [1998] ECR I-4473; Case C-277/02 *EU-Wood-Trading GmbH v Sonderabfall-Management-Gesellschaft Rheinland-Pfalz mbH* [2004] ECR I-11957

[13] Council Directive 91/629/EEC of 19 November 1991 laying down minimum standards for the protection of calves OJ 1991 No. L340/28, emphasis added

The ECJ, however, chose to interpret this provision as well as the Directive as a whole in the context of the goal of the Directive: to ensure that obstacles to trade between Member States were removed by imposing uniform animal welfare standards for goods traded.[14]

The ECJ found that the Directive exhaustively laid down minimum standards for the well-being of calves. It was thus only permissible to take more stringent measures in so far as the Directive permitted this. As to the interpretation of Article 11 (2) of the Directive, which permitted Member States to take more stringent measures, the Court was clearly influenced by the need to ensure the proper functioning of the common organization of the market for calves and related products. The Court interpreted the sentence 'Member States may, in compliance with the general rules of the Treaty, maintain or apply *within their territories* stricter provisions for the protection of calves' to mean that Member States may only take measures 'which are limited to strictly territorial boundaries, [and] may relate only to cattle-farms falling within the jurisdiction of the Member State in question'.[15] The exception thus did not relate to the export of calves. The reason was that would the United Kingdom be permitted under Article 11 (2) of the Directive to prohibit exports for reasons relating to the welfare of calves, this 'would strike at the harmonization achieved by the Directive'.

It seems that the primary consideration of the Court was to enable trade in goods that complied with the minimum requirements imposed by the Directive. As Dougan notes 'the wider context of Article 11 (2) was one in which free movement and regulatory uniformity, rather than social welfare and regulatory diversity, were thought to demand primary consideration'.[16] If the Court had ruled otherwise, the objective of removing obstacles to trade would have been severely compromised, as Member States would be able to impose stricter standards than those contained in the Directive to imported and exported products. On the other hand, Article 11 (2) explicitly permitted Member States to do so. The Court thus had to balance the interest of free movement against the interest of animal welfare protection, and it chose to give preference in this respect to the interest of free movement. Of course, the Directive did lay down minimum standards for the protection of the welfare of calves,

[14] Case C-1/96, *Compassion in World Farming Limited* (n 9), para 44

[15] Case C-1/96, *Compassion in World Farming Limited* (n 9), para 59

[16] Michael Dougan, 'Minimum Harmonization and the Internal Market'

and this interest was also to a limited extent safeguarded beyond the minimum requirements of the Directive by permitting Member States to go beyond the level of protection set with respect to cattle-farms falling within the jurisdiction of the regulating Member State. Nonetheless, such measures are economically less viable if other Member States maintain lower levels of protection.[17]

Compassion in World Farming is in line with other cases in which secondary legislation adopted in the context of an internal market goal and which provide for minimum harmonization was interpreted in favour of free movement rules, permitting Member States to apply more stringent standards to domestic production only and not to goods exported or imported to the extent that the matter was regulated by the secondary rules in question. The most well-known case in that respect is *Gallaher*, in which the Court held that the United Kingdom could apply certain more stringent health protection measures to its domestic industry, but not to imported cigarettes from other Member States complying with the minimum requirements imposed by Directive 89/622/EEC on the labelling of tobacco products.[18] The Directive in question had regulated minimum surface requirements to which warning signs need to be fixed (4%), whereas the UK rules went beyond those surface requirements. The ECJ found consequently that 'this interpretation of the provisions may imply less favourable treatment for national products in comparison with imported products and leaves in existence some inequalities in conditions of competition. However, those consequences are attributable to the degree of harmonization sought by the provisions in question, which lay down minimum requirements'.[19]

That being said, if secondary legislation adopted on the basis of internal market legislation only results in *partial* harmonization, Member State measures in those areas which have not been harmonized

[17] Moreover, as Munoz has noted, the Court did not address the issue of the extensive time periods allowed for Member States to postpone the implementation of the Directive. These derogations result in different levels of protection within the Member States, and the Court's decision to preclude recourse to Article 36 TFEU therefore punishes Member States that comply at an early stage with the Directive's animal welfare standards. See Rodolphe Munoz, 'Case C-1/96, The Queen v. Minister of Agriculture, Fisheries and food, ex parte Compassion in World Farming Limited. Judgment of 19 March 1998, [1998] ECR I-1251' (1999) 36 *Common Market Law Review*, 831, at 838

[18] Case C-11/92, *The Queen v Secretary of State for Health, ex parte Gallaher Ltd, Imperial Tobacco Ltd and Rothmans International Tobacco (UK) Ltd* [1993] ECR I-3545, para. 17

[19] Ibid., para 22

remain possible, even if this results in obstacles to trade.[20] In the recent judgments *Philip Morris* and *Canadian Oil Company Sweden*, the ECJ has been taking a more deferential approach than in relation to minimum harmonization in that respect. In *Philip Morris*, the ECJ indicated that whereas harmonized rules prevented Member States from prohibiting the marketing of tobacco products on grounds relating to the aspects of packaging harmonized by that Directive, it did not do so in relation to those aspects of packaging not harmonized by the Directive.[21] In *Canadian Oil Company Sweden*, the ECJ accepted that Member States could introduce registration requirements for imported chemicals in their territory in addition to the registration requirements under the REACH Regulation for those aspects not regulated by REACH.[22]

The difference between *Gallaher* and *Philip Morris* is that in Gallaher the additional Member State rules concerned something that was explicitly regulated by EU rules (minimum surface area containing a warning on packaging), whereas in *Philip Morris* the ECJ was referring to Member State measures that were not regulated in relation to tobacco products, such as plain packaging.[23] While a lot depends on the particularities of the harmonized rules in place, the ECJ's case-law suggests therefore that, for example, a Member State rule banning the marketing of dolphin-unsafe tuna could not be applied to imported products if EU rules already exhaustively regulated the marketing of dolphin-unsafe tuna. However, if EU rules only partially cover the marketing of dophin-safe tuna, for example, by only laying down such conditions for certain species, Member States may introduce additional rules for those products relating to the other species.

Gallaher and *Compassion in World Farming* can be contrasted with the Court's judgment in *Aher-Waggon* and *EU-Wood-Trading*. In *Aher-Wagon*, the Court had to decide on stricter environmental measures adopted in

[20] Case C-547/14, *Philip Morris Brands SARL and Others v Secretary of State for Health*, EU:C:2016:325, paras. 66–84. See also Protocol 25 of the Lisbon Treaty which states that '[w]ith reference to Article 2(2) of the Treaty on the Functioning of the European Union on shared competence, when the Union has taken action in a certain area, the scope of this exercise of competence only covers those elements governed by the Union act in question and therefore does not cover the whole area'.

[21] Case C-547/14, *Philip Morris Brands SARL and Others v Secretary of State for Health*, EU:C:2016:325, paras. 66–84

[22] Case C-472/14, *Canadian Oil Company Sweden AB and Anders Rantén v Riksåklagaren*, EU:C:2016:171, paras. 26–41

[23] See Case C-547/14, *Philip Morris Brands SARL and Others v Secretary of State for Health*, EU:C:2015:853, Opinion of AG Kokkott, paras. 105–120

the context of secondary environmental legislation which created obstacles to trade. Directive 83/206/EEC laid down minimum noise emission limits for aircraft and Germany had imposed more stringent standards.[24] As a result, Aher-Waggon could not register an imported aircraft, while already registered similar aircraft in Germany was exempted from the noise emission limits. Despite this, the Court accepted the justification on environmental grounds put forward by Germany, as 'limiting noise emissions from aircraft is the most effective and convenient means of combating the noise pollution which they generate'.[25] The Court was quite deferential towards Germany's discretion to apply stricter noise standards as it did not consider the exemption in the German rules for already registered aircraft (essentially a grandfathering clause) to be disproportionate.[26] As such, the Court permitted a Member State from unilaterally imposing stricter standards than the minimum agreed upon at EU level on imported products with the result of creating obstacles to trade within the EU. However, such stricter requirements clearly contribute to the primary objective of the Directive, which was to reduce environmental harm by limiting the amount of noise emissions throughout the EU.[27]

EU-Wood-Trading concerned objections raised by German authorities to a shipment of wood waste from Germany to Italy for recovery on the basis of Regulation 259/93 on shipments of waste.[28] While the Italian authorities did not oppose the shipments, the German authorities did on the basis that the planned recovery in Italy could not be carried out without endangering human health and the environment. In permitting the German authorities to do so, the Court emphasized the context and the objective of the Regulation.[29] In contrast to *Gallaher* and *Compassion in World Farming*, the Court accepted that obstacles to trade may arise out of such objections, but that they were permitted as long as they complied with the principle of proportionality.[30] Member States were thus entitled to object to shipments of waste according to criteria for the protection

[24] Council Directive 83/206/EEC of 21 April 1983 amending Directive 80/51/EEC on the limitation of noise emissions from subsonic aircraft OJ 1983 No. L117/15

[25] Case C-389/96, *Aher-Waggon GmbH v Bundesrepublik Deutschland* [1998] ECR I-4473, para. 21

[26] Ibid., paras. 22–23 [27] Ibid.

[28] Case C-277/02, *EU-Wood-Trading GmbH v Sonderabfall-Management-Gesellschaft Rheinland-Pfalz mbH* [2004] ECR I-11957

[29] Ibid., para. 34. The Court referred to its earlier judgment Case C-187/93, *Parliament v Council* [1994] ECR I-2857, paras. 22–23

[30] Ibid., para. 49

of human health and the environment that were stricter than those in the Member State of dispatch.[31]

A last point to be noted here is the Court's reluctance, in light of the forgoing, to accept derogations and justifications on grounds *other* than protected by rules adopted in the context of the functioning of the internal market. It is settled case-law of the Court that recourse to Article 36 TFEU is no longer possible where EU rules provide for harmonization of measures necessary to achieve the specific objective which would be furthered by reliance upon Article 36.[32] Equally, recourse to mandatory requirements is only possible 'in the absence of common rules' relating to the area covered by national rules.[33] If the harmonized rules therefore do not achieve the specific objective which the Member State is seeking to protect through a process-based measure, this case-law suggests that obstacles to trade might still be justified. However, the Court has been reluctant in accepting such derogations and justifications when the purpose of those rules is to remove obstacles to trade between Member States.

In *Compassion in World Farming*, the Court rejected the argument that public morality was a separate ground for justifying obstacles to trade than the protection of the life and health of animals. In principle, these two grounds for derogation are separate public interests, even with respect to animal welfare. Public morality is more about the perception of the public about certain objectionable things, such as cruelty to animals.[34] The protection of the health and life of animals is not necessarily connected with public morality, as measures can also be taken to prevent diseases from spreading in order to protect economic interests. It could have been argued, however, that the considerations underlying the

[31] Ibid., para. 54

[32] Case 148/78, *Criminal proceedings against Tullio Ratti* [1979] ECR 1629, para. 36; Case C-5/94, *The Queen v MAFF ex parte Hedley Lomas* [1996] ECR I-2553, para. 18; Case C-1/96, *Compassion in World Farming Limited* (n 9), para 47; Case C-350/97, *Wilfried Monsees and Unabhängiger Verwaltungssenat für Kärnten* [1999] ECR I- 2921, para. 24

[33] Case 120/78, *Rewe -Zentral AG v. Bundesmonopolverwaltung für Branntwein (Cassis de Dijon)* [1979] ECR 650, para. 8

[34] As de Witte has put it, 'moral or ethical norms ascribe a normative quality to at type of life, typically, as the reflection of a communal, political understanding of what is "good". They reflect first principles, which are essentially emotive knee-jerk reactions on question such as when life starts or ends, which range of action is considered morally "sinful", and how the State's obligations to look after the individual relate to the individual's own responsibility'. Floris de Witte, 'Sex, Drugs & EU Law: The Recognition of Moral and Ethical Diversity in EU Law' (2013) 50 *Common Market Law Review*, 1545, at 1547

Directive in question were related to a perception of the European public of how animal cruelty could be limited, while creating a level playing field throughout the EU as well as protecting economic interests of farmers which had invested in the veal crate system. But the Court did not see the need to distinguish public morality from the protection of health and life of animals, simply stating that 'in reality, public policy and public morality are not being invoked as a separate justification but are an aspect of the justification relating to the protection of animal health, which is the subject of the harmonising directive'.[35]

The outcome in *Compassion in World Farming* would have probably been the same, as the Directive's implicit aim was also based on moral concerns over animal cruelty (although there was no textual support for this in the Directive),[36] but the Court's reasoning underpins the urge to ensure the smooth operation of the internal market and demonstrates reluctance to consider certain considerations as separate from the considerations underpinning secondary legislation adopted to remove obstacles to trade.

A similar reluctance to that in *Compassion in World Farming* can be found in the Court's judgment in *Commission v. Poland (GMOs)*.[37] In that case, the Court rejected the Polish claim that a ban on GMOs in Poland was justified on grounds of public morality, because (1) it was not a 'separate justification' but an aspect relating to the protection of human health and environment which was the objective of Directive 2001/18 on the release of genetically modified organisms, and (2) Poland had failed to demonstrate in any event that the ban was adopted on those grounds.[38]

[35] Case C-1/96, *Compassion in World Farming Limited* (n 9), para. 66. The Advocate General, by contrast, did consider a derogation on grounds of the protection of public morality still possible. After noting that that concept should be interpreted with the necessary judicial restraint ('it is no part of the Court's task to judge values characterizing the public morality of a Member State and which are therefore quite specific to it'), allowing Member States the necessary discretion, the Advocate General considered that 'the fact that a Member State should consider that harm unjustifiably caused to the life or health of domestic animals, even for economic purposes, through the use of a particular rearing method is a matter of public morality in that State does not appear to be manifestly contrary to Article 36'. See Case C-1/96, *The Queen v Minister of Agriculture, Fisheries and Food, ex parte Compassion in World Farming Ltd.* [1998] ECR I-1251, Opinion of AG Léger, para. 104

[36] The Directive merely refers to a European Parliament resolution: European Parliament Resolution on animal welfare policy OJ 1987 No. C76/185

[37] Case C-165/08, *Commission v Poland* [2009] ECR I-6843

[38] In particular, Poland maintained that the ban was 'inspired by the Christian and Humanist ethical principles adhered to by the majority of the Polish people'. Those

The ECJ did not rule out the possibility of relying on Article 36 TFEU to justify restrictions of trade on grounds other than pursued by EU rules already in place. It simply held that Poland had failed to demonstrate that the rules in question pursued religious and ethical objectives both as an independent ground for justification as well as an aspect related to the protection of the environment and human health. The Court first denied that Poland had 'properly established' that the 'true purpose' of the rules in question was to protect public morality as such.[39] In particular the general statements Poland made in this regard were insufficient, as well as the 'references to fears regarding the environment and public health and to the strong opposition to GMOs manifested by the Polish people' and resolutions adopted by regional assemblies rejecting the use of GMOs. The Court concluded from this that 'public morality is not really being invoked as a separate justification, but as an aspect of the justification relating to protection of human health and the environment, which is precisely the concern of Directive 2001/18 in the present context'.

The Court continued by rejecting reliance on Article 36 TFEU if the justification involved was not a separate, but an aspect of a justification which was part of the objective of secondary rules. Reliance upon the views of a section of public opinion was therefore insufficient to unilaterally challenge the Directive in question, and Poland had in any event failed to establish that the rules in question were in fact adopted on the basis of religious or ethical considerations. The Court dismissed the arguments put forward by Poland that Polish society attaches great importance to Christian and Roman Catholic values and that Polish parliamentarians called for adherence to those values at the time the contested rule was adopted. According to Poland, parliamentarians were more likely to base their choices for the adaptation of rules on ethical and religious grounds than on the basis of complex scientific assessments relating to environmental protection. The Court simply stated that this was not 'sufficient', especially because Poland had in an earlier stage of the procedure tried to defend the rules on the basis of environmental protection and the precautionary principle in particular.[40]

principles opposed GMOs, firstly, because they transformed living organisms into material objects which are the subject of intellectual property rights, second, because GMO technology is contrary to the quest for harmony between man and nature, and lastly, because the reduction of living organisms to the level of products for purely commercial ends undermines the foundations of society. See Case C-165/08 *Commission v Poland* [2009] ECR I-6843, paras 18–21, 30–31, 41

[39] Ibid., para. 53 [40] Ibid., para. 59

The Court was clearly very hesitant to accept any rules adopted by Poland which would compromise the functioning of the collective rules adopted at EU level. At EU level (in which, notably, Poland at the time could not participate) the necessary compromises were made to reach the level of protection agreed upon in order to create a level playing field throughout the EU and remove obstacles to trade in GMO products. Unilateral deviation from such an attempt to create a level playing field for a particular group of products is thus clearly problematic if the purpose of positive integration through approximation of laws is to remove technical barriers to trade. Nonetheless, it remains possible that trade restrictions result out of a public interest that was not taken into account in the harmonized rules: product standards for a particular product might be regulated at EU level for consumer protection purposes, but environmental characteristics of products might not have been the subject of those rules. It should remain open, therefore, for Member States to regulate products for reasons that are not the subject of EU rules. This is essentially recognized by the Court when it states that Article 36 TFEU 'cannot be applied where [EU] directives provide for harmonisation of the measures necessary *to achieve the specific objective which would be furthered by reliance upon it*'.[41] The Polish ban might therefore have been permitted under free movement law if it could have made a better case that the ban was primarily the result of ethical concerns by the Polish people, which potentially would have been possible if Poland had attempted to justify the restriction on ethical considerations from the beginning, as well as provided clearer evidence that the Polish legislature indeed adopted the measures for those reasons.

Member States may therefore encounter legal difficulties if they wish to adopt process-based measures which have already been subject to harmonization at EU level in the context of the proper functioning of the internal market. The fundamental purpose of such rules is, at the very least, to remove 'some' obstacles to trade.[42] Process-based rules by Member States are, in principle, no longer possible if EU rules lay down production requirements, or production requirements to be met by

[41] Case C-319/05, *Commission v. Germany* [2007] ECR I-9811 para. 82; Case C-102/96, *Commission v Germany* [1998] ECR I-6871, para. 21; Case C-99/01, *Criminal Proceedings against Gottfried Linhart and Hans Biffl* (n 9), para 24; Case C-1/96, *Compassion in World Farming Limited* (n 9), para. 47; Case C-350/97, *Wilfried Monsees and Unabhängiger Verwaltungssenat für Kärnten* [1999] ECR I- 2921 para. 24

[42] Case C-547/14, *Philip Morris Brands SARL and Others v Secretary of State for Health*, EU: C:2016:325, para. 81

goods, and the process-based rule lays down different or more stringent rules for products on aspects covered by EU rules and for the same purpose as those EU rules. Such rules seek to establish a level playing field, and unilateral derogation from them by applying more stringent rules is only possible if those rules do not protect the interest relied upon, only results in partial harmonization, or by use of the limited possibilities in Article 114 (4–9) TFEU.[43]

Moreover, the ECJ is suspicious of Member States invoking public interest grounds different than the purpose of the EU rules in question, and requires Member States to unequivocally demonstrate that the national rule serves a different purpose than the EU rule already in place.

On the other hand, to the extent that a process-based measure regulates different aspects than an already existing EU rule and the EU rule only results in partial harmonization, Member States can, in principle, still enact process-based measures. This equally holds true to the extent that such process-based rules serve different objectives than EU rules. Thus, if the EU food safety rules apply to tuna, Member States may still apply rules to tuna on animal welfare grounds. Lastly, EU measures adopted on the basis of different legal bases than those related to the internal market do not impose the same constraints as internal market legislation, because their objective is not to facilitate trade within the EU.

4.2 The Principle of Mutual Recognition

The second legal obstacle process-based measures face within free movement law that is linked to the challenge of unilateralism is the principle of mutual recognition. Despite the permissibility, in principle, of unilaterally adopting process-based measures in the context of regulating the internal market by Member States, there are limits to applying technical rules seeking environmental or social protection on imported goods. There is a certain inherent hostility in the EU towards regulatory blindness for a diversity of solutions employed in other Member States to the substance of the problem underlying process-based measures. One of the cornerstones of free movement law is the principle of mutual recognition.[44] Goods 'lawfully produced and marketed in another Member

[43] See for a detailed discussion of these exceptions Sadeleer, *EU Environmental Law and the Internal Market*

[44] Case 120/78, *Rewe-Zentral AG v. Bundesmonopolverwaltung für Branntwein (Cassis de Dijon)* [1979] ECR 650; JHH Weiler, 'Mutual Recognition, Functional Equivalence and

State' are presumed to comply with the technical regulations of the Member State of import, unless that Member State can demonstrate that it has sufficiently good reasons to apply its technical regulations to the imports in question. The application of the principle of mutual recognition has not only given a strong impetus to the completion of the internal market – by reducing the technical barriers to trade encountered by producers marketing products in multiple jurisdictions – but has also required Member State authorities to be fundamentally more 'outward-looking' in the design and application of their technical regulations. Member State authorities can no longer unilaterally apply their technical regulations with complete disregard of the legislative history of an imported product in another Member State: if an imported product already meets functionally equivalent regulations in the Member State of production, the authorities are required to take this into account in their assessment whether it is necessary to apply the technical rules to the imported product in question.

The principle of mutual recognition is, therefore, fundamentally a principle which is based on cooperation and mutual trust and not on unilateralism: the principle of sincere cooperation is at the core of the principle of mutual recognition: Member States are 'under a duty to assist in bringing about a relaxation of the controls existing in intra-[EU] trade'.[45] What the principle of sincere cooperation adds to mutual recognition is the obligation of the importing Member State to have a certain openness in its technical regulations, in the sense that the Member State should take into account the legislative history of the product in order to determine whether the standards met by the

Harmonization in the Evolution of the European Common Market and the WTO' in Fiorella Kostoris and Padoa Schioppa (eds.), *The Principle of Mutual Recognition in the European Integration Process* (London: Palgrave Macmillan 2005), 25–84; A Mattera 'Principle of Mutual Recognition and Respect for National, Regional and Local Identities and Traditions' in Fiorella Kostoris and Padoa Schioppa (eds.), *The Principle of Mutual Recognition in the European Integration Process* (London: Palgrave Macmillan 2005), 1; A Mattera, 'L' article 30 du traité CEE, la jurisprudence «Cassis de Dijon» et le principle de la reconnaissaince mutuelle' [1992] *Revue du Marché Unique Européen*, 13; Kenneth A. Armstrong, 'Mutual Recognition' in Catherine Barnard and Joanne Scott (eds.), *The Law of the Single European Market: Unpacking the Premises* (Hart Publishing, 2002), 225; see more critically Gareth Davies, 'Is Mutual Recognition an Alternative to Harmonisation: Lessons on Trade and Tolerance of Diversity from the EU' in Ortino and Bartels (eds.), *Regional Trade Agreements and the WTO Legal System* (Oxford University Press, 2006) 265; Laurens Ankersmit, 'What if Cassis de Dijon were Cassis de Quebec? The Assimilation of Goods of Third Country Origin in the Internal Market' (2013) 50 *Common Market Law Review*, 1387

45 Case 188/84, *Commission v France* [1986] ECR 419, para.16

product are equivalent to its own.[46] It should not only trust other Member States' administrative procedures, such as conformity assessment procedures carried out, but also maintain a certain openness towards the recognition of functionally equivalent standards set by other Member States.

Thus, as Armstrong notes,

> the principle of mutual recognition seeks to manage market access under conditions of regulatory pluralism by negotiating between the application of home and host state regulatory controls. Mutual recognition requires that the regulatory history of a product, service or worker acquired in the home state cannot be ignored when it comes to considering what legitimate regulatory controls may be applied in the host state.[47]

This 'other regarding' nature of the principle is exemplified in *Bouchera*, where the ECJ found that, while Member States may require prior approval of products even if those products have been approved in another Member State, the principle of mutual trust between the authorities of the Member States requires the authorities of the importing Member State to take into account documentation from authorities of other Member States in assessing whether the product met the importing Member States' technical rules.[48]

Similarly, in cases such as *Biologische Producten* and *Harpegnies* concerning prior approval schemes of products by the authorities, the Court noted that 'the authorities of the Member States are nevertheless required *to assist in bringing about a relaxation of the controls existing in intra-Community trade*'.[49] In *Foie gras* the Court went even further. Here, the Court required the *legislature* of Member States to be 'other-regarding' in general when drafting new technical rules by requiring the legislature to introduce a mutual recognition clause.[50]

[46] Armstrong, 'Mutual Recognition', 225, at 231–232 [47] Ibid., at 230

[48] Case 25/88, *Criminal proceedings against Esther Renée Bouchara, née Wurmser, and Norlaine SA* [1989] ECR 1105, para. 18

[49] Case C-400/96, *Criminal proceedings against Jean Harpegnies* [1998] ECR I-5121

[50] Case C-184/96, *Commission v France (foie gras)* [1998] ECR I-6197, para. 28. However, in subsequent cases the Court has been more nuanced, focussing on the necessity and proportionality of the measures at hand, and not so much deciding on a prima-facie breach of Articles 34 and 36 TFEU. See Case C-24/00, *Commission v. France* [2004] ECR I-1277, Case C-270/02, *Commission v. Italy* [2004] ECR I-1559 Stefan Enchelmaier 'Article 36: General', in P Oliver (ed.) *Oliver on Free Movement of Goods in the European Union* (Oxford: Hart Publishing, 2010), 215–312, at 231–235

The application of the principle of mutual recognition in a way that requires Member States to trust each other's activities – in this case the verification of composition of textile products – is a remarkable outcome that seems only possible if countries have chosen such a strong level of cohesion, integration, and cooperation. In the case of the EU, this is self-evident, and outside the EU this might be possible through mutual recognition agreements which set in place procedures and rules in order to reach such a level of mutual confidence.[51] The fact that the Court had no difficulty in deciding that the French authorities should trust results obtained from authorities of other Member States in *Bouchera* without there being any harmonization in place on the particular subject matter exemplifies the exceptional level of integration and cohesion achieved in the EU. It exemplifies how each Member State should trust another and his legislation, administrative and control activities. As Mattera has written:

> La mise en œuvre de ces principes constitue un facteur exceptionnel d' intégration et de cohésion entre États qui, malgré leurs traditions et leurs législations différentes, puisent à des sources culturelles et scientifiques communes, unis par des liens toujours plus étroits et soumis à un ordre juridique commun, à des institutions communes et à une juridiction supranationale dont les décisions s'appliquent à tous États. Il en découle que les garanties offertes sont telles qu'elles justifient – même en l'absence d'une réglementation commune – la confiance que chaque État membre est tenu d'accorder à l'État membre «voisin», à sa législation, à ses structures administratives, à ses organes et à ses procédures de contrôle.[52]

It is no different for process-based measures. In fact, the reference to 'lawfully *produced* and marketed' as a precondition to mutual recognition explicitly makes clear that rules relating to production are relevant for the assessment whether the imported goods comply with functionally equivalent legislation of the importing Member State. Thus, if a

[51] Mattera has held that 'The adoption of those principles [mutual confidence and mutual recognition] constitutes an exceptional element of cohesion and integration between States which, in spite of their different traditions and legislations, have common cultural and scientific roots and belong to the same Community, which is held together by links stemming from a common-body legislation, common institutions and a supranational jurisdiction within which rulings apply to all states.' See Mattera, 'Principle of Mutual Recognition and Respect for National, Regional and Local Identities and Traditions', 1

[52] A Mattera, 'L' article 30 du traité CEE, la jurisprudence «Cassis de Dijon» et le principle de la reconnaissaince mutuelle' [1992] *Revue du Marché Unique Européen*, 13, at 53–54

Member State enacts a process-based measure it is required to take into account the legislative history of the product related to the production of the goods in another Member State and it must demonstrate why the product in question does not meet a standard that is equivalent to its own. If a Member State already has certain animal welfare standards in place, for instance, an importing Member State must demonstrate the necessity of the process-based measure in relation to the standard in place in the exporting Member State. Only to the extent that the production rules in the home Member State are not equivalent to that of the host Member State will it be able to apply the process-based measure to the imported product.

The situation is more complex in relation to process-based measures applied to goods of third country origin in free circulation. The problem with process-based measures is that they address social and environmental concerns at the production stage of products, something that by definition has happened in that third country. An exporting Member State has not necessarily regulated that situation through its own process-based measures. In such a situation, Member State authorities might be faced with the question of whether they should recognize potentially equivalent production standards and documents attesting to this of third country governments, or whether application of their own rules is justifiable under free movement law.

This could result in two readings of the principle of mutual recognition at the justification stage in free movement law for process-based measures. The first is a more narrow 'European' view: as the principle of sincere cooperation only applies to relations among Member States and the Union, there is no need to recognize equivalent production standards in third countries. Nonetheless, to the extent that other Member States have process-based measures in place, Member State authorities are under a duty to take into account and accept process-based measures that comply with those process-based measures of the home state if such measures are equivalent to that of the importing Member State. This view is based on the principle of mutual recognition as a device for cooperation among Member States, and not a device for exclusively furthering trade liberalization within the EU internal market. An example would be where two Member States have slightly divergent but broadly equivalent labelling rules in place for 'fair trade' products. As soon as a product of third country origin is labelled according to the requirements of one Member State, it should in principle be permitted on the market of the other Member State as well.

However, if the product in question complies with certain fair trade standards of a third country and labelled accordingly, there is no obligation on Member State authorities to recognize such standards if they do not comply with the standards of one of the Member States themselves.

The second broader 'international' view would be that Member States are under an obligation to take into account the legislative history relating to the production of the product in a third country, in order to avoid unnecessary obstacles to trade within the EU. According to this view, applying a process-based measure to goods which comply with equivalent production rules elsewhere would simply be disproportionate and an unjustified hindrance to the proper functioning of the internal market. This view is based on a reading of the principle of mutual recognition as an obligation of Member States towards the Union to facilitate inter-state trade within the EU as much as possible. Mutual recognition understood under this reading is therefore more based on the principle of proportionality than inter-state cooperation. As a result, Member States would have to recognize 'fair trade' standards of third countries if they are equivalent to that of the importing Member State.

From an EU legal point of view, there seems to be more legal support for the first 'European' view, simply because the principle of sincere cooperation does not apply in relations between a Member State and a third country. One legal argument that could be employed in support of the broader 'international' view, however, is that Article 34 TFEU should be interpreted consistently with the EU's obligations under the WTO Agreements in line with the duty of consistent interpretation.[53] In particular, the WTO's national treatment standard and the rules under the TBT Agreement could be relevant in that regard.[54]

[53] Case C-61/94, *Commission v Germany* [1996] ECR I-3989, para. 52

[54] In particular Article III:4 GATT and Articles 2.1, 2.2, 2.7, and 5 TBT Agreement. See General Agreement on Tariffs and Trade 1994, (Marrakesh, Morocco, 15 April 1994), Marrakesh Agreement Establishing the World Trade Organization, Annex 1A, THE LEGAL TEXTS: THE RESULTS OF THE URUGUAY ROUND OF MULTILATERAL TRADE NEGOTIATIONS 17 (1999), 1867 U.N.T.S. 190, 33 I.L.M. 1153 (1994); Agreement on the Technical Barriers to Trade (Marrakesh, Morocco, 15 April 1994), Marrakesh Agreement Establishing the World Trade Organization, Annex 1A, THE LEGAL TEXTS: THE RESULTS OF THE URUGUAY ROUND OF MULTILATERAL TRADE NEGOTIATIONS 121 (1999), 1868 U.N.T.S. 120.

4.3 The Principle of Sincere Cooperation and 'Enforcement' of Agreed Production Standards

The third and final legal obstacle process-based measures face within free movement law that is linked to the challenge of unilateralism is the principle of sincere cooperation and 'enforcement' of EU production standards. A type of process-based measure that is usually considered less 'unilateral' than others is where market access is conditioned upon compliance with mutually agreed standards. For example, in order to ensure that animals in other Member States are treated in accordance with animal welfare standards adopted at EU level, an importing Member State only allows meat and dairy products on its market that come from animals certified to have been treated in accordance with those EU rules. The unilateral aspect here is the 'enforcement' through trade measures, not the substantive social or environmental production standards as such on which both the exporting and importing countries agree. From a legitimacy perspective, such process-based measures are less problematic – and in some instances even welcome – than process-based measures that lay down substantive standards of their own, since both countries agree with the level of protection sought and have participated in the development of the agreed norm. Indeed, it seems that such measures can actually contribute to solving globalization's social and environmental deficits through the use of process-based measures over which both the importing and exporting countries agree.

A good example in that regard is the EU's FLEGT initiative which prohibits the marketing of timber on the EU market that has not been harvested in accordance with the rules of the exporting third country, which is almost always a developing country. The FLEGT initiative contains both mutually agreed 'enforcement' process-based measures based on voluntary partnership agreements, as well as a complementary scheme that prohibits the marketing of illegally harvested wood without the explicit consent of the exporting country.[55] As a result, the incentives in developing countries to violate social and environmental legislation is diminished because there is no European market for illegally harvested timber anymore, aiding developing countries lacking the necessary enforcement capabilities considerably.

As this section will demonstrate, however, such 'enforcement' process-based measures are particularly problematic within the EU internal

[55] See Chapter 1 Section 1.1.2

market because of the EU's unique legal infrastructure. Although one could argue that such rules strengthen compliance with EU rules collectively agreed upon and ensure that the level of protection sought at EU level is obtained, such measures are problematic as they call into question the mutual trust among Member States to comply with EU rules. In this respect, the Treaty explicitly provides for means to address problems relating to non-compliance. Nonetheless, if there is consent between the two trading Member States on this type of enforcement, the Court does not condemn it. In addition, it is unlikely that the same arguments used to condemn Member States for such 'enforcement' process-based measures will succeed in relation to goods of third country origin.

The issue of unilateral enforcement through trade measures was addressed in *Hedley Lomas*.[56] In that case the UK authorities refused an export license for live sheep from the United Kingdom to Spain on the basis of a conviction that there was a significant risk that the animals in question would be slaughtered in slaughterhouses that did not comply with Directive 74/577/EEC on stunning animals before slaughter.[57] The ECJ held that the United Kingdom was not entitled to rely on Article 36 TFEU because of the existence of EU rules, even if those rules did not contain specific enforcement measures. The Court held that 'recourse to Article 36 is no longer possible where [EU] directives provide for harmonization of the measures necessary to achieve the specific objective which would be furthered by reliance upon this provision. This exclusion of recourse to Article 36 cannot be affected by the fact that, in the present case, the Directive does not lay down any [EU] procedure for monitoring compliance or any penalties in the event of breach of its provisions. The fact that the Directive lays down no monitoring procedure or penalties simply means that the Member States are obliged, in accordance with [Article 4 (3) TEU] and [Article 288 TFEU], to take all measures necessary to guarantee the application and effectiveness of [EU] law [...]. In this regard, the Member States must rely on trust in each other to carry out inspections on their respective territories'.[58]

The Court continued, more generally, by stating that a 'Member State may not unilaterally adopt, on its own authority, corrective or protective measures designed to obviate any breach by another Member State of

[56] Case C-5/94, *The Queen v MAFF ex parte Hedley Lomas* [1995] ECR I-2557, see also Case C-169/89, *Gourmetterie van den Burg* [1990] ECR I-2151, Opinion of AG van Gerven, para. 7

[57] Case C-5/94,*The Queen v MAFF ex parte Hedley Lomas* [1995] ECR I-2553, para. 4

[58] Ibid., paras 18–19

rules of [EU] law'.[59] The Court essentially followed the Advocate General who had been more elaborate on this point. He opined that

> [n]othing is more alien to [EU] law than the idea of a measure of retaliation or reciprocity proper to classical public international law. A Member State paralyses the free movement of goods on the ground that the higher interest of the protection of animals has allegedly been violated in another Member State. In other words, the first Member State reacts to an alleged breach of the Treaty (animals are allegedly not protected in Spain) by a separate breach of the Treaty (sheep originating in the United Kingdom are no longer exported to Spain). [. . .][EU] law does not allow reliance to be placed on the principle of reciprocity for ensuring compliance with Treaty obligations. A Member State cannot take unilateral action against defaults by other Member States. The Treaty of Rome created an original legal order in which the procedures necessary for establishing and penalizing a breach of its provisions are strictly regulated. It is through proceedings for a declaration that a Member State has failed to fulfil its obligations under the Treaty, whether instituted by another Member State or by the Commission, that an infringement of [EU] law can be established.[60]

There are, however, two points which could nuance this judgment in relation to other process-based measures which are linked to enforcement of agreed standards. First of all, in *Hedley Lomas* the Court was confronted with a country-based measure[61]: the United Kingdom laid down a general export prohibition to Spain because it thought there was a significant risk that animals might end up in slaughterhouses which did not comply with the EU Directive. The measure was thus primarily targeted at the Spanish government for its failure to comply with EU rules and not to ensure that the slaughterhouses in question complied with EU rules. On the other hand, a measure aiming at compliance with EU rules of the producer is much less trade restrictive, since the regulating Member State will permit trade with the country in question as long as the specific producer in question complies with EU rules. Thus for

[59] Ibid., para 20

[60] Case C-5/94, *The Queen v MAFF ex parte Hedley Lomas* [1995] ECR I-2553, Opinion of AG Léger, para 27. The Advocate General cited a number of cases in this respect in which the Court held that Member States cannot take the law in their own hands. Joined Cases 90/63 and 91/63, *Commission v Luxembourg and Belgium* [1964] ECR 625, at 631 (also cited by the ECJ); Judgment in Case 325/82, *Commission v Germany* [1984] ECR 777, para. 11; Judgment in Case 232/78, *Commission v France* [1979] ECR 2729, para. 9

[61] Robert Howse and Donald Regan, 'The Product/Process Distinction: An Illusory Basis for Disciplining Unilateralism in Trade Policy' (2000) 11 *European Journal of International Law*, 249–289; Steve Charnovitz, 'The Law of Environmental PPMs in the WTO: Debunking the Myth of Illegality' (2002) 27 *The Yale Journal of International Law*, 59

process-based measures this difference means that imports from a Member State are allowed - even if the Member State does not comply with agreed standards - if the imported products are manufactured according to the agreed rules. Nonetheless, the fact remains that process-based measures create barriers to trade that the Directive seeks to eradicate, and that the Treaty provides for specific legal instruments to make sure that the Directive is properly transposed in another Member State.[62]

Second, the judgment itself highlights that the United Kingdom did not have any strong evidence that Spain did not comply with the Directive or that the sheep exported were transported to a specific slaughterhouse that did not comply with the norms laid down in the Directive. If the United Kingdom had produced this evidence, and had tailored its measure accordingly to those slaughterhouses not complying with the norms in question, the Court might have decided differently. The Court has recently carved an exception into the principle of mutual trust in this respect, although this exception is confined to evidence of breaches of the Charter of Fundamental Rights. In *N.S.*, the Court decided that contrary to the principle of mutual confidence – which the Court coined 'the raison d'être of the European Union' – Member States were entitled in exceptional situations to not comply with EU asylum rules requiring asylum seekers to be sent to a Member State which would result in a breach of Charter provisions. This was so if there were 'systemic flaws' 'resulting in inhuman or degrading treatment, within the meaning of Article 4 of the Charter, of asylum seekers'.[63] Although this judgment makes clear that the principle of mutual trust should not be equated with 'blind trust', as one commentator has put it, the emphasis by the Court placed on the importance of the principle of mutual confidence evidences that the Court is unlikely to easily care in similar exceptions with respect to trade in goods if there is no clear evidence of breach of fundamental rights.[64]

The question becomes more complicated if one considers that a process-based measure can be a means to verify compliance with legislation

[62] Articles 259 and 260 TFEU

[63] Joined Cases C-411 and 493/10, *N.S. v Secretary of State for the Home Department and M.E. and Others v Refugee Applications Commissioner, Minister for Justice, Equality and Law Reform* [2011] ECR I-13905, para. 86

[64] Maarten den Heijer, 'Joined Cases C-411 & 493/10, N.S. v. Secretary of State for the Home Department and M.E. and Others v. Refugee Applications Commissioner, Minister for Justice, Equality and Law Reform, Judgment of the Court (Grand Chamber) of 21 December 2011' (2012) 49 *Common Market Law Review*, 1735

implementing a Directive which might have extraterritorial effects. Under the Directive at issue in *Hedley Lomas,* Member States were free to choose the means of enforcement. A Member State could thus have opted to require all meat sold on its territory to have a certificate demonstrating compliance with the substantive provisions of the Directive. In fact, many Directives require such measures to be taken with respect to goods of third country origin. *Hedley Lomas* suggests that such certificates cannot be required from meat imported from another Member State, which would jeopardize the effectiveness of the system of enforcement chosen by the importing Member State. This would thus restrict the choice over the means of enforcement and complicate the realization of process-based measures merely seeking compliance with agreed norms at EU level.

This is a somewhat paradoxical result. In the absence of common rules, or where only minimum harmonization is in place, process-based measures with extraterritorial effects may be permitted, whilst process-based measures merely intended to strengthen agreed collective standards are not. The explanation is of course to be found in the fairly unique EU legal system, which provides for its own set of remedies as well as the instrument of a Directive which is addressed to the Member States. Other Member States must therefore, in principle, trust Member States to ensure compliance and effectiveness of EU legal norms. The result is that process-based measures which appear to be less unilateral – as they are based on agreed standards – are actually sanctioned under EU law, while more unilateral measures are permitted in the absence of common rules.

Nonetheless, the Court will condone 'enforcement' of mutually agreed standards through trade measures if the other Member State explicitly consents to it. There have been a number of cases in which a Member State has restricted trade on behalf of another Member State, either in the context of a bilateral agreement or in the context of cooperation between Member States. In the absence of harmonization, Member States might still want to cooperate or act in accordance with each other's interests and, as solidarity among Member States is explicitly mandated by the Treaties, the Court does not prohibit trade restrictions that enforce a mutually agreed public interest.[65] In *Bauhuis*, the ECJ stated that veterinary inspections for livestock destined for export that

[65] See the preamble and Article 3 (3) TEU

replaced such inspections of the importing Member State were permissible.[66] In *Exportur v LOR*, the Court upheld trade restrictive measures taken as a result of a convention concluded by France and Spain to protect the geographic denominations on each other's territory. According to the Court, Article 36 'does not preclude such protection from being extended to the territory of another Member State' by means of concluding such a convention.[67]

A final issue relating to enforcement is the situation in which a Member State uses a process-based measure to enforce internationally or bilaterally agreed standards with third countries, but do not agree on the enforcement itself. When goods traded within the EU are denied market access in an importing Member State because those goods do not comply with such a process-based measure – for instance, where textile products do not have a certificate that demonstrates compliance with ILO standards – the arguments in *Hedley Lomas* do not apply. The principle of mutual trust only applies to Member States and EU institutions, as well as among Member States, not between Member States and third countries.[68] Moreover, the instruments for enforcement – infringement procedures and preliminary references – are not available in such a situation. The assessment of the permissibility of such enforcement of process-based measures should arguably therefore be based on the merits of the particular justification invoked and traders will not be able to rely on *Hedley Lomas* to argue against such a measure.

4.4 Member States as Co-Regulators of the EU Internal Market

Provided that Member States properly take into account the legal obstacles identified above, free movement law does not oppose unilateralism in market regulation by Member States. Indeed, as noted in the introduction of this chapter, obstacles to trade resulting from disparities in market regulation must be accepted pending EU regulatory action.[69] Unilateralism is therefore inherent in how the EU internal market is regulated. Regulating the internal market is, after all, a *shared* competence,

[66] Case 46/76, *W.G.J. Bauhuis v the Netherlands State* [1977] ECR 6, paras. 43–47

[67] Case C-3/91, *Exportur v LOR* [1992] ECR I-5553, para. 39; See also Case C-469/00, *Ravil SARL v Bellon import SARL* [2003] ECR I-5085

[68] Ankersmit, 'What if Cassis de Dijon were Cassis de Quebec? The Assimilation of Goods of Third Country Origin in the Internal Market', 1387

[69] See the introduction of this chapter, Article 36 TFEU, and Case 120/78, *Rewe-Zentral AG v. Bundesmonopolverwaltung für Branntwein (Cassis de Dijon)* [1979] ECR 650, para. 8

something that Member States are entitled to regulate pending EU action and in conformity with primary law.[70] This means that both the EU and Member States may adopt legally binding acts in the area of the internal market 'to the extent that the Union has not exercised its competence'.[71]

Member States can thus be seen as co-regulators of the internal market, laying down the conditions of economic activity in the interest of at least part of the EU and its citizens. In that sense, it may come as no surprise that the ECJ sees measures that contribute to the goals and ambitions of the EU in a favourable light as the EU has an interest in the protection of such values, too. As such, a Member State might not be cooperating with another Member State to resolve an issue, but it is trying, in accordance with the principle of sincere cooperation between the Member State and the *Union*, to facilitate the achievement of the Union's tasks.[72]

The Court often refers to primary law, international agreements concluded by the Union and secondary legislation, when stating that the justification or derogation invoked not only contributes to a public interest as defined by the Member State, but to a public interest of the Union as a whole. Thus, in *Josemans*, the Court stated that banning non-residents from coffeeshops in the Netherlands was justified 'given the commitments entered into by the European Union and its Member States' which concern 'both the maintenance of public order and the protection of the health of citizens, at the level of the Member States and also of the European Union'.[73] The Court noted that this common interest in protecting the health of citizens as well as the maintenance of public order 'has been recognized by various international conventions which the Member States, and even the European Union, have cooperated on or acceded to'.[74] In addition, the ECJ referred to EU

[70] Article 4 (2) (a) TFEU

[71] Article 2 (2) TFEU further states 'The Member States shall again exercise their competence to the extent that the Union has decided to cease exercising its competence.' Furthermore, Protocol 25 of the Lisbon Treaty states that '[w]ith reference to Article 2(2) of the Treaty on the Functioning of the European Union on shared competence, when the Union has taken action in a certain area, the scope of this exercise of competence only covers those elements governed by the Union act in question and therefore does not cover the whole area.'

[72] Article 4 (3) TEU

[73] Case C-137/09, *Marc Michel Josemans v Burgemeester van Maastricht* [2010] ECR I-13019, paras. 65–66

[74] Ibid., para 67

Treaty ambitions in drug policy as well secondary legislation mentioning these amibitions.[75]

In the free movement cases on green electricity discussed in Chapter 3, the ECJ noted that combatting climate change was a goal of both the EU and of its Member States and noted not the international commitments entered into in that regard.[76] In *Ålands Vindkraft*, for example, the ECJ recalled its judgment in *PreussenElektra* and stated that the national measure intended to promote green electricity production 'contributes to the reduction in greenhouse gas emissions, which are amongst the main causes of climate change that the European Union and its Member States have pledged to combat' and 'the increase in the use of renewable energy sources constitutes [...] one of the important components of the package of measures needed to reduce greenhouse gas emissions and to comply with the Kyoto Protocol to the United Nations Framework Convention on Climate Change, and with other [Union] and international greenhouse gas emission reduction commitments'.[77] In *Ålands Vindkraft*, the ECJ also noted for the first time that the Treaties state that combatting climate change is one of the energy objectives that must guide EU energy policy, whereas in the other cases the ECJ referred to the goals of EU environmental policy in the Treaties.[78]

And in *Gysbrechts*, the ECJ highlighted the complementary nature of the Belgian measure in question to existing EU legislation which sought to protect consumers, but did not prohibit suppliers from requiring credit card numbers in advance. It held that the Belgian measure aimed at protecting consumers and, 'in particular, the effectiveness of the right

[75] In para. 68 the ECJ states 'the need to fight drugs, in particular by preventing drug addiction and punishing the illicit trafficking in such products or substances, has been set out in Article 152(1) EC and in Articles 29 EU and 31 EU. As regards provisions of secondary law, the first recital in the preamble to Framework Decision 2004/757 states that illicit drug trafficking poses a threat to health, safety and the quality of life of citizens of the European Union, and to the legal economy, stability and security of the Member States. Furthermore, as is apparent from paragraph 10 of this judgment, certain instruments of the European Union relate expressly to the prevention of drug tourism'.

[76] Case C-379/98, *PreussenElektra AG v Schleswag AG* [2001] ECR I-2159, paras. 73–81; Case C-573/12, *Ålands Vindkraft AB v Energimyndigheten* EU:C:2014:2037, paras. 77–82; Joined Cases C-204/12, C-205/12, C-206/12, C-207/12, C-208/12, *Essent Belgium* EU:C:2014:2192, paras. 90–95

[77] Case C-573/12, *Ålands Vindkraft AB*, para. 78–79; Case C-379/98, *PreussenElektra AG v Schhleswag AG*, para 73–74; Joined Cases C-204/12, C-205/12, C-206/12, C-207/12, C-208/12, *Essent Belgium*, paras. 91–92

[78] Case C-573/12, *Ålands Vindkraft AB*, para. 81

of withdrawal guaranteed' to the consumer by the Directive in question.[79]

These cases highlight how Member State regulatory activity can contribute to the achievement of EU goals and that in the context of free movement law, the ECJ considers this contribution relevant in considering whether such measures can be justified. The EU trade system thus permits frontrunners and regulatory leadership in environmental and social protection and does not condemn them. This is not surprising, since there is no *legal* means which permit Member States to initiate legislation at EU level that seeks to protect the environment or workers at EU level. With the right to propose secondary legislation at EU level firmly in the hands of the EU Commission, Member States have no formal legal means to initiate regulation of production standards consensually. Thus, while one might prefer European cooperation to address the issues process-based measures seek to address, Member States are, legally speaking, not able to initiate such cooperation.

Moreover, it is exactly EU competence that is triggered as soon as Member States enact legislation that creates obstacles to trade. *Tobacco Advertising* makes clear that the EU only has competence to approximate laws for the proper functioning of the internal market on the basis of Article 114 TFEU, if this results in the removal of obstacles to trade or distortions of competition that are the result of nationally divergent rules.[80] The EU is, therefore, dependent on the existence of such divergent rules or their likely adoption.[81] Thus, as soon as a Member State adopts process-based measures, this results not only as an incentive for the Commission to initiate legislation that may level the playing field, it also provides the EU with express competence to do so.[82]

The EU regime on trade in seal products is exemplary in that regard. This Regulation was adopted after the Netherlands and Belgium had

[79] Case C-205/07, *Criminal proceedings against Lodewijk Gysbrechts and Santurel Inter BVBA* [2008] ECR I-9947, para. 48

[80] Case C-376/98, *Germany v European Parliament and Council* [2000] ECR I-8419, paras 81–89; Case C-547/14, *Philip Morris Brands SARL and Others v Secretary of State for Health*, EU:C:2016:325, paras. 57–64

[81] Case C-58/08, *Vodafone and Others* [2010] ECR I-4999, paras. 32–36; Case C-547/14, *Philip Morris Brands SARL and Others v Secretary of State for Health*, EU:C:2016:325, paras. 57–64

[82] See most recently, Case C-58/08, *The Queen, on the application of Vodafone Ltd and Others v Secretary of State for Business, Enterprise and Regulatory Reform* [2010] ECR I-4999, paras. 32–36 Case T-526/10, *Inuit Tapiriit Kanatami and Others v Commission* EU:T:2013:215, paras. 25–48; Case C-547/14, *Philip Morris Brands SARL and Others v Secretary of State for Health*, EU:C:2016:325, paras. 57–64

imposed a marketing ban of seal products because of the cruel hunting methods employed in the Arctic region. This triggered EU competence to initiate an EU wide ban on seal products on the basis of Article 114 TFEU. The preamble of Regulation 1007/2009 notes that in response to animal welfare concerns among the public, several but not all Member States adopted rules regulating the trade in seal products, and that as a consequence, the differences in legislation among Member States 'adversely affect the operation of the internal market in products which contain or may contain seal products'.[83] Therefore, the Regulation in question, 'should therefore harmonise the rules across the [EU] as regards commercial activities concerning seal products, and thereby prevent the disturbance of the internal market in the products concerned, including products equivalent to, or substitutable, for seal products'.[84] On this basis, the EU courts in *Inuit Tapiriit Kanatami and Others* accepted recourse to Article 114 TFEU as a legal basis for the adoption of the Regulation.[85]

Conclusion

Unilateralism is not necessarily problematic in free movement law. Member States may in principle regulate their markets to protect social and environmental interests, and it is not apparent from the case-law of the ECJ that Member States are required to consult with affected parties abroad or calibrate their measures to take into account extraterritorial interests. Nonetheless, this chapter has identified three legal obstacles Member States face that can be linked to a preference for common solutions and recognition of interests of outsiders. First, harmonized rules in the internal market context impede Member States' ability to take more stringent or divergent measures. Second, the principle of mutual recognition requires Member State authorities to be 'other-regarding' and disciplines regulatory blindness for measures of other Member States laying down equivalent levels of protection. Third and

[83] Regulation 1007/2009 of the European Parliament and of the Council of 16 September 2009 on trade in seal products providing for restrictions on the placing on the market of the European Union of seal products, OJ 2009 No. L286/36 (subsequently amended by Regulation 2015/1775 of the European Parliament and of the Council of 6 October 2015, OJ 2015 No. L262/1), recitals 5–6

[84] Ibid., recital 8

[85] Case T-526/10, *Inuit Tapiriit Kanatami and Others v Commission* EU:T:2013:215, paras. 25–48 confirmed by Case C-398/13P, *Inuit Tapiriit Kanatami and Others v Commission* EU:C:2015:535, paras. 26–32

last, the ECJ requires Member States to trust each other in the implementation and enforcement of EU secondary legislation, thus primarily viewing trade restrictions as 'retaliation' rather than 'facilitation' of the achievement of common objectives.

While Member States are thus under an obligation to cooperate with each other both in terms of removing unnecessary obstacles to trade and in trusting each other to implement secondary legislation, Member States are entitled, in the absence of common internal market rules and as co-regulators of the internal market, to unilaterally set levels of protection for the protection of public interests. There is no obligation on, or even a possibility for, Member States to look for a European common solution within the EU legal framework, while there are possibilities to justify trade restrictions that result out of measures seeking to protect public interests. In that respect, the Court endorses restrictions of trade that seek to protect a common European interest. Nonetheless, in applying such measures, Member States are under a duty to facilitate intra-EU trade by taking into account the functional level of protection obtained at the production stage in other Member States. In addition, Member States must trust each other in the implementation of secondary legislation and cannot use trade restrictions to ensure that the level of protection laid down by secondary legislation is obtained. Lastly, Member States cannot unilaterally lay down more stringent rules than adopted at EU level in the context of the proper functioning of the internal market if such rules are contrary to those rules or obstruct their goal. This means that if a measure is adopted in the context of the internal market, Member States cannot lay down process-based measures that create obstacles to trade for essentially the same reasons as foreseen in secondary legislation.

In light of the EU's frequent use of process-based measures in order to protect social and environmental interests abroad, both through regulation and procurement, it seems unlikely that the EU Courts will take a principled stance against process-based measures as GATT panels have done in the past. Such opposition would also be contrary to the EU's own interests and ambitions which are not solely aimed at trade liberalization, but also at environmental protection, the protection of fundamental and social rights, the eradication of poverty and the protection of the welfare of animals, both domestic *and* abroad.

5 Process-Based Measures and EU Competition Law

Introduction

The application of EU competition rules may also have implications for private process-based measures. The cartel prohibition in Article 101 TFEU prohibits coordination or cooperation among undertakings which restricts competition. While some firms actively seek to compete on the basis of green or social process attributes of their goods, others may seek contribution to social and environmental goals through cooperation with rivals. There are several examples of such cooperation. The European garment industry has an initiative to prevent the marketing and importation of textile products from Bangladesh that have not been made in accordance with basic labour standards.[1] Dutch electricity producers have, in a joint initiative with the Dutch government and civil society interest groups, decided to close down old coal-fired plants because these plants are environmentally unfriendly and pose potential health risks.[2] And there have been two initiatives in the Netherlands in the meat and retail industry to restrict the sale of factory-farmed chicken[3] and more

[1] This is a hypothetical example based on the Bangladesh safety accord whose participants (which include retailers in the West) agree to fund producers in Bangladesh for higher safety standards in the working environment, even if this results in higher prices for the consumer. Information can be found about this accord on www.bangladeshaccord.org/

[2] The Dutch coal closure plan can be found at www.ser.nl/nl/publicaties/overige/2010–2019/2013/energieakkoord-duurzame-groei.aspx. See for a preliminary competition law assessment by the Dutch competition authority ACM: ACM, 'Notitie ACM over sluiting 5 kolencentrales in SER Energieakkoord' www.acm.nl/nl/publicaties/publicatie/12033/Notitie-ACM-over-sluiting-5-kolencentrales-in-SER-Energieakkoord/

[3] ACM, 'Analyse ACM van duurzaamheidsafspraken Kip van Morgen', www.acm.nl/nl/publicaties/publicatie/13758/Analyse-ACM-van-duurzaamheidsafspraken-Kip-van-Morgen/, 26 January 2015

generally, to commit to the sale of more sustainable meat – introducing binding commitments to improve animal welfare.[4]

These private process-based initiatives by undertakings can raise competition law issues: first, because, from a 'traditionalist' understanding of competition law, they result in potential constraints on the economic freedom of the undertakings involved to independently operate on the market[5]; and second, from a more 'economic' understanding, the effects of the agreements may result in loss in welfare if the agreements result in potential price increases and limitation of output, reduced choice of products, or restrictions on innovation.[6] The limits imposed by competition law upon these private process-based measures relate to the important question of *who regulates:* competition law may pose significant constraints upon the enactment of process-based measures by private parties, in contrast to the more limited constraints imposed by public process-based measures in the EU legal order, especially when compared to the legality of process-based measures enacted by the EU itself.

Nonetheless, there are two approaches within EU competition law that can accommodate the protection of social or environmental interests through private process-based measures restrictive of competition: (i) an economic approach and (ii) an approach which tries to integrate public interests within competition law analysis without resorting to quantifying those interests economically. First, an economic approach of Article 101 TFEU to the incorporation of social and environmental issues holds that such incorporation is justified to the extent that it

[4] Commissie van Doorn, 'Al het vlees Duurzaam: De doorbraak naar een gezonde, veilige en gewaardeerde veehouderij in 2020' www.rijksoverheid.nl/bestanden/documenten-en-publicaties/rapporten/2011/11/23/al-het-vlees-duurzaam-de-doorbraak-naar-een-gezonde-veilige-en-gewaardeerde-veehouderij-in-2020/al-het-vlees-duurzaam.pdf 2 September 2011; Laurens Ankersmit, 'Het einde van de kiloknallers? De grenzen aan zelfregulering van duurzaam vlees onder het kartelverbod' (2011) *Actualiteiten Mededingsrecht*, 149–155

[5] Giorgio Monti, *EC Competition Law* (Cambridge: Cambridge University Press, 2006), 20–52; Renato Nazzini, 'Article 81 EC Between Time Present and Time Past: A Normative Critique of "Restriction of Competition" in EU Law' (2006) 43 *Common Market Law Review*, 497–536; Giorgio Monti, 'Article 81 EC and Public Policy' (2002) 39 *Common Market Law Review*, 1057–1099

[6] Richard Whish, *Competition Law*, 7 edn (Oxford: Oxford University Press, 2012), 1; Commission Guidelines on the application of Article 81(3) of the Treaty OJ 2004 C101/97; Commission Guidelines on the applicability of Article 101 of the Treaty on the Functioning of the European Union to horizontal co-operation agreements OJ 2011 C11/1; Lars Kjølbye, 'The New Commission Guidelines on the Application of Article 81 (3): an Economic Approach to Article 81'(2004) 25 *European Competition Law Review*, 566–577

makes sense economically. This approach is based on relying on Article 101 (3) TFEU which exempts restrictive agreements that contribute to economic or technical progress. Within this economic approach, there are two views on when and how social and environmental interests can be subsumed under this article. Under a narrow view, a relatively narrow use of neoclassical economic theory is employed to interpret Article 101 (3) TFEU.[7] A broad view, by contrast, makes use of economic reasoning that is more accommodating to quantifying public interests by, for example, calculating the environmental costs and benefits of an agreement or going beyond an economic understanding of the text of Article 101 (3) TFEU.[8]

The second approach is to exclude restrictive agreements from the scope of Article 101 (1) TFEU altogether if such agreements are necessary for the pursuit of a public interest goal.[9] This approach takes into

[7] Guidelines on the application of Article 81(3) of the Treaty OJ 2004 C101/ 97; Guidelines on the applicability of Article 101 of the Treaty on the Functioning of the European Union to horizontal co-operation agreements OJ 2011 C11/1; Okeoghene Odudu, *The Boundaries of EC Competition Law: The Scope of Article 81* (Oxford: Oxford University Press, 2006); Okeoghene Odudu, 'The Wider Concerns of Competition Law' (2010) 30 *Oxford Journal of Legal Studies*, 599; Lars Kjølbye, 'The New Commission Guidelines on the Application of Article 81 (3): an Economic Approach to Article 81' (2004) 25 *European Competition Law Review*, 566–577; see for a critical assessment Paul Lugard and Leigh Hancher, 'Honey, I Shrunk the Article! A Critical Assessment of the Commission's Notice on Article 81(3) of the EC Treaty' (2004) 25 *European Competition Law Review*, 410–420; Anne C. Witt, 'Public Policy Goals under EU Competition Law: Now Is the Time to Set the House in Order'(2012) 8 *European Competition Journal*, 443–471

[8] Suzanne Kingston, *Greening Competition Law and Policy* (Cambridge: Cambridge University Press, 2012); Christopher Townley, *Article 81 EC and Public Policy* (Oxford: Hart Publishing 2009); Donal Casey, 'Disintegration: Environmental Protection and Article 81 EC' (2009) 15 *European Law Journal*, 362–381; Anna Gerbrandy, 'Competition Law and Private-Sector Sustainability Initiatives' in A.L.B. Colombi Ciacchi and others (eds.) *Law & Governance – Beyond the Public-Private Divide?* (The Hague: Eleven International Publishing, 2013), 81–103; Rein Wesseling, *The Modernisation of EC Antitrust Law* (Oxford: Hart Publishing, 2000). For a broader economic assessment (which is narrower) Hans Vedder, *Competition Law and Environmental Protection in Europe: Towards Sustainability?* (Groningen: Europa Law Publishing, 2003); Nicole Rosenboom, 'How Does Article 101(3) TFEU Case Law Relate to EC Guidelines and the Welfare Perspective?' (2013) SEO Working Paper, http://acle.uva.nl/events/competition–regulation-meetings/conference-papers-9th-cr-meeting-2013.html

[9] Giorgio Monti, 'Article 81 EC and Public Policy' (2002) 39 *Common Market Law Review*, 1057–1099; Kamiel Mortelmans, 'Towards Convergence in the Application of the Rules on Free Movement and Competition?' (2001) 38 *Common Market Law Review*, 613; Kingston, *Greening Competition Law and Policy*; Assimakis P. Komninos, 'Non-competition Concerns: Resolution of Conflicts in the Integrated Article 81 EC' (2008) The University of Oxford

account other public interest requirements within a competition law analysis and is based on a more contextual and purposive reading of the EU Treaties. It is not so much based on the idea that competition authorities and judges should pursue a multitude of goals in applying competition law, but rather the idea that the application of competition law takes place in a broader context, justifying a more modest approach which allows other public interests to be balanced against the goal of undistorted competition on the EU internal market. In a way, this approach is similar to the 'rule of reason' employed within the free movement of goods context, which also enables the goal of trade facilitation and market integration to be balanced against legitimate public interests.

These two approaches are not uncontroversial in literature. Both the broader economic approach and the embedded approach have been criticized on a number of grounds based on arguments which include maintaining the workability of Article 101 TFEU, preserving its 'impartial' nature, and the lack of legitimacy of undertakings to regulate in the public interest. Especially this last point raises interesting and difficult questions. Can undertakings claim to act in the public interest and under which conditions? What is the role of courts in adjudicating those claims and how should they assess whether anti-competitive conduct contributing to the public interest should be permitted when applying EU competition law?

This chapter will assess when private process-based measures fall within the scope of Article 101 TFEU and under which conditions process-based measures may be exempted from its application. First, this chapter will identify when process-based measures result in restrictions of competition sufficient to *prima facie* trigger the application of Article 101 (1) TFEU (Section 5.1). Second, this chapter will discuss how such restrictions may nonetheless be exempted from the application of EU competition rules either through (1) the interpretation of the Treaty exemption of Article 101 (3) TFEU, or (2) through the Court's case-law based exceptions in *Wouters* and *Albany* (Section 5.2). The subsequent section (Section 5.3), will critically assess the main points of criticism towards including social and environmental considerations in the application of Article 101 TFEU, and offer a means of identifying when

Centre for Competition Law and Policy Working Paper (L) 08/05 http://intranet.law.ox.ac.uk/ckfinder/userfiles/files/CCLP%20L%2008-05.pdf

process-based measures restrictive of competition can, nonetheless, be exempted from the application of Article 101 TFEU.

5.1 Process-Based Measures and Restrictions of Competition under Article 101 (1) TFEU

Undertakings are not necessarily required to enter into restrictive agreements with competitors on a competitive market in order to be able to produce in a socially or environmentally conscious way. Many corporate social responsibility initiatives do not take the form of collusion, but are rather independent decisions made by undertakings to address the impact their conduct has on society. Producing in more environmentally friendly ways can in that sense be a way of competing with other firms by distinguishing their products through their specific environmental or social properties at the production stage of the product. These 'process-attributes' can pursue environmentally or socially conscious consumers to procure such products, and therefore provide economic incentives for undertakings to produce in environmentally or socially responsible ways.[10] This is especially the case in societies in which consumers are becoming more and more conscious of the social or environmental impact of their purchasing decisions.[11]

However, it may also be that unilateral conduct of undertakings to address social and environmental concerns at the production stage is not conceivable from an economic point of view and that an agreement between undertakings is necessary in order to ensure that products have been marketed in socially or environmentally responsible ways.

First of all, it might be that consumers are simply indifferent in their purchasing decisions to the social and environmental attributes of the products concerned or may value a lower price more. If production costs rise because of the socially or environmentally conscious production methods employed, undertakings may risk losing their competitive advantage or could even be driven off the market. An agreement with competing undertakings would neutralize the competition and level the playing field on the particular method of production concerned.[12]

[10] Gaëlle Balineau and Ivan Dufeu, 'Are Fair Trade Goods Credence Goods? A New Proposal, with French Illustrations' (2010) 92 *Journal of Business Ethics*, 331–345

[11] Michele Micheletti, *Political Virtue and Shopping* (London: Palgrave McMillan, 2003)

[12] An example is the initiative mentioned in the introduction of the Dutch meat industry which recalls the preference of the consumer on the Dutch market for cheap meat

Second, an agreement between undertakings might also be necessary if an individual undertaking is simply not in the position to signal the process-attributes of its products to its consumers, even if the consumers have a preference for socially or environmentally friendly produced products. Signalling and creating consumer confidence in the quality of an aspect of a product is a costly and difficult exercise.[13] Consumers might be willing to pay an extra premium to address social and environmental concerns at the production stage of products, but they might be sceptical as to whether a product that promises to deliver this quality can in reality deliver this quality which results in so-called attitude-behaviour gaps.[14] This can be the result of the fact that consumers are not in the position to verify themselves whether the product was made in the way promised or are only able to do so at very high costs.[15] Moreover, even if consumers trust the message that the

instead of meat produced sustainably which takes into account animal welfare. As a result of this preference, the initiative calls for binding commitments which are aimed at eliminating 'free-riders' Commissie van Doorn, 'Al het vlees Duurzaam: De doorbraak naar een gezonde, veilige en gewaardeerde veehouderij in 2020' www.rijksoverheid.nl/bestanden/documenten-en-publicaties/rapporten/2011/11/23/al-het-vlees-duurzaam-de-doorbraak-naar-een-gezonde-veilige-en-gewaardeerde-veehouderij-in-2020/al-het-vlees-duurzaam.pdf 2 September 2011; Laurens Ankersmit, 'Het einde van de kiloknallers? De grenzen aan zelfregulering van duurzaam vlees onder het kartelverbod' (2011) *Actualiteiten Mededingingsrecht*, 149–155

[13] Gaëlle Balineau and Ivan Dufeu, 'Are Fair Trade Goods Credence Goods? A New Proposal, with French Illustrations' (2010) 92 *Journal of Business Ethics*, 331–345; M. Darby and E. Karni, 'Free Competition and the Optimal Amount of Fraud' (1973) 16 *Journal of Law and Economics*, 67–88

[14] S. Castaldo, F. Perrini, N. Misani and A. Tencati, 'The Missing Link Between Corporate Social Responsibility and Consumer Trust: The Case of Fair Trade Products' (2009) 84 *Journal of Business Ethics* 84, 1–15; P. De Pelsmacker and W. Janssens, 'A Model for Fair Trade Buying Behaviour: The Role of Perceived Quantity and Quality of Information and of Product-Specific Attitudes' (2007) 75 *Journal of Business Ethics*, 361–380; Gaëlle Balineau and Ivan Dufeu, 'Are Fair Trade Goods Credence Goods? A New Proposal, with French Illustrations' (2010) 92 *Journal of Business Ethics* 331–345

[15] M. Darby and E. Karni, 'Free Competition and the Optimal Amount of Fraud' (1973) 16 *Journal of Law and Economics*, 67–88; O. Bonroy and C. Constantatos, 'On the Use of Labels in Credence Goods Markets' (2008) 33 *Journal of Regulatory Economics*, 237–252; M. L. Loureiro and J. Lotade, 'Do Fair Trade and Eco-Labels in Coffee Wake up the Consumer Conscience?' (2005) 53 *Ecological Economics*, 129–138; T. Steinrücken and S. Jaenichen, 'The Fair Trade Idea: Towards an Economics of Social Labels' (2007) 30 *Journal of Consumer Policy*, 201–217; B. Roe and I. Sheldon, 'Credence Good Labeling: The Efficiency and Distributional Implications of Several Policy Approaches' (2007) 89 *American Journal of Agricultural Economics*, 1020–1033; S. Baksi and P. Bose, 'Credence Goods, Efficient Labelling Policies, and Regulatory Enforcement' (2007) 37 *Environmental & Resource Economics*, 411–430; M. Fridell, I. Hudson and M. Hudson, 'With Friends

product conforms to a certain production process, consumers might not be sure as to whether the particular production process actually contributes to the social or environmental goal at issue.[16] This is a common problem for fair-trade products, for instance, where different methods of ensuring development and addressing social injustice can create confusion among consumers as to whether one particular policy chosen might be effective.[17]

In order to address these problems that are the result of information asymmetries between the producer and the consumer, undertakings might want to set up a signalling device, a labelling scheme for instance, which ensures that consumers are properly informed without unnecessary confusion on the market.[18] This has the advantage of giving undertakings a relatively cheap means (by not having to set up a certification system themselves and investing in the necessary branding) of signalling certain process-attributes of products as well as avoiding too much confusion on the market. Examples of such agreements are were undertakings join certain labelling schemes such as the Marine Stewardship Council (MSC) label, the Forest Stewardship Council (FSC) label, and the Max Havelaar label.[19]

Third, an agreement between undertakings might be necessary in order to maintain the reputation of a given economic sector. Public naming and shaming campaigns might lead to an agreement between undertakings in order to restore the public image of a given economic sector as well as consumer confidence in particular products, by excluding those undertakings that produce or procure from producers that produce in environmentally unfriendly or harmful ways. An example is the Kimberley Process Certification Scheme, which seeks to preserve

Like These: The Corporate Response to Fair Trade Coffee' (2008) 40 *Review of Radical Political Economics*, 8–34

16 S. Lupton, 'Shared Quality Uncertainty and the Introduction of Indeterminate Goods' (2005) 29 *Cambridge Journal of Economics*, 399–421; Gaëlle Balineau and Ivan Dufeu, 'Are Fair Trade Goods Credence Goods? A New Proposal, with French Illustrations' (2010) 92 *Journal of Business Ethics*, 331

17 Gaëlle Balineau and Ivan Dufeu, 'Are Fair Trade Goods Credence Goods? A New Proposal, with French Illustrations' (2010) 92 *Journal of Business Ethics*, 331–345

18 A. Lizzeri, 'Information Revelation and Certification Intermediaries' (1999) 30 *The Rand Journal of Economics*, 214–231; on information asymmetries generally see the seminal work of G. A. Akerlof, 'The Market for "Lemons": Quality Uncertainty and the Market Mechanism' (1970) 84 *Quarterly Journal of Economics*, 488–500

19 Fred Gale, *Global Commodity Governance: State Responses to Sustainable Forest and Fisheries Certification* (London: Palgrave Macmillan, 2011)

the reputation of the diamond industry by eliminating conflict diamonds from the market through public-private cooperation.[20]

Such coordination may result in a restriction of competition under Article 101 (1) TFEU. The Court has held that Article 101 (1) TFEU 'is intended to prohibit any form of coordination which deliberately substitutes practical cooperation between undertakings for the risks of competition'.[21] Nonetheless, not every restriction on the economic freedom of an undertaking will result in a restriction of competition under Article 101 (1) TFEU because the Court considers that prohibition to protect a market of 'workable competition'.[22] Only appreciable restrictions of competition therefore fall within the scope of Article 101 (1) TFEU.[23]

Generally, process-based measures will be deemed to restrict competition if, to an appreciable extent, they limit the ability of undertakings to compete on one of the relevant parameters of a market, such as price, output, and quality of a product, or results in the exclusion of a rival. Thus, the agreement to close down polluting factories, can, depending on the particular economic and legal context, lead to a limitation of output which may result in higher prices. Similarly, the agreement to set up a common label among undertakings can restrict competition if the agreement limits the participating undertakings in their ability to offer different types of products, set prices, or results in the exclusion of rival undertakings from the market. Excluding upstream undertakings from the market, by imposing production conditions upon them collectively by undertakings on the downstream market, may also have a negative impact on price or quality of products. This might be the case, for instance, when undertakings agree to no longer sell blood diamonds, or where they agree to no longer sell unsustainable meat.

Significantly for process-based measures, Article 101 TFEU also applies to agreements concluded by undertakings established outside the EU and

[20] Virginia Haufler, 'The Kimberley Process Certification Scheme: An Innovation in Global Governance and Conflict Prevention' (2010) 89 *Journal of Business Ethics*, 403–416. The Kimberly Process Certification Scheme Core document can be found at www.kimberleyprocess.com/en/kpcs-core-document

[21] Case C-209/07, *Competition Authority v Beef Industry Development Society Ltd and Barry Brothers (Carrigmore) Meats Ltd.* [2008] ECR I-8637, para 34

[22] Case 26/76, *Metro SB-Großmärkte GmbH & Co. KG v Commission (Metro I)* [1977] ECR 1875, para 20

[23] Case 5/69, *Völk Vervaecke* [1969] ECR 295, paras 5–7

concluded outside the EU, as long as they are 'implemented' within the EU.[24] Any type of private regulatory arrangement between undertakings in third world countries seeking to ameliorate environmental or social conditions there, even with the explicit or implicit approval of the government and societal actors there, will, in principle fall within the scope of Article 101 TFEU if that arrangement has negative effects for the EU internal market. EU competition law, therefore, serves as a *de facto* prohibition of private regulatory arrangements in other countries if the undertakings participating in the arrangement implement the restrictive aspects of it within the EU internal market through changing their participation on the EU internal market, for instance, by limiting the amount of products sold or the range of different products sold.

5.1.1 *Process-Based Measures that are Restrictions by Object*

Article 101 (1) TFEU distinguishes between restrictions of competition by object and restrictions of competition by effect. While the dividing line between these two types of restrictions is not entirely clear, the distinction has important practical effects.[25] If an agreement is found to restrict competition by object, no economic analysis of the effects of an agreement on the relevant market is necessary to demonstrate the negative effects on competition the agreement has. Object restrictions function similar to traffic rules, certain conduct is considered to pose such a risk to the competitive process that it is not necessary to prove that conduct actually leads to detrimental effects, although undertakings can refute this finding by proving that the agreement does not, in fact, restrict competition.[26]

[24] Damien Geradin, Marc Reysen and David Henry, 'Extraterritoriality, Comity, and Cooperation in EU Competition Law' in by Andrew T. Guzman (ed) *Cooperation, Comity, and Competition Policy* (Oxford: Oxford University Press, 2011); Florian Wagner-von Papp, 'Competition Law and Extraterritoriality' in Ariel Ezrachi (ed.) *Research Handbook on International Competition Law* (Cheltenham: Edward Elgar Publishing, 2012), 21–59; W. van Gerven, 'EC Jurisdiction in Antitrust Matters: The Wood Pulp Judgment' [1989] *Fordham Corporate Law Institute*, 470; Case 48/69, *Imperial Chemical Industries Limited v Commission* [1972] ECR 619; Joined Cases 89, 104, 114, 116, 117 and 125 to 129/85, *A. Ahlström Osakeyhtiö and others v Commission* [1988] ECR 5193; Case T-102/96, *Gencor Ltd v Commission* [1999] ECR II-753. See for those advocating for the introduction of an effects-based test: Case 48/69, *Imperial Chemical Industries Limited v Commission* [1972] ECR 619, Opinion of AG Mayras, at 699–700; Joined Cases 89, 104, 114, 116, 117 and 125 to 129/85, *A. Ahlström Osakeyhtiö and others v Commission* [1988] ECR 5193, Opinion of AG Darmon

[25] David Bailey, 'Restrictions of Competition by Object under Article 101 TFEU' (2012) 49 *Common Market Law Review*, 559

[26] Case C-209/07 *Competition Authority v Beef Industry Development Society Ltd and Barry Brothers (Carrigmore) Meats Ltd.* [2008] ECR I-8637, Opinion of AG Trstenjak, para 46 and

The most important situations for process-based measures are when the agreement limits output or seeks to exclude undertakings from the market. Therefore, process-based agreements may be considered restrictions of competition by object if they have as their object the limitation of output. In *BIDS*, for instance, an agreement between members of the Irish beef industry to restructure the industry by reducing the number of meat processors operating on the market to combat overcapacity, was considered to be a restriction by object.[27] One may wonder, therefore, whether an agreement such as the agreement by the Dutch electricity suppliers to close down polluting production facilities can also be considered a restriction by object. Similarly, the Commission has stated in its horizontal cooperation guidelines that an agreement 'whereby a national association of manufacturers sets a standard and puts pressure on third parties not to market products that do not comply with the standard' would be considered a restriction by object.[28] Arrangements such as the Dutch initiatives to ban unsustainable meat or broiler chickens from Dutch supermarkets are therefore liable to be considered restrictions by object.[29]

Importantly, the Court has considered additional public interest motives irrelevant for the determination if an agreement is a restriction by object. In *BIDS*, the Court rejected the argument that the need to restructure the Irish beef industry meant that the restrictions on output agreed upon should not be considered a restriction by object.[30] The Court held that considerations such as remedying the effects of a crisis in a particular sector 'are irrelevant for the purposes of applying [Article 101 (1) TFEU]. Indeed, an agreement may be regarded as having a restrictive object even if it does not have the restriction of

C-8/08 *T-Mobile Netherlands BV, KPN Mobile NV, Orange Nederland NV and Vodafone Libertel NV v Raad van bestuur van de Nederlandse Mededingingsautoriteit* [2009] ECR I-4529, Opinion of AG Kokott, para 47; see David Bailey, 'Restrictions of competition by object under Article 101 TFEU' (2012) 49 *Common Market Law Review*, 559, at 563–564

27 Case C-209/07, *Competition Authority v Beef Industry Development Society Ltd and Barry Brothers (Carrigmore) Meats Ltd.* [2008] ECR I-8637, paras 34–36

28 Commission Guidelines on the applicability of Article 101 of the Treaty on the Functioning of the European Union to horizontal co-operation agreements OJ 2011 C11/1, para 273. The Commission mentions its decision in *Pre-insulated pipes* (Case IV/35.691) Commission Decision 1999/60/EC OJ 1999 L 24/1

29 See ACM, 'Kip van Morgen' (*n* 3)

30 Case C-209/07, *Competition Authority v Beef Industry Development Society Ltd and Barry Brothers (Carrigmore) Meats Ltd.* [2008] ECR I-8637, para 21

competition as its sole aim *but also pursues other legitimate objectives.*'[31] In *Akcenta*, the Court also rejected the argument that illegal behaviour of competitors is relevant for the determination of whether an agreement is restrictive by object.[32]

5.1.2 Process-Based Measures that are Restrictions by Effect

If a process-based agreement between undertakings does not amount to restriction by object, it may still be considered to restrict competition by effect. Here, a fully-fledged market analysis is required in order to demonstrate that the agreement has a negative impact on one of the parameters of competition within a particular market and therefore restricts competition to an appreciable extent.[33] This presupposes an assessment of the effects the conduct of undertakings will have in the relevant market, and therefore, it is imperative that the relevant market is properly identified.[34] This is of particular relevance to process-based measures, because if a market is narrowly defined, products with process-attributes might be considered to exist on a separate market, making it more likely that undertakings participating on that market will have market power.[35] As a consequence, these undertakings may be perceived to negatively affect competition on the market by coordinating

[31] Ibid.

[32] Case C-68/12, *Protimonopolný úrad Slovenskej republiky v Slovenská sporiteľňa a.s. (Akcenta)* [2013] ECR I-71 (ECLI), para 19

[33] Case T-328/03, *O2 (Germany) GmbH & Co. OHG v Commission* [2006] ECR II-1231, para 68; Case 56/65, *Société Technique Minière (L.T.M.) v Maschinenbau Ulm GmbH (M.B.U.)* [1966] ECR 235, at 249–250. The courts emply a counterfactual analysis for that purpose: the competition will be assessed 'within the actual context in which it would occur in the absence of the agreement in dispute'. See further Damien Geradin, Damien and Ianis Girgenson, 'The Counterfactual Method in EU Competition Law: the Cornerstone of the Effects-based Approach' in Jacques Bourgeois, Denis Waelbroeck (eds.) *Ten Years of Effects-based Approach in EU Competition Law: State of Play and Perspectives* (Brussels: Bruylant, 2012)

[34] Case 6/72, *Europemballage Corporation and Continental Can Company Inc. v Commission* [1973] ECR 215, para 32; Case 85/76, *Hoffmann-La Roche & Co. AG v Commission* [1979] ECR 461, para 28; the approach is summarized in Case C-49/07, *Motosykletistiki Omospondia Ellados NPID (MOTOE) v Elliniko Dimosio* [2008] ECR I- 4863, para 32 'the relevant product or service market includes products or services which are substitutable or sufficiently interchangeable with the product or service in question, not only in terms of their objective characteristics, by virtue of which they are particularly suitable for satisfying the constant needs of consumers, but also in terms of the conditions of competition and the structure of supply and demand on the market in question'.

[35] Case T-427/08, *Confédération européenne des associations d'horlogers-réparateurs (CEAHR) v. Commission* [2010] ECR II- 5865, para 74

their economic behaviour. For example, if fair trade coffee is considered to be a separate market from regular coffee, the market share of undertakings making fair trade coffee will be much higher, and, as a result, standardizing certain aspects of 'fair trade' would more likely lead to an 'appreciable' restriction of competition. In that sense, competition law does take into account consumer perception and the image certain products may have.[36]

The question of the existence of an effects-based restriction for process-based measures is whether the agreement restricts actual or potential competition that would have existed without the agreement. Would undertakings have competed with each other in relation to the production standard agreed upon and does the standard therefore have an effect on one of the parameters of competition (price, output, quality of products)? For example, what would be the situation on the market for textile products if the EU garment industry would not agree to no longer market and import products that have not been verified as being produced in accordance with certain ILO standards? Would more products be available? Would there be lower prices for these products? Another counterfactual could be done for the 'electricity example': if the agreement to shut down coal-fired power plants had not been concluded, what would be the situation on the market? Would the undertakings have not shut down these plants and would that have resulted in more output and lower prices?

Setting up a label to enable a number of undertakings to effectively signal process-attributes to consumers, may not be restrictive of competition at all. As long as such an agreement does not require producers to only sell products adhering to the underlying production standard, but is of a voluntary nature, it is unlikely that the agreement will be considered to restrict competition. In fact, it may be considered to be pro-competitive if the voluntary label enables undertakings to penetrate a market, for instance. However, if the agreement imposes constraints upon the undertakings in relation to one of the parameters of competition, or is set up as to drive

[36] Case T-19/92, *Groupement d'achat Edouard Leclerc v Commission* [1996] ECR II- 1851, para 114; see also *Airtours/First Choice* (Case IV/M.1524) Commission Decision 2000/276/EC OJ 1999 L93/1; *Unilever/Sara Lee Body Care* (Case COMP/M.5658) Commission Decision available at http://ec.europa.eu/competition/mergers/cases/decisions/m5658_20101117_20600_2193231_EN.pdf, para 44

competitors off the market, and does so to an appreciable extent, it is more likely that the agreement will be found to be restrictive in effect.[37]

In that respect, whether a process-based measure has restrictive effects on the market is a matter of degree and is greatly dependent on the economic context in which the agreement is implemented. The more an agreement reduces the decision-making independence on a market, because the degree of uncertainty is reduced or because the agreement lays down obligations, the more likely the agreement is to have restrictive effects.[38] Factors that matter in this sense are the market share of undertakings that are part of the agreement, the degree of voluntariness to adhesion to production standards and the extent to which the particular production standard has an impact on the overall price, quality, and quantity of the products involved. The more the undertakings concerned are able to negatively affect prices, quality, output and innovation, the more likely the agreement will be considered to be restrictive in effect.[39]

5.2 Public Interest Justifications

5.2.1 *Article 101 (3) TFEU*

The first means of accommodating the potential conflict between the cartel prohibition in Article 101 TFEU and social and environmental interests underlying private process-based measures is the exception found in Article 101 (3) TFEU. That provision allows restrictive agreements to be exempted if such agreements contribute to 'improving the production or distribution of goods or to promoting technical or economic progress'.[40]

[37] In APB, for instance, the Commission considered the use of an environmental quality mark to be restrictive of competition because it was used to create exclusive sale and purchasing networks which had the effect of excluding certain competitors from participating in the network *APB* (Case IV/32.202) Commission Decision 90/33/EEC OJ 1990 L18/35

[38] Guidelines on horizontal co-operation agreements (n 7), para 27; see in particular the section on standardization agreements, paras 257–335; Case C-238/05, *Asnef-Equifax* [2006] ECR I-11125, para 51

[39] Guidelines on horizontal co-operation agreements (n 7), para 35; see also Kingston (n 8), 245–257

[40] Article 101 (3) TFEU sets four cumulative criteria in total. The restrictive agreement further needs to allow consumers a fair share of the resulting benefit, and should not impose on the undertakings concerned restrictions which are not indispensable to the

The exemption can be interpreted narrowly – not leaving much room for process-based measures restrictive of competition to be exempted under Article 101 (3) TFEU – as well as broadly. The narrow interpretation supported by the Commission in its 'more economic approach' only allows for the consideration of social and environmental factors to the extent that it can be subsumed under a narrow economic analysis.[41] The broad interpretation – advocated by Townley, Casey, Kingston, and Vedder, among others – allows social and environmental considerations to be weighed into the analysis more favourably either by adopting a social welfare standard or by arguing that public interests can be taken into account even if this is not economically efficient.[42] The narrow view makes such agreements only permissible to the extent that the consumers of the regulated product benefit from the agreement in an economic sense, while a broader societal perspective under the broad view enables the adjudicator to go beyond the narrow interests of the consumer of the regulated product and take into account other interests, too.

Under the narrow view, exemplified by the Commission's 'more economic approach' in its White Paper on Modernization, the purpose of the exemption provision of Article 101 (3) TFEU 'is to provide a legal framework for the economic assessment of restrictive practices and not to allow application of the competition rules to be set aside because of political considerations'.[43] Although an 'economic approach' is in itself

attainment of these objectives and afford such undertakings the possibility of eliminating competition in respect of a substantial part of the products in question.

41 Guidelines on the application of Article 81(3) of the Treaty; Guidelines on horizontal co-operation agreements (n 7); Okeoghene Odudu, *The Boundaries of EC Competition Law: The Scope of Article 81* (Oxford: Oxford University Press, 2006); Okeoghene Odudu, 'The Wider Concerns of Competition Law' (2010) 30 *Oxford Journal of Legal Studies*, 599; Lars Kjølbye, 'The New Commission Guidelines on the Application of Article 81 (3): an Economic Approach to Article 81'(2004) 25 *European Competition Law Review*, 566–577

42 Kingston, *Greening Competition Law and Policy*; Christopher Townley, *Article 81 EC and Public Policy* (Oxford: Hart Publishing, 2009); Donal Casey, 'Disintegration: Environmental Protection and Article 81 EC' (2009) 15 *European Law Journal*, 362–381; Gerbrandy, 'Competition Law and Private-Sector Sustainability Initiatives', 81–103; Rein Wesseling, *The Modernisation of EC Antitrust Law* (Oxford: Hart Publishing, 2000). For a broader economic assessment (which is narrower) Hans Vedder, *Competition Law and Environmental Protection in Europe: Towards Sustainability?* (Groningen: Europa Law Publishing, 2003); Nicole Rosenboom, 'How does article 101(3) TFEU case law relate to EC guidelines and the welfare perspective?' (2013) SEO Working Paper, http://acle.uva.nl/events/competition–regulation-meetings/conference-papers-9th-cr-meeting-2013.html

43 European Commission, 'White Paper on Modernisation of the Rules Implementing Articles 85 and 86 of the EC Treaty' OJ 1999 No. C132/1, para 57

a political choice, the Commission seems to consider a utilitarian outlook using neoclassical economic methodology to be a neutral way of assessing the EU competition rules. As a result, only public interest goals 'pursued by other Treaty provisions can be taken into account to the extent that they can be subsumed under the four conditions of Article [101(3) TFEU]' by using the economic methodology employed by it.[44]

The 'more economic approach' of the Commission has three core features. First of all, the Commission applies a narrow cost-benefit analysis: the exemption under Article 101 (3) would apply only to the extent that economic benefits for *consumers* outweigh the economic disadvantages of the restriction on competition. According to the Commission, 'When the pro-competitive effects of an agreement *outweigh* its anti-competitive effects the agreement is on balance pro-competitive and compatible with the objectives of the Community competition rules.'[45] The Commission notes that 'The concept of "fair share" implies that the pass-on of benefits must at least compensate consumers for any actual or likely negative impact caused to them by the restriction of competition found under Article [101(1)].'[46] This approach is not strictly supported by the text of Article 101 (3) TFEU, which merely refers to the consumer's 'fair share' of the benefit, nor by the case-law of the Court, which holds that the advantages must be 'appreciable objective advantages of such a kind as to compensate for the resulting disadvantages for competition' generally without stating that this should reflect advantages for consumers only.[47]

For process-based restrictive agreements, the environmental and public health benefits resulting from the closure of polluting coal plants, need to be 'counted' in economic terms from the perspective of consumer welfare, and these benefits need to outweigh the negative economic effects of the restrictive agreement. This makes it less likely that moral and more economically diffuse interests such as worker protection and animal welfare are to be exempted under this test. Improvements in the working conditions of textile workers in Bangladesh made

[44] Guidelines on the application of Article 81(3) of the Treaty (n 7), para 42
[45] Ibid., para 33 [46] Ibid., para 85
[47] Joined cases C-501/06 P, C-513/06 P, C-515/06 P and C-519/06 P, *GlaxoSmithKline* [2009] ECR I-9291, para 92 Joined Cases 56 and 58/64, *Établissements Consten S.à.R.L. and Grundig-Verkaufs-GmbH v Commission* [1966] ECR 299, at 348–349

possible through a restrictive agreement will, for instance, not be taken into account under the narrow view.

The second feature of the Commission's approach is the narrow construction within which consumers are to be considered when taking into account the benefits. Under the narrow view, only consumers (direct and indirect users) within the relevant market where the restriction is taking place may be counted, not consumers in other markets or even economic benefits for society at large.[48] Even within the economic paradigm this approach is controversial. From a social welfare perspective it makes no sense to exclude the benefits that an agreement may accrue for other actors than just the direct and indirect consumers of the products within a given market.[49] If in the 'electricity example' the benefits for consumers of electricity in the Dutch market do not outweigh the costs, but society as a whole benefits because of reduced health risks and pollution abatement, this is something that would be problematic in the eyes of the Commission.[50]

The third feature is that the Commission requires a direct link between the benefits and the agreement. The Commission states that 'The causal link between the agreement and the claimed efficiencies must normally also be direct. Claims based on indirect effects are as a general rule too uncertain and too remote to be taken into account.'[51] This approach is again more prone to excluding environmental and social benefits which can be more diffuse and distant.[52]

[48] Guidelines on the application of Article 81(3) of the Treaty (n 7), paras 43 and 84

[49] See Rosenboom, 'How does article 101(3) TFEU case law relate to EC guidelines and the welfare perspective?' (n 8) and Casey, 'Disintegration' (n 8)

[50] However, in the Article 81 (3) EC Guidelines the Commission does add, after stating that normally only the benefits for the users of the product in a given market are considered, that 'society as a whole benefits where the efficiencies lead either to fewer resources being used to produce the output consumed or to the production of more valuable products and thus to a more efficient allocation of resources.' See, Guidelines on the application of Article 81(3) of the Treaty (n 7), para 85

[51] Ibid., para 54

[52] One potential beneficial aspect for the consideration of social and environmental interests within Article 101 (3) TFEU by the Commission, however, is the willingness to take into account future benefits of the agreement. The guidelines state that the 'fact that pass-on to the consumer occurs with a certain time lag does not in itself exclude the application of Article [101(3]). However, the greater the time lag, the greater must be the efficiencies to compensate also for the loss to consumers during the period preceding the pass-on. In making this assessment it must be taken into account that the value of a gain for consumers in the future is not the same as a present gain for consumers.' See Guidelines on the application of Article 81(3) of the Treaty (n 7), paras 87–88

The broad view, by contrast, is more accommodating towards exempting process-based measures restrictive of competition that address social and environmental concerns. Basically, within the broad view two approaches can be identified. The first approach uses economic analysis in a way that is more accommodating to societal interests, for instance, through the use of a social welfare standard.[53] This approach uses economic methodology in a way to quantify and put a value on both the costs and benefits certain conduct by undertakings can have. The use of environmental and ecological economics is a prominent example of such an approach which goes well beyond the use of neoclassical welfare analysis.[54] The second approach argues for taking into account public interests even if this does not result in economically efficient results.[55] This less utilitarian approach does not, however, exclude the use of the first approach to the extent that public interests can be weighed within the utilitarian calculus.

The first approach would be more favourable to process-based measures that create economic benefits for other actors than the consumers of the regulated product. If, for instance, society as a whole benefits from the agreement to close down the coal-fired power plants in the Netherlands, but the consumers of electricity on the Dutch electricity market would not have a net benefit, this approach would not be in favour of applying the competition rules to such an agreement. The notion of 'fair share to consumers' could also be widened to include cross-market benefits that might accrue from process-based competition restrictions. The criterion for direct benefits could also be loosened according to this approach, and the impact of maintaining or agreeing to abandon certain production methods could be calculated over a longer period of time.

The quintessential example of a broader economic approach is the Commission decision in *CECED*, which was made just before the publication of the Article 81 (3) EC Guidelines. In *CECED*, the Commission had to assess whether an agreement between washing machine manufactures and importers to take environmentally unfriendly washing machines off the market was not contrary to Article 101 TFEU.[56] In assessing whether the agreement contributed to economic or technical progress, the Commission took a broader view on the impact of the agreement on society as

[53] Roosenboom (n 8) [54] See Kingston (n 8), pp. 163–193

[55] Christopher Townley, *Article 81 EC and Public Policy* (n 8), 201–311; Casey (n 8), Kingston (n 8), Commission practice before the 'more economic approach' (discussed below)

[56] *CECED* (Case IV.F.1/36.718) Commission Decision 2000/475/EC OJ 2000 No. L187/47

a whole. It found that the reduction of up to 20 per cent energy consumption achieved led to reduced pollution from electricity generation.[57] According to the Commission, the 'future operation of the total of installed machines providing the same service with less indirect pollution is more economically efficient than without the agreement',[58] noting that the energy savings produced by the agreement were 'remarkable'.[59]

The analysis of the benefits passed on to consumers did not only focus on the individual benefits for consumers, but also considered *collective environmental benefits*. In relation to these collective environmental benefits, the Commission started by pronouncing that the agreement can contribute to a goal of the EU outside the goal of protecting competition, namely, environmental protection, and emphasized that account must be taken of the costs of pollution and the EU's environmental objective of rationale utilization of natural resources.[60] After calculating the costs of externalities relating to carbon dioxide emissions, nitrous oxide and sulphur dioxide, the Commission stated that '*the benefits to society* brought about by the CECED agreement appear to be more than seven times greater than the increased purchase costs of more energy-efficient washing machines. Such environmental results for society would adequately allow consumers a fair share of the benefits *even if no benefits accrued to individual purchasers of machines.*'[61]

Despite the obviously more accommodating tone towards environmental considerations in *CECED*, this economic approach has disadvantages as well. First of all, if the myopic understanding of consumer welfare of the Commission is abandoned, one would have to define the borders of social welfare: does social welfare only encompass members of a particular country or jurisdiction? If, for example, the economic benefits mainly flow to the workers in textile factories in Bangladesh, does this mean that such benefits cannot be taken into the equation? Second, even a very broad *economic* approach cannot disguise the fact that certain public interests are more readily quantifiable economically speaking than other public interests. Environmental costs and benefits are easier to calculate than moral and ethical concerns such as animal welfare concerns, human rights violations, and culture. An economic approach, no matter how broadly construed, will therefore, due to its utilitarian focus, inherently be more beneficial to certain public interests.

[57] Ibid., paras 47–48 [58] Ibid., para 48 [59] Ibid., para 49 [60] Ibid., para 55
[61] Ibid., para 56

The second approach has been used by the EU courts and the Commission and has strong academic support.[62] The ECJ in *Metro I & II* and the General Court in *Métropole* held that the Commission may reconcile safeguarding public interest objectives with the maintenance of workable competition under its Article 101 (3) TFEU assessment.[63] There are many Commission decisions prior to the 'more economic approach' in which this discretion was put into practice.[64] In a number of environmentally relevant cases – mostly joint ventures resulting in either environmentally friendlier production or the production of environmentally friendlier products – the Commission referred to the interest of environmental protection, although the reference to environmental protection was more of a supportive nature than decisive for the outcome of the case.[65]

This broader approach under Article 101 (3) TFEU is also reflected in a number of decisions which concern social policy. In *Ford/Volkswagen*, job creation was a consideration in the Commission's 101 (3) TFEU decision to authorize a joint venture for the production of cars noting that the joint venture 'contributes to the promotion of the harmonious development of the [Union] and the reduction of regional disparities which is one of the basic aims of the Treaty. It also furthers European market integration by linking Portugal more closely to the Community through one of its important industries.'[66] Similarly, in the *Stichting Baksteen* and *Synthetic fibres* decisions, the Commission exempted so-called 'crisis cartels' under Article 101 (3) TFEU for social policy reasons, in essence condoning limitation of production under acceptable social conditions.[67]

[62] See in particular Townley (n 8), Casey (n 8), Kingston (n 8)

[63] Case 75/84, *Metro SB-Großmärkte GmbH & Co. KG v Commission (Metro II)* [1986] ECR 3021, para 65; Joined Cases T-528, 543 and 546/93, *Metropole and Others v. Commission* [1996] ECR II-649, para 118; Case 26/76, *Metro I* (n 22), para 43

[64] See for a good discussion of these decisions Casey (n 8), 268

[65] Ibid., *BMW* (Case IV/14.650) Commission Decision 75/73/EEC OJ 1974 No. L 29/1; *BBC Brown Boveri* (Case IV/32.368) Commission Decision 88/541/EEC OJ 1988 No. L301/68, para 23; *Exxon/Shell* (Case IV/33.640) Commission Decision 94/322/EC OJ 1994 No. L144/20, paras 68–71; *Philips/Osram* (Case IV/34.252) Commission Decision 94/986/EC OJ 1994 No. L378/37, paras 25–27; *DSD* (Cases COMP/34493 – DSD and others) Commission Decision 2001/837/EC OJ 2001 No. L319/1, para 143

[66] *Ford/Volkswagen* (Case IV/33.814) Commission Decision 93/49/EEC OJ 1993 L20/14, para 36

[67] See Monti, 'Article 81 EC and Public Policy' (n 9), 1071; *Stichting Baksteen* (Case IV/34.456) Commission Decision 94/296/EC OJ 1994 No. L 131/15, para 27–28; *Synthetic fibres* (Case IV/30.810) Commission Decision 84/380/EEC OJ 1984 No. L207/17, para 37

5.2.2 The ECJ's Case-Law in Wouters and Albany

The second approach, in addition to the approach based on Article 101 (3) TFEU, enables public interests to be taken into account by integrating them within competition law analysis within Article 101 (1) TFEU on the basis of the Court's judgments in *Wouters* and *Albany*.[68] This approach excludes restrictive agreements from the scope of Article 101 (1) TFEU altogether if such agreements are necessary for the pursuit of a public interest goal, either based on recognition of this goal in EU legal sources (*Albany*) or on the basis the interest itself (*Wouters*). It differs from the approach under Article 101 (3) TFEU, in that, first, restrictions of competition do not need to give consumers a 'fair share' of the benefits of the agreement, and second, that it is based on a reasoning more akin to a proportionality analysis and not on the basis of a cost-benefit analysis which is more inherent in Article 101 (3) TFEU. As such, this approach is more suitable for restrictive process-based agreements where consumers are indifferent towards process-attributes, but which nonetheless contribute to public interest goals. Thus, if consumers of textile products are indifferent, in their purchasing decisions, to the working conditions in Bangladesh, this approach could provide a pathway for undertakings, labour unions, and other grassroots organizations wishing to contribute to improving those conditions through restrictive agreements.

This book will refer to this approach as the integrationist approach because it is a means of embedding public interests into competition law analysis based on a more contextual and purposive reading of the EU Treaties. This approach is more forthcoming in acknowledging that the EU competition rules apply in the wider context of the EU's goal and ambitions, and the rules should not be applied if restrictions are necessary for the pursuit of public interest goals. It is not so much based on the idea that competition authorities and judges should pursue a multitude of goals in applying competition law, but rather the idea that the application of competition law takes place in a broader context, justifying a more modest approach which allows other public interests to be balanced against the goal of undistorted competition on the EU internal market. In a way, this approach is similar to the 'rule of reason' employed within the free movement of goods context, which also enables the goal of trade facilitation and market integration to be balanced against legitimate public interests. To be sure, this approach is not without controversy as

[68] Case C-309/99, *Wouters* [2002] ECR I-1577; Case C-67/96, *Albany* [1999] ECR I-5751

many authors have opposed or tried to interpret the *Wouters* and *Albany* judgments in a way as limited as possible.[69] These arguments will be explored in the subsection below (Section 5.3). First, however, this book will discuss the *Wouters and Albany* judgments and argue how it can be employed to exclude process-based agreements restrictive of competition from the scope of Article 101 (1) TFEU.

First, this book argues that, on the basis of *Albany*, agreements restrictive of competition can be exempted from the application of Article 101 (1) TFEU to the extent that the restrictions are necessary for the protection of an interest recognized by EU legal sources, especially those interests recognized in the EU treaties such as social and environmental protection and the protection of (social) fundamental rights. However, to the extent that the EU or other relevant public authorities have already exhaustively regulated the issue, recourse to the *Albany* exception is no longer possible. This would entail that process-based measures, such as the agreement to close down coal-fired plants in the Netherlands or an agreement to guarantee safe working conditions for workers in the garment industry in Bangladesh, would be exempted from the scope of application of Article 101 (1) TFEU to the extent that they are necessary for the achievement of that goal and that the issue has not been exhaustively regulated.

In the *Albany* line of cases, the Court exempted agreements necessary for the achievement of social policy goals recognized in EU legal sources from the application of the competition rules.[70] *Albany, Brentjes*, and *Drijvende Blokken* all concerned cases relating to collective bargaining agreements between employers and employees in order to improve employment conditions.[71]

The judgments very clearly place the EU competition rules in the wider context of the EU's goals and ambitions, referring not only to the fundamental aims of the EU, but also to another policy area of the EU as well as an interim addition to the internal market. For the ECJ, because certain restrictions of competition are 'inherent' in collective agreements between employers and workers, 'social policy objectives pursued by such agreements would be seriously undermined if management and

[69] See in particular Edith Loozen, 'Professional Ethics And Restraints Of Competition' [2006] *European Law Review*, 28

[70] Case C-67/96, *Albany* [1999] ECR I-5751

[71] Ibid.; Joined Cases C-115–117/97, *Brentjens* [1999] ECR I-6025; Case C-219/97, *Drijvende Blokken* [1999] ECR I-6121; Joined Cases C-180 and 184/98, *Pavlov* [2000] ECR I-6451

labour were subject to Article [101] (1) of the Treaty when seeking jointly to adopt measures to improve conditions of work and employment.'[72] Consequently, the ECJ concluded 'from an interpretation of the provisions of the Treaty as a whole' that such restrictions must, by virtue of their nature and purpose, be regarded as falling outside the scope of Article [101] (1) of the Treaty.'[73]

However, while the Court has recently expanded its approach, it is not without its limits: only agreements that genuinely contribute to those goals fall within the scope of the exception. Thus, in *Pavlov* the Court held that a collective pension fund set up by self-employed medical specialists could not be excluded from the competition rules for similar reasons as in *Albany* because it was not specifically encouraged by Treaty provisions.[74] The Court noted that the agreement was not concluded in the context of collective bargaining between employers and employees and aimed at improving employment conditions, but merely at working conditions of self-employed persons.[75] The General Court came to a similar conclusion in *FNCBC and others*, where it did not find an agreement among farmers and slaughterers which had fixed prices and applied an import ban to contribute to improving conditions of work and employment.[76]

While some have argued that *Pavlov* reduces the *Albany* exception to collective bargaining agreements only, it seems more appropriate to consider the agreement in *Pavlov* not to genuinely be about social protection, since the case concerned self-employed people hardly in any social need: the medical specialists in question could not substantiate, by reference to EU legal sources, that they required social protection through a collective pension scheme. This appears to be confirmed by the ECJ's recent ruling in *FNV Kunsten Informatie en Media* where the ECJ decided on the basis of *Albany* that competition law does not apply to arrangements among freelance substitute orchestra musicians (collectively negotiating a minimum fee for their services) that aim to improve their working conditions if they can be qualifed as 'workers'.[77] The ECJ considered that if these freelancers could be considered workers, the arrangement to collectively negotiate a minimum fee directly contributed to the employment and working conditions.[78] The *FNV Kunsten*

[72] Ibid., para 59–60 [73] Ibid., para 59–60

[74] Joined Cases C-180 and 184/98, *Pavlov* [2000] ECR I-6451, paras 67–69 [75] Ibid.

[76] Joined Cases T-217 and 245/03, *FNCBC and others* [2006] ECR II-4987, para 100

[77] Case C-413/13, *FNV Kunsten Informatie en Media* EU:C:2014:2411, paras 30–37

[78] Ibid., para 40

Informatie en Media case demonstrates therefore that the Court is more concerned with the actual social purpose and effect of an agreement than whether it can formally be considered a collective bargaining agreement.

Second, on the basis of the *Wouters* line of cases and in line with other literature on the case, agreements restrictive of competition can be exempted from the application of Article 101 (1) TFEU to the extent that the restrictions are necessary for the protection of public interests not recognized in EU legal sources, such as the proper functioning of the legal profession or the regulation of sports.[79] This doctrine has more limited practical use for process-based measures, since most public interests underlying process-based measures relate to a specific EU goal or interest, such as animal welfare protection, social policy, or environmental protection. Nonetheless, these cases demonstrate the Court's willingness to embed public interests in the application of the competition rules, and as such exclude the application of those rules to the extent that they are necessary for the pursuit of the public interest goal.

In *Wouters*, the Court accepted that a rule by the Dutch bar council which prohibited professional partnerships between accountants and lawyers interest fell outside the scope of Article 101 TFEU. While the Court considered the rule to be restrictive of competition, it did not violate Article 101 TFEU because it was necessary for the protection of a public interest, namely the proper functioning of the legal profession and more particularly to ensure the independence and professional secrecy of lawyers. In its analysis, the ECJ looked into the context of the rule in question and its objectives in order to determine whether the restriction of competition was 'inherent' in the pursuit of these objectives and did not go beyond what was strictly necessary, effectively introducing a proportionality test.[80] In relation to the context, the Court found that the rule operated within a national legal framework in which the Dutch Bar was required to ensure legal independence of lawyers.[81] The Court concluded that the Dutch Bar regulation 'could therefore *reasonably* be considered to *be necessary in order to ensure the proper practice of the legal profession*, as it is organised in the Member State concerned.'[82] The fact that other Member States had different systems set up and

[79] Monti, 'Aritcle 81 EC and Public Policy' (n 9)

[80] Case C-309/99, *Wouters* [2002] ECR I-1577, para 97–109

[81] Ibid., para 101–104

[82] Ibid., para 107

allowed partnerships between accountants and lawyers was immaterial because the Bar was entitled to consider that the objectives pursued 'cannot, having regard in particular to the legal regimes by which members of the Bar and accountants are respectively governed in the Netherlands, *be attained by less restrictive means*'.[83] Therefore, the restrictive effects on competition of the measure at issue did not 'go beyond what is necessary in order to ensure the proper practice of the legal profession'.[84] In *OTOC*, the ECJ confirmed *Wouters* in relation to private rules of conduct for accountants but came to a different conclusion on the facts when applying the proportionality test.[85]

The *Wouters* rule is not a limited doctrine only applicable to certain deontological rules, as some have argued, or to situations in which regulatory powers have been delegated to undertakings or an association of undertakings.[86] In relation to the latter point, the judgment in *Meca-Medina*, demonstrates that the *Wouters* rule also applies to a regulatory scheme that was entirely private and that did not concern deontological rules. At issue were the the penalties as well as the anti-doping rules themselves of sporting bodies, such as the International Olympic Committee (IOC). The ECJ found that while such rules could have adverse effects on competition, it nonetheless found that such rules could be justified if they were 'limited to what is necessary to ensure the proper conduct of competitive sport'.[87]

The *Wouters* line of cases demonstrate the Court's willingness to investigate public interest objectives that might be served by excluding the agreement from the scope of Article 101 TFEU, even if these objectives are not recognized or defined in EU legal sources, nor recognized by other public authorities. As such, *Wouters* appears to be different from *Albany*. Moreover, the Court has employed an elaborate proportionality test in the *Wouters* line of cases, whereas this requirement has so far not been explicitly mentioned in the *Albany* line of cases. Some authors have argued, therefore, that there is a difference between these two cases, in that on the basis of *Albany*, agreements are excluded generally from the application of Article 101 TFEU, whereas on the basis of *Wouters*, agreements are exempted to the extent that they are necessary for the

[83] Ibid., para 108 [84] Ibid., para 109
[85] Case C-1/12, *OTOC* [2013] ECR I-127, paras 98–99
[86] Edith Loozen, 'Professional ethics and restraints of competition' [2006] *European law review*, 28
[87] Case C-519/04P, *Meca-Medina* [2006] ECR I-6991, para 47

achievement of the public interest goal.[88] This would imply that no proportionality test should be applied in case of the former, but it should be applied in the latter. However, it would appear logical that the Court will apply some form of proportionality test in relation to *Albany* as soon as a restrictive agreement pursuing a social policy goal would go beyond what is necessary to attain it, for example, a hypothetical collective bargaining agreement which includes a price-fixing arrangement unrelated to social protection.

5.3 The Legitimacy of Public Interest Justifications under Competition Law

The inclusion of public interests within competition law outside the narrow neoclassical economic framework (the narrow approach) has come under considerable criticism in literature.

Four main arguments can be identified and will be discussed in detail below:

- Competition law should only pursue the 'modest' aim of economic efficiency (*the modesty argument*);
- The application of competition law should be 'freed' from political interference (*the independence argument*);
- Including societal interests in the application of competition law would undermine legal certainty (*the legal certainty argument*);
- There is no democratic legitimacy for exempting anti-competitive conduct from the competition rules (*the democratic legitimacy argument*).

The first argument has its origins in US antitrust jurisprudence, but has found support within the EU context as well. Originally, in the United States at least, this argument was used to argue against over-enforcement of competition law, and not under-enforcement as is the issue here. Bork, and the Chicago school more generally, objected to the use of American antitrust rules to punish large efficient undertakings in order to protect small undertakings for social justice reasons, for instance. They therefore

[88] Alison Jones, 'Regulating the Legal Profession: Article 81, the Public Interest and the ECJ's Judgment in Wouters' (2008) 19 *European Business Law Review*, 1079; Edith Loozen, 'Reactie op 'Economisch recht en het Verdrag van Lissabon I: mededinging en interne markt' van prof. dr. F. Amtenbrink en prof. mr. J.W. van de Gronden (SEW 2008, 146)' [2009] *Sociaal Economische Wetgeving*, 108

argued for 'modesty' on part of the government when interfering in the market through antitrust legislation. Their objective was to argue for less application of competition rules, not more.[89]

However, ironically, some scholars use this reasoning to argue for *more* governmental intervention in the market, not less, by arguing against public interest *exceptions*. Odudu, for instance, argues that the legitimate task of EU competition law is modest – economic efficiency – and that accepting public interest *exceptions* within the competition law framework 'exceeds the limited competences conferred on the Union and the limits of justifiability'.[90] This reasoning appears illogical: Odudu wants public authorities to interfere more, not less, because otherwise they would exceed the powers they have been attributed by the Treaties. According to him, competition law should be applied in a way to ensure that economic efficiency is realized at all costs, irrespective of the consequences for other societal interests, and as such would be in line with the 'limited' powers public authorities have on the basis of Article 101 TFEU. This approach is however anything but a modest application of competition law.

Moreover, besides this equivocation by Odudu, the EU competition rules do not operate in isolation, but within the broader framework of the EU Treaties, which explicitly call for the accommodation of other public interests within the EU's policies and activities, including competition policy. This is true with respect to environmental protection (Article 11 TFEU), animal welfare protection (Article 13 TFEU), and the various social rights enshrined in the Charter. Much has been written about the nature and strength of the so-called integration articles, which require a certain coherence of EU policy.[91] It is still not clear what the exact nature of these obligations are within EU competition law, but in order for those articles to have a meaning and added value

[89] Robert H. Bork, *The Antitrust Paradox. A Policy at War with Itself* (New York: Basic Books, 1978)

[90] Okeoghene Odudu, 'The Wider Concerns of Competition Law' (2010) 30 *Oxford Journal of Legal Studies*, 599

[91] Nele Dhondt, *Integration of Environmental Protection into Other EC Policies: Legal Theory and Practice* (Groningen: Europa Law Publishing, 2003), Kingston (n 8), Casey (n 8), Vedder (n 8). Three possible interpretations have been identified in relation to Article 11 TFEU: a 'weak interpretation' whereby policy makers are only required to take environmental considerations into account, a 'stronger interpretation' whereby policy makers are obliged to choose for the environmentally friendliest option if more than one option is available and a 'strongest interpretation' whereby environmental protection requirements should be applied at all times. See Kingston (n 8) 113

they must be able to change the interpretation of competition rules so that they are interpreted differently from an interpretation of the competition rules in isolation of other policies.[92]

In addition to the integration articles, the Charter of Fundamental Rights also poses limits on the application of EU competition rules. Article 51 of the Charter thus requires the EU courts as well as the Commission to respect the rights, observe the principles and promote the application thereof in accordance with their respective powers. In addition, Member State adjudicators, be it NCAs or national judges, are under the same obligation to respect the rights, observe the principles and promote the application of the Charter rights when they are implementing Union law.[93]

If national courts, EU courts, the Commission or NCAs are to apply the EU competition rules, this entails that they have to respect the rights, observe the principles and promote the application of the rights contained in the Charter. It is here that our hypothetical 'garment industry' example shows the legal limits of applying EU competition law in a way that does not respect those rights, observes the principles and promotes the application of those rights if competition rules were applied with only economic efficiency in mind. To recall, this would require adjudicators to prohibit an agreement that seeks to ensure that textile products sold on the EU market have not been made in violation of certain core labour standards so that workers making textile products for the EU market work in safe and healthy working conditions, and that no children are employed in the manufacturing process to the extent that the agreement either impedes economic efficiency or economic freedom. This would, however, be quite the opposite of respecting and promoting a number of articles in the Charter.[94] How and to what extent the Charter will operate in practice will be dependent on the interpretation of the Court, but it is submitted that it is doubtful that competition

[92] See Chapter 1 Section 1.3, 64–66

[93] As the Court has made clear in *Åkerberg Fransson*, 'implementing' should be equated with 'acting within the scope of EU law'. The Court held that 'in essence' 'the fundamental rights guaranteed in the legal order of the European Union are applicable in all situations governed by European Union law, but not outside such situations. To put it simply: 'the applicability of European Union law entails applicability of the fundamental rights guaranteed by the Charter.' Case C-617/10 *Åklagaren v Hans Åkerberg Fransson* [2013] ECR I-105 (ECLI), paras 19–21

[94] See for instance Articles 31 and 32 Charter

rules will be interpreted so as to actively frustrate the realization of the rights contained in the Charter.

In addition, the argument that EU competition law should be about economic efficiency only has very little legal support. The competition rules themselves do not mention this, nor can they be extrapolated from the general goals of the EU, of which the EU competition rules are a means to achieve them, nor has the Court ever stated that competition law is solely about economic efficiency. The Court has made clear that competition rules are part of the internal market rules,[95] which have a long history of balancing trade facilitation with public interest regulation. The competition rules are therefore necessary for the functioning of the internal market.[96] If competition rules serve to achieve the aims of the internal market more generally, they should be applied in a way that is consistent with what the internal market is about. And Article 3 TEU makes clear that the internal market is not about economic efficiency, but about promoting a host of economic, social, environmental and other public interest goals.

It is evident that much room for interpretation is left as to what the terms in Article 3 TEU entail, such as 'social market economy', for instance.[97] However, it cannot be inferred from this text that the internal market solely aims at economic efficiency to the exclusion of social and environmental interests. If competition rules are to be interpreted in light of the goals of the internal market, it would follow that the articles are interpreted similarly as to their ultimate results.[98] The Court has always interpreted the internal market rules in a way that respects and embeds trade restrictions to the extent that they contribute to recognized public interests. The Court, of course, has done the same with competition law, as cases such as *Wouters* and *Albany* demonstrate.

[95] Case C-52/09, *Konkurrensverket v TeliaSonera Sverige AB* [2011] I-527, para 20 See also Protocol 27 on the internal market and competition which states that 'the internal market as set out in Article 3 of the Treaty on European Union includes a system ensuring that competition is not distorted'

[96] Ibid., para 21

[97] Giorgio Monti, 'EU Competition Law from Rome to Lisbon - Social Market Economy' in Caroline Heide-Jorgensen, Christian Bergqvist, Ulla Neergaard & Sune Troels Poulsen (eds.), *Aims and Values in Competition Law* (Kopenhagen: DJØF Publishing, 2013), 27; Dragana Damjanovic, 'The EU Market Rules as Social Market Rules: Why the EU can be a Social Market Economy' (2013) 50 *Common Market Law Review*, 1685

[98] Kingston (n 8), 119–124; Mortelmans, 'Towards Convergence in the Application of the Rules on Free Movement and Competition?' (n 8)

The second argument (*the independence argument*) against the inclusion of societal interests in the application of competition law is that competition law should remain 'independent' from political influence, 'freed' from it as Amato has argued. This also seems central to the Commission's 'more economic' approach discussed above.[99] As many ordo-liberals would argue, competition law is about restricting private economic power so that liberal democracy can function properly. Competition law applied independently of political influence ensures that certain private economic power is not favoured over another private power.

Two points can be made here. First, full independence of public powers from societal interests is not only in itself questionable from an accountability point of view, it is also contrary to the system of the Treaties which clearly require policy integration. Second, embedding societal interests in competition law analysis does not amount to a 'usurpation of democracy' as Odudu has put it.[100] Quite the contrary, the adjudicator, through the application of competition law, is able to assess and check private power in a way that enables it to verify whether allowing anti-competitive conduct is truly in the public interest. Intervention by public authorities will inevitably lead to favouring some private economic power over other such power.

The third argument (*the legal certainty argument*) is that a clear rule – economic efficiency – with no exceptions enhances legal certainty and is to be preferred over a rule with many exceptions.[101] Non-inclusion of societal interests keeps the provision of Article 101 TFEU workable and sufficiently clear for national courts and authorities to apply, which would be more difficult if other public interest considerations could be taken into account outside the economic approach.[102] However, the truth is that not many firms will engage in anti-competitive conduct for altruistic reasons. Most firms are still profit-maximizing entities, thus it is unlikely that the corporate social responsibility movement will ensure that firms no longer care about their subsistence. In many instances, the legislator has already regulated matters, which makes the public interest defence usually superfluous. After all, in the more

[99] See above section III. a.; Commission, 'White Paper on Modernisation of the Rules Implementing Articles 85 and 86 of the EC Treaty', para 57

[100] Odudu, 'The Wider Concerns of Competition Law' (*n* 90)

[101] Okeoghene Odudu, *The Boundaries of EC Competition Law: The Scope of Article 81* (Oxford University Press, 2006) 170–173

[102] Giuliano Amato, *Antitrust and the Bounds of Power: The Dilemma of Liberal Democracy in the History of the Market* (Oxford: Hart, 1997) 118–122

than fifty years that competition law has been applied in the EU, only a handful of cases have involved the consideration of public interests. Legal certainty is unlikely to be hampered if competition law is used in a way that embeds societal interests in those limited situations in which those interests might be affected. Moreover, the practice of internal market law demonstrates that it is very well possible for national and European judges to apply the internal market rules and take into account public interest justifications when applying the fundamental freedoms.

The fourth and last argument (*the democratic legitimacy argument*) criticizes including societal interests in competition law analysis with two separate but related points. First, undertakings lack the necessary democratic tools to make a legitimate claim on acting in the public interest, and second, that adjudicators are not in the best position to verify whether such coordination is in the public interest.

The first point of criticism is that undertakings are not accountable to the public through democratically held elections and they lack the means of deliberating and making a careful assessment of what is in the public interest.[103] However, it is not so much that in this approach that undertakings are capable of assessing what is in the public interest or should be able to do so, it is the adjudicator that is making this assessment, carefully determining whether the application of the competitition rules is in the public interest. In the absence of specific legislation, this is something that adjudicators entrusted with a public task are

[103] This is the view for instance by Advocate General Darmon. In Case 228/84, *British Leyland Public Limited Company v Commission* [1986] ECR 3263, Opinion of AG Darmon, Advocate General Darmon concluded that the alleged safety problem resulting from parallel imports of left-hand-drive Metro cars into the United Kingdom where right-hand-drive Metro cars were being marketed by its manufacturer British Leyland was not an objective justification for preventing these parallel imports: 'As regards the problems relating to the safety of consumers and therefore the reputation of the model, the solution can only be legislative. If there is a gap in the British system of type approval – the apparent lack of a right on the part of a manufacturer or any authority appointed to that effect to check that a conversion has been properly carried out after the issue of the certificate of conformity – the solution must be found in the adoption of appropriate laws or regulations, and not in a measure which by distorting the normal competition represented by prices of re-imported vehicles, itself encouraged by BL's initial decision, amounts to depriving dealers and therefore private individuals of the possibility of purchasing vehicles at a lower price. It may be noted, in addition, that the cases of defects submitted by BL, which were identified during the period subsequent to the re-establishment of the approval, clearly cannot justify the decision taken in October 1981.'

verifying when applying the competition rules. Thus, only if the adjudicator is convinced that it is not in the public interest to prohibit the anti-competitive behaviour that the agreement at issue is prohibited.

Competition authorities have discretion in which cases they are willing to spend their limited resources on, for instance, by focussing only on secretive price-fixing arrangements and market partitioning. Similarly, courts can opt for the application of rules in a reasonable way, something the Court has a lot of experience with in the context of the other internal market rules.[104] It does not matter for the Court that the parties infringing the internal market rules are private parties or public authorities.[105] In *Bosman*, for example, the Court had no difficulty in allowing the FIFA and UEFA to rely on public interest justifications for restrictions of the free movement of workers. The Court held that 'there is nothing to preclude individuals from relying on justifications on grounds of public policy, public security or public health. Neither the scope nor the content of those grounds of justification is in any way affected by the public or private nature of the rules in question.'[106] The Court went on to find that it did not accept any of the justifications put forward by the FIFA and UEFA as being sufficient or convincing as to override the interest of the free movement of workers.

This brings us to the second point: are adjudicators capable of understanding what is in the public interest? Isn't the legislator, which is democratically accountable and benefits from the ability of deliberating in public, more competent to assess what is in the public interest?[107]

[104] See for instance Case 120/78, *Rewe-Zentral AG v. Bundesmonopolverwaltung für Branntwein (Cassis de Dijon)* [1979] ECR 650, para 8; Case C-384/93, *Alpine Investments BV v Minister van Financiën* [1995] ECR I-1141, paras 40–44; Case C-55/94, *Reinhard Gebhard v Consiglio dell'Ordine degli Avvocati e Procuratori di Milano* [1995] ECR I-4165, para 37

[105] Case C-415/93, *Union royale belge des sociétés de football association ASBL v Jean-Marc Bosman* [1995] ECR I-4921, para 86; Case C-438/05, *International Transport Workers' Federation and Finnish Seamen's Union v Viking Line ABP and OÜ Viking Line Eesti* [2007] ECR I-10779, paras 75–77

[106] Case C-415/93, *Bosman*, para 86

[107] Francis Kieran suggests as much, even stating that administrative agencies are in a better position to determine what is in the public interest than judges. See Francis Kieran, 'A Separation of Powers Approach to Non-efficiency Goals in EU Competition Law'(2013) 19 *European Public Law*, 189. See also for an interesting comparative example the US *Topco* case (United States v Topco Associates 405 US 596 (1972), 611–612): 'There have been tremendous departures from the notion of a free-enterprise system as it was originally conceived in this country. These departures have been the product of congressional action and the will of the people. If a decision is to be made to sacrifice competition in one portion of the economy for greater competition in another portion this too is a decision that must be made by Congress and not by private forces or by the

The answer is yes, albeit to a limited extent, since legislators are also bound to constitutional restraints guarded by judges. But it does not follow that if a legislator has not enacted legislation, judges should be barred from the possibility to take into account the public interest.[108] In fact, constitutional judges do this all the time as well as judges applying free movement law. It is also not true that the legislator has prohibited the adjudicator from taking into account the public interest when applying Article 101 TFEU. It has entrusted the task of interpreting this provision to the Court, and the Court has not ruled that economic efficiency is the only interest that can be taken into account when applying competition law.

In the absence of the means that the legislator has to determine what is in the public interest – accountability and deliberation – how and when should an adjudicator decide when anti-competitive conduct is in the public interest? It is submitted that guidance can be found in the actions of the legislator. This entails, first, that where the legislator has already exhaustively regulated a particular situation, and, as a consequence, has already weighed all the different interests involved, the adjudicator should take a deferential stance and presume that the anti-competitive conduct is not in the public interest. This is in line with the approach taken by the Commission and the General Court in *Hilti.*[109] Hilti, a producer of nail guns, cartridges, and nails, had tried to justify its exclusionary conduct (requiring consumers of Hilti cartridges for their nail guns to also buy Hilti nails) on health and safety grounds.

courts. Private forces are too keenly aware of their own interests in making such decisions and courts are ill-equipped and ill-situated for such decision-making. To analyze, interpret, and evaluate the myriad of competing interests and the endless data that would surely be brought to bear on such decisions, and to make the delicate judgment on the relative values to society of competitive areas of the economy, the judgment of the elected representatives of the people is required.'

108 The General Court in Case T-83/91, *Tetra Pak International SA v Commission (Tetra Pak II)*[1994] ECR II-755 seems to conflate the issue of the roles played by the adjudicator and that of the undertakings engaging in anti-competitive conduct. The General Court refuted the argument made by Tetra Pak that separating aseptic cartons and aseptic filling machines might lead to serious public health concerns. See paras 83–84 of that judgment where the General Court held that it was not for Tetra Pak to decide on safety requirements in the public interest and stated that 'the remedy must lie in appropriate legislation or regulations, and not in rules adopted unilaterally by manufacturers, which would amount to prohibiting independent manufacturers from conducting the essential part of their business.'

109 Case T-30/89, *Hilti AG v Commission* [1991] ECR II-1439; *Eurofix-Bauco v Hilti* (Cases IV/30.787 and 31.488) Commission Decision 88/138/EEC OJ 1987 No. L65/19

The Commission dismissed this argument on procedural grounds, finding that Hilti had not taken any action towards public authorities or other retailers to address the issue.[110] The General Court dismissed the argument on the basis of already existing legislation. The General Court pointed out that there were already laws relating to health and safety standards in place in the United Kingdom and that they were enforced. According to the General Court, 'in those circumstances it is clearly not the task of an undertaking in a dominant position to take steps on its own initiative to eliminate products which, rightly or wrongly, it regards as dangerous or at least as inferior in quality to its own products'.[111]

A related point is that of enforcement. What if the legislator has exhaustively laid down rules, and undertakings agree to restrict competition in order to enforce such rules? Again, there should be a presumption that this should, in principle, be left over to the authorities and that undertakings should notify the authorities if competitors are not complying with legislation. In *Akcenta*, the Court seems to suggest as much, noting that it was 'for public authorities and not private undertakings [. . .] to ensure compliance with statutory requirements' and emphasising that 'the application of statutory provisions may call for complex assessments which are not within the area of responsibility of those private undertakings'.[112] However, it is submitted that this should be a presumption as there might be instances in which public authorities are not in the position to verify compliance with legislation or entrust undertakings with the task of enforcement. This may be particularly relevant to process-based measures. It might be very difficult for public authorities to verify compliance with legislation if activities do not fully take place within the jurisdiction of the legislator for instance. The Bangladesh government, due to its limited resources and lack of jurisdiction on the European market, may be supportive of initiatives within the EU which lower the incentives of factories in Bangladesh to not comply with basic labour standards. This kind of public-private cooperation is also central to the Kimberley Certification process, in which the diamond industry plays an important role in the enforcement of the agreed standards.

If a situation has not been exhaustively covered by the legislator, then second, the adjudicator can identify a public interest by having recourse

[110] *Eurofix-Bauco v Hilti*, paras 88–92

[111] Case T-30/89, *Hilti AG v. Commission* (n 109), para 118

[112] Case C-68/12, *Akcenta* (n 32), paras 19–20

to goals and obligations formulated in legislation. Within the EU this means that the goals and obligations formulated within the EU Treaties, international agreements of which the EU or its Member States are party, and secondary legislation can be guiding in determining when anti-competitive conduct is in the public interest. These goals can be vaguely formulated, not providing much guidance, but can also be surprisingly precise. This was the approach of the Court in *Albany* in formulating the public interest of improving the conditions of work and employment.[113]

The *DSD* decision of the Commission provides an example in which both the goals of the EU as formulated in the Treaties as well as secondary legislation can be guiding in the formulation of the public interest and the proper assessment of the contribution made by the anti-competitive conduct to that public interest. In assessing whether the long-term service agreements between DSD and the collectors contributed to technological and economic progress, the Commission found that DSD was giving effect to national and EU environmental legislation and policy with regard to the prevention, recycling and recovery of waste packaging and thereby providing a high level of environmental protection.[114]

This approach is different from the approach of the Court in *Wouters*. In that case, it was not the EU legislature which was providing guidance for the Court in determining whether the anti-competitive conduct was in the public interest, but a legislature of a Member State. In *Wouters*, the Court found guidance in identifying the public interest of ensuring the proper functioning of the legal profession in the Dutch Advocatenwet.[115] The Court used that Dutch legislative framework of what was in the public interest to verify whether the conduct of the Dutch Bar was suitable for the achievement of those public interests and did not go further than necessary.

Lastly, there is the situation in which there is no guidance by the legislature in identifying a public interest. This is the most difficult situation for an adjudicator since it will have to assess the public interest on its own. The Court, however, has not shied away from excluding the application of the competition rules in such a situation. In *Meca-Medina*,

[113] Case C-67/96, *Albany* (n 70), para 55–58
[114] *DSD* (Cases COMP/34493 – DSD and others) Commission Decision 2001/837/EC OJ 2001 No. L319/1, para 143
[115] Case C-309/99, *Wouters* (n 80), para 98–102

it could not rely on any rule of a public nature, but it nevertheless considered the proper conduct of competitive sport to be a public interest that could justify the exclusion of the application of the competition rules to the extent that they were necessary for the achievement of that goal.

If an adjudicator establishes that the anti-competitive conduct contributes to a public interest, how should it assess whether this contribution justifies the exclusion of the competition rules? In principle, the answer is relatively simple. To the extent that the public interest can be subsumed under Article 101 (3) TFEU, it requires an investigation into the extent to which the agreement meets all four cumulative requirements. If not, in line with *Wouters*, a proportionality test should be applied to ensure that the agreement is not more restrictive of competition than strictly necessary for the protection of the public interest. The two limbs of the proportionality test – suitability and necessity – can be applied with flexibility on a case-by-case basis depending on the context, nature, and purpose of the restrictive agreement. Within the proportionality test a number of factors can be taken into account in order to ensure that the agreement at issue is actually in the public interest. Account can be taken of the importance of the issue at hand, both formally and substantively. Thus, if the measure contributes to a public interest that is given great importance by the legislator, for example, if it is featured in the Charter of Fundamental Rights, this should be taken into account as well as the impact the agreement has on the public interest. The relative contribution to the public interest and the degree of restrictiveness of the agreement can also play a determining factor in this respect. In fact, this is inherent in the fourth criterion of Article 101 (3) TFEU, which requires that at least some competition remains intact on a given market.

Moreover, consideration can be given to the extent that stakeholders affected by the agreement endorse it.[116] If societal actors such as NGOs, labour unions, environmental or consumer organizations endorse a certain initiative, this can be an indication of both the fact that the agreement goes beyond the narrow self-interest of the undertakings as well as an indication that the agreement is well balanced and an adequate reflection of the consensual nature of the outcome. The Dutch agreement to close down five out-of-date coal-fired electricity plants, for

[116] Sébastien Mena and Guido Palazzo, 'Input and Output Legitimacy of Multi-Stakeholder Initiatives' (2012) 22 *Business Ethics Quarterly*, 527–557

instance, had broad grass-roots support: not only did the Dutch government endorse the agreement, over forty different organizations supported it, among them labour unions, employers organizations, environmental organizations and – notably – consumer organizations.[117] Similarly, the endorsement of labour organizations, human rights organizations, the garment industry in Bangladesh, and the Bangladeshi government can give the adjudicator guidance on whether the process-based standards are well-balanced. The more consensual in nature the agreement is, and the more various stakeholders endorse the standard, the more likely it is that the restrictions of competition do not go beyond what is strictly necessary to achieve the public interest goal. The Commission in its horizontal cooperation guidelines also refers to the importance of stakeholder endorsement. It states that 'If participation in the standard-setting process is open in the sense that it allows all competitors (and/or stakeholders) in the market affected by the standard to take part in choosing and elaborating the standard, this will lower the risks of a likely restrictive effect on competition by not excluding certain companies from the ability to influence the choice and elaboration of the standard.'[118]

In addition, an adjudicator can take into account the quality of the regulation if the agreement takes the form of a standardization agreement. This can include aspects such as the unambiguous nature of the wording of the process-based standards, transparency both in relation to procedure as well as outcome, and independent enforcement or verification of the process-based standard. Transparency both at procedural and outcome level enables the adjudicator to evaluate the activities of the undertakings involved in the formation and enforcement of the process-based standard. Moreover, independent verification of compliance and enforcement can be an important factor in determining whether the process-based standard is in the public interest. Generally speaking, self-monitoring greatly increases the risks of the undertakings to cheat, report falsely on compliance and makes compliance verification more difficult in general.[119] Second-party monitoring, whereby an external audit company monitors compliance, improves compliance although third-party monitoring is a better way of enforcement of the norms if

[117] See above (*n* 2)

[118] Guidelines on horizontal co-operation agreements (n 7), para 295, see also *X/Open Group* (Case IV/31.458) Commission Decision OJ 1987 No. L 35/36

[119] Mena and Palazzo (n 116), 542

public interests need to be secured. Third-party monitoring is monitoring done by independent civil society or government organizations that do not have any incentive to cover-up for the undertaking involved.[120]

Finally, especially in relation to process-based standards, an adjudicator can look carefully into whether the measure is actually effective. There is the danger that process-based measures are mere dress-ups to improve the image of a given sector and do not actually contribute to the public interest that the anti-competitive conduct seeks to address. Process-based measures can result in green-washing or blue-washing, in which the standards result in too low standards or wrongly calibrated measures that do not lead to social or environmental improvement.[121] Wrong calibration can lead to unjustifiably excluding undertakings from the market over others, for instance, if a process-based standard is mainly developed for Western brands and detrimental to smaller firms in developing countries without any objective justification.[122]

Conclusion

The EU competition rules seek to accomplish workable competition on the EU internal market in order to ensure the well-being of the European Union. Process-based measures enacted by undertakings may violate Article 101 (1) TFEU if their conduct enables them to create market power on a given market and use that market power with negative consequences for one of the parameters of competition, even if the conduct is beneficial to social and environmental interests. This is particularly so if a process-based measure takes the form of a binding standardization agreement which may have negative effects on the price, innovation and diversity of the products concerned.

There are, however, two ways in which social and environmental interests may be accommodated within a competition law analysis.

[120] Ibid., 543

[121] Ibid., 542; Debora L. Spar and Lane T. La Mure, 'The Power of Activism: Assessing the Impact of NGOs on Global Business' (2003) 45 *California Management Review*, 78–101; Virginia Haufler, 'New Forms of Governance: Certification Regimes as Social Regulations of the Global Market' in E. Medinger, C. Elliot and G. Oesten (eds.) *Social and Political Dimensions of Forest Certification* (Remagen-Oberwinter: forstbuch.de, 2003), 237–247; Labour Rights in China, 'No illusions: Against the global cosmetic SA8000' (1999) www.lancaster.ac.uk/fass/law/intlaw/ibuslaw/docs/noillusions.doc

[122] David Vogel, 'The private regulation of global corporate conduct'(2010) 49 *Business & Society*, 68–87; Mena and Palazzo (n 116) 542

The first way is through a broad interpretation of the explicit exemption created in Article 101 (3) TFEU. The second way is through case-law based justifications. The Court's case law is, in both respects, very similar to its case-law on the fundamental freedoms: public interests other than competitive free markets are embedded within the internal market rules. It is not surprising, however, that not much case-law on these public interest defences has emerged since undertakings are not primarily concerned with promoting public interests in the way Member State governments are. Much of the future development and concrete implications of the Court's case law on accommodating public interests within competition law analysis, therefore, lies ahead of us.

Nevertheless, literature on Article 101 TFEU has opposed and played down the significance of the Court's case law on the public interest defence, which is mainly of a utilitarian and ordo-liberal nature. Few of these arguments are convincing, but adjudicators should be wary as to the claims that undertakings make in relation to contributions to the public interests. Process-based standards developed by undertakings might be entirely self-serving, badly designed and overly restrictive. Moreover, they can be superfluous if the legislator has already made an assessment of all the different interests involved and has exhaustively regulated the particular issue. Adjudicators should therefore carefully assess process-based measures under EU competition law. Deference towards the legislator is necessary in most instances, and guidance on the identification of the public interest can be found in the formulation of public interest goals by the legislator. Moreover, through a careful analysis of the regulatory design of the process-based measure, as well as the use of the proportionality principle, adjudicators can embed social and environmental interests in competition law analysis in a way that is reflective of the aims of the Treaties.

Conclusion

Process-based measures (or PPMs as they are often referred to in the WTO context) are a particular response to globalization, deriving, in part, from the lack of a competent regulator at the international level and an increasing awareness that consumption at home of goods produced abroad may have an adverse impact on the environment, animal welfare, or social conditions elsewhere. Process-based measures have stirred controversy for over two decades in the WTO context. Opponents of such measures argue that they interfere impermissibly with the domestic affairs of exporting countries and eliminate their comparative advantages, and that importing countries should 'mind their own business'. Proponents see process-based measures as a way to fill global governance gaps and address the negative effects of international trade, and argue that it is an importing country's right to determine which goods may be sold on its market.

This book has argued that process-based measures challenge our common conceptions of how trade is and ought to be regulated in three fundamental ways. First, process-based measures – in contrast to more traditional product rules – address societal concerns that manifest themselves outside the jurisdiction of the host state, and thus challenge our understanding of trade regulation as a predominantly domestic affair. Process-based measures regulate products not because they present a danger to the host state or its people, but rather because they present a danger in the state of production, as they are made in a way that harms the environment, is detrimental to animal welfare, or affects workers' health and safety. Process-based measures therefore seek to engage in extraterritorial social or environmental protection.

Second, process-based measures challenge our conception of how trade is and ought to be regulated, because of the process by which this environmental and social protection is accomplished. Instead of looking for common and mutually agreeable solutions among states, process-based measures seek to address transnational issues unilaterally, conditioning market access on compliance with the social and environmental production standards applicable in the importing state without necessarily or adequately consulting the country of production.

Third, process-based measures challenge our conception of how trade is and ought to be regulated because increasingly these type of norms are laid down by private parties, rather than through traditional channels of public power. Labelling initiatives such as the MSC, FSC, and Fairtrade labels, standardization agreements among undertakings engaging in corporate social responsibility, and more ad hoc private arrangements such as boycotts and promotional campaigns all seek to influence trade in goods to limit the social or environmental footprint of production. These initiatives can affect trade in the same manner as traditional state market regulation, but do so without the institutional arrangements that guarantee a level of legitimacy for state authority. On the other hand, since such arrangements are not bound by the confines of state territorial jurisdiction, they may have more legitimacy than state-created process-measures, as a host of transnational 'stakeholders' may participate in norm creation.

Process-based measures are, therefore, a different response to globalization and the liberalization of markets than traditional regulatory arrangements. The origins of process-based measures are different from traditional forms of trade regulation which concern more clear-cut domestic regulatory issues. They are not a traditional 'inward-looking' reaction towards the opening-up of markets, seeking to protect interests that are confined to domestic harm, but, more broadly, seek to protect transnational social and environmental interests and are therefore more 'outward-looking' and globalized in nature. Private process-based measures can even be seen as transnational regulatory efforts that operate outside the realm of the state, connecting different social groups that have previously only been able to address social and environmental issues through concerted efforts of their respective governments. Within this context, the question this book has sought to address is how the EU legal order copes with these challenges and to what extent these distinctive regulatory aspects of process-based measures affect their legality under EU law. While process-based measures have given rise to considerable controversy within WTO law and scholarship, this debate has remained largely absent in the EU context. In a way, this is surprising because similarly to the WTO, the EU seeks to liberalize trade among its constituent members via provisions that prohibit restrictions on trade while at the same time permit trade restrictions for legitimate public interest purposes. One would expect, therefore, that such a fundamental debate on the (territorial) scope and (unilateral) means of regulating trade on the basis of those interests would also exist within the EU. Moreover, given the EU's normative commitment to tolerance for diversity, one would expect controversy over unilateral sanctions on products that do not conform to a regulator's social and environmental normative preferences. Also, the EU not only has more far more extensive provisions on trade liberalization than the WTO – including detailed rules on public procurement and competition – its legal system also enables many more measures to come before courts, which would suggest that the debate surrounding process-based rules would have materialized more prominently than it has.

On the other hand, the lack of discussion regarding the permissibility of process-based measures is less surprising if one takes into account that the EU has a constitutional mandate to spread its norms (which includes environmental and social protection), and its primary means of doing so is through internal and external market regulation. It might therefore be less controversial for the EU to permit extraterritorial social and environmental protection through its trade rules. In addition, concerns over extraterritoriality and unilateralism are less likely to surface in a legal system such as the EU, since regulatory measures are predominantly challenged by traders and other individuals, rather than by states. Whereas within the WTO a country might feel that a process-based measure unduly infringes upon its prerogative to regulate production within its borders, individual traders are more concerned with obtaining market access than with principled notions of regulatory autonomy.

Lastly, the EU has both the tools and the political will to undertake harmonization measures that help avoid the need for process-based measures. Process-based measures often result from a lack of 'like-mindedness' among states, where one state wishes to address dolphin mortality during tuna harvests, whereas another may have fewer moral scruples. EU Member States, by contrast, share a wide range of values that are not solely restricted to trade liberalization, and seek to translate these values into common policies. The EU has social and environmental policies, a Charter that guarantees a level of fundamental rights protection within the EU legal order, and seeks to accommodate animal welfare concerns in its regulatory policies. The EU, therefore, also has the tools to deal with transnational concerns related to EU-produced goods, as production can be harmonized or regulated across the EU within the confines of EU competence. Products sold within the EU internal market are not always manufactured within the EU internal market, however, reintroducing the potential need for process-based measures at the EU, Member State and private levels. As such, there remains a need to find an answer to the question to what extent such measures are permitted within the EU legal order. This is particularly so, as trade with third countries and the globalizing dissemination of production and consumption is expanding.

This book has identified three main types of EU process-based measures, differentiated on the basis of whom they target: countries (country-based measures), producers (producer-based measures), and consumers (consumer-based measures). Country-based measures seek to persuade governments to change their production standards by restricting market access for products that originate from countries without adequate production standards. These measures are by their very nature discriminatory, as they distinguish products based on their origin, irrespective of whether they are actually made in accordance with the desired standard, and are only effective to the extent that the targeted government can be 'persuaded' by the measure in question. Country-based measures are, generally speaking, also more likely to face opposition on the grounds of extraterritoriality and unilateralism, because there is a more direct link between the measure in question and the regulatory autonomy of the home state.

Producer-based measures, on the other hand, are not necessarily discriminatory, and seek to influence producers, not their governments. Producer-based measures restrict producers' market access to the extent that they do not comply with the relevant production standards. The policies of a producer's home state are irrelevant, so long as the producer itself complies with the production standard underlying the process-based measure. Producer-based measures are, therefore, not unlike product rules in their restrictive effects on trade, as both rules lay down requirements that a manufacturer must meet in order to market its products in the host state.

Lastly, consumer-based measures target consumer behaviour on the market. Measures like voluntary labelling schemes, tax incentives and disincentives, advertising restrictions, boycotts, and advertising campaigns depend for their success entirely upon the willingness of consumers to change their purchasing behaviour. The responsibility to make socially or environmentally conscious purchasing decisions is left to the individual consumer, rather than made by society collectively. Consumer-based measures are, therefore, less effective than producer-based measures, as the decision of whether or not to purchase certain products is not collectively made *a priori*. Generally, at least some non-conforming products will still be marketed.[1] On the other hand, consumer-based measures will have more normative appeal for those who wish to empower consumers, rather than making decisions for them. In addition, consumer-based measures are less likely to raise concerns over extraterritoriality, as the rule-targets (consumers) provide for a greater nexus with the territory of the regulating state.

Within this context, this book has argued that process-based measures raise the same essential balancing issues as are always found when the economic and the non-economic, the public and the private, or the interests of multiple states, interact within a legal order. However, they do so in a new way, and the EU legal system has not yet fully developed a response to the specific issues they raise. In order to assist in this project, this book has sought to provide a map of the legality of process-based measures in the EU, demonstrating where there are gaps and inconsistencies in EU law and policy, and investigating how process-based measures might be designed so as to be compatible with EU law.

This book has assessed each category of process-based measures at three different levels: the EU level, the Member State level, and the private level. Chapter 1 explored the wide range of process-based measures currently in force at the EU level. It not only made clear that the regulatory practice of the EU legislator demonstrates the adoption of country-based, producer-based, and consumer-based measures, but also that, on the basis of the case law of the ECJ, process-based, measures are unlikely to be annulled on grounds of extraterritoriality or unilateralism.

First, the ECJ interprets the territoriality principle broadly, refusing to distinguish between prescriptive and enforcement jurisdiction, as international legal jurisprudence often does. The ECJ considers that a measure complies with the territoriality principle in international law so long as it is enforced within EU territory, regardless of the potential

[1] Generally, at least some non-conforming products will still be marketed unless there is a strong preference among consumers (potentially as a result of the consumer-based measure) to purchase the products that respect the production standard laid down in the measure. See for instance the observations of the Mexican government in *US Tuna II*: WTO Panel Report, *United States – Measures Concerning the Importation, Marketing and Sale of Tuna and Tuna Products*, 15 September 2011 (WT/DS381/R), paras. 7.87–7.90

extraterritorial aims or effects the measure has. This means that as soon as a product enters EU territory, the EU legislator has the competence to regulate that product on the basis of the territoriality principle, irrespective of whether the rules themselves take into account matters that have occurred outside EU territory and irrespective of extraterritorial economic or legislative effects.

Second, the ECJ takes a deferential approach towards the legislator, both in terms of complying with obligations under WTO law, as well as in terms of respecting the proportionality principle, applying the so-called 'manifestly inappropriate' test in relation to the latter. The ECJ has found no legal requirement that the legislator must consult those affected (within or outside the EU) by the norm or accommodate their concerns. This holds true even if the measure in question affects individual rights that may fall within the scope of the Charter (such as in the case of the Inuit seal hunters who invoked their right to property before EU courts, to no avail). The case law further suggests, both in relation to extraterritoriality and unilateralism, that it is irrelevant whether a measure either targets governments, producers, or consumers. Moreover, the EU Treaties themselves mandate the EU to enact process-based measures, and to a certain extent encourage the use of trade measures to achieve other policy goals. The 'integration' articles, which require environmental and other interests to be integrated across all EU policy fields, explicitly enable or even require the EU legislator to take into account social, environmental, and animal welfare considerations when enacting market legislation.

The picture at the Member State level (discussed in Chapters 2, 3, and 4) is more ambiguous. Member State process-based measures are to a large extent disciplined by EU law. First of all, the broad scope of Article 34 TFEU ensures that any measure with actual, potential, or indirect effects on intra-EU trade must be either justified or fall under one of the derogations listed in Article 36 TFEU. Except for a limited number of consumer-based measures that can be characterized as selling arrangements within the meaning of *Keck*, most process-based measures will be characterized as quantitative restrictions on imports or measures of equivalent effect. Moreover, EU tax and procurement rules impose additional limitations on the ability of Member States to adopt process-based measures.

The free movement of goods regime is also applicable to goods of third country origin that are in free circulation within the Union. The principle of assimilation enables traders to rely on Article 34 TFEU to protect third country goods in the same manner as goods of EU origin once they have cleared customs in any Member State. Process-based measures that seek to address social and environmental considerations in countries outside the EU will therefore have to contend with Article 34 as well.

Despite the limitations imposed by internal market law, Member State process-based measures may still very well be permissible. Chapters 3 and 4 analyse the ECJ's case law on justifications of and derogations from Article 34 TFEU in relation to the challenges of extraterritoriality (Chapter 3) and unilateralism (Chapter 4). The law on the free movement of goods does not in principle prevent Member States from relying on derogations and justifications to save trade-restrictive measures that contribute to social and environmental protection abroad. Measures with extraterritorial effects may raise suspicion, but there is no clear doctrinal or policy support to be found in the case-law of the ECJ to oppose measures which have the effect of protecting social and environmental interests abroad. In fact, more often than not, most 'extraterritorial' interests can also be construed as having either national or European interests as well, permitting the ECJ to uphold trade restrictive measures on those grounds.

Equally, while Member States are under an obligation to cooperate in removing unnecessary obstacles to trade and trusting each other to implement secondary legislation, they are also entitled, in the absence of common rules and as co-regulators of the internal market, to act unilaterally to set the level of protection necessary for safeguarding public interests. Member States have no obligation to look for a common European solution to every problem, and may act on their own to protect public interests through justified trade restrictions. In that respect, the ECJ endorses restrictions on trade that seek to protect common European interests. Nonetheless, in applying such measures, Member States are under a duty to facilitate intra-EU trade by taking into account the level of protection of those interests in other Member States. In addition, Member States must trust each other to implement secondary legislation, and cannot use trade restrictions in order to 'second guess' their neighbours, and ensure that the level of protection laid down by EU rules is obtained. Lastly, Member States cannot unilaterally lay down more stringent rules than those adopted at the EU level if they are contrary to those rules or obstruct their goal. This means that if a measure is adopted in the context of the internal market, Member States cannot lay down process-based measures that create obstacles to trade for essentially the same reasons as foreseen in the EU secondary legislation.

While EU free movement law disciplines Member State process-based measures and procurement measures explicitly, as shown in Chapter 2, it does allow Member States to differentiate between products on the basis of their production processes where such factors do not form part of their material substance.

In relation to taxation, as shown in Chapter 2, EU law allows Member States to introduce additional taxes to encourage the consumption of environmentally or socially friendly goods, but is less permissive when it comes to allowing reductions or exemptions from EU harmonized tax rates. All EU harmonized tax rules permit additional taxes, and Articles 30 and 110 TFEU only prohibit customs duties and discriminatory internal taxation. The ECJ has given Member States considerable leeway to introduce product specific taxes for public policy reasons, only prohibiting taxes that introduce discrimination between imported and domestic goods and result in protectionism. The ECJ has explicitly stated that Member States can differentiate among products on the basis of their production methods. Because discrimination on the basis of origin is prohibited, the ECJ requires that similar or competing foreign products that meet the production standards set by the taxing authority must be allowed to profit from the lower tax rate. Therefore, domestic incentives to produce in an environmentally or socially friendly way are extended extraterritorially.

In relation to public procurement, EU law explicitly allows public authorities to base their purchasing decisions on social and environmental production characteristics. The new regime even enables public authorities to refer to a specific label to verify that the supplies in question meet the required standards. Nonetheless, EU public procurement law also imposes a number of constraints on public authorities wishing to procure socially or environmentally friendly goods. First of all, such process-based considerations must be linked to the subject-matter of the contract. This limits the possibility for contracting authorities to reward undertakings for their general corporate social responsibility policies by awarding them public supplies contracts. EU public procurement law thus enables contracting authorities to purchase green electricity, for example, but not to purchase electricity from an undertaking that only makes green electricity. The only general requirement that can be imposed on undertakings is that they comply with legislative requirements. This means that public authorities may only require undertakings to comply with applicable social and environmental legislation, and cannot require that they go beyond those legal requirements. Undertakings can only be excluded from a public tender if they are guilty of 'grave professional misconduct', not on the basis of whether they can produce goods in a socially or environmentally friendly way. This has consequences for the ability of the EU and its Member States to encourage Corporate Social Responsibility through market incentives, which is more limited than EU policy would suggest.

EU law imposes the most significant constraints on process-based measures that are enacted at the private level. First, while free movement of goods rules have so far not been applied horizontally to entirely private arrangements, the personal scope of Article 34 has been applied broadly to encompass measures for which there was some sort of public involvement. Private parties therefore might be constrained by Article 34 TFEU to the extent that they collaborate with public authorities or are put by those public authorities in a position of commanding influence in national markets and are able to prevent or significantly restrict trade in goods imported from another Member State (Chapter 2).

Second, private process-based measures are significantly constrained by EU competition law under Article 101 TFEU. Competition law (Chapter 5) constrains the ability of private parties to enact process-based measures because competing undertakings may not coordinate their economic behaviour in a way that appreciably restricts competition. This may be the case for instance when undertakings agree to go beyond voluntary production standards in their facilities (for example by collectively shutting down polluting factories), or to collectively impose production standards upon their suppliers (for example by refusing to sell unsustainable meat or textile products made by children). This type of coordinated action may be necessary to achieve social and environmental objectives that manifest themselves at the production stage. As a result of information asymmetries between producers and consumers and differences in consumer attitudes and behaviour, it may be very difficult for a single undertaking to compete if it unilaterally adopts superior social or environmental production standards. To address these concerns, therefore, restrictions on competition (for example introducing binding commitments and punishing 'free-riders') might be necessary. This may, however, result in an appreciable restriction of competition prohibited by Article 101 TFEU. Moreover, because EU competition law applies extraterritorially to undertakings established outside the EU as well, coordination designed to protect the environment or core labour standards in developing countries also fall within the scope of Article 101 TFEU to the extent it is 'implemented' in the EU, thus extending the reach of this restriction considerably.

Nonetheless, there are two ways in which competition law may be interpreted to accommodate social and environmental interests. The first way is through a broad interpretation of the explicit exemption created in Article 101 (3) TFEU (the economic approach). The second way is through case-law based justifications (the integrationist approach). The economic approach to Article 101 TFEU would allow for coordination for social and environmental protection to the extent that it also makes sense economically. This approach relies on Article 101 (3) TFEU, which exempts restrictive agreements that contribute to economic or technical progress. The integrationist approach would exclude restrictive agreements from the scope of Article 101 (1) TFEU altogether if such agreements are necessary for the pursuit of a public interest goal. This approach takes into account other public interest requirements within a competition law analysis and is based on a more contextual and purposive reading of the EU Treaties. The second approach is not unlike the ECJ's approach towards other internal market rules, balancing public interests with free movement law. It is not surprising, however, that not much case-law on these public interest defences has emerged since undertakings are not primarily concerned with promoting public interests in the way Member State governments are.

Allowing restrictions of competition on public interest grounds does, however, raise legitimacy issues. Judges and competition authorities are required to identify the public interests that undertakings are protecting in order to exempt their conduct from competition rules. While these authorities are required to take social and environmental interests into account, it is not entirely clear how they should establish whether a restriction of competition is legitimately in the public interest. Chapter 5 suggests that adjudicators should verify whether the public interest identified has already been exhaustively regulated. To the extent that it has, economic coordination by undertakings should not be exempted from the application of competition rules. However, if the legislator has *not* regulated the interest exhaustively, the adjudicator can use other legal sources (such as the Treaties and the Charter) as well as the tools of input and output legitimacy to verify whether economic coordination is necessary for the protection of the public interest. For example, if the economic coordination results from a broader grassroots effort to pursue social or environmental goals, and is endorsed by a wide range of stakeholders, this would indicate that it is legitimately pursuing public interest goals. In such a situation, adjudicators should be permitted to use the proportionality principle to exempt the economic coordination from the EU competition rules. Through a careful analysis of the regulatory design of the process-based measure, as well as the use of the proportionality principle, adjudicators could thus embed social and environmental interests in competition law analysis in a way that reflects the aims of the Treaties.

All in all, despite the characteristics that make process-based measures analytically distinct, EU law does not treat them differently or more strictly than other types of market regulation. The EU legislature and the ECJ have endorsed the use of procurement as a means of incentivizing producers to manufacture their goods in ethically, socially, or environmentally responsible ways. Similarly, the ECJ endorses tax incentives that seek to encourage socially or environmentally friendly production. Moreover, the EU legislator has itself made frequent use of process-based measures as a means to advance social and environmental objectives outside EU borders, and the ECJ's case law suggests that such measures are in principle compatible with EU law. This lenient approach toward EU process-based measures generally, and Member State process-based tax and procurement policies could inform other areas of EU law as well, in particular the interpretation of Article 34 TFEU and the approach towards derogations and justifications from that article. If, for instance, the ECJ takes a principled stance on permitting EU measures on the basis of the territoriality principle, it would require a strong argument why this approach would be different for Member States operating within Article 34 TFEU. The Treaties, in fact, suggest that the treatment should be the same, as such measures contribute to the achievement of the EU's wider goals and ambitions, such as environmental, animal welfare, social, and fundamental rights protection.

This does not mean, however, that process-based measures are immune from legal challenge, nor that their particular features should not be taken into account by regulators and judges. While process-based measures need to comply with internal market rules in the same way as other forms of market regulation, these obligations may be more difficult to meet. This is most visible in the case of private process-based measures enacted by undertakings that are in competition with each other. In order to successfully address social or environmental harm at the production stage, private actors may attempt to 'level the playing field' collectively to prevent compliant undertakings from being outcompeted—something that is at odds with EU competition rules. Similarly, the principle of loyal cooperation and the existence of harmonization measures can significantly impede the possibilities for Member States to adopt process-based measures.

In addition to these legal hurdles, process-based measures also present regulatory design and legitimacy issues of which regulators and judges should be aware. It can be challenging to address social and environmental concerns abroad: a rule might not be adequately calibrated to take into account the different circumstances and preferences of those affected by the norm, and it may be more difficult to verify its impact on the interests addressed. For one thing, the rule's effects occur in a place not within immediate reach and affect people that have not taken part in its development. For another, undertakings might pretend to aspire to social and environmental protection, while not actually delivering results or adequately taking into account the concerns of those affected by their conduct. EU courts do have the option, within the powers invested to them, to take these factors relating to regulatory design into account when reviewing process-based measures that fall under the scope of EU law. They have done so in the past for many other types of measures, and process-based measures will likely be no exception.

Process-based measures thus highlight some interesting points regarding the relative power of the EU, its Member States, and private actors. At the EU level, process-based measures are seen as a legitimate use of European legislative authority. The EU is one of the world's largest markets, and its product rules are of considerable economic importance for third country exporters. EU process-based measures therefore can influence these undertakings and their governments' decisions on how to produce, and as such can contribute to more socially and environmentally conscious ways of producing globally. The EU is willing and able as a collective of states and peoples to regulate its social and environmental footprint abroad through collective purchasing decisions.

Member States are more constrained by EU law in resorting to process-based market regulation. The EU's free movement rules ensure that Member States need to take into account the imperatives of the EU's internal market. Moreover, Member States may be deterred from enacting process-based measures due to the relative ease with which such rules can find their way to the ECJ. This does not mean that Member States cannot enact process-based measures, but rather that they need to take into account both existing harmonized EU rules, as well as the legislative history of the product in other Member States.

When Member States do enact process-based measures, they must therefore also take into account EU legal requirements. The EU's procurement rules, for instance, explicitly allow Member State contracting authorities to procure goods that were produced in an environmentally or socially friendly way.

The EU's regulatory response is most constraining for private process-based measures. The EU's normative imperative to protect competition acts as a significant legal constraint for private parties that desire to standardize production processes on the basis of environmental and social considerations. EU competition rules prohibit initiatives among undertakings that have a negative impact on price, output, or consumer choice. As such, EU competition rules represent the interests of consumers and undertakings unwilling to participate in the social or environmental standard. EU's competition rules therefore favour those who seek to compete on the basis of lower environmental and social norms or prefer to purchase such goods. Nonetheless, private process-based standards may still survive the scrutiny of the ECJ even if they result in restrictions of competition – so long as they are carefully designed.

EU law offers opponents of process-based measures several tools with which to challenge them. However, carefully designed process-based measures – whether promulgated by the EU, Member States, or private actors – can be lawful under EU law. Moreover, even if a process-based measure cannot be taken at one level, proponents can always look for alternatives, and in the end the EU itself can generally enact such measures without much opposition from the ECJ.

To return to an issue raised in this book's Introduction, we can now draw some comparisons between the EU's response to process-based measures with that of the WTO – the forum in which this category was originally defined and problematized. As we have seen, in the EU process-based measures have been explicitly endorsed by the ECJ as a legitimate means by with the EU and Member States may distinguishing among products. By contrast, in the WTO context, process-based measures are not necessarily inconsistent with WTO law, but they have been singled out as a suspicious and problematic category of product rules. What institutional features might explain this difference in approach?

Part of the explanation for these diverging approaches is undoubtedly that the EU, unlike the WTO, can adopt social and environmental legislation, and can resort to positive integration to harmonize Member State rules within the internal market. This has two implications for the EU's regulatory response. First, the fact that the EU pursues goals in addition to trade liberalization gives its institutions, and the ECJ in particular, the mandate to give weight to those other interests. This manifests itself not only in legitimizing process-based measures at EU level, but also accepting Member State measures that pursue interests common to the EU.

Second, trade restrictions within the internal market caused by Member State process-based measures create EU competence to undertake positive integration. A Member State process-based measure is therefore less of a threat to the system, not only because it triggers EU authority, but also because the EU has an institutional solution available to deal with obstacles to trade. While the WTO Dispute Settlement Body certainly can refer to international instruments, and does so, the WTO does not have a constitutional framework that enables (let alone requires) it to pursue social and environmental goals through market regulation. This makes the EU inherently more open and less defensive towards measures that use trade to advance social and environmental interests.

More generally, the EU's ultimate economic goal is creating a uniform market that has the characteristics, as much as possible, of a genuine domestic market.[2] This presumes the creation of a level playing field for all economic actors operating in the EU market. The WTO's goals are less ambitious, and do not seek to create a global level playing field, but rather to allow its Members to benefit from their comparative advantage, not least in terms of lower environmental or social standards.[3] For the EU and its Member States this is less of an issue, because creating a level playing field is the ultimate goal, rather than a threat to the system.

Another factor that may explain the difference in regulatory response is that the WTO is a global organization, whereas the EU is a regional organization. The EU, more so than the WTO, therefore regulates trade with 'outsiders', countries that are not Member States of the EU, as well as trade among its Member States. The EU is therefore inherently more outward-focussed than the WTO. This has, not surprisingly, resulted in the EU's adoption of process-based measures. Moreover, whereas both the EU and WTO regulate trade among their members, the EU's shared goals and ambitions in social and environmental policy suggest that its Member States may have less cause to resort to using process-based

[2] Case 207/83 *Commission v United Kingdom (origin marking)* [1985] ECR 1207, para 17

[3] WTO Ministerial Conference, 'Singapore Ministerial Declaration' (Adopted on 13 December 1996) www.wto.org/english/thewto_e/minist_e/min96_e/wtodec_e.htm

measures to address social and environmental harms *in other Member States*. Generally speaking, EU Member States' environmental and social goals and ambitions are not widely divergent.

Finally, one may point out a significant difference between the EU and WTO in dispute settlement, which may have consequences for legal discourse or how the discussion around process-based measures is framed. Disputes among WTO members are settled in accordance with public international law. While the WTO legal system has undergone a certain level of juridification in recent years, it remains a diplomatic process driven by sovereign states. EU free movement law, by contrast, correlates more closely with domestic legal systems. Individuals can bring cases in front of domestic courts and directly rely on the relevant EU rules in order to set aside Member State rules that create unjustified obstacles to trade. It is not surprising, therefore, that issues of extraterritoriality and sovereignty have surfaced more prominently before the WTO system where disputes are brought by sovereign countries under a system of public international law, than in the EU system, which hears cases brought by individuals in domestic courts. The legal discourse within the EU is focused on balancing individuals' free movement rights against Member State responsibilities to regulate in the public interest, a discourse that does not necessarily involve the exporting country's interests or legal entitlements.

This is not to say that the EU is necessarily more deferential to process-based measures than the WTO in every single respect. In fact, the EU's legal system is a great deal more intrusive. Not only do the EU's competition rules discipline private actors, with respect to whom the WTO has no jurisdiction, but the broad personal and substantive scope of free movement law also requires many process-based measures to be justified. One of the key features of the WTO over process-based measures is whether products that were produced in different ways but are nevertheless physically indistinguishable are 'like'. The EU's *Dassonville* formula, by contrast, brings any measure with potential or indirectly trade-restrictive effects within the scope of EU law. Moreover, the EU's legal system sees a great deal more litigation than the WTO's. While the EU's legal system may not take a principled stance against process-based measures, therefore, the broad scope of EU law means that more measures are subject to its disciplines. This has particularly disempowering effects for private actors at the EU level compared to the WTO, as the WTO does not discipline private actors at all.

Nonetheless, there is an important similarity in the EU and WTO regulatory responses to process-based measures. Both organizations have a certain aversion to 'regulatory blindness' for to the choice of solutions employed by other countries. In the WTO, the Appellate Body in its *US – Shrimp* decision condemned the 'rigid and unbending standard' employed by the United States that did not take into consideration 'different conditions which may occur in the territories of those other Members'. Similarly, the principle of mutual recognition in EU free movement law requires Member State authorities to be fundamentally more 'outward-looking' in the design and application of their process-based measures. As a consequence, in both instances authorities cannot unilaterally apply their process-based measures with complete disregard for the legislative history of an imported product in the exporting country.

From the point of view of legitimacy, this book has argued that process-based measures face considerable challenges. Process-based measures often seek to address social and environmental concerns abroad, without necessarily or adequately consulting local inhabitants or governments or adequately calibrating process-based measures to their needs and capabilities. Similarly, private measures seeking to address recognized public interests such as environmental and social protection are not necessarily constituted in the same way as public measures developed under elaborate democratic institutional frameworks. Interestingly, EU law appears to only take issue in this regard in relation to private rule-making under the constraints imposed by EU competition law, and measures enacted by Member States. The challenge of unilateralism resonates only to a very limited extent to EU process-based measures. The EU's legal system therefore empowers certain public actors vis-à-vis private actors in particular. In a way, it is not surprising that the EU's legal system criticizes its own decision-making the least from the point of legitimacy. The other levels of decision making (Member State and private level), on the other hand, are construed outside its own decision-making procedures and can therefore more easily be criticized as something more distant to the EU's own norms. Moreover, and perhaps most importantly, they may clash with the EU's own economic constitution, the fundamental freedoms and the EU competition rules. This forces the ECJ to scrutinize such rule-making more carefully, because its own constitutional norms are at stake.

Taking a step back and placing the EU's regulatory response to process-based measures in the broader debate on whether the EU has a preference and willingness to 'export' its social and environmental norms abroad, one may question whether the EU's response strengthens or undermines the arguments made in that debate. Does the EU's response to process-based measures underline or undermine the idea that the EU as an international actor seeks to change third countries' social and environmental policies in a way that is more reflective of its own normative preferences? And if so, does the EU's regulatory response say anything about how the EU goes about inducing such change?

Process-based measures enacted by the EU can indeed be seen as a means by which the EU seeks to spread its norms abroad. However, because they are economic instruments, conditioning market access to social or environmental aspects of production abroad, these measures are more examples of economic power than normative power of the EU. They are therefore not so much exemplary of the EU's ideational influence abroad, but more about the use of economic power to achieve social and environmental goals abroad. In that sense, the EU's process-based measures are not unlike the EU's GSP+ programme which also conditions market access upon compliance with core international environmental and labour standards. Only the EU's rules on illegal timber and the importation of illegal, unreported, and unregulated fish bear closer resemblance to the idea of a normative power Europe, because these rules seek to support international and domestic policies abroad that are important to the EU's normative leadership in those areas. With the ban on the marketing of illegal timber, for example, the EU supports domestic rules in third countries that promote sustainable forest management, an aspect of the EU's climate change and environmental policy.

On the other hand, the EU's internal market rules can act as a constraint on efforts in the EU to promote social and environmental goals abroad through process-based measures. These rules discipline and regulate the extent to which private actors and Member States may enact process-based measures. These rules therefore do not unambiguously demonstrate the EU's willingness and ability to spread its social and environmental preferences abroad. However, the ECJ's willingness to accept justifications in the context of free movement law and competition law in light of the EU's social and environmental objectives underpin that such measures remain feasible. Even if the EU's internal market is based on free intra-EU trade and a system of undistorted competition, it does integrate and balance these economic rights against the EU's other objectives.

In that sense, the EU's qualified willingness to endorse process-based measures is perhaps a cautious endorsement of the idea that within the EU, private actors, Member States, and the EU itself may counter the vices of free markets in what Karl Polanyi has historically classified as a 'double movement' in international trade regulation. In 1944, Karl Polanyi coined the term 'double movement' to describe the processes by which the economy, in a 'first movement', became separated from the rest of society through economic liberalization, and was then, in a 'second movement' reintegrated by those seeking societal protection against the dislocation and insecurities unleashed by liberalizing markets.[4] Polanyi's double movement described the liberalization and subsequent re-integration that occurred over a period from roughly 1830 until the Second World War, and resulted in what John Ruggie later famously termed 'embedded liberalism': the post-war compromise of balancing a commitment to free trade with national economic regulation.[5]

The EU's qualified endorsement of process-based measures can be seen in light of and as a continuation of that embedded liberalism compromise. While the EU on the one hand promotes free trade both with and within the EU, the EU's regulatory system also has legal room for counter-movements that seek to address the dislocation, inequality, insecurity, and disruption trade liberalization may cause. The EU's regulatory response to process-based measures is certainly not an unqualified endorsement of such counter-movements. However, its response does demonstrate that the EU's legal structure permits such measures to be taken, therefore balancing a commitment to free trade with other social and environmental interests.

All in all, one may wonder whether the future will bring more process-based measures enacted by the EU, its Member States, or by private parties. So far, such measures have been scarce, certainly at Member State level. Competition authorities' push for a more 'economic' approach to competition enforcement in recent years may certainly complicate the enactment of process-based measures at the private level in the coming years. The two Dutch initiatives to shut down coal fired

[4] Karl Polanyi, *The Great Transformation: The Political and Economic Origins of Our Time* (2nd edn, Boston: Beacon Press, 2001); John Gerard Ruggie, 'International Regimes, Transactions, and Change: Embedded Liberalism in the Postwar Economic Order' (1982) 36 *International Organization* 379

[5] Ibid

power plants and restrict the marketing of factory farmed chicken have, in that sense, already been a victim to this approach.

At the EU level, the EU's current trade policy 'Trade for All' is more centred around concluding deep and comprehensive trade agreements at bilateral level, with far-reaching provisions on investment and regulatory cooperation. While such agreements contain social and environmental chapters, they do not fundamentally seek to address the process-related problems process-based measures seek to address. If anything, these chapters merely restate and legitimize existing EU process-based measures, such as the EU Timber Regulation. These bilateral trade agreements have come under public criticism in recent years, in particular the envisaged trade agreement with the United States, the Transatlantic Trade and Investment Partnership.

Perhaps in response to this criticism and pushed by the European Parliament and Member States, the Commission may propose to initiate more measures such as the EU Conflict Minerals Regulation.

The Commission, in its 'Trade for All' strategy document does pay tribute to its process-based measures and has committed itself to 'ensure responsible management of supply chains' in the future.[6] The Commission seems to be particularly concerned about ensuring consumers right to know what they are buying in light of labour and environmental rules, and corporate social responsibility and due diligence across the production chain. However, it is not clear whether the Commission will pursue these ambitions through proposing more process-based measures. In the past, EU process-based measures have often been a response to Member State regulatory action rather than an initiative leg by DG Trade. In that sense, the Commission's commitment to promote social and environmental pillars of sustainable development 'in a positive, incentive-based way, without any hidden protectionist agenda' suggest an approach more along the lines of the GSP programme and environmental and social chapters in free trade agreements. Indeed, the focus lies with implementation of sustainable development dimensions of free trade agreements as well as multilateral efforts to promote existing EU rules on illegal logging and conflict minerals. While the Communication does explicitly refer to the 'promoting fair and ethical trade schemes', the Commission is only seeking to raise 'awareness' of them and not by engaging in any fair trade regulatory initiatives.

[6] Commission, 'Trade for All: Towards a more responsible trade and investment policy' (Communication) COM (2015) 497 final, 17–18

The question is whether the Commission's trade policy is adequate in addressing citizens' concerns on trade policy. While much of the current scepticism towards trade is inspired by the failure of trade policy and trade liberalization to address those that 'lose out' on trade liberalization, scepticism also derives from the perception that trade liberalization primarily benefits multinational corporations that can use 'global value chains' with few strings attached.[7] In that sense, it will perhaps not be DG Trade but others that will seek process-based measures. The current rules on illegal timber, seal products, organic and eco-labelling, biofuels, and fishing have been developed and are the responsibility of other Directorate's General in the Commission, in particular DG Environment. Moreover, there may be a push from the Member States to have more stringent rules on production processes of products at EU or Member State level, as we have seen in the past. And, of course, private initiatives, in particular labelling initiatives, will continue to be present on EU markets. The EU's economic constitutional framework, as this book has shown, introduces legal complexities for the realization of such measures, but certainly does not oppose them in principle.

[7] Dani Rodrik, *The Globalization Paradox: Why Global Markets, States, and Democracy Can't Coexist* (Oxford: Oxford University Press, 2012); John Gerard Ruggie, *Just Business: Multinational Corporations and Human Rights* (Norton & Company, 2013)

Bibliography

Akerlof GA, 'The Market for "Lemons": Quality Uncertainty and the Market Mechanism' (1970) 84 *Quarterly Journal of Economics*, 488

Alemanno A, 'The Better Regulation Initiative at the Judicial Gate: A Trojan Horse within the Commission's Walls or the Way Forward?' (2009) 15 *European Law Journal*, 382–400

'The European Reform of Organic Farming: Balancing Consumer Preferences and Free Movement Imperatives' [2009] *European Food and Feed Law Review*, 406

Amato G, *Antitrust and the Bounds of Power: The Dilemma of Liberal Democracy in the History of the Market* (Oxford: Hart 1997)

Ankersmit L, 'Het einde van de kiloknallers? De grenzen aan zelfregulering van duurzaam vlees onder het kartelverbod' (2011) *Actualiteiten Mededingingsrecht*, 149

'The Scope of the Common Commercial Policy after Lisbon: The Daiichi Sankyo and Conditional Access Services Grand Chamber Judgments' (2014) 41 *Legal Issues of Economic Integration*, 193

'What if Cassis de Dijon were Cassis de Quebec? The Assimilation of Goods of Third Country Origin in the Internal Market' (2013) 50 *Common Market Law Review*, 1387

Ankersmit L and Lawrence JC, 'The Future of Environmental Labelling: US – Tuna II and the Scope of the TBT' (2012) 39 *Legal Issues of Economic Integration*, 127

Ankersmit LJ, Lawrence JC, and Davies GT, 'Diverging EU and WTO Perspectives on Extraterritorial Process Regulation' (2012) 21 *Minnesota Journal of International Law Online*, 58

Armstrong KA, 'Mutual Recognition' in Catherine Barnard and Joanne Scott (eds.) *The Law of the Single European Market: Unpacking the Premises* (Oxford: Hart, 2002), 225

Arnould J, 'Secondary Policies in Public Procurement: The Innovations of the New Directives' [2004] *Public Procurement Law Review*, 191

Arrowsmith S, 'The Purpose of the EU Procurement Directives: Ends, Means and the Implications for National Regulatory Space for Commercial and Horizontal Policies' (2011–2012) 13 *The Cambridge Yearbook of European Legal Studies*, 1

Arrowsmith S and Kunzlik P (eds.), *Social and Environmental Policies in EC Procurement Law: New Directives and New Directions* (Cambridge: Cambridge University Press, 2009)

Azoulai L, 'The Court of Justice and the Social Market Economy: The Emergence of an Ideal and the Conditions for Its Realization' (2008) 45 *Common Market Law Review*, 1335

Bailey D, 'Restrictions of Competition by Object under Article 101 TFEU' (2012) 49 *Common Market Law Review*, 559

Baksi S and Bose P, 'Credence Goods, Efficient Labelling Policies, and Regulatory Enforcement' (2007) 37 *Environmental & Resource Economics*, 411

Balineau G and Dufeu I, 'Are Fair Trade Goods Credence Goods? A New Proposal, with French Illustrations' (2010) 92 *Journal of Business Ethics* 331

Baquero Cruz J, *Between Competition and Free Movement: The Economic Constitutional Law of the European Community* (Oxford: Hart Publishing, 2002)

'Free Movement and Private Autonomy' (1999) 24 *European Law Review*, 603

Barnard C, *EU Employment Law*, 4th edn, (Oxford: Oxford University Press, 2012)

'Fitting the Remaining Pieces into the Goods and Persons Jigsaw' (2001) 26 *European Law Review*, 35

The Substantive Law of the EU: The Four Freedoms Third Edition (Oxford: Oxford University Press, 2010)

Barrett Lydgate E, 'The EU, the WTO and Indirect Land-Use Change' (2013) 47 *Journal of World Trade*, 159

Bartels L, 'Article XX of GATT and the Problem of Extraterritorial Jurisdiction: The Case of Trade Measures for the Protection of Human Rights' (2002) 36 *Journal of World Trade*, 353

Basaran HR, 'How Should Article 81 EC Address Agreements that Yield Environmental Benefits', (2006) 9 *European Competition Law Review*, 479

Bayefsky AF, 'Cultural Sovereignty, Relativism, and International Human Rights: New Excuses for Old Strategies' (1996) 9 *Ratio Juris*, 42

Beqiraj J, 'The Delicate Equilibrium of EU Trade Measures: The Seals Case' (2013) 14 *German Law Journal*, 279

Bernstein S and Cashore B, 'Can Non-State Global Governance Be Legitimate? An Analytical Framework' [2007] *Regulation & Governance*, 347

Bhagwati J, 'After Seattle: Free Trade and the WTO' in Roger B, Jagdish Porter and others (eds.), *Efficiency, Equity, and Legitimacy: the Multilateral Trading System at the Millennium* (Washington: Brookings Institution Press, 2001), 50

In Defense of Globalization (Oxford: Oxford University Press, 2007)

Black J, 'Constitutionalising Self-Regulation' (1996) 59 *The Modern Law Review*, 24

Bodansky D, 'What's So Bad about Unilateral Action to Protect the Environment?' (2000) 11 *European Journal of International Law*, 339

Boedeltje M and Cornips J, 'Input and Output Legitimacy in Interactive Governance' (No. NIG2-01) *NIG Annual Work Conference 2004 Rotterdam*

Bogaert S van den, 'Horizontality: The Court Attacks?' in Catherine Barnard and Joanne Scott (eds.), *The Law of the Single European Market: Unpacking the Premises* (Oxford: Hart Publishing, 2002), 123

Bonroy O and Constantatos C, 'On the Use of Labels in Credence Goods Markets' (2008) 33 *Journal of Regulatory Economics*, 237

Bork RH, *The Antitrust Paradox. A Policy at War with Itself* (New York: Basic Books, 1978)

Bronckers M, 'The Relationship of the EC Courts with other International Tribunals: Non-Comittal, Respectful or Submissive?' (2007) 44 *Common Market Law Review*, 601

Brown C, 'Case C-112/00, Eugen Schmidberger, Internationale Transporte und Planzüge v. Austria' (2003) 40 *Common Market Law Review*, 1499

Brus M, 'Case C-510/99, Procureur de la République v. Xavier Tridon' (2003) 40 *Common Market Law Review*, 169

Camm T and Bowles D, 'Animal Welfare and the Treaty of Rome-Legal Analysis of the Protocol on Animal Welfare and Welfare Standards in the European Union' (2000) 12 *Journal of Environmental Law*, 197

Caporaso JA, 'International Relations Theory and Multilateralism: The Search for Foundations' (1992) 46 *International Organization*, 599

Casey D, 'Disintegration: Environmental Protection and Article 81 EC' (2009) 15 *European Law Journal*, 362

Castaldo S, Perrini F, Misani N and Tencati A, 'The Missing Link Between Corporate Social Responsibility and Consumer Trust: The Case of Fair Trade Products' (2009) 84 *Journal of Business Ethics* 1

Chalmers D, Davies G, and Monti G, *European Union Law; Cases and Materials*, 2nd edn, (Cambridge: Cambridge University Press, 2010)

Chang H, 'An Economic Analysis of Trade Measures to Protect the Global Environment' (1995) 83 *Georgetown Law Journal*, 4

Charnovitz S, 'Free Trade, Fair Trade, Green Trade: Defogging the Debate' (1994) 27 *Cornell International Law Journal*, 459

'The Law of Environmental PPMs in the WTO: Debunking the Myth of Illegality' (2002) 27 *The Yale Journal of International Law*, 59

Conford R, *The Origins of the Organic Movement* (Edinburgh: Floris Books, 2001)

Cornish W, *Intellectual Property: Omnipresent, Distracting, Irrelevant?* (Oxford: Oxford University Press, 2004)

Damjanovic D, 'The EU Market Rules as Social Market Rules: Why the EU can be a Social Market Economy' (2013) 50 *Common Market Law Review*, 1685

Darby M and Karni E, 'Free Competition and the Optimal Amount of Fraud' (1973) 16 *Journal of Law and Economics*, 67

Davies G, 'Freedom of Movement, Horizontal Effect, and Freedom of Contract' [2012] *European Review of Private Law*, 805

'Is Mutual Recognition an Alternative to Harmonisation: Lessons on Trade and Tolerance of Diversity from the EU' in Lorand Bartels and Federico

Ortino (eds.), *Regional Trade Agreements and the WTO Legal System* (Oxford: Oxford University Press, 2006) 265
'Process and Production Method Based Restrictions on Trade in the EU' in C. Barnard (ed.), *Cambridge Yearbook of European Legal Studies 2007–2008* (Oxford: Hart Publishing, 2008), 69
de Mars S, 'The Limits of General Principles: A Procurement Case Study' (2013) 38 *European Law Review*, 316
de Sadeleer N, 'Environmental Governance and the Legal Bases Conundrum' (2012) 31 *Yearbook of European Law*, 373
EU Environmental Law and the Internal Market (Oxford: Oxford University Press, 2014)
de Vries S, 'Case C–470/03, A.G.M.–COS.MET Srl v. Suomen valtio, Tarmo Lehtinen' (2008) 45 *Common Market Law Review*, 56
de Witte B, 'Non-market Values in Internal Market Legislation' in Niamh Nic Shuibhne (ed.), *Regulating the Internal Market* (Cheltenham: Edward Elgar, 2006), 61
de Witte F, 'Sex, Drugs & EU Law: The Recognition of Moral and Ethical Diversity in EU Law' (2013) 50 *Common Market Law Review*, 1545, 1553
Dhondt N, *Integration of Environmental Protection into Other EC Policies: Legal Theory and Practice* (Groningen: Europa Law Publishing, 2003)
Dougan M, 'Minimum Harmonization and the Internal Market' (2000) 37 *Common Market Law Review*, 853
Doukas D, 'Untying the Market Access Knot: Advertising Restrictions and the Free Movement of Goods and Services' (2007) 9 *Cambridge Yearbook of European Legal Studies*, 177
Dragos D and Neamtu B, 'Sustainable Public Procurement: Life-Cycle Costing in the New EU Directive Proposal' [2013] *European Procurement & Public Private Partnership Law Review*, 19
Drijber BJ and Stergiou H, 'Public Procurement Law and Internal Market Law' (2009) 46 *Common Market Law Review*, 805
Dworkin G, 'Paternalism' in R A Wasserstrom (ed.), *Morality and the Law* (Belmont: Wadsworth, 1971)
Eeckhout P, *EU External Relations Law*, 2nd edn (Oxford: Oxford University Press, 2011)
Enchelmaier S, 'Article 36: General' in P Oliver (ed.), *Oliver on Free Movement of Goods in the European Union* (Oxford: Hart Publishing, 2010), 215
Fitzgerald PF, '"Morality" May Not Be Enough to Justify the EU Seal Products Ban: Animal Welfare Meets International Trade Law' (2011) 14 *Journal of International Wildlife Law & Policy*, 85–136
Fridell M, Hudson I and Hudson M, 'With Friends Like These: The Corporate Response to Fair Trade Coffee' (2008) 40 *Review of Radical Political Economics*, 8
Gaines SE, 'Processes and Production Methods: How to Produce Sound Policy for Environmental PPM-Based Trade Measures?' (2002) 27 *Columbia Journal of Environmental Law*, 383

Gale F and Haward M, *Global Commodity Governance: State Responses to Sustainable Forest and Fisheries Certification* (London: Palgrave Macmillan, 2011)

Geraerts D and Natens B, 'The WTO Consistency of the European Union Timber Regulation' (2014) 48 *Journal of World Trade*, 433

Gerbrandy A, 'Competition Law and Private-Sector Sustainability Initiatives' in A.L.B. Colombi Ciacchi and others (eds.), *Law & Governance – Beyond the Public-Private Divide?* (The Hague: Eleven International Publishing, 2013), 81–103

Gormley L, 'Competition and Free Movement: Is the Internal Market the Same as a Common Market?' [2002] *European Business Law Review*, 517

'Reasoning Renounced? The Remarkable Judgment in Keck & Mithouard' [1994] *European Business Law Review*, 63

'Silver Threads among the Gold . . . 50 Years of the Free Movement of Goods' (2007) 31 *Fordham International Law Journal*, 1637

Haas E B, *The Uniting of Europe: Political, Social and Economic Forces*, 1950–57 (Notre Dame: University of Notre Dame Press, 1958)

Habermas J, *The Postnational Constellation: Political Essays* (Cambridge: MIT Press, 2001)

Harbo TI, 'The Function of the Proportionality Principle in EU law' (2010) 16 *European Law Journal*, 158, 185

Harrems N, 'The Leghold Trap Regulation and Potential Pitfalls during the Dutch Presidency of the EU' (1998) *European Environmental Law Review*, 7

Harvey D, *A brief history of neoliberalism* (Oxford: Oxford University Press, 2005)

Haufler V, 'The Kimberley Process Certification Scheme: An Innovation in Global Governance and Conflict Prevention' (2010) 89 *Journal of Business Ethics*, 403

Hedemann-Robinson M, 'Defending the Consumer's Right to a Clean Environment in the Face of Globalisation. The Case of Extraterritorial Environmental Protection under European Community Law' (2000) 23 *Journal of Consumer Policy*, 25

Hertel M, 'Climate-Change-Related Trade Measures and Article XX: Defining Discrimination in Light of the Principle of Common but Differentiated Responsibilities' (2011) 45 *Journal of World Trade*, 653

Hojnik J, 'Free Movement of Goods in a Labyrinth: Can Buy Irish Survive the Crises?' (2012) 49 *Common Market Law Review*, 291

Horsley T, 'Unearthing Buried Treasure: Art 34 TFEU and the Exclusionary Rules,' (2012) 37(6) *European Law Review*, 737

Howse R and Langille J, 'Permitting Pluralism: The Seal Products Dispute and Why the WTO Should Accept Trade Restrictions Justified by Noninstrumental Moral Values' (2012) 37 *Yale Journal of International Law*, 367

Howse R and Regan D, 'The Product/Process Distinction: An Illusory Basis for Disciplining Unilateralism in Trade Policy' (2000) 11 *European Journal of International Law*, 249

Jack B, *Agriculture and EU Environmental Law* (Farnham: Ashgate, 2009)

Jackson JH, *The World Trading System: Law and Policy of International Economic Relations* 2nd edn (Cambridge, MIT Press, 1997)

Jans JH, 'Stop the Integration Principle?' (2009–2010) 33 *Fordham International Law Journal*, 1533

Jans JH and Vedder HHB, *European Environmental Law* (Groningen: Europa Law Publishing, 2008)

Jansen B, 'The Limits of Unilateralism from a European Perspective' (2000) 11 *European Journal of International Law*, 309

Jarvis MA, 'Case C-325/00, Commission v. Germany, Judgment of the Court of Justice of 5 November 2002. Full Court' (2003) 40 *Common Market Law Review*, 71

Jones A, 'Regulating the Legal Profession: Article 81, the Public Interest and the ECJ's Judgment in Wouters' (2008) 19 *European Business Law Review*, 1079

Kieran F, 'A Separation of Powers Approach to Non-efficiency Goals in EU Competition Law' (2013) 19 *European Public Law*, 189

Kingston, S, *Greening EU Competition Law and Policy* (Cambridge University Press, 2012)

'Integrating Environmental Protection and EU Competition Law: Why Competition Isn't Special' (2010) 16 *European Law Journal*, 780

Kjølbye L, 'The New Commission Guidelines on the Application of Article 81 (3): an Economic Approach to Article 81' (2004) 25 *European Competition Law Review*, 566

Komninos AP, 'Non-competition Concerns: Resolution of Conflicts in the Integrated Article 81 EC' (2008) The University of Oxford Centre for Competition Law and Policy Working Paper (L) 08/05

Krämer L, 'Sustainable Development in EC Law' in H Bugge and C Voigt (eds.), *Sustainable Development in International and National Law* (Groningen: Europa Law Publishing, 2008)

Krenn C, 'A Missing Piece in the Horizontal Effect "Jigsaw": Horizontal Direct Effect and the Free Movement of Goods' (2012) 49 *Common Market Law Review*, 177

Kröger J, 'Nationally Exclusive Support Schemes for RES Electricity Production and the Free Movement of Goods' (2013) 10 *Journal for European Environmental & Planning Law*, 378–393

Kuijper PJ and Bronckers M, 'WTO Law in the European Court of Justice' (2005) 42 *Common Market Law Review*, 1313

Kulovesi K, Morgera E and Muñoz M, 'Environmental Integration and Multi-faceted International Dimensions of EU Law: Unpacking the EU's 2009 Climate and Energy Package' (2011) 48 *Common Market Law Review*, 829

Kunzlik P, 'From Suspect Practice to Market-Based Instrument: Policy Alignment and the Evolution of EU Law's Approach to "green" Public Procurement' [2013] *Public Procurement Law Review*, 97

Laïdi Z, *La norme sans la force: L'énigme de la puissance européenne*, 2nd edn (Paris: Les Presses de Sciences Po, 2008)

Lang ATF, 'Reconstructing Embedded Liberalism: John Gerard Ruggie and Constructivist Approaches to the Study of the International Trade Regime' (2006) 9 *Journal of International Economic Law*, 81

Levashova Y, 'How Effective is the New EU Timber Regulation in the Fight against Illegal Logging?'(2011) 20 *Review of European Community and International Environmental Law*, 294

Lohse EJ, 'Fundamental Freedoms and Private Actors – Towards an "Indirect Horizontal Effect"' 13 (2007) *European Public Law*, 159

Loozen E, 'Professional Ethics and Restraints of Competition' [2006] *European Law Review*, 28

Loureiro ML and Lotade J, 'Do Fair Trade and Eco-Labels in Coffee Wake up the Consumer Conscience?' (2005) 53 *Ecological Economics*, 129

Ludwig R and O'Gorman R, 'A Cock and Bull Story? – Problems with the Protection of Animal Welfare in EU Law and Some Proposed Solutions' (2008) 20 *Journal of Environmental Law*, 363

Lugard P and Hancher L, 'Honey, I Shrunk the Article! A Critical Assessment of the Commission's Notice on Article 81(3) of the EC Treaty' (2004) 25 *European Competition Law Review*, 410

Lupton S, 'Shared Quality Uncertainty and the Introduction of Indeterminate Goods' (2005) 29 *Cambridge Journal of Economics*, 399

Maduro MP, *We the Court: the European Court of Justice and the European economic constitution: a critical reading of Article 30 of the EC Treaty* (Oxford: Hart Publishing, 1998)

Manners I, 'Normative Power Europe: A Contradiction in Terms?' (2002) 40 *Journal of Common Market Studies*, 235

Martens M and de Margerie S, 'The Link to the Subject-Matter of the Contract in Green and Social Procurement' [2013] *European Procurement & Public Private Partnership Law Review*, 8

Matsushita M, Schonebaum TJ and Mavroidis PC (eds.), *The World Trade Organization: Law, Practice And Policy* (2nd edn, Oxford University Press 2006) 808

Mattera A, 'L' article 30 du traité CEE, la jurisprudence «Cassis de Dijon» et le principle de la reconnaissaince mutuelle' [1992] *Revue du Marché Unique Européen*, 13

'Principle of Mutual Recognition and Respect for National, Regional and Local Identities and Traditions' in Fiorella Kostoris and Padoa Schioppa (eds.), *The Principle of Mutual Recognition in the European Integration Process* (Houndmills, Basingstoke, Hampshire: Palgrave Macmillan, 2005)

Mena S and Palazzo G, 'Input and Output Legitimacy of Multi-Stakeholder Initiatives' (2012) 22 *Business Ethics Quarterly*, 527

Micheletti M, *Political Virtue and Shopping: Individuals, Consumerism, and Collective Action* (London: Palgrave Macmillan, 2003)

Moïsé E and Steenblik R, 'Trade-Related Measures Based on Processes and Production Methods in the Context of Climate-Change Mitigation', (2011) *OECD Trade and Environment Working Papers*, 2011/04

Monti G, 'Article 81 EC and Public Policy' (2002) 39 *Common Market Law Review* 1057

'EU Competition Law from Rome to Lisbon – Social Market Economy' in Caroline Heide-Jorgensen, Christian Bergqvist, Ulla Neergaard & Sune Troels Poulsen (eds.), *Aims and Values in Competition Law* (Kopenhagen: DJØF Publishing, 2013), 27

Mortelmans K, 'Towards Convergence in the Application of the Rules on Free Movement and on Competition?' (2001) 38 *Common Market Law Review*, 613

Munoz R, 'Case C-1/96, The Queen v. Minister of Agriculture, Fisheries and food, ex parte Compassion in World Farming Limited. Judgment of 19 March 1998, [1998] ECR I-1251' (1999) 36 *Common Market Law Review*, 831

Nicoaïdis K and Howse R, '"This is my EUtopia . . .": Narrative as Power' (2002) 40 *Journal of Common Market Studies*, 767–792

Nocolaides P, 'The Balancing Myth: The Economics of Article 81 (1) and (3)' (2005) 32 *Legal Issues of Economic Integration*, 123

Nollkaemper A, 'The Legality of Moral Crusades Disguised in Trade Laws: An Analysis of the EC "Ban" on Furs from Aimals taken by Leghold Traps' (1996) 8 *Journal of Environmental Law*, 237

Notaro N, 'The New Generation Case Law on Trade and Environmnent' (2000) 25 *European Law Review*, 467

Obradovic D, Alonso Vizcaino JM, 'Good Governance Requirements Concerning the Participation of Interest Groups in EU Consultations' (2006) 43 *Common Market Law Review*, 1049

Odudu O, *The Boundaries of EC Competition Law: The Scope of Article 81* (Oxford: Oxford University Press, 2006)

'The Wider Concerns of Competition Law' (2010) 30 *Oxford Journal of Legal Studies*, 599

Ogus A, 'The Paradoxes of Legal Paternalism and How to Resolve Them' (2010) 30 *Legal Studies*, 61

Oliver P (ed.), *Oliver on Free Movement of Goods in the European Union* (Oxford: Hart Publishing, 2010)

Organisation for Economic Co-operation and Development (OECD) 'Processes and Production Methods (PPMs): Conceptual Framework and Considerations' (OECD 1997)

Partiti E, 'The Appellate Body Report in US – Tuna II and Its Impact on Eco-Labelling and Standardization' (2013) 40 *Legal Issues of Economic Integration*, 73

Pauwelyn J, 'Carbon Leakage Measures and Border Tax Ajdustments under WTO Law' in Denise Prevost and Geert van Calster (eds.), *Research Handbook on Environment Helath and the WTO* (Cheltenham: Edward Elgar, 2012)

Pijnacker Hordijk EH, 'Oordeel over verenigbaarheid van verbod van invoer en verhandeling van uitheemse vogelsoorten met art. 36 EEG-Verdrag en Richtlijn inzake het behoud van de vogelstand' [1991] *Sociaal-Economische Wetgeving*, 261

Pirker B, *Proportionality Analysis and Models of Judicial Review: A Theoretical and Comparative Study* (Groningen: Europa Law Publishing, 2013)

Polanyi K, *The Great Transformation: The Political and Economic Origins of Our Time* (2nd edn, Beacon Press 2001)

Pollack MA, 'Unilateral America, Multilateral Europe?' in John Peterson and Mark A. Pollack (eds.), *Europe, America, Bush: Transatlantic Relations in the Twenty-first Century* (London: Routledge, 2003), 115
Roe B and Sheldon I, 'Credence Good Labeling: The Efficiency and Distributional Implications of Several Policy Approaches' (2007) 89 *American Journal of Agricultural Economics*, 1020
Romppanen S, 'Regulating Better Biofuels for the European Union' [2012] *European Energy and Environmental Law Review*, 123
Rosenboom N, 'How does article 101(3) TFEU case law relate to EC guidelines and the welfare perspective?' (2013) SEO Working Paper
Roth WH, 'Case C-205/07, Lodewijk Gysbrechts, Santurel Inter BVBA, Judgment of the Court of Justice (Grand Chamber) of 16 December 2008' (2010) 47 *Common Market Law Review*, 509
Ruggie JG, 'International Regimes, Transactions, and Change: Embedded Liberalism in the Postwar Economic Order' (1982) 36 *International Organization*, 379
Just Business: Multinational Corporations and Human Rights (New York: Norton & Company, 2013)
Ryland D and Nurse A, 'Mainstreaming after Lisbon: Advancing Animal Welfare in the EU Internal Market' [2013] *European Energy and Environmental Law Review*, 101
Ryngaert C, *Jurisdiction in International Law* (Oxford: Oxford University Press, 2008)
Sands P, '"Unilateralism", Values, and International Law' (2000) 11 *European Journal of International Law*, 291
Sauter W and Schepel H, *State and Market in European Union Law: The Public and Private Spheres of the Internal Market before the EU Courts* (Cambridge: Cambridge University Press, 2009)
Scharpf FW, *Governing in Europe: Effective and Democratic?* (Oxford: Oxford University Press, 1999)
Schepel H, 'Case C-171/11 Fra.bo Spa v Deutsche Vereinigung des Gas- und Wasserfaches' 9 (2013) *European Review of Contract Law*, 186
'Constitutionalising the Market, Marketising the Constitution, and to Tell the Difference: On the Horizontal Application of the Free Movement Provisions in EU Law' 18 (2012) *European Law Journal*, 177
'The New Approach to the New Approach: The Juridification of Harmonized Standards in EU Law' 20 (2013) *Maastricht Journal of European and Comparative Law*, 521
'Private Regulators in Law' in Joost Pauwelyn, Ramses Wessel, and Jan Wouters (eds.), *Informal International Lawmaking* (Oxford: Oxford Scholarship Online, 2013), 356
Scherer G and Palazzo G (eds.), *Handbook of Research on Global Corporate Citizenship* (Cheltenham: Edward Elgar Publishing 2008), 249
Schiff Berman P, 'Global Legal Pluralism' (2007) 80 *Southern California Law Review*, 1155

Schütze R, 'Supremacy without Pre-emption? The Very Slowly Emergent Doctrine of Community Pre-emption' (2006) 43 *Common Market Law Review*, 1023

Scott J, *EC Environmental Law* (Longman, London 1998)

'Extraterritoriality and Territorial Extension in EU Law' (2014) 62 *The American Journal of Comparative Law*, 87

'The Multi-level Governance of Climate Change' in Paul Craig (ed.), *The Evolution of EU Law* (Oxford: Oxford University Press, 2011), 805

'The New EU "extraterritoriality"' (2014) 51 *Common Market Law Review*, 1343

Sevenster H, *Eco-imperialisme binnen de Europese Unie; een juridisch probleem?* (Deventer: W.E.J. Tjeenk Willink, 1998)

Shuibhne NN and Maci M, 'Proving Public Interest: The Growing Impact of Evidence in Free Movement Case Law' (2013) 50 *Common Market Law Review*, 965

Snell J, *Goods and Services in EC Law: A Study of the Relationship between the Freedoms* (Oxford: Oxford University Press, 2002)

Spar DL and La Mure LT, 'The Power of Activism: Assessing the Impact of NGOs on Global Business'(2003) 45 *California Management Review*, 78

Steinrücken T and Jaenichen S, 'The Fair Trade Idea: Towards an Economics of Social Labels' (2007) 30 *Journal of Consumer Policy*, 201

Stolze M and Lampkin N, 'Policy for Organic Farming: Rationale and Concepts' (2009) 34 *Food Policy*, 237

Temple Lang J, 'The Development by the Court of Justice of the Duties of Cooperation of National Authorities and Community Institutions under Article 10 EC' (2007–2008) 31 *Fordham International Law Journal*, 1483

Thaler RH and Sunstein CR, *Nudge: Improving Decisions About Health, Wealth, and Happiness* (New Haven: Yale University Press, 2008)

The American Law Institute, *Restatement (third) of Foreign Relations Law* (The American Law Institute 1987)

Townley C, *Article 81 EC and Public Policy* (Oxford: Hart Publishing, 2009)

Trebilcock M, *Howse R and Eliason A eds, The Regulation of International Trade*, 4th edn (London: Routledge, 2013)

Van Calster G, 'Export Restrictions – A Watershed for Article 30' (2000) 25 *European Law Review*, 335

International & EU Trade Law: The Environmental Challenge (London: Cameron May, 2000)

van Eijndthoven J, 'Energy Taxation at European Level: What does it do for the Environment and Sustainability?' [2011] *EC Tax Review*, 283

van Hoek A, 'Het proces tegen Shell wegens olielekkages in de Ogonidelta (Nigeria)' (2013) 62 *Ars Aequi*, 482

van Leeuwen B, 'From Status to Impact, and the Role of National Legislation: The Application of Article 34 TFEU to a Private Certification Organisation in Fra.bo' [2013] *European Journal of Risk Regulation*, 405

Vedder H, *Competition Law and Environmental Protection in Europe: Towards Sustainability?* (Groningen: Europa Law Publishing, 2003)

Vogel D, 'The Private Regulation of Global Corporate Conduct' (2010) 49 *Business & Society*, 68

'Trading up and Governing Across: Transnational Governance and Environmental Protection' (1997) 4 *Journal of European Public Policy*, 556

Vranes E, *Trade and the Environment: Fundamental Issues in International Law, WTO Law, and Legal Theory* (Oxford: Oxford University Press, 2009)

Wasmeier M, 'The Integration of Environmental Protection as a General Rule for Interpreting Community Law' (2001) 38 *Common Market Law Review*, 159

Weiler JHH, 'In the Face of Crisis: Input Legitimacy, Output Legitimacy and the Political Messianism of European Integration' (2012) 34 *Journal of European Integration*, 825

'Mutual Recognition, Functional Equivalence and Harmonization in the Evolution of the European Common Market and the WTO' in Fiorella Kostoris and Padoa Schioppa (eds.), *The Principle of Mutual Recognition in the European Integration Process* (Houndmills, Basingstoke, Hampshire: Palgrave Macmillan, 2005), 25

Wiers J, *Trade and Environment in the EC and the WTO: a Legal Analysis* (Groningen: Europa Law Publishing, 2002)

Wiesbrock A, 'An Obligation for Sustainable Procurement? Gauging the Potential Impact of Article 11 TFEU on Public Contracting in the EU' (2013) 40 *Legal Issues of Economic Integration*, 105

Witt AC, 'Public Policy Goals under EU Competition Law: now is the Time to set the House in Order' (2012) 8 *European Competition Journal*, 443

Wright C, 'Tacking Conflict Diamonds: The Kimberley Process Certification Scheme' (2004) 11 *International Peacekeeping*, 697

Index